The Phantom
of the Ego

Studies in Violence, Mimesis, and Culture

The Phantom of the Ego

MODERNISM
AND THE MIMETIC
UNCONSCIOUS

Nidesh Lawtoo

Michigan State University Press · *East Lansing*

♾ The paper used in this publication meets the minimum requirements of ANSI/NISO
Z39.48-1992 (R 1997) (Permanence of Paper).

 Michigan State University Press
East Lansing, Michigan 48823-5245

Printed and bound in the United States of America.

19 18 17 16 15 14 13   1 2 3 4 5 6 7 8 9 10

LIBRARY OF CONGRESS CATALOGING-IN-PUBLICATION DATA
Lawtoo, Nidesh.
The phantom of the ego : modernism and the mimetic unconscious / Nidesh Lawtoo.
pages cm. — (Studies in violence, mimesis, and culture series)
Includes bibliographical references and index.
ISBN 978-1-60917-388-3 (ebook) — ISBN 978-1-61186-096-2 (pbk. : alk. paper)
1. Modernism (Literature) 2. Mimesis. 3. Ego (Psychology) in literature. 4. Literature—
Philosophy. I. Title.
PN56.M54L38 2013
809'.9112—dc23
2012049425

Book design by Charlie Sharp, Sharp Des!gns, Lansing, Michigan
Cover design by David Drummond, Salamander Design, www.salamanderhill.com
Cover art is a detail of Joan Miro's *Femme et Oiseau dans la Nuit* (1947) and is used with
permission of the Calder Foundation, New York / Art Resource, NY, and the estate of
Joan Miro, © 2012 Successió Miró / Artists Rights Society (ARS), New York / ADAGP,
Paris. All rights reserved.

g green press INITIATIVE Michigan State University Press is a member of the Green Press Initiative
and is committed to developing and encouraging ecologically responsible
publishing practices. For more information about the Green Press Initiative and the use of
recycled paper in book publishing, please visit *www.greenpressinitiative.org*.

Visit Michigan State University Press at *www.msupress.org*

For Michi

Contents

Acknowledgments

I am grateful to the Comparative Literature program at the University of Washington for providing the intellectual freedom necessary to conceive this ghost-hunt, to the Collège International de Philosophie in Paris for a transdisciplinary spirit that allowed me to pursue it, and to the committee of the Pembroke College Fellowship for a research grant that made time to finally corner the ghost at the University of Cambridge. In particular, I would like to thank Leroy Searle, Carolyn Allen, Rod Mengham, Michael Bell, Herman Siemens, Michael Groneberg, and Neil Roberts for reading different sections of the manuscript and for offering valuable indications along the road. My colleagues at the University of Lausanne I wish to thank for offering a friendly and stimulating environment to revise the manuscript, and my students for responding to my mimetic phantasms with original questions. Many thanks to Roelof Overmeer, Martine Hennard Dutheil de la Rochère, and Rachel Falconer for keeping me on track, and to Philip Lindholm for helping with the bibliography. I am very grateful to the editorial team at MSUP, in particular to Kristine Blakeslee and Elise Jajuga for their careful editorial work, and to William Johnsen for his flexibility, openness and, above all, for finding a house for this *Phantom*.

Special thanks go to Mikkel Borch-Jacobsen, Henry Staten, and Gary

Handwerk. They have been behind this project from beginning to end, and have provided the perfect combination of friendly advice, merciless critiques, and inspiring suggestions. *The Phantom of the Ego* owes much of its materialization to their unflagging support, which kept me grounded—while being on the move. I am confident they will spot traces of my gratitude in what follows. Many solutions to the mimetic riddles that haunt this book have emerged from communications with my closest *socius*, Michaela Lawtoo. What this diagnostic of the modern soul owes to her inimitable patience and psychological finesse goes well beyond what I can acknowledge here.

Sections of this book have appeared before in a modified form in the following articles and chapters:

- "Nietzsche and the Psychology of Mimesis: From Plato the *Führer*," in *Nietzsche Power and Politics: Rethinking Nietzsche's Legacy for Political Thought,* eds. Herman Siemens and Vasti Roodt (New York: W. de Gruyter, 2008), 667–693.
- "The Horror of Mimesis: 'Enthusiastic Outbreak[s]' in *Heart of Darkness," Conradiana* 42.1–2 (2010): 45–74.
- "Bataille and the Birth of the Subject: Out of the Laughter of the *Socius*," *Angelaki* 16.2 (2011): 73–88.
- "The Horror of Mimesis: Echoing Lacoue-Labarthe," in *Conrad's "Heart of Darkness" and Contemporary Thought: Revisiting the Horror with Lacoue-Labarthe,* ed. Nidesh Lawtoo (London: Bloomsbury, 2012), 239–259.

Introduction

The greatest part of our being is unknown to us.... We have a phantom of the "ego" in our heads, which determines us many times over.
—Friedrich Nietzsche, *Nachlass*

A phantom is haunting the modern world—the phantom of the ego. This ghostly presence is not confined to the darkness of the night; nor is it simply the product of the oneiric imagination of the sleeping subject, something that can be willed away, at daybreak, when the light of reason returns. Rather, the modern ego seems to be tracked, haunted, perhaps even possessed by such a phantom, during its waking daily life. This, at least, is what Friedrich Nietzsche claims as he writes that "the greatest part of our being is unknown to us. . . . We have a phantom of the 'ego' in our heads, which determines us many times over."[1] What does it mean to have a phantom in place of the ego? Does it mean that the ego copies, shadow-like, another ego from without? Or, alternatively, that an external ego has mysteriously penetrated one's head and taken control of it from within? What is sure is that, for Nietzsche, this "phantom" should not be dismissed as a rare

1

psychic illusion, but is symptomatic of a quite common mimetic confusion. As he explains in *Daybreak*, this phantom is born out of an unconscious process of psychic "communication" that spreads contagiously from self to others, one head to another head, depriving "the great majority" of their own thoughts, values, and opinions and, thus, turning their ego into what he calls, once again, a "phantom of the ego [*Phantom von Ego*]."[2]

Disscuss This

Mimesis not as straightforward imitation, then, but rather mimesis as a disconcerting form of unconscious communication that troubles the boundaries of individuation: this is, in a nutshell, the single yet protean problem I struggle with in this book. Elusive, masked, always on the move, mimesis is a dramatic, phantasmal concept that changes form at will, slipping into a variety of related conceptual characters and personae. From hypnosis to identification, sympathy to trance, hysterical pathologies to fascist ideologies, "primitive" magical actions to a variety of "modern" bodily reactions, contagious affective realities to mass-mediatized virtual hyperrealities, we shall see that mimesis participates in most of the battles that are constitutive of the crisis of modernity. This book, then, does not propose a return to the old conception of "mimetic realism"[3] but rather opens up a new interdisciplinary investigation of a fragmented, slippery, and polymorphous phenomenon that haunts "the mind of modernism" as a whole.[4]

Nietzsche's warning that a phantom is taking possession of the modern ego is not an isolated, original cry from the last decades of the nineteenth century directed towards future centuries yet to come. A mimetic undercurrent in literary and philosophical modernism, which runs from Nietzsche to Joseph Conrad, from D. H. Lawrence to Georges Bataille, via a panoply of fin de siècle theories in the human sciences—including crowd psychology, religious anthropology, psychoanalysis, and different schools of dynamic psychology—sense the same phantom coming and warn modernity against the psychic, ethical, and political dangers of appearing to be oneself, while being someone other. And yet, Nietzsche comes first. And not only for obvious, historical reasons, but also for deeper, theoretical reasons. Nietzsche's thought occupies a privileged position in both the diachronic and the synchronic development that guides my entire investigation. As an introductory gesture, then, I turn to a figure that has been called "the apotheosis of aesthetic modernism,"[5] in order to articulate my approach to the old, yet always new, question of mimesis and open up an alternative door to the modernist unconscious—a Nietzschean back door that does not hinge on a repressive hypothesis but on a mimetic hypothesis instead.

Pathos of Distance

The Nietzschean concept of "pathos of distance" provides this book with a moving frame to investigate the fundamental double-bind that mimetic affects have the power to generate in modernist literary and philosophical authors. This double bind stems from the fact that Nietzsche's concept, like the god Janus, is at least double-faced. On one side, it marks a critical, philosophical *distance* from forms of mimetic behavior Nietzsche—as well as other modernists after him—frequently denounces in modern subjects. His targets are often subjects he derogatively calls "the many" or, more often, "the herd": gregarious, unoriginal people who, in his view, are not in conscious possession of their egos and are, thus, easy prey to different forms of psychic dispossession. This is the well-known side of Nietzsche as a "master of suspicion," the psychologist who relentlessly unmasks what he considers pathological forms of behavior at the heart of modernity. On the other, less known side, the concept of "pathos of distance" points towards Nietzsche's own emotional vulnerability to the mimetic *pathos* he so eloquently denounces in others. There is, in fact, something surprising in Nietzsche's use of the Greek concept of πάθος to qualify his scornful "distance" from the multitude. As E. R. Dodds reminds us, for the Greeks the word *pathos* testifies to "the experience of passion . . . something mysterious and frightening, the experience of a force that was in [a man], possessing him, rather than possessed by him."[6] I argue that if Nietzsche is so passionately opposed to the affective force of pathos, it is because this force has already taken possession of him, in a mimetic way. This is true of that pathos he considers "his greatest danger," namely compassion, but also of what he calls the "Wagnerian pathos" and the different forms of contagious pathologies it entails.

This fundamental oscillation towards/away from mimetic reactions is a structuring feature that has tended to elude readers of Nietzsche who are uniquely attentive to his philosophical *logos*. Yet it has not escaped a theorist of mimesis like René Girard, who, already in the 1970s, noticed this "contradiction" at the heart of one of Nietzsche's texts.[7] This study begins by taking Girard's realization seriously. It argues that the contradiction Girard identifies in a specific, unpublished fragment runs not only through the entirety of Nietzsche's published corpus, but also resurfaces in all the modernist authors I subsequently consider: from Conrad's take on sacrificial horrors, to Bataille's conception of contagious "communication," via Lawrence's analysis of the "old stable ego," all the thinkers of mimesis we shall encounter oscillate towards/away from different forms of mimetic pathologies that infect the ego. In a specific sense, then, this book picks up and amplifies a Girardian question in order to extend mimetic theory to the field of "new modernist studies."[8] Its general ambition is to rethink the problematic of mimesis in its ambivalent, affective, and infective manifestations so as to continue accounting for what the French philosopher and theorist of mimesis Philippe Lacoue-Labarthe calls "the imitation of the moderns."[9]

Like the Romantic figures at the origin of the Girardian system, the modernist authors I examine prove to be insightful theorists of mimesis themselves. Figures like Nietzsche, Conrad, Lawrence, and Bataille are, indeed, acute, introspective writers who are not only extremely sensitive to different forms of emotional contagion but also diagnose different symptoms of mimetic sickness with extreme clinical precision. My goal, then, in what follows, is not simply to "apply" Girard's mimetic theory to modernist texts—though Girard's insights will be central for my argument. Nor am I solely concerned with offering new readings of literary and philosophical modernists via the theoretical filter of mimesis—though we shall see that this filter is immensely productive and allows us to resolve hermeneutical riddles that have haunted critics for a while. Instead, the primary focus of this book is on unearthing a specific brand of mimetic theory that is already internal to the Nietzschean current of modernism I explore—a theory that, as figures like René Girard and Philippe Lacoue-Labarthe have shown, can be made visible through an interpretative effort that takes seriously the theoretical potential of the literary works themselves.

Clearly, some of the modernist insights into the ambivalence, rivalry, and violence mimetic affects have the power to generate involve an extension of preoccupations that were already articulated by Girard in his earliest and most influential works, *Deceit, Desire and the Novel* (1961) and *Violence and the Sacred* (1972).[10] For instance, the Nietzschean current in modernism I engage with continues to undermine the stability of the subject of

Aufklärung, characterized by faith in progress, rationality, and the capacity of the mind to control one's thoughts, opinions, and desires in the modern (post-Romantic) period. The Nietzsche-Conrad-Lawrence-Bataille axis of modernism also encourages us to explore subjectivity in relational, intersubjective terms, terms that challenge reassuring notions of originality, autonomy, and solipsistic self-sufficiency. Above all, these figures open up the boundaries of literature to a transnational, interdisciplinary context, encouraging readers to move across disciplines as diverse as philosophy, anthropology, sociology, and crowd psychology. The modernist brand of mimetic theory that emerges from this study is, thus, in a relation of continuity with its Romantic predecessors. It extends their preoccupations into the twentieth century in order to address disquieting phenomena of psychic depersonalization, affective contagion, ideological indoctrination, and the all too human violence that often still ensues.[11]

And yet, despite these similarities, important differences will also have to be signaled. Modernists writing roughly from the 1870s to the 1940s are shaped by the experience of major technical innovations, increasing urbanization, colonial expansions, the diffusion of mass media, not to speak of globalized wars based on fascist forms of collective psychology that subjugate not only individual bodies but also the entire body politic. These historical experiences shake the psychic, ethical, political, religious, and metaphysical foundations of the Western world. It is thus not surprising that significant shifts of emphasis appear in the modernist brand of mimetic theory I set out to unearth. For instance, unprecedented forms of sacrificial violence are indeed enacted in the modern period. And yet these massive outbreaks of violence do not offer cathartic resolutions to the horrors of mimesis. On the contrary, they seem to spread contagiously, generating more violence.[12] Moreover, the problematic of desire, and the rivalries that ensue, continues to be part of modernist preoccupations; but the focus is less on mimetic *desire* as such than on a mimetic *loss of the ego* instead. From Nietzsche to Conrad, Lawrence to Bataille, the experience of mimesis dissolves the modern ego in such a fundamental way that, strictly speaking, there is no ego left for intensely desiring, in the Romantic sense. As we shall see, it is as if, for the modernists, the problematic of desire is peeled off from the problematic of mimesis—and what is left over is not an ego, but a phantom of the ego instead.

The specificity of the modernist approach to mimesis will progressively emerge from the engagement with the literary and philosophical texts themselves, and its strengths and weaknesses will have to be tested on those specific textual grounds. As Girard also recognized, "one cannot map out the way mimesis works with writers in general. Each one demands an entirely different demonstration, although a critic who is interested in the mimetic mechanism knows that ultimately he or she will unveil the same mimetic principles."[13] Indeed, variations of the same mimetic pathos of distance will emerge from the Nietzschean modernist axis I explore, and this movement will provide us with a distinctive methodology to approach the problem of mimetic dispossession in the modern period. What we must add now is that this clinical, diagnostic methodology emerges from an affective implication in the pathologies these authors critically dissect from a distance.

Mimetic Patho(-)logies

Rather than celebrating the ambivalence at the heart of modernist accounts of mimesis as a contradiction, this book sets out to reconstruct the logic informing the double movement that swings these authors back and forth from pathos to distance, and vice versa. This logic transgresses the principle of noncontradiction. It is situated at the juncture of the *both-and*, rather than at the disjunction of the *either/or*. In fact, I argue that it is only because modernist thinkers are themselves affected or, better, infected by the mimetic pathologies that haunt the mind of modernism that they can manage to effectively critique them from a distance. Out of this back-looping movement, whereby the infected subject turns upon itself in order to reflect on its pathology, emerges a method of reading that is as attentive to the logical structure of mimetic thought as to the affects that animate this thought. Given the distinctive *clinical* dimension of this approach, I have called it mimetic patho(-)logy—in the dual sense of mimetic sickness, and critical discourse (*logos*) on mimetic affects (*pathos*).

The clinical assumption that informs the movement of mimetic patho(-) logy is not mapped onto modernism from the outside; it emerges rather directly from the inside, out of a close textual investigation of what Nietzsche already called his "longest exercise." Here is how this self-proclaimed "philosophical physician" defines this clinical exercise in *Ecce Homo*:

Ego -?

to look from a morbid perspective towards *healthier* concepts and values, and again conversely to look down from the abundance and certainty of *rich* life into the secret labour of the instinct of *décadence*—that is what I have practiced most [*meine längste Übung*], it has been my own particular field of experience, in this if in anything I am a master.[14]

Nietzsche was, indeed, well trained in the art of psychological dissection of what is "sick" in the modern ego, his critical tools all the sharper insofar as he tirelessly practiced his clinical art of recognizing the symptoms he denounces in the modern "herd" in his own self. This is not simply symptomatic of a logical inconsistency in Nietzsche's *logos*. Nor should it be easily dismissed as a sign of perspectival confusion and loss of orientation characteristic of the modernist sensibility. On the contrary, this reversal of perspectives is predicated on a lucid methodological recognition that is at least as old as the origins of mimetic theory itself. As Plato had already suggested in Book III of the *Republic*, physicians, by which he means, primarily, physicians of the soul, "would prove most skilled . . . if they themselves had suffered all diseases and were not of very healthy constitution."[15] To be sure, Nietzsche is a self-proclaimed anti-Platonic philosopher; yet he remains a Platonic philosophical physician in his assumption that "sickness is instructive . . . even more instructive than health."[16] Indeed, Nietzsche's unhealthy constitution gave him much clinical material on which to practice his diagnostic skills. This study takes this Nietzschean/Platonic realization literally as it sets in motion the movement of mimetic patho(-)logy that guides our entire investigation—a movement informed as much by the *pathos* that infects the inquiring subjects, as by the *logos* these subjects use to clinically dissect contagious phenomena from a distance.

Important

In my diagnostic approach to mimesis I have been guided by the methodological assumption that a shift of perspectives from a personal vulnerability to mimetic sickness (or pathology) to the rigor of a *logos* that dissects different forms of *pathos* (or patho-logy) does not only entail an indecisive, back-and-forth oscillation from pathos to distance, affect to logos, and vice versa. This movement, in other words, is not linear; nor is it predicated on a safe and neat distinction between the "healthy" subject who carries out the clinical investigation and its "sick" object of inquiry. Rather, it involves a complex, patho(-)logical movement where the object of study (*pathos*) retroacts on the subject who investigates it through the tools of reason (*logos*). It does so in two opposed ways, one disabling and the other enabling. On the one hand, the movement of mimetic patho(-)logy makes the critical observer vulnerable to the affects she or he dissects and is thus not without risks of infection. Indeed, all the authors I examine capitulate, at some point or other, to the same forms of imitative behavior they denounce in others in terms of sickness (or pathology). On the other hand, this modernist vulnerability to different forms of mimetic sickness also informs their critical logos on mimetic pathos (or patho-*logy*) with an experiential, affective knowledge that has the paradoxical effect of sharpening, rather than blunting, their clinical tools and diagnostic lenses—at least among self-proclaimed "philosophical physicians" who make this reversal of perspective their "longest exercise." Out of this feedback loop emerges the *spiraling* movement of mimetic patho(-)logy that serves as the distinctive feature of modernist mimetic theory.

Across the shifts of perspective, the same approach will always be at issue everywhere: a dual, Janus-faced approach that not only uses the filter of mimesis to offer new readings of Nietzschean pathologies in literary modernism, but also attempts to come to a better understanding of mimetic phantoms on the basis of authors who are "most skilled" in the art of psychic dissection. A characteristically modernist self-consciousness and psychic sensibility join hands with an equally typical modernist critical distance and diagnostic attitude towards modernity. Out of this conjunction of *both* pathos *and* distance, the clinical motor of mimetic patho(-)logy is set in motion: a back-looping, spiraling motion that turns hermeneutics into theoretical logos, cultural critique into self-critique. The goal of this critique of mimesis, I hasten to add, is not to reiterate ancient quarrels but, rather, to diagnose the power of mimetic pathos in a spirit of modern reconciliation.

Ancient Quarrels, Modern Reconciliations

The paradigmatic choice of two authors who, while not being traditional philosophers, are associated with modernist and postmodernist philosophical trends (Nietzsche and Bataille), and two British novelists who fall neatly within the modernist literary tradition (Conrad and Lawrence), via the literary-philosophical concept of mimesis may require a word of explanation.

Most especially since, in the Western tradition, the split between philosophy and literature, specialists of concepts and specialists of affects, is predicated on what Plato famously called in Book X of the *Republic* an "old quarrel"[17] over the value of mimetic art. Mimesis is, thus, traditionally, a locus of disciplinary disputes rather than of friendly reconciliations; it does not bring philosophy and literature together, but wrests them apart in two competing and rivalrous fields. As Nietzsche succinctly puts it: "Plato versus Homer: that is the complete, the genuine antagonism."[18] It may therefore seem misguided to lock together two literary authors and two philosophers via the very question that caused such a quarrel in the first place.

And yet an approach attentive to the paradoxical reactions mimesis generates in the modernist period immediately complicates such neat disciplinary distinctions, as well as clear-cut ruptures between modern and ancient approaches to mimesis. Already in Plato, the distinction between the philosopher and the poet is not as clear-cut as it initially appears to be, the violent rivalry between the two figures already masking an underlying, mimetic affinity.[19] And if this is already partially true of the founder of philosophy, it is certainly true of that philosopher-poet of anti-Platonic inspiration who is Nietzsche, a philosopher whose thought emerges precisely out of a struggle between an artistic celebration of what he considers to be "good" mimesis (e.g., Dionysian mimesis) on the one hand, and a philosophical critique of what he values as "bad" mimesis (e.g., Wagnerian mimesis) on the other. Conversely, on the literary front, a modernist figure of direct Nietzschean inspiration like D. H. Lawrence openly voices his discontent about such an ancient, disciplinary quarrel. Anticipating the new turn in modernist studies, Lawrence advocates the necessity for a reconciliation between literature and philosophy as he writes: "it was the greatest pity in the world when philosophy and fiction got split"; "you've got to marry the pair of them. Apart, they are no good."[20] And in order to remarry this split pair, his fictions and essays concentrate precisely on the cause of this ancient quarrel, namely mimesis.

At the most general level, then, my choice of authors indicates an attempt to consider the contagious affects that take possession of the modern ego not so much as the source of disciplinary disputes between poets and philosophers but as a productive locus of articulation between two exemplary traditions. This also means that at work in this project is an attempt to both interpret and theorize. Following Girard, I shall take seriously the theoretical potential of literary texts (literature *as* theory), and in a mirroring countermovement, following Lacoue-Labarthe, I will also pay attention to the literary dimension of theoretical texts (theory *as* literature).[21] If we are right in claiming that mimesis, like the god Janus, is double-faced, both philosophical in theoretical conception and artistic in affective dramatization, then, in order to understand its workings, mimetic patho(-)logy will have to confront *both* its conceptual *and* its affective face, both the *pathos* and the *logos* that transect this Janus-faced concept.

And yet things are not so clear-cut. A split, divided concept can easily multiply identities. And indeed, in fin de siècle Europe, states of psychic confusion between self and other(s) tend to mask themselves under a panoply of different conceptual personae. These conceptual masks include emotional contagion, enthusiasm, crowd behavior, and psychic depersonalization, but also compassion, sympathy, mimicry, automatic reflexes, hypnotic suggestion, hysteria, trance, participation, and identification. Mimesis, as the modernists understand it, constantly transgresses disciplinary boundaries, all too easily coming to mean different things to everyone who approaches it through different theoretical lenses. This transgression of boundaries is particularly accentuated at the turn of the century, at a time when mimesis and the psychic confusion it entails split into a multiplicity of emerging disciplinary perspectives (or *logoi*). Hence, the phenomena I treat under the heading of "mimesis" can no longer be confined to a dual literary/philosophical tradition, but must extend in order to include multiple, and at times conflicting, interdisciplinary traditions. Not only philosophy and literature, but now also emerging new disciplines in the human sciences such as sociology, religious anthropology, crowd psychology, psychoanalysis, psycho-physiology, and different schools of dynamic psychology attempt to account for the disconcerting phenomenon that leads the ego to confuse itself with a multiplicity of other egos.

Mimesis is, indeed, a protean, mimetic concept that changes name, identity, and appearance as it crosses disciplinary borders. It challenges the all too comfortable temptation of limiting oneself to one of its disciplinary manifestations, while ignoring its other protean masks, under the false pretense that they do not respond to the official name, "mimesis." This multiplicity of identities is, of course, not new. From the very beginning of mimetic theory in Plato's thought, mimesis operates as a concept without a fixed, stable essence and is difficult to define.[22] But in the modernist period, this concept continues, perhaps more than ever, to be in search of an identity. Called "imitation" by social psychologists, "contagion" by crowd psychologists, "trance" by religious anthropologists, "identification" by psychoanalysts, "hypnotic suggestion" by pre-Freudian psychologists, mimesis is a chameleon concept that changes color if set against different disciplinary backgrounds. It is then no wonder that this mimetic concept, as it moves through the modernist period, has so far largely escaped critical attention and has remained unexplored. In addition to its unfashionable association with copying,[23] mimesis is, indeed, seriously at odds with still dominant tendencies in the humanities to compartmentalize knowledge in specific fields of disciplinary specialization—a tendency that was not yet solidified in the period that concerns us.[24]

An attempt to track the phantom that takes possession of the modern ego requires a flexible, dynamic approach that troubles disciplinary distinctions and does not lose sight of this chameleon-like phenomenon as it crosses over into another field of knowledge. Consequently, this book takes the trouble to situate specific mimetic affects against the disciplinary, historical, and theoretical backgrounds that are most directly linked to the phantom of the ego's particular appearance in a particular text and author, at a particular historical moment. It is only by doing so that the phantom that haunts modernism can be made to appear. And as we shift from Nietzsche's writings of the 1870s and 1880s to the Bataille of the 1930s, 1940s, and 1950s, via Conrad's texts of the first decade of the twentieth century, and Lawrence's writings of the 1920s, we shall see that this background will be constantly moving, presenting the phantom that concerns us in a kaleidoscope of constantly changing light.

This last point should make clear that despite the author-oriented dimension of this study, a mimetic approach to subject formation does not allow an exclusive understanding of four heroic, original authors considered in isolation, but must take into consideration the larger theoretical and historical context from which their conception of the subject or ego emerges.
[25] If the *pathos* that runs through their writings is truly singular and must be understood on the basis of a hermeneutical effort that is as attentive to the "literary" dimension of their work as to the personal "confessions" expressed through this work, the *logos* they rely on in order to dissect mimetic *pathos*

is borrowed from a variety of disciplinary traditions that emerge, for the first time in a systematized way, in the modern period. Hence, as we move historically from Nietzsche to Conrad, Lawrence to Bataille, spanning a period of nearly a century, these four writers—who are, of course, also voracious and eclectic readers—will urge us to deal with an impressive array of theories and theorists of subjectivity. These include, but are not limited to, research on hypnosis (Jean-Martin Charcot and Hippolyte Bernheim), crowd psychology (Gustave Le Bon, Gabriel Tarde, and the "heir" of this tradition, Sigmund Freud), religious anthropology (Lucien Lévy-Bruhl, Jane Harrison, and Émile Durkheim), as well as much-neglected figures who develop different models of dynamic psychology (from the American dissident psychoanalyst Trigant Burrow to the French philosopher and psychologist Pierre Janet).

I engage with such a heterogeneous set of theorists not only because they are integral to the heterogeneous cultural phenomenon that is modernism,[26] but also because they are already internal to the literary and philosophical investigations of the primary authors I examine, providing them with the conceptual logos to develop a distinctive modernist brand of mimetic theory. If mimetic patho-logy is not concerned with applying a stabilizing meta-theory of mimesis from the outside, it pays considerable attention to the different strands of mimetic theory that in-*form* (gives form to) modernist thought from the inside. From Nietzsche's psychological critique of modernity to Conrad's concerns with colonial power, from Lawrence's critique of Freud to Bataille's focus on the birth of the ego, we understand little of their diagnostic insights if we do not consider the theoretical foundations on which their conception of the ego relies.

What we must add now is that since this ego is not a rational, fully conscious, volitional entity, our inquiry calls for an investigation of yet another key modernist discovery: the so-called discovery of the unconscious. Girard is indeed right to say that "in imitation there is always some degree of 'unconsciousness' involved."[27] We shall go further and say that mimesis provides an alternative door to the much-discussed question of the unconscious, offering us a new key to solve its riddles. And here is where the *mimetic* unconscious enters the modernist stage.

The Mimetic Unconscious

For a long time, European modernism has been viewed through a distinctly Freudian lens. That slant has been enormously productive in many ways, unsurprisingly, since the "fit" of Freud to both canonical and noncanonical modernist texts can be very close. These Freudian tendencies, for all their innovations and explicative power, share an idealist bias that can be traced back to Plato. My goal here is a different one. Informed, I would hope, by all that Freudian readings of modernist literature have brought us, I aim to recover some of what Freud and his successors have blinded us to: modernism without Freud or, better, modernism through a pre-Freudian, but still emphatically psychological lens. Rather than with Freud as the father of modernism, I begin with Nietzsche's antimetaphysical reorientation of philosophy, his insistence that psychology informs philosophical reflection, the detachment of psychological analysis from its metaphysical overlays, a residual tendency, I would argue, in Freud and Freudian-influenced renderings of modernism.

Given the success of this approach in literary studies, it is not surprising that psychoanalysis has been the most trodden path to approach the question of the modernist unconscious, especially since the unconscious has been loudly proclaimed to be a Freudian "discovery."[28] And yet, outside the confines of literary studies, historians of psychology have demonstrated, for quite some time now, that the concept of the unconscious is far from being Freud's original invention and has a long and complicated history, a history that cannot be dissociated from the mimetic phenomena that haunt the modern period. As Henri Ellenberger puts it, in his monumental *The Discovery of the Unconscious* (1970), at the turn of the century, hypnosis, rather than dreams, functions as what he calls, mimicking Freud, the "*via regia* to the unconscious."[29] And in the process of recovering this neglected (some would say suppressed) tradition, Ellenberger sets out to retell the long forgotten pre-Freudian history of dynamic psychology, from its magical origins in Anton Mesmer's "animal magnetism" to Hippolyte Bernheim's "hypnotic suggestion," via Jean-Martin Charcot's "*grande hystérie*" to Pierre Janet's "psychology of the socius."[30] In the wake of Ellenberger's historical reframing of the unconscious, other historians and theorists have continued exploring this pre-Freudian road. Thus, figures as diverse as Marcel Gauchet, Raymond Saussure, Jean-Michel Oughourlian, Ian Hacking, Sonu Shamdasani, and Mikkel Borch-Jacobsen, to name a few, have stressed the importance of the model of hypnotic suggestion to access a pre-Freudian model of the unconscious, a model that did not rely on a repressive hypothesis but on what Borch-Jacobsen calls a "mimetic hypothesis" instead.[31]

Due to this confrontation of psychoanalysis with its prehistory, old debts were brought to the fore; old battles that were thought to have been won by Freud were reconsidered from a more impartial historical perspective; old mimetic concepts (such as the "riddle of suggestion") that psychoanalysis never managed to fully dissipate reappeared on the forefront of the analytic scene. This historical reevaluation of hypnosis and related concepts entails a rediscovery of the unconscious that is currently dismantling received Freudian notions about the psyche; and the recent "Freud wars" on both sides of the Atlantic testify to the liveliness, virulence, and timeliness of this debate. I take it to be a positive sign that the echoes of these theoretical and historical battles are now beginning to be registered in literary studies as well. In fact, modernist scholars informed by recent developments in the history of psychology have begun to propose a correction to "Freudocentric" approaches to literature. For instance, Judith Ryan's *The Vanishing Subject* opened up modernist concerns with the dissolution of the subject to a more inclusive, pre-Freudian psychology.[32] More recently, Mark Micale, in his wide-ranging introduction to *The Mind of Modernism*, extends this innovative line of inquiry: building on both Ellenberger's and Ryan's studies, Micale provides a historical "map" that urges critics to "move beyond Freud" in order to include what he calls a "gallery of physicians, psychiatrists, and psychologists whose work was known to and resonated with artists and intellectuals between 1880 and 1920."[33] *The Phantom of the Ego* contributes to these post-Freudian theoretical developments in literary and philosophical studies by considering the specific, and thus far largely neglected, role mimetic reflexes play in the modernist dissolution of the ego. It also opens up psychological approaches to modernism to a wider, Nietzschean interdisciplinary tradition that roots the unconscious back in the immanence of bodily affects.

It is well known that Nietzsche paves the way for many of Freud's major intuitions and has often been considered an unacknowledged precursor of psychoanalysis. Less known is that Nietzsche's immanent approach to the unconscious is truly pre-Freudian in the sense that it is predicated on a psycho-physiological model of the psyche that has hypnosis—or as Plato used to call it, mimesis—as its *via regia*. This model has nothing to do with a repressive hypothesis. Neither does it propose a universalist account of familial dramas based on an idealist topography of the mind. Rather, the Nietzschean unconscious roots the ego in the immanence of bodily, psycho-physiological reflexes, mimetic reflexes that are not under the volitional control of consciousness and are, in this sense, *un*-conscious. Paradigmatic manifestations of this bodily unconscious—or as the historian of psychology Marcel Gauchet calls it, "cerebral unconscious" (*inconscient cérébral*)— include contagious reactions such as yawning, laughter, and mimicry, but also hypnotic swoons, hysteria, somnambulism, sympathy, compassion, suggestibility, suggestion, identification, and mass behavior.

Although Freud struggled with some of these psychic issues, the difference between the Freudian and the Nietzschean underlying theoretical assumptions are many and fundamental. For instance, if Freud constantly uncovers "repressed" sexual contents of Oedipal configuration, modernists discover a variety of altered states of consciousness of multiple mimetic orientations. If the Freudian unconscious is based on solid (metaphysical) structures rendered intelligible via the abstractions of a metapsychology, the Nietzschean unconscious concentrates on the fluid (physical) affects unmasked by the clinical observation of genuine physio-psychology. Above all, the modernist unconscious is not located in a solipsistic model of the psyche interrogated in isolation, but emerges from intersubjective forms of lived, affective communications experienced in daily social situations. This account of the unconscious is thus not private but social; not egocentric but relational; it does not claim to have a universal, transhistorical validity, but is self-consciously informed by the historical conditions of modernity. Finally, this model does not frame the ego in an ideal topography of the mind or a mirror image of oneself, but opens up the boundaries of the ego to the immanent experience of becoming other. As we shall have occasion to see, the contagious affects that have the power to turn the ego into a phantom, to deprive it of its rational presence to selfhood, rendering it open, for better or worse, to the influence of others, open up an alternative road to the modernist unconscious. Given that "mimesis" in its modernist, patho(-)logical manifestations will serve as our Ariadne's thread to find our way in the labyrinth of the pre-Freudian unconscious, I shall call this new modernist unconscious the "mimetic unconscious."

Once again, Nietzsche is not alone in relying on a mimetic model of the psyche to diagnose the modern ego. The Nietzschean current in modernism I explore pursues his patho-*logical* investigation of mimesis on the basis of the same psycho-physiological assumptions. Given the tremendous popularity of theories of hypnosis at the turn of the century, psychological concerns about contagion, depersonalization, suggestion, affective communication, and crowd behavior moved freely across linguistic, national, and disciplinary frontiers, informing not only *mass* opinion but also *public* opinion: that is, an opinion generated by the power of mass media to generate consensus (from Latin, *con-sensus*, to feel with) from a distance.[34] It is thus not surprising that despite their different disciplinary affiliations and national belongings, we find among European modernists of literary and philosophical orientation similar preoccupations with states of psychic dissolution symptomatic of what Nietzsche calls "the phantom of the ego." From Nietzsche's "genuine physio-psychology," to Bataille's contagious "communication," via Conrad's horror of the "crowd," and Lawrence's critique of psychoanalysis, we understand little of the modernist dissolution of the "old stable ego" if we do not take into consideration the model of the mimetic unconscious that makes such a dissolution possible in the first place. One of the goals of this book is thus to recuperate this mimetic tradition in order to open up modernist studies, as well as mimetic theory, to a more inclusive line of investigation; by doing so, we shall reveal a conception of the unconscious that has been much neglected in our past Freudian century, but that haunts the mind of modernism nonetheless.

In this sense, then, this study looks back to the history of the *pre*-Freudian unconscious in order to propose an alternative genealogy of the modernist ego and the mimetic unconscious that animates it. And yet, turning backwards also allows us to better see what lies ahead. In fact, this Nietzschean current in modernism is in line with contemporary *post*-Freudian developments in mimetic theory that have recently established that automatic reflexes and influences are much more fundamental to the formation of the ego than past Freudian approaches had realized. Empirical studies in developmental psychology have, in fact, demonstrated that newborns are, quite literally, imitative from the very beginning: records of mimetic reflexes so far being set by thirty-minute-olds! As developmental psychologist Andrew

Meltzoff summarizes it, "newborn imitation . . . demonstrates that self-other connectedness and communication exists at birth. *Humans imitate before they can use language; they learn through imitation but don't need to learn to imitate.*"[35] This is indeed an empirical confirmation of the Aristotelian realization that what "distinguishes man from other creatures [is] that he is thoroughly mimetic."[36] And the discovery of "mirror neurons," as well as of the human brain's ongoing "plasticity,"[37] gives additional neurophysiological explanations to this well-known philosophical lesson, opening up new interdisciplinary possibilities that are vital to stimulating the promising dialogue between "mimesis and science."[38]

These are revolutionary discoveries that involve a Copernican turn away from ego-centric approaches to subject formation and cast serious doubts on the monadic conception of the Oedipal (or linguistic) subject that has dominated the past, Freudian century. And yet, in a sense, these discoveries are far from being *new* discoveries. A historically informed account of the unconscious demonstrates that they are important empirical confirmations of well-known modernist realizations. Gabriel Tarde, for instance, in *The Laws of Imitation* already based his account of the interpersonal social bond on the mimetic hypothesis that "there is, in the nervous system, an innate tendency towards imitation."[39] And virtually all the modernists we shall consider, writing from the 1870s to the 1950s, share the untimely and, at the time, still unfashionable realization that the ego is not born in isolation but in a relation of mimetic and unconscious communication with others. For them, imitation is not a consequence of learning and development but its fundamental presupposition: it is because newborns are imitating from the very first hours of life and automatically respond to facial expressions and gestures that they learn to understand the affects, intentions, and thoughts of privileged others (what Pierre Janet calls *socii*). From Nietzsche to Tarde, Conrad to Lawrence, Bataille to Janet, we shall repeatedly confirm that it is through an unconscious process of imitation characteristic of the "psychology of the socius" that the subject emerges as a relational, affective, and mimetic human being. Well before the empirical sciences, then, modernist writers attentive to the bodily forces that shape our psychic lives urge readers to rethink the foundations of the ego in relational, intersubjective terms.

This theoretical imperative is more timely than ever. In fact, if empirical research on imitation has now convincingly shown that the ego is not a solipsistic, mythical monad nor the precipitate of a narcissistic image reflected in a mirror, but rather responds mimetically to the affects of the other from the very first hours of life, then, if we want to understand how humans come into being, much more theoretical attention needs to be given to the formative function of these intersubjective, unconscious, responses that give birth to the ego—out the *pathos* of the other. One of the aims of this study is to focus on mimetic phenomena that turn the ego into a phantom of the ego in order to provide the missing link between the modernist, pre-Freudian unconscious and the new, post-Freudian unconscious that is currently emerging on the theoretical scene.

The realization that the ego emerges from an unconscious communication with the other does not fit easily within psychoanalytical accounts of ego formation in terms of Oedipal triangulations or specular identifications, yet it comes as no surprise to a genealogical approach of Nietzschean inspiration that roots the modernist unconscious back in the immanence of bodily reflexes. The authors I now turn to consider all agree that the experience of mimesis, in its polymorphous manifestations, informs the subject from the very beginning, and that it is through such bodily, affective relations, where imitation plays a decisive role, that the ego is born as a relational, communicative being. Their intuition that the ego is formed *by* the other, *through* the other, in a relation of unconscious communication *with* the other, is theoretically ahead of their times and testifies to the modernity and relevance of their approach. Opening up a line of inquiry that contemporary psychology is barely beginning to explore, these authors are *modern* in the sense that they manage to make our understanding of the psyche *new*. They also call our attention to the empirical fact that mimetic relations are the very condition that brings the ego into life as a relational, affective being. Thus understood, the ego is not a subject that precedes the experience of communication but, rather, a much more elusive, porous, and malleable entity that emerges from a type of mimetic communication that challenges the boundaries of individuation.

Furthermore, for the modernists, it is clear that such a relational ego open to the pathos of others in childhood continues to respond automatically to affects that are not under the control of consciousness in adulthood. This realization allows modernist writers to supplement current empirical approaches by considering mimesis outside of the objectifying walls of the laboratory and to account for the subjective, cultural implications of unconscious forms of mimetic behavior in the modern world. Extending the study of mimesis from individual bodies to the entire body politic, modernists explore the wider social, political, ethical, and philosophical implications of the power of the mimetic unconscious to infect and affect subjects in a world increasingly haunted by the power of affective contagion to turn selves into others, egos into phantoms. If the modernist insights into the patho(-)logical sides of imitation remain important for us today, it is also because we are barely beginning to foresee the unconscious phenomena our illustrious predecessors tried to warn us against.

The story of a phantom taking possession of the modern ego was once well-known in fin de siècle Europe. This phantom was even seen as constitutive of European history, a mimetic history concerned with the emergence of crowd behavior, the power of suggestion, and a general awareness that the laws of imitation informed both personal and public opinions. Yet, over time, not without violent struggles, and at great theoretical and practical costs, the emergence of a supposedly more "scientific" approach to the psyche imposed a single road to the unconscious and took possession of a century enthralled with the myth of scientific progress. The result is that in the past Freudian century, the history of this mimetic phantom—with its legendary power of possession, its magical generation of an ego that is not one, and its alternative key to open up bodily back doors to what was once called the soul—was all too quickly dismissed as a fiction. *The Phantom of the Ego* returns to tell this long-forgotten history. And in an ironic reversal of perspectives characteristic of the modernist Weltanschauung, it suggests that these so-called fictions turn out to be based on empirical facts, while the "scientific" approach is now revealed to a fable.

Diagnostic Program

Chapter 1 offers an alternative genealogy of Nietzsche's thought that roots the modernist ego back in the immanence of the mimetic unconscious. I argue that the German philosopher's most discussed concepts (from the Dionysian to slavery, from mastery to the will to power) emerge out of Nietzsche's affective implication in different forms of mimetic sickness he denounces in others (from hysteria to compassion, mimicry to hypnosis).

This is, indeed, a "contradiction" (Girard's term) that Nietzsche does not manage to fully resolve and that runs through the entirety of his thought, from *The Birth of Tragedy* (1872) to *Nietzsche contra Wagner* (1895). Consequently, the critiques Nietzsche addresses to his models are also inevitably attacks upon his own mimetic ego.

Yet this is what Nietzsche himself is ready to avow, and this avowal is constitutive of his diagnostic, perspectival method that informs his critique of modernity. Nietzsche's affective vulnerability to mimetic pathology has patho-*logical* relevance insofar as it lays bare a typically modern vulnerability to contagious affects that have the power to turn the ego into a mere phantom of the ego. In a second moment we shall thus see that Nietzsche's mimetic rivalry with his major intellectual models (Plato, Schopenhauer, and Wagner) is not only personally disabling, but also theoretically enabling insofar as it allows him to articulate an untimely critique of the mimetic pathologies that infect not only his ego but also modernity as a whole. Above all, his "psychology of 'looking around the corner'"[40] diagnoses a modern world haunted by the hypnotic will to power of charismatic leader figures who can take possession of masses of egos and generate unprecedented forms of horrors. In short, Nietzsche turns his mimetic sickness to productive theoretical use and offers a rich starting point for an alternative genealogy of the modernist unconscious.

Chapter 2 considers how Conrad extends this Nietzschean critique of the pathological effects of the mimetic unconscious towards the field of postcolonial studies, stretching—through the mediation of Francis Ford Coppola's *Apocalypse Now*—into the present. Late nineteenth-century disciplinary discourses as diverse as crowd psychology, hypnotic theory, and evolutionary anthropology tend to project mimetic, irrational affects onto subordinate "others," such as children, women, and racial others. Conrad, like Nietzsche before him, is not immune to this ethnocentric and patriarchal bias. A close reading of "An Outpost of Progress" (1896) and, especially of that milestone in literary modernism, *Heart of Darkness* (1899), demonstrates that Conrad is steeped in fin de siècle mimetic prejudices against women and Africans. Consequently, the much-discussed critiques of Conrad's "racism" and "sexism" must be radically reconsidered in the light of the mimetic theories and prejudices that already inform his work: Conrad's sexism turns out to be mimetic sexism, his racism, mimetic racism.

Yet Conrad, like Nietzsche before him, does not simply reproduce dominant stereotypes. On the contrary, he re-presents them (i.e., presents them again) only in order to better critique them from a distance. Thus, in a second moment, he unmasks how the dominant colonial subject of *Aufklärung* is imbued by the mimetic, irrational pathos he initially projects onto subordinate others. The mimetic subject, for Conrad, is not only the "primitive" other but is also and above all the "modern" ego. Consequently, the terms of the race debate, famously defined by the Nigerian novelist Chinua Achebe in "An Image of Africa" (1977), need to be reframed in the light of Conrad's mimetic critique of modernity. A close investigation of the formal structure of *Heart of Darkness* makes us see that the white male subject of *Aufklärung* is radically vulnerable to mimetic forms of subjection not only in childhood but also in adulthood, as the modern subject is impressed by the power of mass media to inform both mass opinion and public opinion. This process of in-formation—what social psychologist Gabriel Tarde calls "imitation" and Lacoue-Labarthe calls "typography"—is responsible for rendering the white, male subject of ideology vulnerable to "atrocious phantom[s]" like Mr. Kurtz, endowed with the will to power to put colonizing theories into practice and for the ethico-political horrors that, as Coppola's *Apocalypse Now* (1979) reminds us, continue to ensue. For Conrad, then, the horror of modernity must be reconsidered in the light of what I call "the horror of mimesis."

Chapter 3 shows that Nietzsche and Conrad are not alone among modernists to advocate the centrality of the mimetic unconscious. D. H. Lawrence's later period marks a theoretical shift from the much-discussed problematic of desire to the so far unnoticed problematic of mimesis. I argue that questions that have been central to Lawrence studies from the very beginning of his reception—such as Lawrence's implication in authoritarian forms of will to power, his fascination with primitivism, fascist psychology, and the dissolution of the "old stable ego"—must be reconsidered against the generalized background of the mimetic theories that inform his writings of the postwar period, from the so-called political novels (*Aaron's Rod* [1922], *Kangaroo* [1923], and *The Plumed Serpent* [1926]) to his books on the unconscious (*Psychoanalysis and the Unconscious* and *Fantasia of the Unconscious* [1921/1922]), as well as the anthropological essays collected in *Mourning and Mexico* (1927) and the posthumous papers *Phoenix* I & II (1936/1968). These theories include anthropological accounts of sympathetic magic (Frazer, Lévy-Bruhl), philosophical accounts of mimesis (Nietzsche, Plato), and different schools of dynamic psychology (Burrow, Freud). This transdisciplinary reframing is important for mimetic theory because it helps us theorize *both* the violent effects of affective contagion emphasized by Lawrence's predecessors (or "bad mimesis") *and* the vitalizing, communal function of affective participation (or "good mimesis"). It also reveals that the same model of the mimetic, or as he also calls it, "vertebral unconscious," is constantly at work in Lawrence's critique of the modern ego. His much-discussed quarrel with Freud will be reconsidered in the light of this pre-Freudian realization.

And yet, like Nietzsche and Conrad, Lawrence is not only looking backwards, towards a pre-Freudian tradition; he is also looking forwards, towards contemporary post-Freudian developments. I shall argue that Lawrence continues to be central in our postmodern period because he gives us the theoretical tools to understand why, exactly, a culture that privileges the eye over the body, mimetic representations over mimetic impersonations, continues to be haunted by what he calls "phantasmal consciousness." This realization is of theoretical value because it challenges dominant accounts of the ego in terms of specular identification (Lacan), anticipates anti-Oedipal critiques of psychoanalysis (Deleuze and Guattari), and foreshadows postmodern concerns with simulacra of the real (Baudrillard). Who would have thought that this often marginalized modernist is so theoretically ahead of his times in his diagnostic of mimesis? Lawrence is an untimely Nietzschean thinker who will indeed help us engage with cutting-edge theoretical developments, extending the modernist insights into mimetic theory to our mediatized, postmodern world.

Chapter 4 pursues this interdisciplinary investigation of the phantom of the ego by showing how Georges Bataille, one of the most celebrated precursors of the postmodern death of a linguistic subject (the subject of the signifier), is above all a modernist thinker who offers us an account of the birth of an affective subject (the subject of mimesis). Critics still tend to read Bataille through surrealist, postmodern, or deconstructive lenses, and quite rightly so, since he is conventionally associated with such contexts. However, in this chapter, I shall transgress conventional approaches to Bataille in order to reinscribe his heterogeneous thought into the modernist, transdisciplinary, pre-Freudian, and above all, Nietzschean tradition to which he belongs. If it is true that among postmodern quarters Bataille's heterogeneous thought still tends to recuperate him within a "metaphysics of the subject," I argue that the central concept of his thought (i.e., "sovereign communication") needs to be reread in the light of the modernist tradition of the mimetic unconscious that transgresses precisely such metaphysics. More precisely, Bataille, following one of the leading philosophers and psychologists of his time, Pierre Janet, considers that significant others (or *socii*) are from the beginning constitutive of the formation of the ego. For him the ego emerges from a nonlinguistic form of contagious "experience" that he misleadingly calls "interior" but that opens the ego to its affective outside.

As this study draws to an end, we shall progressively realize that at the origins of the ego there is no secret essence that is already interior to oneself, but a mimetic communication with an other who is neither fully interior nor exterior insofar as this unconscious communication transgresses the boundaries of individuation. From his early writings of the 1930s to some of his major theoretical texts of the 1940s and 1950s—*Inner Experience* (1943), *Guilty* (1944), *On Nietzsche* (1945), and *Eroticism* (1957)—Bataille shows that the ontological distinctions between "self" and "other," "interior" and "exterior," "private" and "public," which modernist figures have been questioning all along, no longer hold by the beginning of the postmodern period, a period haunted by the phantom of fascism and Nazism. Directly informed by the ethical and political horrors of modernity his predecessors had foreseen, Bataille returns to the foundations of subjectivity in order to open up new theoretical possibilities for what the ego could possible become. He may even offer a possible answer to the much discussed question, "Who comes after the subject?"[41]

Proposing an alternative to celebrated accounts of ego formation in terms of a specular identification with an image (or *imago*), Bataille advocates a model of unconscious communication that gives birth to the ego via the pathos of the other (or *socius*). Like his predecessors, Bataille continues to be critical of the pathological effects of imitation. But in his patho-*logical* countermovement, he also develops a gay science of mimesis that focuses on vitalizing and life-affirming forms of communications—sovereign communications like laughter that tickle the ego into being as a relational, mimetic being. After the much-discussed death of the linguistic subject, Bataille then turns to advocate the birth of a bodily ego—out of the laughter of the other. He does so in order to unmask the relational and communicative foundations that animate the process of subject formation along immanent, psycho-physiological lines that contemporary developments in the neurosciences are now beginning to rediscover. Finally, Bataille also offers an answer the question, "Who comes after the subject?" by echoing the Nietzschean realization that behind the mask of subjectivity lurks not so much the ego but the phantom of the ego.

In the end, then, the Nietzschean account of the mimetic unconscious will turn out to be more untimely than previously realized. It anticipates, by more than a century, cutting-edge insights into the dynamic of mimetic reflexes, affective communication, and the ongoing malleability of the human brain. The discoveries of "mirror neurons," of newborn imitation, and of the brain's neuroplasticity are decisive confirmations of mimetic principles our authors have been dissecting all along. Their diagnostic findings about the mimetic unconscious will thus have to be reevaluated in light of these empirical confirmations. For modernists of Nietzschean inspiration, in fact, as for contemporary developments in mimetic theory and the empirical sciences, the ego is a more malleable material than previously realized and continues to be formed, informed, and deformed by different types of personal, social, and political impressions. These impressions require close diagnostic operations because, for better or worse, they give form to an ego that is not one, but is animated by someone else. As we shall see, this phantom easily takes possession of the modern ego because it is through a phantom that the ego is born. Articulating the theoretical implications of this mimetic realization is what this study sets out to do.

The book ends with a coda that articulates the continuities and discontinuities between René Girard's mimetic theory and modernist mimetic theory. What emerges from this study is that in the modernist period the problematic of mimesis can no longer be restricted to the problematic of mimetic *desire* (and the rivalrous-violent triangles it entails) but must be supplemented by a more generalized investigation of the impersonal workings of what I call mimetic *pathos* (and the patho(-)logies it entails). This coda draws the conclusion of this theoretical realization. It also fleshes out some new lines of inquiry concerning the life-enhancing side of mimesis, the experience of community, and an ethics of mimesis that is aware that the other is both external and internal to the ego. These lines of inquiry have their origins in modernism, but they stretch in order to affect our own hyper-mimetic, postmodern times. As such, they call for further explorations by mimetic theorists yet to come.

CHAPTER 1

Nietzsche's Mimetic Patho(-)logy

From Antiquity to Modernity

I am still waiting for a philosophical *physician* in the exceptional sense of that word.

—Friedrich Nietzsche, *Twilight of the Idols*

The Phantom

When Nietzsche claims that a phantom is haunting the modern ego, he is not only expressing a personal, mimetic anxiety; he is also diagnosing a wider cultural sickness that affects and infects modernity as a whole. This mimetic pathology condemns the modern ego to live in a world of phantoms where one is not oneself, but someone other instead. As Nietzsche diagnoses in *Daybreak* (1881):

> Whatever they may think and say about their "egoism," the great majority nonetheless do nothing for their ego their whole life long: what they do is done for the phantom of their ego [*Phantom von ego*] which has formed itself in the heads of those around them and has been communicated [*mitgeteilt*] to them;—as a consequence they all of them dwell in a fog

of impersonal, semi-personal opinions, and arbitrary, as it were poetical
evaluations, the one forever in the head of someone else, and the head of
this someone else again in the head of others: a strange world of phantasms. (105)[1]

This is a world where what is most intimate about oneself is indistinguishable
from others, where one's opinions are someone else's opinions, one's head
part of someone else's head. This is a strange world of phantoms, indeed. And
since Nietzsche feels that the phantom of the ego has possessed the "great
majority" of modern subjects, it is perhaps not surprising that, philosophical
ghost-buster that he is, he will spend a good part of his career chasing this
mimetic phantom. This chapter tells the story of Nietzsche's ghost hunt, a
mimetic hunt where the hunter is himself haunted by the unconscious phantoms he sets forth to unmask.

Nietzsche is a self-proclaimed "philosophical physician" who frequently
practices the art of psychological dissection. On his operating table one can
find psychic phenomena as diverse as compassion, identification, theatrical
impersonation, crowd behavior, hysteria, intoxication, emotional contagion,
and mass opinion, to name but the most prominent mimetic pathologies.
These phenomena are mimetic in the psychic sense that they create a confusion between self and other characteristic of the "phantom of the ego."
Mimesis, for Nietzsche, is thus not simply understood as imitation or representation, but as a polymorphous phenomenon that troubles the boundaries
of individuation. Indeed, mimesis is at the heart of Nietzsche's most insistent
concerns with modernity. It not only informs his account of masters and
slaves, the Apollonian and the Dionysian, compassion and will to power, but
also occupies center stage with respect to his agonistic confrontation with his
most significant models and rivals: that is, Schopenhauer, Wagner, and Plato.
Indeed, the problematic of affective mimesis, though rarely discussed, is not
only at the heart of Nietzsche's most constant philosophical preoccupations;
it also goes to the foundations of his thought and persona.

What does not remain constant, however, is Nietzsche's diagnostic
evaluation of mimesis. Nietzsche's position oscillates, like a pendulum,
between two opposed poles. Most often, as his account of the "phantom of
the ego" already indicates, this "physician of the soul" (D 52) posits himself
at a radical distance from the psychic phenomena that lie on his dissecting

[handwritten margin notes: "Anti-Christianity / criticizes Wagner"]

table. This distance, or as he often calls it, this "pathos of distance," splits his conception of the subject in two and sets up a sharp contrast between non-mimetic and mimetic subjects: the master contra the slave, the individual contra the herd, Nietzsche contra Wagner, and so on. Yet the primary characteristic of affective mimesis, as Nietzsche knows, is precisely to challenge the boundaries that divide and oppose subjects. Thus, not only the "great majority," but also the conceptual types Nietzsche consistently promotes—including "Herr Nietzsche" himself—will prove vulnerable to the contaminating power of contagious communication he so effectively diagnoses in others. Nietzsche, like Plato before him and other modernists after him, is deeply implicated in the modern forms of mimetic sickness he vehemently critiques. This is true with respect to that mimetic "pathos" (from Greek suffering, passion related to *penthos*, sorrow) par excellence which is compassion, but is equally true if we consider Nietzsche's confrontation with what he calls "Wagner's pathos" (*CW* 8) and the theatrical mimesis it entails.[2] We can thus say that tacitly at work in the notion of "pathos of distance" is a fundamental structural oscillation towards / away from mimesis, a conjunctive-disjunction generated by the fact that Nietzsche's "distance" is constantly undermined by his own entanglement in (and, at times, even enthusiasm for) mimetic "pathos."

This fundamental tension at the heart of Nietzsche's thought has largely gone unnoticed, yet it has not escaped René Girard's reading of Nietzsche. In a series of essays that open up Nietzsche studies to mimetic theory, Girard has shown that a fundamental "contradiction" is at the heart of Nietzsche's take on compassion. And in a characteristically provocative gesture, he invites future readers of Nietzsche "who do not praise contradiction only in the abstract" to address this point.[3] To my knowledge, Girard's challenge has not been directly addressed, and, as a consequence, it has not received the attention it deserves. In this chapter, I pick up this thought-provoking line of inquiry in an attempt to further Girard's insights into Nietzsche's contradictory stance on mimetic affects. Building on the work of two major figures in Nietzsche studies and mimetic theory aligned with rigorous forms of deconstruction, the American critic and theorist Henry Staten and the French philosopher Philippe Lacoue-Labarthe,[4] I shall argue that such a "contradiction" traverses the entirety of Nietzsche's corpus, from his early account of the Dionysian to his late critique of the mimetic crowd, passing

[handwritten margin note: "Plan for this chapter"]

via his paradoxical take on compassion, poetic enthusiasm, and massive outbreaks of hypnotic depersonalization. Or, if you prefer Nietzsche's diagnostic language, the problematic of mimesis informs his Schopenhauerian, Platonic, and Wagnerian sicknesses.

A mimetic approach suggests that Nietzsche's most valuable insights into the workings of affective mimesis progressively emerge if we closely consider this contradictory push-pull as it surfaces throughout his work of the early, middle, and, especially, later period. If distance from mimesis is obviously necessary for the development of a critical practice that leads him to evaluate contagious affects in pathological terms (i.e., as a "sickness"), Nietzsche's own mimetic *pathology* should not be dismissed as a mere contradiction; nor should it be celebrated as an aporia. Rather, following Nietzsche's insight that "sickness is instructive . . . even more instructive than health" (*GM* III, 9; 92), I will argue that his "mimetic disease" furnishes him with the affective raw material necessary for the development of a mimetic patho-*logy* (i.e., a critical discourse, or *logos, on* mimetic *pathos*). Out of this oscillation between "distance" from and affective proximity to mimetic "pathos," the spiraling motor of Nietzsche's "patho(-)logy"—now understood in the dual sense of both disease and diagnosis—is set in motion. Both infected and critical aspects of Nietzsche's thought will be instrumental in taking hold of the process of unconscious communication responsible for the formation of that "strange world of phantoms" in which the modern subject, *volens nolens*, is condemned to find his or her way.

The Logos of Sympathy

Nietzsche's considerations on the "phantom of the ego" are part of his disturbing aristocratic radicalism that violently splits his conception of the subject in two; and this *Spaltung* is tacitly predicated on the question of mimesis. On the one hand, we are told, there is the "great majority" whose moral opinions are "adopted" (i.e., mimetic subjects) and, on the other, the "free spirits" whose opinions are "original" (i.e., nonmimetic subjects) (*D* 104). This moral distinction between individuals functions as a leitmotif in Nietzsche's conception of morality and anticipates the much-debated typology he posits in *On the Genealogy of Morals* (1887). If the master/slave distinction introduces new criteria to evaluate human types (such as "active-ness" and "reactiveness," "life affirmation" and "life negation," "strength" and "weakness," "health" and "sickness"), the fundamental distinction between imitative and nonimitative subjects remains firmly in place. In fact, Nietzsche defines the noble as an "autonomous" subject who creates his own values and "resembles no one but himself" (*GM* II, 2; 41). And, as is well known, he repeatedly defines slavery in terms of passive submission to moral conven-tions, dismissing such a psychic docility via the telling image of the mimetic "herd." The "pathos of distance" Nietzsche posits between these two types of men at the opening of *Genealogy of Morals* allows him to "contrast," as he puts it, the "noble, the powerful, the superior and the high-minded" to "everything low, low-minded, common and plebeian" (*GM* I, 2; 12). In short, this notion guarantees the stability of what David Krell aptly calls a *"disjunc-tive typology."*5

Mimetic Infections

Nietzsche's critique of the mimetic status of the "herd" is predicated on a physiological/medical terminology that leads him to conflate slavery with "sickness." Nietzsche's insistence on the diagnostic notion of sickness to denounce slavery pervades his later work, but is especially apparent in the third essay of *On the Genealogy of Morals*, devoted to a critique of "ascetic ideals." There he speaks of the "sickliness of the type of man which has existed so far" (*GM* III, 13; 99) as well as of the "sick herd" (15; 105). This theoreti-cal gesture is most often read as a direct expression of Nietzsche's *"aggres-sive* pathos" (*EH* 7; 47): that is, a sovereign, philosophical attack explicitly directed against Christianity, but which also encompasses the sphere of morality or, as he dismissively calls it, "the herd instinct in the individual" (*GS* 116). From this perspective, Nietzsche's critique of slavery in terms of sickness is launched from a superior position based on what he calls a scorn-ful "looking down on subjects" (*BGE* 257) and can be read as just one of the many derogatory attributes he refers to in order to define "herd morality." The sick human being, Nietzsche repeatedly affirms, is a "life-negating" sub-ject characterized by "weakness," the *"Wille zum Ende,"* "ressentiment," and the inability to affirm, enjoy, and celebrate life here and now. Needless to say that at such textual moments the pathos of distance that divides the master's (healthy) life affirmation from the slaves' (sick) life negation is at its sharpest. As Nietzsche puts it, there is an "*abyss* between the healthy and the sick" (*GM* III, 16; 107). This romantic story is often told, well known, and often passes as the only version of Nietzsche's thoughts on morality.

And yet a closer look at *Genealogy* shows that at work in Nietzsche's notion of "sickness" is also a more insidious, less transparent, early-modernist level of thought that tends to complicate the violent hierarchical disjunction between mimetic and antimimetic types. In fact, at times, Nietzsche loses his self-assurance in the stability of his hierarchical typology and admits, for instance, that "the sick represent the greatest danger [*grösste Gefahr*] for the healthy" (14; 100). In this section of the essay the notion of "pathos of distance" surfaces for the second time, but now this notion is no longer intro- duced to guarantee the distinction between the "high-minded" and the "low- minded," the "healthy" and the "sick," and the tone of aristocratic superiority has left space for an anxiety concerning the dangers of mimetic infection:

> That the sick should *not* infect the healthy with their sickness . . . this ought to be the prime concern on earth [*der oberste Gesichtspunkt auf Erden*]— but that requires above all that the healthy should remain *segregated* from the sick, protected even from the sight of the sick, so that they do not mis- take themselves for the sick. . . . the pathos of distance [*Pathos der Distanz*] *should* keep even their missions separate to all eternity! (14; 103)

The masters need to be protected "even from the sight of the sick, so that they do not mistake themselves for the sick." Such a claim casts serious doubts on the radical distinction Nietzsche had initially posited between human types and makes clear that inherent in his "pathos of distance" is not only an affirmative gesture, which posits a disjunction between noble and slave, but also a self-preservative move intended to protect the so-called "strong" from the "weak." As Henry Staten aptly recognized, "Nietzsche's text is pervaded by a fear of the power of the weak."[6] Or, to put it in Nietzschean parlance, inherent in the pathos of distance is not only an "aggressive pathos" but also a "defensive ability"—not only "action" but also "reaction."

This is already the moment to pause in order to ask a series of questions concerning such a defensive/reactive movement in Nietzsche's text: How can a look be sufficient to turn the most aristocratic subject who "resembles no one but himself" into the despised mimetic other? Is the conceptual and the affective distance between noble and slave so thin? Or is the slave's power of contagion—what Nietzsche also calls "will to power of the weakest" (14; 102)—so strong? And if the latter, how is such contagion communicated (*mitgeteilt*)? In *Genealogy*, Nietzsche does not provide a direct answer to these clinical questions; yet he tells us where to look for it. In fact, a few lines after mentioning that "it is not the strongest but the weakest who spells disaster for the strong," Nietzsche attributes this "disastrous effect" to "great *disgust* at man; as well as great *compassion* [*Mitleid*] for man" (14; 101). Let us recall that elsewhere Nietzsche says that compassion "makes suffering contagious" (*A* 7; 573), and he adds that Aristotle considered it "a pathological and dangerous condition" (7; 574)—dangerous, that is, for its power of infection, whereby pathos breaks down what he also calls "the delicate feeling for distance" (*EH* 4; 44). It is thus to this instinct that I now turn in order to define the precise modality of that affective, infective, or as we shall call it, *mimetic pathology* that threatens to bridge the so-called abyss that divides the healthy from the sick.

The purpose of this "detour" via the problematic of compassion is at least twofold. On the one hand, a focus on *Mitleid*, or if you want, sympathy (from Greek *sym-pathos*, suffering together) is instrumental in solving a fundamental contradiction in Nietzsche's text. And insofar as this shared pathos threatens to bridge the distance that Nietzsche posits within his "disjunctive" human typology, this side of the argument allows us to turn our diagnostic lenses inwards, to dissect the infections of his mimetic thought (or pathology). On the other hand, a focus on the problematic of compassion allows us to reconstruct Nietzsche's theoretical discourse *on* mimetic pathos (or patho-logy), to start an inquiry into the infectious nature of mimesis in the modern period, and to open up an alternative model of the unconscious. In short, this detour is the detour via mimesis, a detour instrumental in setting in motion the spiraling motor of Nietzsche's mimetic patho(-)logy that will guide us during our clinical investigation.

The Power of Mitleid

Compassion is one of Nietzsche's most persistent targets and can obviously not be dissociated from his equally persistent critique of Christianity. In fact, a dissection of this psychic phenomenon allows him to reach the heart of what he denominates "the religion of *pity*" (*die Religion* des Mitleidens) (*A* 7; 572). It is thus not surprising that his vehement attack on this psychic phenomenon can be found in most of his works dealing with Christianity; basically, everywhere from *Human, All Too Human* (1878) to the *Antichrist* (1895).[7] It is, however, in *Daybreak*, especially, that Nietzsche's critique of compassion is most thoroughly developed, and more precisely in Book II, the book where the notion of "the phantom of the ego" appears. Nietzsche, in fact, relentlessly exposes the psychological motivations that hide under the mask of that "sympathetic affection" (*sympathische Affektion*) (*D* 143) par excellence which is compassion. His approach is, once again, initially launched from a position of critical distance and is predicated on what Nietzsche calls the "art of psychological dissection" (*HH* 35). And as the phenomenon of compassion is progressively taken apart, Nietzsche takes some pleasure in exposing his readers to what he calls the "horrible sight of the psychological operating table" (37). Nietzsche uncovers in compassion a pathological, life-negating tendency that he considers a "harmful affect" because it "*increases* the amount of suffering in the world" (*D* 134). And in the *Antichrist*, he goes as far as rooting in compassion the source of all modern ailments. As he puts it: "In our whole unhealthy modernity there is nothing more unhealthy than Christian pity [*Mitleid*]. To be physicians *here*, to be inexorable *here*, to wield the operating knife *here* [*das Messer füh-ren*]—that is our part" (*A* 7; 574; trans. modified).[8] Such a critical approach is part of Nietzsche's project of reevaluation of all values. And insofar as it is in line with his critique of slave morality as fundamentally nihilistic, it leaves the distinction between strong and weak, healthy and sick, firmly in place. Furthermore, as Nietzsche sharpens his operating knife, his critique of compassion cuts even deeper. Reactive psychic phenomena as diverse as "fear," "egoism," "pleasure," "revenge," and "honor" are, according to his diagnosis, among the unconscious motives at the origin of compassionate acts (*D* 133). This patho-*logical* approach leads him to conclude that it is "misleading to call the *Leid* (suffering) which we experience . . . *Mitleid* (pity)," for this suffering "is our own, as the suffering he feels is his own" (133). In other words, the pathos at work in this "sympathetic affection" is far from being a *shared* pathos. Consequently, compassion and the sickness it entails is far from being contagious.

And yet, even in this text of the middle period, a closer look at Nietzsche's operating table allows us to see that a parallel discourse underlies his confident patho-logical considerations. This second discourse on compassion begins to surface as Nietzsche's degree of emotional implication in the phenomenon under consideration increases. If the suffering other is not a stranger, nor a Christian, but, let us say, a friend or somebody one admires, Nietzsche shifts from a position of "suspicion" with respect to compassion to one that is alert to the mimetic aspect inherent in this pathos. "There are cases where sympathy is stronger than the actual suffering," he writes. And he adds: "We feel it as more painful, for instance, if one of our friends incurs the guilt of something disgraceful than if we ourselves do" (HH 46). And in *Daybreak*, continuing this emotional line of inquiry, he adds: "If we love, honor, admire someone and then afterwards discover that he is *suffering* . . . the gulf between us and him seems to be bridged, and an approximation of identity [*Annäherung an Gleichheit*] seems to occur" (138). Contrary to what he had previously said, Nietzsche now argues that inherent in compassion is a true *Mit-leid*, in the literal sense that we suffer (*leiden*) *with* (*mit*) the other, experience the suffering *of* the other, suffer *as* the other does, and perhaps even more. As Nietzsche had put it in his account of the communication of the phantom of the ego, *Mitleid* places one, quite literally, "in the head of someone else." Inherent in this shared pathos, then, is a mimetic indistinction that troubles the boundaries of individuation and allows the phantom to take possession of the ego.

It is true that such examples seem to indicate that an initial identificatory relationship with a (male) subject, such as a friend or a model, facilitates the "approximation of identity" inherent in compassion. In this sense, compassion would only bring to full completion a preexisting mimetic bond; identification would thus be the necessary precondition for a *sympathetic* mimesis to take place. Yet, for Nietzsche, this bond is far from being limited to such intimate cases. Thus, he extends such personal intuitions in order to develop a general "theory of empathy" that accounts for the precise modality of this process of mimetic communication. And insofar as Nietzsche's theory is a direct response to his former "educator," Arthur Schopenhauer, we need to consider Nietzsche's critical engagement with a philosopher who posited *Mitleid* at the "foundation of morality," this being also the title of Schopenhauer's study devoted exclusively to ethics.

Nietzsche is extremely critical of Schopenhauer's theory of compassion. In his view, his former educator promotes a life-negating attitude or, to use Schopenhauer's terminology, a negation of the "Will," which runs against Nietzsche's life-affirming philosophy. The conflation of one of the first philosophers to openly embrace atheism with the life-negating tendency Nietzsche sees in Christianity is made clear as he writes that "Schopenhauer was an enemy of life and therefore turned compassion into a virtue" (*A* 7; trans. mine). And already in *Human, All Too Human* (the book that marks the break with his two youthful intellectual models and, later, mimetic rivals, Wagner and Schopenhauer) he writes that "the whole medieval Christian way of viewing the world and perceiving humanity could again celebrate its resurrection in Schopenhauer's teaching, despite the long-since achieved annihilation of all Christian dogmas" (26).⁹ This "resurrection" of the "Christian world" via Schopenhauer's take on compassion is partly responsible for that dispossession characteristic of the "phantom of the ego." In fact, Nietzsche says that Christianity entails a "'loss of the self,' sanctification; in physiological terms hypnosis" (*GM* III, 17; 110). We shall return to hypnosis and the "loss of the self" it entails later on. For the moment suffice to say that for Nietzsche, Schopenhauer's "much loved and sanctified theory" is itself also endowed with a contagious power to affect "clear and not-so-clear heads" (*D* 142; 90). Schopenhauer's *thought* on compassion is thus defined in the same contagious terms characteristic of the *affect* under consideration, which also means that, for Nietzsche, Schopenhauer's *logos* is infected by the *pathos* it attempts to analyze.

Nietzsche's critique of the philosopher of pessimism does not stop at the latter's *evaluation* of compassion, but extends to encompass his psychological insights as well. Still in *Daybreak*, Nietzsche says that Schopenhauer "observed [*Mitleid*] so imperfectly, and described [it] so badly" (133; 85). Furthermore, he goes on to ridicule and, eventually, dismiss his theory as a "mystical process by virtue of which *pity* makes two beings into one and in this way makes possible the immediate understanding of the one by the other" (142; 90). This is a strong and rather antagonistic critique. Hence, it would be quite reasonable to expect Nietzsche's descriptions and observations to radically diverge from Schopenhauer's. And yet, strangely enough, this does not seem to be the case. In fact, Schopenhauer's account of compassion is predicated on a mimetic indistinction between self and other that is practically isomorphous with the "bridging" or "approximation of identity" Nietzsche describes in the case of *Mitleid* with a friend. Here is Schopenhauer on compassion:

> to a certain extent I have identified myself with the other man, and in consequence the barrier between the ego and non-ego is for the moment abolished; only then do the other man's affairs, his need, distress, and suffering, directly become my own. . . . I share the suffering with him despite the fact that his skin does not enclose my nerves.[10]

On this fundamental mimetic point, Nietzsche and Schopenhauer tend to agree, after all: inherent in compassion is a pathos that disrupts the distance of individuation and traverses the skin that divides self and other, putting two nervous systems in communication, wiring them together, as it were. In *Mit-Leid*, then, one feels the pathos of the other; what is proper to the other becomes part of the self; the ego slowly turns into what Nietzsche calls "phantom of the ego."

Is Nietzsche, then, simply reproducing Schopenhauer's logos on mimesis, introducing difference where there is only sameness? It is not so simple. It is only if we consider the precise modality whereby this state of mimetic indistinction is achieved that a difference between the two theories of *Mitleid* begins to appear. Schopenhauer's theory, contrary to what Nietzsche says, does not entail an "immediate understanding of the other." And if it is true that Schopenhauer himself, at times, defines compassion as a "wholly direct and even instinctive participation in another's suffering," the most rigorous articulation of his conception of compassion makes clear that for him, this phenomenon is far from being based on an "immediate," "direct participation" devoid of critical reflection.[11] In fact, Schopenhauer continues,

> But this requires that I am in some way *identified with him*, in other words, that this entire *difference* between me and everyone else, which is the very basis of my egoism, is eliminated, to a certain extent at least. Now since I do not exist *inside the other man's skin*, then only by means of the *knowledge* I have of him, that is of the representation of him in my head, can I identify myself with him to such an extent that my deed declares that difference is abolished.[12]

Mimesis, for Schopenhauer, is not a matter of direct bodily affects transgressing the physical boundaries that divide self from other, as Nietzsche
wants us to believe. Instead, for the philosopher of pessimism, sympathetic identification is mediated by *knowledge* of the other. It follows that
identification does not take place with the *other* as such, nor with the *suffering* of the other but, rather, with the other as he or she appears to me, in a
mental *representation* (*Vorstellung*). This mediated, mimetic process suggests
that no matter how deeply I sympathize with the other, I can never fully slip
under the "skin" of the other and experience the suffering of the other as the
other does. Strictly speaking, for Schopenhauer, the compassionate subject
remains always and only in its own head. For him, the only thing compassion
can achieve is *a fiction* of "approximation of identity." That is, we can act *as
if* such dividing skin did not exist, *as if* the "barrier between the ego and the
non-ego" were no longer a reality. The phantom, in other words, never really
takes possession of the ego, only fictionally so.

Now, Nietzsche's "theory of empathy" (*Mitempfindung*)[13] offers an interesting variation on this mediated possibility. His most thorough elucidation
of the mimetism at work in "empathy" appears, once again, in *Daybreak*. In
this work of the middle period, he places his mimetic considerations within
the context of a wider theory of communication (*Mitteilung*) that equally
informs his account of the phantom of the ego. The passage begins as follows:

> To understand another person, that is, to *imitate his feelings in ourselves*
> [*sein Gefühl in uns nachzubilden*], we do indeed often go back to the *reason*
> for his feeling thus or thus and ask for example: *why* is he troubled?—so as
> then for the same reason to become troubled ourselves. (*D* 142; 89)

With Schopenhauer, Nietzsche seems to posit the mediating necessity of "reason" (i.e., of a mental representation) in order to be sympathetically affected
by the "feelings" of the other. Notice also how such an account introduces a
critical distance between the compassionate subject and the type of affect at
work in the suffering other. In fact, if the "reasons" at the origin of the other's
suffering, or pathos, are considered to be weak or invalid, no *Mit-Leid* can
possibly occur. The immediate theoretical consequence of this account is that
the power of reason can keep the "contagious instinct" of compassion under
control, while at the same time preserving a "pathos of *distance*."

Yet, according to Nietzsche, such a rational, mediated approach with respect to the suffering of the other is far from being the norm. After admitting this possibility, he moves on to a second, what he calls a "more usual," dynamic, a dynamic that comes awfully close to what he condemns in the theory of his first philosophical model: namely, an "immediate" understanding of the other. Here is the core of Nietzsche's theory of empathy:

> it is much more usual to omit to do this [i.e., consider the reasons of suffering] and instead to produce the feeling in ourselves after the *effects* it exerts and displays on the other person by imitating [*nachbilden*] with our own body the expression of his eyes, his voice, his walk, his bearing (or even their reflection in word, picture, music). Then a similar feeling arises in us in consequence of an ancient association between movement and sensation. . . . We have brought our skill in understanding the feelings of others to a high state of perfection and in the presence of another person we are always almost involuntarily [*unwillkürlich*] practicing this skill. (142; 89)

Nietzsche is now taking his distance from Schopenhauer's theory, but this distance brings him considerably closer to the suffering of the other, this time not a friend, but an anonymous other. In fact, according to this second, mimetic hypothesis, compassion no longer involves the mediation of the other's affects via the tribunal of reason. As Nietzsche explains, the association is now no longer between *reason* and sensations, but between *movement* and sensation. And he claims that an imitation of the *bodily manifestation* (or even its representation) of the inner pain leads the sympathetic subject to experience the pain of the other. According to this "ancient association between movement and sensation," pathos turns into sym-pathos, *Leid* into *Mit-Leid*.

This is a fundamental mimetic realization that is central to the modernist account of the unconscious and will traverse our entire investigation. At this stage, we wonder: How is this association triggered in the first place? And why does Nietzsche say that it is "ancient"? For Nietzsche, such an "ancient association" underscores not only his account of communication of suffering but also his understanding of the origin of communication *tout court*. This amounts to saying that all communication, for Nietzsche, is predicated on a mimetic principle and, thus, that what he excoriates as a pathology is in reality a most normal, ordinary human phenomenon. As he puts it already in *Human, All Too Human*, in a key section aptly titled "Gesture and Speech,"

> older than speech is the mimicking of gestures, which takes place invol-
> untarily and is even now, despite a general repression of gestural language
> and a cultivated mastery of the muscles, so strong. . . . The imitated [*nach-*
> *geahmte*] gesture led the person who was imitating [*den, der nachahmte*]
> back to the sensation that expressed itself in the face or body of the person
> being imitated [*des Nachgeahmten*]. Thus people learned to understand
> one another; thus the child still learns to understand its mother. (216)[14]

Here we see how deep Nietzsche's theory of the mimetic subject actually goes. This passage, in fact, makes strikingly clear that both at the level of ontogenesis (the development of the child) and phylogenesis (the develop-ment of the human species) mimesis, for Nietzsche, precedes language and allows communication to take place. For Nietzsche, in fact, it is the uncon-scious reproduction of a facial gesture of the other that allows the self to understand the sensation of the other and, thus, to communicate with the other. In the beginning, then, according to Nietzsche, there is no rational *logos* but a bodily *mimesis* instead. Mimesis is at the origin of subjectivity, communication, and culture.

This may appear to be a disconcerting realization in a world still imbued with solipsistic accounts of ego formation, yet it is perfectly in line with contemporary empirical accounts of the role of "unconscious mimesis" in self-others relations.[15] Now that Nietzsche's "genuine physio-psychology" has found a neurophysiological confirmation, we can go further and suggest that modernists may provide an account of the cultural and philosophical *implications* of this ordinary phenomenon, so ordinary that it should be vis-ible to a slightly attentive parent. Still, the psychic, cultural, political, and philosophical implications of this Nietzschean realization are extraordinary and will occupy us in what follows.

For the moment, let us draw some provisional theoretical conclusions concerning Nietzsche's account of mimetic communication. Two crucial points need to be underscored. First, the mimetic disposition of the subject should not be dismissed as an archaic trait belonging to our cultural or per-sonal prehistory that has been suppressed by civilization. On the contrary,

Nietzsche, anticipating key insights in mimetic theory, makes clear that it "goes on even now," even among the "educated"—a point that should not surprise us since it is clearly in line with his account of the phantom of the ego. Second, such a mimesis is not under the control of a rational, volitional subject who imitates at will and with discrimination. As Nietzsche makes clear, this bodily/affective mimesis "goes on involuntarily." Nietzsche is insistent about the involuntary dimension of mimesis. For him, imitative reflexes are not under the volitional control of consciousness and are in this sense, *un*-conscious. And in order to make his theory more tangible he offers us a paradigmatic example of the contagious power of the mimetic unconscious: the imitation of a gesture, he writes "is so strong that *we cannot look upon facial movements without innervation of our own face* (one can observe that feigned yawning evokes a natural yawning in someone who sees it)" (*HH* 216; my emphasis). We begin to see that the mimetic unconscious troubles the logic that clearly divides true and false affects, copy and original, the ego and the phantom of the ego. As the example of yawning suggests, it is a *feigned* yawning that engenders a *real* yawning, not the other way round. The "copy" brings the "original" into being, in a mimetic way, opening up the theoretical possibility that the phantom might actually give birth to the ego itself.

Nietzsche's theory of reflex, unconscious communication is far from being limited to his early period, but informs his conception of the subject until the very end. In a fragment of March–June 1888 collected in *The Will to Power*, for instance, he writes:

> Empathy with the souls of others is originally nothing moral, but a physiological susceptibility to suggestion: "sympathy," or what is called "altruism" is merely a product of that psychomotor rapport which is reckoned a part of spirituality (*induction psycho-motrice*, Charles Féré thinks). One never communicates thoughts: one communicates movements, mimic signs, which we then trace back to thoughts. (*WP* 809)

We shall see later that Nietzsche is not saying anything absolutely original here. He is advocating a conception of the suggestible, hypnotic, or as we call it, *mimetic* unconscious that was very much *en vogue* during the second half of the nineteenth century, and not only among the scientific community, but also among modernist writers concerned with rooting subjectivity back in the immanence of psycho-physiological affects and bodily reactions. For the moment, it is important to realize that such unconscious, mimetic reflexes are constitutive of Nietzsche's theory of the subject. In fact, for Nietzsche, communication (of which compassion is a specific instance) is predicated on an involuntary-instinctual-passive-reflex-psycho-physiological mimesis, which translates body language into affective language, involuntary gestures into intelligible emotions, and, by doing so, bridges the gap that divides self from other, one ego from another ego. Surprisingly, it is not Schopenhauer but, rather, Nietzsche, a philosopher who still tends to be considered a champion of linguistic mediation, who proposes a direct, bodily mimesis, which is precisely *not* mediated by *logos*, at the origin of human communication. How, then, is *Mitleid* possible? Like any other form of affective communication, for Nietzsche, it is through an unconscious, mirroring reflex that we experience and understand the feelings of the other. Unconscious reflexes are thus at the origin of rational thought; mimetic *pathos* opens up the possibility of rational *logos*. This is a mimetic hypothesis we shall have to bear in mind.

If the Nietzschean model of unconscious communication seems straightforward, some of its implications are perhaps not as easily acceptable and open the door to a variety of possible objections. Here are but a few. First, Nietzsche's account of communication deprives the subject of rational control over his cogitations and makes it vulnerable to any sort of psychic influences. In our post-Freudian era, the irrational status of the subject may seem a truism, but the ethico-political implications of a type of subjectivity that mimetically reacts to any movement or gesture and develops thoughts on the basis of such gestures, as we shall see, are troubling enough. Second, Nietzsche challenges a Romantic sense of individuality that posits a deep, original, authentic interiority at the source of one's ego and shows that the psychic life of the subject is formed by external social pressures. Third, this model makes no essential difference between "primitive" and "civilized" subjects. On this point, Nietzsche is perhaps less entangled in the evolutionary biases characteristic of modernist accounts of primitivism. But, more problematically, this model equates children and adults, as well as noneducated and educated, suggesting that age and education are not necessarily a guarantee against the dangers of mimetic infection. Finally, this account is equally troubling for philosophical reasons. We have become so accustomed to think of mimesis in terms of mediation and representation that such a direct, affective mimesis may initially sound suspect, if not theoretically naive. This is not yet the moment to put these important objections to rest, but simply to acknowledge them as internal to Nietzsche's critique of the phantom of the ego. In what follows, we shall discover that Nietzsche is in good company, both ancient and modern, in advocating such a troublesome mimetic conception of the ego.

Mimesis Reconstructed

These considerations of Nietzsche's early theory of communication allow us to confront and resolve our initial questions concerning the defensive move inherent in the master's pathos of distance. As the German philosopher, towards the end of his career, defines compassion as a "contagious instinct," he means exactly what he says. Namely, that compassion is contagious precisely because it is an *instinctual* mirroring reflex that can be contained but not completely suppressed—as a yawn can be contained but not suppressed. We are thus now in a better position to understand his claim that the healthy need to be "protected even from the *sight* of the sick." In fact, if Nietzsche explains compassion via the paradigm of yawning, it is indeed understandable that any subject who is exposed to the simple sight of suffering risks capitulating to the unconscious power of mimetic contagion. This "pathological and dangerous condition" (*A* 7; 574), as he also calls it, is endowed with the power of "action at distance." Furthermore, Nietzsche's account of the origin of communication postulates an unconscious, imitative tendency in every human subject that is, by definition, indifferent to hierarchical typological distinctions. In other words, the mimetic instinct, which Nietzsche tries to cast to the outside by relegating it to the sphere of slavery, is already internal to sovereignty. The master turns out to be *as* mimetic *as* the slave; the sick *as* strong *as* the healthy! Needless to say, such a mimetic pathos introduces an *affective conjunction* in Nietzsche's *disjunctive typology*.

As we move to a higher level of generality, we can push the theoretical consequences of patho(-)logical reading in two divergent directions. On the one hand, this analysis challenges the consistency of Nietzsche's human typology: the "appropriate" conclusion of a reading *against* Nietzsche devoted to pointing out the contradictions in his thoughts on morality. I acknowledge this "conclusion" as an initial effect of my reading insofar as

I consider Nietzsche's aristocratic distinction between human "types" a problematic characteristic of his thought, whose political implications we shall later consider. On the other hand, our attention to the oscillating dimension of Nietzsche's thought on mimesis functions as a reading *with* Nietzsche, a reading that is not so much a "conclusion" as a "beginning" of the problematic that informs this book. It is thus primarily in this second sense that I understand it: that is, as a critical effort devoted to reconstructing Nietzsche's thought on subjectivity and the theoretical implications this thought entails for mimetic theory. From this perspective, Nietzsche's insights into the workings of affective communication can be supplemented by his more personal "confessions" that are already internal to his philosophy and bear testimony to the relevance and power of mimetic pathos.[16] This last methodological point involves a shift of attention from a theory of mimesis to an experience of mimetic affects; from a patho-*logy* Nietzsche controls to a *pathology* that controls the thinker and his thought; from Nietzsche's *distance* with respect to mimesis to his personal implication in the mimetic *pathos* he so deftly analyzes.

Nietzsche is even more insistent about the need to posit a pathos of *distance* with respect to his fellow men when he appears in propria persona in his philosophical discourse. In *Ecce Homo,* for instance, he links "a forgetting of one's distance" with the danger of "self-dissolution" (*Selbstlosigkeit*) (2; 56). It is thus not surprising that this autobiographical book is pervaded by a defensive language with respect to forms of affects that threaten to penetrate the subject ("Nietzsche") "from the outside" (*von aussen her*). Thus, he speaks of the necessity of "walling in the self" (*Selbst-Vermauerung*), "self-containment" (*Selbst-Erhaltung*), and "self-defense" (*Selbst-Verteidigung*) (8; 63). And if this were not enough, Nietzsche articulates his need for a radical defense from the power of external affects that throng the modern city to penetrate the interior life of the ego by asking, in a Schopenhauerian mood: "Would I not in face of it have to become a *hedgehog* [zum *Igel* werden]?" (8; 63). It is clear that this tropological language implies a self-preservative move that defensively reacts to the contaminating power of the mimetic pathology inherent in the sick herd.

Nietzsche is the first to admit that he is directly implicated in the mimetic conception of the subject he otherwise diagnoses as a mimetic sickness. This is most apparent, once again, with respect to compassion itself, a mimetic affect that he calls his "greatest danger" (*GS* 271). As he confesses: "I know just as certainly that I only need to expose myself to the sight of some genuine distress and I am lost. And if a suffering friend said to me, 'Look, I am about to die; please promise to die with me,' I should promise it" (*GS* 338; 270). If we consider this statement against the background of Nietzsche's "theory of *Mitempfindung*" we have just outlined, we could say that Nietzsche is revealing the affective sources of his theory of communication. The fact that Nietzsche's vulnerability to mimetic *pathos* informs his philosophical *logos* should not come as a surprise. It is perfectly in line with Nietzsche's claim that "every great philosophy" is actually based on a "personal confession," a definition that equally applies to his thought. In fact, Nietzsche's critical thought on mimesis stems directly from his personal susceptibility to contagious affects, his patho-logy from his pathology. This inversion of perspectives is, after all, what he calls his "longest exercise." And this point is confirmed as he candidly admits that "For a psychologist there are few questions that are as attractive as that concerning the relation of health and philosophy, and if he should himself become ill, he will bring all of his scientific curiosity into his illness" (*GS* "Preface 2nd Ed." 2; 33).

In this first section, we have followed Nietzsche's diagnostic curiosity into the secret workings of the sympathetic logos of mimesis. What we have noticed is that Nietzsche's insights into mimetic affects do not always flow on the surface of his text, but inform it from within. Nietzsche's thought often moves in contradictory directions, at times helplessly "attracted," at times repulsed by the working of mimesis, so repulsed as to disavow it. And as we have seen, it is precisely out of this double movement towards/ away from pathos that his philosophical logos progressively emerges. This process of emergence continues if we now push our inquiry into Nietzsche's mimetic patho(-)logy further and turn to consider what René Girard calls Nietzsche's "mimetic disease" as it appears in his confrontation with his "mimetic rival" par excellence, Richard Wagner.

Beyond the Rivalry Principle

Nietzsche's mature philosophy can be read as an attempt at cathartic purgation from his youthful contamination by the Wagnerian touch. In the preface to *The Case of Wagner* (1888) he puts it clearly: "My greatest experience was a recovery [*Genesung*]. Wagner is merely one of my sicknesses." And a few pages later, he adds: "Is Wagner a human being at all? Isn't he rather a sickness? He makes sick whatever he touches" (5; 164). Wagner, at the end of Nietzsche's career, shares with the herd the main characteristic of being "sick." And, once again, Nietzsche defines this pathology in contagious terms. Even the structure of Nietzsche's position with respect to sickness repeats itself. In fact, he begins by proclaiming his state of health (in this case a "recovery") and by casting this sickness on the outside (Wagner is dismissed as "merely" a sickness). Yet, at the same time, his passionate tone, as well as the acknowledgment that this sickness is internal to his system (Wagner *belongs* to Nietzsche's diseases), strongly indicates that, at the end of his career, the Wagnerian "infection" (*CW* "Postscript") is far from being cured.

This time, however, the contaminating power of mimesis is firmly located in a specific subject who occupies a crucial role in Nietzsche's development both personal and intellectual. In a way, we could even say that Wagner constitutes the alpha and omega of Nietzsche's philosophical career—a career that begins with *The Birth of Tragedy* (written under the inspiration of both Schopenhauer and Wagner) and concludes with two books entirely devoted to Wagner (clearly written as an attempt at agonistic differentiation from his former hero and mentor). This kind of contagious pathology endemic to "Wagner's pathos" (*CW* 8; 172) involves a con-fusion between self and other symptomatic of the phantom of the ego, which also means that the question of "mimesis" is once again central to this pathos. This, at least, is René Girard's thesis.

The Girardian Challenge

In a series of essays devoted to Nietzsche, Girard has convincingly argued that Nietzsche's "sickness" should be understood in mimetic terms.[17] Girard's notion of "mimesis," not unlike the Freudian notion of "identification" we shall later encounter, is understood as a desire to "be the other." In fact, he tells us that "Wagner is the god that Nietzsche would like to be."[18] And yet this identification with the other should not be confused with Freud's, insofar as it is only the first step in Girard's understanding of the "mimetic process." Such a "process" constitutes the center of Girard's theory of mimesis and, as is well known, is generated by the structure of appropriative desire. For Girard, we might recall, desires are mimetic insofar as the subject "models" his or her desire on the figure of a "mediator" and, thus, desires what the model desires. If the emphasis on the triangular structure of desire is still Freudian, in a deft theoretical move that opens up the field of mimetic theory, Girard inverts the Oedipal triangle by positing the primacy of mimesis over desire: "The Oedipal complex roots desire in the maternal object" (the object informs desire), writes Girard. And he adds: "The mimetic process detaches desire from any predetermined object" (mimesis informs desire).[19] Identification (or mimesis) with a model, then, determines the object of desire, and not the other way round. The logical outcome of the "primacy of mimesis" over desire is that the model inevitably turns into a "rival." In fact, "if desires are truly mimetic," Girard explains, "they are bound to clash with other desires,"[20] so that rivalry is revealed to be a direct consequence of mimetic desire, and the mediator to be both a model of desire and an obstacle to the desire it generated. The subject's "ambivalent" relation to the model/obstacle, left unexplained by psychoanalysis, is thus revealed to be a natural consequence of the imitative dynamic of desire. Finally, paving the way for what I call mimetic pathology, Girard says that mimetic desire has the contagious characteristic of a sickness. As he puts it in *Deceit, Desire and the Novel*, "one 'catches' a nearby desire just as one would catch the plague or cholera, simply by contact with an infected person."[21]

It is in this specific sense that for Girard, the sickness Nietzsche "catches" from the exposure to the Wagnerian infection should be understood as a "mimetic disease,"[22] a disease that relegates Nietzsche's psychic life to the status of a phantom of Wagner's ego. And indeed, "the history of Nietzsche's relationship to Wagner," as Girard puts it, "corresponds perfectly to the various stages of the mimetic process," a process whereby a "model" turns into a "rival" or "obstacle" in the path towards the desired object, in this case, Cosima Wagner.[23] Girard also suggests that this "mimetic rivalry" is directly responsible for Nietzsche's final "plunge into madness"[24] and, thus, implies that Nietzsche, despite his claims of "recovery," ultimately fails to heal his mimetic pathology. This is an important and still unexplored thesis. Girard's reading constitutes one of the earliest attempts to reinscribe behavioral mimesis within the frame of Nietzsche studies, to focus on Nietzsche's personal susceptibility to mimesis, as well as to give an elaborate psychological account of Nietzsche's complicated relationship to his mimetic rival, Richard Wagner. Girard's reading confirms thus what we have seen in the preceding chapter on compassion and the theoretical rivalry with Schopenhauer it entailed. Namely, that as Nietzsche posits himself at radical distance from contagious forms of mimetic pathologies, an infection has already taken place. Hence, Nietzsche's "pathos of distance" is not only disjunctive but also conjunctive. Hence again, the theoretical patho-logy that leads Nietzsche, the thinker, to diagnose others in terms of sickness cannot be dissociated from a mimetic pathology that affects Nietzsche, the man.

Now, if we do not simply "apply" Girard's mimetic theory to Nietzsche, but pursue this innovative line of inquiry, we need to take seriously Girard's invitation to engage with the "contradiction" mimesis generates in Nietzsche's text. In order to do so, a few specifications are in place. First, even though the importance of desire cannot be underestimated, at stake in Nietzsche's mimetic rivalry with Wagner is not only a clash of desires over a shared object (i.e., Cosima Wagner) but something much more fundamental. In fact, Wagner's influence over the young Nietzsche has the power to deprive the latter of a sense of proper identity *tout court*. Nietzsche expresses such anxiety of nonbeing caused by an overbearing presence of the "model" already in the fourth of his *Untimely Meditations* (1876). In "Richard Wagner in Bayreuth," he characterizes the "central point of his [Wagner's] power" in terms of "the demonic *transmissibility* [*dämonischen* Übertragbarkeit] and self-relinquishment of his nature, with which others are able to communicate [*mitteilen*] just as readily as it communicates with other natures (*UM* IV, 7; 222). Notice that the verb Nietzsche uses here to define communication (*mitteilen*) is the same as the one he uses to denote the process of communication of the phantom of the ego, a verb that nicely captures the movement of conjunctive (*mit*) disjunction (*teilen*) so characteristic of the pathos of distance that concerns us. Moreover, the effect of this "*Mitteilung*" is that the *Beobachter* (Nietzsche himself) is led to ask himself a fundamental existential question: namely, "To what end are *you* actually here?" And since he fails to find an adequate answer to this question, the inevitable result, concludes Nietzsche, is that "he *feels alienated from his own being*" (er *sich seinem Wesen entfremdet fühlt*) (IV, 7; 222). This also means that the model's powerful intrusion in the ego deprives the latter not only of a desired object, but also, and more problematically, of a purpose (*wozu?*) or, better, of its very "being" (*Wesen*).

This psychological point has not gone unnoticed both inside and outside the field of Nietzsche studies. Herman Siemens, for instance, in an analysis of this early text aptly defines the early Nietzsche's position of dependency as a "moment of non-identity,"[25] a loss of self that brings about an agonistic confrontation with the model in order to overcome him. And within the field of mimetic theory, Mikkel Borch-Jacobsen gives the following account of mimetic rivalry:

> the rage that overwhelms me at the sight of him does not come from the fact that he is dispossessing me of something, but from the fact that he is robbing me, inexplicably, of and from myself. Hence the total, totalitarian character of the war that is begun then and that no satisfaction can appease: "Either him or me."[26]

This account of rivalry is Girardian in inspiration and directly addresses the psychic struggle that confronts the young Nietzsche. And yet what is at stake in this life and death struggle is not so much the possession (or "appropriation") of the desired object, as something more intimate and troubling, namely the proper being (or "propriation") of the subject itself. Such a conflict springs from the subject's attempts to resist the smashing, intrusive impression of the model in order to maintain its sense of proper identity. Nietzsche's anxiety of a loss of "purpose" and "being" is symptomatic of mimetic rivalry; and yet this rivalry is not primarily focused around the question of mimetic *desire*, but around the question of *mimesis* itself.[27] The problem, in other words, is not one of having or not having the object, but one of being or not being a subject. To be or not to be, that is the question Nietzsche, along with other modernists, is anxious to address, and in this question lies, perhaps, his mimetic originality.

So much for Nietzsche's personal mimetic pathology. But what about the general structure of Girard's reading and its wider theoretical implications? Girard is a theorist who is extremely attentive not to restrict the problematic of desire within the private interiority of the subject, or within domestic familial structures. His whole theory of mimesis consists in a bold and innovative attempt to unmask the violent social effects that ensue from the imitative structure of desire, a violence that, as he explains, spreads contagiously among the crowd, is responsible for what he calls a "crisis of difference," and threatens to disrupt the wider social order. Such mimetic crises, as we shall see, haunt the modernist period even more than the Romantic ·period, and the violence that ensues reaches unprecedented proportions. And yet, in his reading of Nietzsche, Girard tends to delimit his problematic within the confines of the Wagnerian family circle. The triangle Nietzsche-Wagner-Cosima (and the mythological counterpart Theseus-Dionysus-Ariadne) functions as a quasi-Oedipal structure where identification has primacy over desire. Why this unusual, reterritorializing move?

Girard's delimitation of the Nietzschean problematic of mimesis within the private sphere appears less striking if we schematically consider the two main underlying theoretical investments that motivate his reading. Nietzsche's mimetic rivalry with Wagner functions as a meeting point where two of Girard's main theoretical axioms come together. The first is obvious and hardly needs to be mentioned: this relationship is instrumental in "marvelously" confirming, as Girard puts it, the triangular structure of desire and, equally important, in clarifying his theoretical position vis-à-vis alternative accounts of desire—in this case, Girard's own theoretical model and rival par excellence, Sigmund Freud.[28] The second is less visible but goes to the heart of Girard's affective engagement with Nietzsche. What is implicitly at stake in Girard's reading of Nietzsche is the celebration of Christianity over and against one of its most formidable critics. The theological implications of Girard's brand of mimetic theory will come progressively to the fore in subsequent books, but they already underscore his reading of Nietzsche. In fact, if the theory of mimetic desire is the alpha of Girard's career, Christianity is the omega. For the French theorist, violence finds resolution in the "scapegoat" mechanism, the innocent victim whose sacrifice allows a cathartic purgation of social violence.[29] Girard finds ample evidence for the need of this sacrificial resolution, from Greek myths to wide-ranging anthropological examples, as well as from the great classics of Western literature. But it is especially in the Christian myth that, for Girard, the mimetic logic is more radically and scandalously unveiled. Christianity, for Girard, has ontological primacy over other religions insofar as it is only in the Christian myth, he claims, that the radical *innocence* of the sacrificial victim on the cross, and thus, of the logic that underscores violence, is finally revealed for all the world to see.

A recognition of this "truth"—and here the theoretical "truth" of mimetic violence and the Christian "truth" of revelation join hands—according to Girard, opens the door for a redemption from social violence.[30] We can thus see that for Girard there is enough at stake in his reading of Nietzsche in order *not* to open up the problematic of mimesis to the wider social sphere, as he is usually inclined to do.

It is certainly true that Nietzsche's personal attacks on Wagner are tainted by the latter's own ressentiment. As we have already had occasion to see, when it comes to mimesis Nietzsche is pathologically implicated in what he denounces, and this is especially clear when compassion is expressed through Wagner's pathos.[31] Equally fundamental is Girard's claim that "any future reading of Nietzsche . . . must be able to account for the contradiction that we found in Nietzsche's judgment of *Parsifal*."[32] Accounting for this contradiction is what we have done in the preceding section. As we have seen, Nietzsche's ambivalent attitude toward compassion—not only as it is expressed in a fragmentary response to *Parsifal*, but *in the entirety of his published corpus*—consistently implicates him in the mimetic pathology he otherwise denounces as a symptom of slavery. And yet, by focusing primarily on Nietzsche's personal relationship with Wagner, Girard, in our opinion, swings that oscillating pendulum that is Nietzsche's pathos of distance too much in the direction of mimetic pathos and the *pathology* that ensues, and does not trace the countermovement that necessarily follows. That is to say, he does not account for the patho-*logical* relevance of Nietzsche's attempt to posit a critical distance between himself and Wagner. In short, Girard tells us only half of the story; I now turn to consider the other half.

It is important to realize that Nietzsche's implication in mimetic affects and rivalries is not only disabling, implicating Nietzsche in what he denounces, but is also potentially empowering; mimetic patho(-)logy is not only a symptom of sickness (or pathology) but also has a critical, clinical interest (or patho-logy). In fact, what Girard calls Nietzsche's ressentiment for "the cultural hero of the German people"[33] also has the paradoxical effect of sharpening Nietzsche's critical lenses with respect to the means through which this success is achieved. There is thus a sense in which Nietzsche turns a capitulation to identificatory pathos into a critical distance of clinical value. In fact, if sickness continues to affect our philosophical physician, there is also a wider diagnostic at stake in Nietzsche's critique of his former "model."

I am thinking in particular of the overwhelming number of references in Nietzsche's late texts concerning that mimetic scene par excellence which is the Wagnerian theater, a scene that for Nietzsche is symptomatic of the mimetic pathologies that infect modernity as a whole.

It is with respect to the "cult" that has the power to affect the "crowd" that Nietzsche's operating knife is, perhaps, at its sharpest. A "cult" is always the product of a highly ritualized relationship to the crowd, and Nietzsche's visits to Bayreuth gave him plenty of occasions to carefully observe this inter-subjective group dynamic. Nietzsche's critique of both the "Wagner cult" and the modern masses that enthusiastically celebrate it, as we now turn to see, is predicated on a wider critique of modern subjectivity, language, and culture. Indeed, the "mimetic disease" that affects Nietzsche contaminates what Nietzsche calls "all of modern 'humanness'" (*die ganze moderne "Menschlichkeit"*) (*CW* "Preface"; 155). Hence, we now shift from the family to the theater, from individual to social psychology. And in this shift of perspectives, which is also his "longest exercise," Nietzsche turns, once again, from mimetic patient to a physician of culture affected by the disease he attempts to cure.

Nietzsche's Platonism

Nietzsche says of the ascetic priest that "he must himself be sick, he must be fundamentally related to the sick and underprivileged in order to understand them" (*GM* III, 15; 104). The same can be said with respect to Nietzsche's relationship to mimetic sickness in general, and to the sickness he sees at work in the "Wagner cult" in particular. It is, indeed, because Nietzsche is himself affected by what he calls Wagner's "infection" (*CW* "Postscript"; 184) that he can "understand" it. But unlike the priest, Nietzsche does not aim at "an understanding *with* them [i.e., the sick]" (*GM* III, 15; 104; my emphasis). Instead, he proposes an understanding *against* them; and, he adds, *against* himself. Thus, he opens *The Case of Wagner* with the radical intention to "take sides [*Partei zu nehmen*] *against* everything sick in [him], including Wagner, including Schopenhauer, including all modern 'humanness'" ("Preface"; 155).

In the two preceding sections, we have considered the mimetic dimension of this "sickness" and its power to affect both the figure of the master and Nietzsche. This analysis involved a movement from Nietzsche's critical *distance* from mimesis to his personal psychic involvement in two major forms of mimetic *pathos*: compassion and rivalry or, if you prefer, his Schopenhauerian and Wagnerian diseases. Taking our clue from Nietzsche's declaration of war against his own mimetic infection, we now follow its perspectival countermovement: We now move from his personal infection (or pathology) to a critical evaluation (or patho-logy) of a mimetic sickness he sees at work not only in himself, but also in that microcosm of modernity which is the Wagnerian theater. This theoretical shift, in turn, should allow us to understand why, after acknowledging his contamination by "Wagner's pathos," Nietzsche immediately adds: "Not that I wish to be ungrateful to this sickness" (preface; 155).

Theatrocracy

In the opening pages of *The Case of Wagner* Nietzsche makes clear that what is at stake in his critique of Wagner is not only a *personal* agonistic confrontation with his former model motivated by mimetic rivalry, nor solely an *aesthetic* attack concerning Wagner's musical pathos (though it is both these things), but also, and more importantly, an *ethico-political* attack directed at Wagner and the modern world he represents. That Wagner and modernity are two sides of the same coin is indicated by Nietzsche as he writes that "Wagner *sums up* modernity" or, as he also puts it, "through Wagner modernity speaks most *intimately*" (*durch Wagner redet die Modernität ihre* intimste *Sprache*) ("Preface"; 156). For Nietzsche, then, Wagner functions as a medium through which the language of modernity is conveyed. Accordingly, he does not limit his medical diagnosis to a consideration of "the case of Wagner"[34] ("Wagner's art is sick" [*CW* 5; 166]), but extends it to modernity as such ("nothing is more modern than this total sickness" [*Gesamterkrankung* 5; 166]). This synecdochal relationship between Wagner and modernity allows Nietzsche to delimit his critical analysis of mimetic behavior to the theatrical sphere, a sphere he is well acquainted with given his philological training in classical antiquity.

In his later period, Nietzsche is insistent about Wagner's language being essentially a theatrical rather than a musical language, which also means that it is a language of dramatic impersonation, or as Plato would say, *mimesis*. References to theatricality are pervasive in Nietzsche's critique of Wagner. In

The Case of Wagner, for instance, the latter is repeatedly defined as an "actor," "genius of the theater" (*CW* 8; 172), "the Protean character of degeneration" (5; 166). Nietzsche goes as far as to claim that he is "an incomparable *histrio*, the greatest mime" (8; 172), or as he emphatically puts it "the most enthusiastic mimomanic of all time" (*GS* 368). Thus, he can say that "only the actor still arouses *great* enthusiasm [*die* grosse *Begeisterung*]" (*CW* 11; 179).[35] But Nietzsche's critique does not confine itself within the boundaries of theatrical walls. Shifting the emphasis from theatrical to political language, he defines Wagner as a "tyrant" (8; 172), and his cult as a "*theatrocracy*" ("Postscript"; 182), a sort of theatrical autocracy that is above all inimical to rational thought: "Above all, no thought! Nothing is more compromising than a thought" (6; 167). And finally, he makes the theoretical stakes behind this vehement attack clear: Wagner, says Nietzsche, "contains the whole psychology of the actor; it also contains—we need not doubt it—his morality" (8; 173). Morality and psychology cross, once again, the path of Nietzsche's mimetic patho(-)logy. But this time it is clear that both the language and the reasons that inform Nietzsche's critique of Wagner are fundamentally indebted to the Platonic critique of affective mimesis. Nietzsche contra Wagner, the philosopher contra the actor or, as he had already said in *Daybreak*, "the cult of reason" against the "cult of feeling" (197). This is, indeed, a modern reenactment of what Plato famously called the "ancient quarrel between philosophy and poetry."[36]

That Nietzsche, the philosopher-poet, sides with Plato, the rational man, against the figure of the enthusiastic artist, may initially surprise. After all, Nietzsche, the anti-Platonic philosopher par excellence, is intent in "overturning Platonism" rather than prolonging Plato's thought. And as is well known, it is difficult to find a philosopher in the history of Western thought who attacks Plato with more ironic distance than Nietzsche. Both the man and his thought are repeatedly defined as sick, life-negating, nihilistic, and so on. And in order to dispel any doubts with respect to his critical stance towards the founder of philosophy, Nietzsche bluntly defines himself as a "complete skeptic about Plato" (*TI* 2; 557). This, at least, is what Nietzsche claims in his well-known anti-Platonic moments. Yet it is crucial to understand that Nietzsche's distance from the father of philosophy, not unlike his relationships with his other intellectual father figures we have encountered (i.e., Schopenhauer and Wagner), is not as abyssal as it initially appears to be. As he himself confesses in *Ecce Homo*, he attacks only "causes that are victorious" and towards which he feels "gratitude" (7; 47). So it is crucial to qualify Nietzsche's position immediately by saying that his critique of Plato concerns ontology rather than ethics, metaphysics rather than psychology, representational mimesis rather than mimetic impersonation.

This is the moment to recall that Nietzsche's debt to the Platonic critique of mimesis was already apparent in his remarks on the "phantom of the ego" with which we began. In *Daybreak*, we have seen, Nietzsche writes that insofar as the "great majority" do not have an ego but a phantom of the ego instead, "they all of them dwell in a fog of impersonal, semi-personal opinions as arbitrary as poetical evaluations." That the notion of "phantom" appears in conjunction with a reference to the arbitrariness of "poetical evaluations" is an unmistakable hint at Plato's epochal critique of mimesis . In Book X of the *Republic*, Plato's metaphysical idealism leads him to consider the world of immanence as a devalued copy of ideal forms, and the sphere of mimetic representation as a copy of a copy. Thus, in order to undermine the epistemological and ontological value of art, Plato famously defines mimetic art as a mere "imitation of a phantasm" (*phantasma*) (823; 598b), and the "imitator" as a "creator of phantoms" (824; 599d) at three removes from reality. In Plato, then, the notion of "phantom" is loaded with his epistemological preoccupations characteristic of his idealist ontology: the "phantom" is opposed to "reality," as "appearance" is opposed to "being."

Nietzsche, of course, is perfectly aware of the fundamental connection between the Platonic notion of *phantasma* and the ontological critique of mimesis. After all, his quarrel contra Plato involves an attempt to overturn precisely this metaphysical opposition. In *The Birth of Tragedy*, for instance, he had already reminded us that Plato's main objection to art was that "it is the imitation of a phantom and hence belongs to a sphere even lower than the empirical world" (14; 90).[37] However, in *Daybreak*, Nietzsche psychologizes the Platonic concept of phantom, shifting the focus of attention from ontology to psychology; from representational mimesis (poetry as a "phantom *of reality*") to psychological mimesis (man as a "phantom *of the ego*"). This shift of emphasis from the empirical world to the psychic world, from "reality" to the "ego" is a way for Nietzsche to mark his distance from Plato's idealistic ontology and the devaluation of life and art it entails. And yet there is also a sense in which such a shift of emphasis towards psychology remains faithful to the Platonic critique of mimesis in general and of the mimetic actor in particular. In fact, Nietzsche, throughout his critique of Wagner, is concerned with a psychological state of confusion between self and other characteristic of the "phantom of the ego" that is also at the root of Plato's concerns with what he calls a "creator of phantoms." Nietzsche, the anti-Platonic philosopher, is thus also implicitly writing *with* Plato, or at least, with Plato's *psychological* insights into mimesis contra the figure of the mimetic actor.

The critique of mimesis that informs Nietzsche's reference to the "phantom of the ego" could even be read as an implicit attempt to answer Plato something that, if made explicit, could run along these lines: "I agree with you, old Plato. Mimesis is linked to a world of phantoms, indeed. And as you taught us, these phantoms are the direct consequence of the subjects' emotional turmoil, which prevents them from seeing reality clearly. Hence, I am sure you don't mind if I say that the cause of the subject's lack of clarity of vision is not so much in those phantoms of *reality* artists reproduce, as in the emotional power of such actors to turn the ego into a mere copy, or phantom of other egos. At least, you seem to suggest so yourself in Book III of the *Republic* and again in Book X, as you switch from painting back to poetry; from representational mimesis back to affective mimesis. But then, as you know, I prefer to stick to this (immanent) psychological line of inquiry, rather than inventing (transcendental) metaphysical fables. In other words, rather than denouncing *reality* itself as a mere phantom, I place the blame directly on the phantom of the *ego* poets and actors have the power to communicate." Indeed, if we follow the silent theoretical moves that underscore Nietzsche's account of the phantom of the ego, we could say that it is *through* Plato's psychological account of mimetic impersonation that Nietzsche fights *against* Plato's ontological devaluation of reality.

But in order to fully take hold of Nietzsche's condemnation of the Wagnerian/modern sickness, we need to recall the main elements of Plato's own *psychological* theory of mimesis—an ancient brand of mimetic theory, knowledge of which Nietzsche is assuming in his modern readers.

The Platonic Ban

Despite the fact that Plato's critique of mimesis is often dismissed as a simple, tyrannical exclusion of the poet from the ideal city, his argument against poetry is complex, multilayered, and escapes easy summaries. My goal here is to schematically point out the fundamental *reasons* that inform Plato's notorious expulsion of mimesis in order to fully convey the theoretical implications inherent in Nietzsche's condemnation of Wagner, and of the "language of modernity" that speaks through him. In order to make sense of this critique we shall have to follow the path first indicated by Plato. This also means that we need to consider both the content (*logos*) and the formal qualities (*lexis*) of this language (*Rep.* 637; 392c), as well as the effects of this language on the actor and the modern audience that listens to him.

At the level of content, the late Nietzsche sees in Bayreuth the crucible of some of the modern ideologies he most strongly opposes. For him Wagner's language is "modern" insofar as it gives expression to ideologies as diverse as idealism, nihilism, German nationalism, and anti-Semitism, ideologies that Nietzsche consistently rejects. Nietzsche makes this point succinctly as he writes that "since Wagner had moved to Germany, he had condescended step by step to everything I despise—even to anti-Semitism" (*NW* 1; 676). Critics attentive to the political dimension of Nietzsche's thought have elaborated on Wagner's problematic political implications. Philippe Lacoue-Labarthe and Jean-Luc Nancy, for instance, argue that Wagner's total work of art "is not only aesthetic: it beckons to the political" and recognize the role of mimesis in this politics.[38] More recently, Jacob Golomb and Robert Wistrich have pointed out that the "Wagnerian ideology and cult that developed in Bayreuth was a ... real precursor of *völkisch* and Hitlerian ideas." In this sense, they add, Nietzsche's "devastating critique of Wagner—prophetic in many ways of what was to come—reveals with what penetrating insights he saw through its dangerous illusions."[39] But of course, if Nietzsche saw through such illusions, not everybody did; especially not the Wagnerian public. And it is precisely in order to understand the specific process whereby the artist communicates such opinions to his public that we need to reconsider the formal qualities of the Wagnerian/modern language Nietzsche critiques. While agreeing with Golomb and Wistrich that Nietzsche's "penetrating insight" into the content of Wagner's "ideas" (*logos*) is unmistakable, I would like to suggest that Nietzsche turns out to be even more "penetrating" and "prophetic" as he turns to critique the modality whereby such *völkisch*, Hitlerian ideas are communicated (*lexis*). As Nietzsche puts it: "This artist offends me by *the manner* in which he presents his ideas" (*GS* 187; my emphasis).

In order to reevaluate the implications of Nietzsche's critique of Wagner's modern *lexis* a detour via Plato's ancient theory of mimesis can no longer be postponed.[40]

It is well known that Plato's condemnation of affective mimesis is concentrated in the *Republic*. But it is perhaps *Ion*—a Platonic dialogue where the *concept* of "mimesis" is not directly invoked but is, nonetheless, imbued in the *problematic* of mimesis—that can best serve to introduce Plato's critical take on the affective consequences of mimetic *lexis*.[41] In *Ion*, Plato focuses on the figure of the rhapsode, a public reciter of poetry specialized in Homer, who perfectly embodies that kind of mimetic subject Plato wants to expel from the ideal state. The rhapsode Ion is a kind of chameleon, an expert in camouflage endowed with the capacity of "assuming every kind of shape and imitating all things" (*Rep.* 642; 398a). Thus, Socrates says that he is "just like Proteus . . . assuming every shape" (*Ion*, 227; 541e). Insofar as Ion's job is to affectively enter into the roles of the characters he is giving voice to, he has a protean personality that leads him, like the god Proteus, to change form at will. This mimetic tendency is, of course, an essential characteristic of all good actors; and Ion, who has just won a poetic contest, is reputed to be the best. It is crucial to recognize that in order to fully express such a protean personality, the actor must rely on a specific linguistic modality. Technically put, the rhapsode does not speak *about* his characters, using the third-person narrative (*diegesis*). Instead, he speaks in the first person (*mimesis*), impersonating different Homeric roles. In this specific sense, Socrates's critique of *Ion* overlaps with his critique of the actor in the *Republic*. In fact, we can say that the mimetic actor "delivers a speech as if he were somebody else," "likening [him]self to another in speech or bodily bearing" (638; 393c). And this is the definition of mimesis, as it first appears in that founding text for mimetic theory that is Book III of the *Republic*.[42]

Why, then, is mimetic speech more conducive to impersonation? And why does Plato so radically distinguish *mimetic* from *diegetic* speech, tolerating the latter and outlawing the former? The answer is apparently simple, but the implications are fundamental. A first person, *mimetic* narrative mode (as opposed to a third-person, *diegetic* one) involves a linguistic indistinction between the "I" of the speaker and the "I" of the other, a sort of linguistic confusion of identities (or egos) triggered by the fact that the actor, in tragic or comic spectacles, speaks in propria persona by impersonating his characters.

Mimetic speech is, thus, the necessary condition for a mimetic imperson-ation to take place; *linguistic* mimesis is at the origin of a *psychic*, affective, and infective mimesis. And it is precisely such a mimetic, theatrical process that allows the subject to stop being itself in order to become someone other. We are here in a position to understand the importance of a literary-affective mechanism that tacitly informs Plato's critique of mimesis. It is not simply a question of banning mimetic representations (or phantoms) of reality that do not tell the truth about the gods, but of banning a mimetic confusion of identity that turns the ego into a phantom of the ego. If we want to fully understand the modernist critique of mimesis we shall have to remember this ancient theoretical lesson.

Another perspective on this psychic confusion consists in saying that mimetic rhapsody involves a state of "enthusiasm" understood in its etymo-logical meaning (from Greek *enthousiazein*, to be possessed by a god). Hence, Socrates can say that through the enthusiastic Ion, it is "the god himself who speaks." As he explains to the hapless rhapsode, "this gift you have of speaking well on Homer is not art [*technē*]; it is a power divine" (*Ion*, 219; 533d). Ion, a character who, while being "inspired" or, better, because of this inspira-tion may be what romantics would call a *poetic* genius, is definitively not an *intellectual* genius; hence his vanity is flattered. But Socrates's statement is, of course, imbued with ironic distance and exposes the fact that the inspired rhapsode is not in a position of rational control over his art. Quite literally, for Socrates, Ion does not know what he is saying. As he puts it, "a poet is a light and winged thing, and holy, and never able to compose until he has become inspired, and is besides himself, and reason is no longer in him" (220; 534b). And moving to the real target, the poets themselves, he adds:

> the deity has bereft them of their senses and uses them as ministers [notice the political reference] . . . it is not they who utter these precious revela-tions while their mind is not within them, but it is the god himself who speaks, and through them becomes articulate to us. (220; 534d)

Enthusiasm, as Plato understands it (being *en-theos*, possessed by a god), entails an unconscious indistinction between self and other that breaks down the boundaries of individuation and deprives the rhapsode of his rational control over himself.[43] This is why Nietzsche, at the beginning of his career, will say that for Plato "the poet is incapable of composing until he has become unconscious [*bewusstlos*] and bereft of understanding" (*BT* 12; 86). The problematic of the unconscious and that of mimesis are, thus, from the origins of mimetic theory, tightly strung together.

Now, both states of mimetic indistinction Plato describes in *Ion* (impersonation and enthusiasm) inform, at the deepest level, Nietzsche's late critique of Wagner. His definition of Wagner as both "Proteus-Character" and "enthusiastic mimomanic" is, indeed, a clear recapitulation of the critical move at work in *Ion*. The goal of this move is equally clear. The philosopher, in his critique of mimesis, is intent on discrediting the artist and his art. Both Plato and Nietzsche poke fun at the mimetician who is not in his right mind and, thus, implicitly tell us that the poet/actor (and his histrionic art) should not be taken seriously, not be bothered with. The mimetic rival is thus unmasked as a figure who is not in control of himself, let alone his *techne*. Plato contra Homer, Nietzsche contra Wagner—that is the real antagonism. So far so good. But then, we may now ask, why should both ancient and modern philosophers bother at all with such irrational characters? If the actor cannot even control himself, why should Nietzsche say that "the actor Wagner is a tyrant; his pathos topples every taste, every resistance" (*CW* 8; 172)? And if this madman is, indeed, a "tyrant," and his theater a "*theatrocracy*," where does his irresistible "pathos" come from? Once again, we find direct answers to such questions in Plato.

If we read *Ion* against the background of Plato's critique of theatrical mimesis as it appears in Books III and X of the *Republic*, it is clear that Socrates's ironic condemnation of the rhapsode is motivated by a profound awareness of the dangerous ethico-political implications of mimetic impersonation for a culture dominated by what Eric Havelock calls "an oral state of mind."[44] The threatening dimension of mimesis is made clear at those moments when Plato's psychology turns to consider the *impact* of the (mimetic) actor on the (mimetic) crowd of spectators. Plato's psychological insights into the effects of mimesis can be schematically divided into two related categories that equally inform Nietzsche's critique of the language of modernity.

The first category concerns education (*paideia*). Mimesis, for Plato, is endowed with a power of impression that has the characteristic to magically infiltrate the subject and shape its psychic life. This is especially true with respect to "young and tender" creatures who are easily impressed by mimetic spectacles, namely children. As Plato puts it, anticipating a key insight in mimetic theory, it is in childhood that the subject is "best molded and takes the impression that one wishes to stamp upon it" (*Rep.* 624; 377b). Plato, in other words, thinks of children's "character" (from Greek *kharassein*, to engrave, stamp) as a formless, malleable psychic mass, a mass that, as Lacoue-Labarthe would put it, is "typographically" in-*formed* by a mimetic power of impression.[45] This initial psychic formation, as Plato's psychological sensibility allows him to recognize, is difficult to shake off. Thus, he famously adds: "imitations, if continued from youth far into life, settle down into habits and second nature, in the body, the speech, and the thought" (640; 395d). With this psychological point in mind, we begin to understand why Plato is getting a little bit nervous—as nervous as parents or educators can be nowadays with respect to children's exposure to certain spectacles on TV, videogames, the Internet, and other avatars of the virtual.[46]

Notice that this process of psychic formation is not the product of parental impression but is, from the very beginning, thought in the wider sociopolitical context represented by the theater. Thus, Nietzsche, once again like Plato, establishes an explicit causal connection between actors and children. That "ideal ape" (*D* 324) characterized by the "capacity for all kinds of adaptations" (*GS* 361) which for Nietzsche is the mimetic actor (i.e., Wagner) does not fail to awaken the mimetic disposition of those "born apes" (*D* 34) that children are and to imprint their characters with a specific trait. As Nietzsche equally puts it, Wagner's theater-rhetoric—what Nietzsche also calls "the whole gesture hocus-pocus of the actor" (*GS* 368)—is endowed with the "magical" power to corrupt the "German youth" (*Jünglinge*) (*CW* 6; 167). Nietzsche, then, like many modernists after him, is still part of a long tradition of thought that is painfully aware of the tyrannical power of mimesis to shape the youth's moral and political opinions.

That children are imitative we all know, and recent discoveries in developmental psychology and the neurosciences, as we shall have occasion to point out in subsequent chapters, have proved on an empirical basis that this primary mimetism is more fundamental than it was thought to be. But Plato's critique goes well beyond childhood. And this takes us to Plato's second psychological insight. For him, in fact, adults are not much better; or at least, they are not much better from the moment that they are part of an enthusiastic, theatrical crowd. Thus, this second Platonic insight takes us

back to the internal dynamic of the theater and the type of affects that are
conveyed, by mimetic *lexis*, to the masses of spectators. Theatrical mimesis,
says in substance Plato, is dangerous because it is a fundamentally "contagious" and "irrational" affect that deprives the mass of spectators (adults as
much as children) of rational control over themselves. It is contagious, one
could even say electrifying, since the spectators are made to feel, via mimetic
speeches and gestures, the pathos of the mime on the stage who is not himself
but someone other instead. And by the time we reach Book X of the *Republic*, it is clear that what Plato has primarily in mind are emotions such as
"laughter," "anger," "sexual desire," and "pity" (831–832; 605c–606d). If effectively dramatized, these emotions appeal to what Plato calls the "irrational
and idle part of us" (830; 604d) and thus deprive the public of its ability to
see clearly and, thus, think rationally. Plato's psychological insights into the
blinding effect of emotions can better be understood in the light of the poets'
emotional power "to win favor with the multitude" (830; 605a). Indeed,
emotions like desire, pity, anger, and laughter, are part of that *pathos* that
spectators of tragedies and comedies expect to be contaminated by. But Plato
goes further. Thus he adds that it is also because the subject who is part of a
crowd is already predisposed to succumb to irrational, pathological, mimetic
behavior that such emotions immediately set the public on fire. Thus, he
rhetorically asks, "does not the fretful part of us present many and varied
occasions for imitation . . . especially by a nondescript mob assembled in the
theater?" (*Rep.* 830; 604e). Anticipating one of the fundamental insights of
mass psychology, Plato clearly sees that irrational affects spread contagiously,
or as he also says, magnetically, in a crowd.[47] In sum, well before the modern
birth of the social sciences, Plato is painfully aware that the subject, especially
as she or he is part of a "nondescript mob," is not a rational subject in control
of its cogitations but, rather, is driven by emotions that are fundamentally
contagious—contagious because mimetic. Perhaps, then, at stake in Plato's
ancient quarrel with poetry is not only the birth of philosophy, but also of its
twin sister, psychology—a psychology that is born out of the same womb as
philosophy, as it were.

Now Nietzsche, the self-proclaimed "philosophical physician," is a
faithful descendant of this dual philosophical-psychological tradition, more
faithful than he is often ready to admit. In fact, this necessarily sketchy overview of Plato's critique of mimesis should suffice to clarify that if Nietzsche

uncompromisingly says that he is a "complete Skeptic about Plato," this skepticism definitively does *not* concern Plato's psychological critique of mimetic impersonation. We have seen that Wagner occupies the role of a modern Ion. Like Ion he is a "Protean character" (*CW* 5; 166), a mimetic actor endowed with "*great* enthusiasm." Moreover, Wagner is defined as a "*scenic artist par excellence*," whose "theatrical rhetoric" (8; 172) aims at "excitement at any price" (*der Affekt um jeden Preis*) ("2nd Postscript"; 187). This strife for affect equally deprives the man on the stage of rational control over himself and, more importantly, allows him to impress, inform, and magnetize the *Jünglinge* and adults alike who are part of the crowd of spectators. Thus, Nietzsche concludes, echoing Plato: "*This is precisely what is proved by the case of Wagner*: he won the crowd" ("Postscript"; 183). In brief, all the elements of Plato's critique of theatrical impersonation (enthusiasm, psychic impression, contagion, possession, etc.), as well as the mimetic conception of the subject inherent to it, are clearly at work in Nietzsche's critique of "the most enthusiastic mimomanic of all times."[48]

And yet if Wagner's language falls so neatly within the framework of the Platonic critique of theatrical mimesis, why, we may now ask, should Nietzsche persist in saying that "through Wagner speaks *modernity* its most intimate language"? Should he not rather say that this sick, mimetic language is most characteristic of ancient Greece? More problematically, isn't the theatrical language of "enthusiasm," "impersonation," and "contagious intoxication" characteristic of Nietzsche's conception of Greek tragedy as it appears in his first book devoted to Wagner under the name of the Dionysian?

The Dionysian Neurosis

Once again, the sickness Nietzsche denounces in his mimetic rivals is already internal to his conception of the subject. In *The Birth of Tragedy* he had defined the Dionysian in terms that are strikingly reminiscent of the contagious affects he now excoriates as mimetic pathology. In fact, for the early Nietzsche, the Dionysian is not only a musical phenomenon, but also a staged, *dramatic* phenomenon. We could even say that his dramatic celebration of the Dionysian cult matches, *à la lettre*, Nietzsche's definition of Wagner's cult; the "Dionysian enthusiast" matches Wagner's "enthusiastic mimomania"; the "dionysicher *Schwärmer*" matches the modern *Theatermensch* who "today raves [*schwärmt*] about Wagner." Is the Dionysian, then, one of those sicknesses Nietzsche is trying to cure himself from? Or is it a sickness for which he is grateful to Wagner? Or both?

The isomorphism between the Dionysian and the Wagnerian cults goes beyond mere terminology and immediately appears if we schematically consider the process of artistic *creation*, the actor's *impersonation*, and the public *contagion* as they emerge from one of *The Birth of Tragedy*'s most often quoted sections. First, Nietzsche tells us, the "dramatist" "feel[s] the urge to transform himself and to speak out of other bodies and souls" (8; 64); second, the choral dramatization involves "act[ing] as if one had actually entered into another body, another character" (8; 64); and third, Nietzsche writes that "The Dionysian excitement is capable of communicating this artistic gift to a multitude [*Masse*]" and that "this phenomenon is encountered epidemically" (8; 64). This mimetic con-fusion between self and other, which spreads contagiously, as "'folk-diseases'" (*Volkskrankheiten*) do (1; 37), and affects entire populations, is indeed as much a Dionysian as it is a Wagnerian phenomenon. Dionysian mimesis, like Wagner's enthusiastic mimomania, is instrumental in depriving acolytes of their egos and setting up a world of phantoms instead.

These analogies between Wagner's pathos and the Dionysian pathos should not come as a surprise. After all, Wagner's music and Schopenhauer's thought were the main source of inspiration for Nietzsche's early conception of the Dionysian. But Nietzsche's sources do not stop with these two exponents of German romanticism. Here is a passage from Plato's *Ion* that should strike readers of Nietzsche with a sense of déjà vu:

> as the worshiping Corybantes are not in their senses when they dance, so the lyric poets are not in their senses when they make these lovely lyric poems. No, when once they launch into harmony and rhythm, they are seized with the Bacchic transport, and are possessed—as the bacchants, when possessed, draw milk and honey from the rivers, but not when in their senses. (220; 534a)

As we see from Plato's account of poetic inspiration, Nietzsche is far from being original in linking dramatic creation to the Dionysian. This connection is, in fact, at least as old as Plato. And if it is true that at this stage Nietzsche's celebration of the Dionysian is radically opposed to the Platonic condemnation of mimesis, it is equally true that Nietzsche, the philologist who in his early years at Basel affirmed that teaching philology allowed him to "infect his students with the philosophy of Plato,"[49] was particularly well placed to elaborate on the mimetic content of this fundamentally Platonic analogy. Not only Schopenhauer's and Wagner's Romantic celebration of bodily pathos, but also Plato's philosophical suspicion of it, is now incorporated in Nietzsche's youthful conceptualization of the Dionysian.

After this bewildering detour via the problematic of mimesis, it is becoming increasingly difficult to stabilize the movements of Nietzsche's mimetic patho(-)logy. But a logic immediately emerges if we understand that the models Nietzsche most vehemently opposes provide him with the very conceptual tools to operate such an opposition. Nietzsche contra Schopenhauer, Nietzsche contra Wagner, Nietzsche contra Plato: these are, indeed, old affairs of mimetic rivalry. Such a rivalry, as Girard explains, is based on a double bind that implicates the subject in what he opposes. But Nietzsche's mimetic rivalry with Wagner not only involves a capitulation to Wagner's "dämonischen *Übertragbarkeit*," which prevented him from being a subject; it equally generates an empowering countermovement against his model who is consciously exploited to become a subject. As Nietzsche puts it, in a confessional tone, quite early in his career, "by apparently succumbing to Wagner's overflowing nature, he who reflects upon it has in fact participated in its energy and has thus as it were *through him* acquired power *against him*" (*UM* IV, 7; 223).[50]

The mimetic movement of Nietzsche's thought becomes increasingly difficult to follow at those moments where Nietzsche is confronting more than one model at once. It is clear that in *The Case of Wagner* Nietzsche is dealing with the same theatrical phenomenon as in *The Birth of Tragedy*, but this time his evaluation radically diverges. The Dionysian mimesis he had celebrated in his youth *with* Wagner, *contra* Plato, he now condemns as a sickness *with* Plato, *contra* Wagner. This reevaluation in Nietzsche's preoccupations with mimesis during his later period involves a shift of emphasis from *aesthetics* to *morality*. If aesthetics entails a celebration of the dissolution of the ego under the rubric of the Dionysian, morality leads Nietzsche to recuperate Apollonian distance to diagnose mimetic behavior under the rubric of the phantom of the ego. This shift, in turn, swings him from one model/rival to another, from Wagner's *mimetic* aesthetics to Plato's *ethical* critique of mimetic art; from *"Wagnerschen Pathos"* to what he calls *"das philosophische Pathos"* (*CW* 1), from pathology to patho-logy. In our language, Nietzsche now reads pathos as a pathology he wants to distance himself from.

Is Nietzsche's early conception of the Dionysian, then, part of the personal sickness he is now siding against? Does the Dionysian, like Schopenhauer and Wagner, "belong merely to his sicknesses"? If we recall Nietzsche's conjoint reference to both his models/rivals as part of what is sick in him (notice Plato's absence), as well as the well-known fact that *The Birth of Tragedy* was written under the influence of both these authors, this should indeed be the logical consequence. Attacking the mimetic pathos at work in the cult of Dionysus in terms of sickness would only be consistent with Nietzsche's process of recovery—a Platonic *Genesung*, as it were.

And yet, Nietzsche's mimetic patho(-)logy never ceases to rotate.

In his "Attempt at Self-Criticism"—added to the second edition of *Birth* in 1886—Nietzsche is severely critical of the kind of music that, to his youthful ears, allowed for the rebirth of the Dionysian in modern culture. He now calls it "a first rate poison for the nerves" (*BT* 6; 25). However, neither in this foreword nor in his subsequent writings will he go as far as distancing himself from his early conception of Dionysian pathos. It is true that in "Attempt" Nietzsche is much more careful about his celebration of Dionysian mimesis. He is ready to admit that the question "what is Dionysian?" is a "difficult psychological question" (4; 20). He even considers the possibility of relegating the "Dionysian madness," as well as the culture that produces it, to the sphere of pathology. Thus, playing off fin de siècle fears of degeneration that were beginning to haunt modern Europe, he writes: "Is [Dionysian] madness perhaps not necessarily the symptom of degeneration, decline, and the final stage of culture?" (4; 21). Still, while considering this possibility, Nietzsche does not take hold of it. Instead, he attempts to pull this "symptom" on the side of "health." Thus he begins to wonder: "Are there perhaps—a question for psychiatrists—neuroses of *health*?" (4; 21).

Nietzsche will keep returning to the Dionysian and to the mimetic conception of the subject it entails until the very end of his career, considering such a phenomenon on the side of health while, paradoxically, diagnosing it through the language of sickness. For instance, in *Twilight of the Idols* (1889) he returns to the aesthetic distinction that had occupied him in *The Birth of*

Tragedy by contrasting "Apollonian *Rausch*" to Dionysian *Rausch*; an excitation of the visual sense (*das Auge erregt*) to an excitation of the whole affective system (*das gesamte Affekt-System erregt*). In the Dionysian state, he writes,

> the whole affective system is excited and enhanced: so that it discharges
> [*entladet*] all its means of expression at once and drives forth simultane-
> ously the power of representation, imitation [*Nachbilden*], transfiguration,
> transformation, and every kind of mimicking and acting [*alle Art Mimik
> und Schauspielerei*]. The essential feature here remains the ease of meta-
> morphosis, the inability *not* to react (similar to certain hysterical types who
> also, upon any suggestion, enter in *any* role [*in* jede *Rolle eintreten*]). It is
> impossible for the Dionysian type not to understand any suggestion [*Sug-
> gestion*]; he does not overlook any sign of an affect. . . . He enters into any
> skin, into any affect: he constantly transforms himself. (*TI* 10; 519–520)[51]

Mimicry, *Schauspielerei*, but also suggestibility to suggestion, and hysteria? The Dionysian artist, when he creates is indeed up to the neck in mimetic sickness! But despite Nietzsche's use of the language of pathology, this state of hyperaffective excitation is in no way interpreted as truly pathological. On the contrary. Affective mimicry, hysterical histrionics, and suggestibility to suggestion are, according to the late Nietzsche, the necessary emotional conditions for a truly healthy creative expression to take place. Nietzsche's patho(-)logy, in other words, manages to turn mimetic pathology into a sign of creative strength, at least as long as his focus is on his own artistic creation.[52]

This is one of those moments when Nietzsche's patho(-)logy remains suspended between contradictory propositions. Two competing evaluations of mimetic subjectivity simultaneously transect his late writings. One of them attacks Wagner and his art in pathological terms out of *moral* concerns; the other enthusiastically celebrates hypnotic suggestibility and hysteria for its *aesthetic* potential. Hence, the critical distance he posits with respect to the mimetism at work in the Wagnerian pathos is openly undermined by the Dionysian pathos he is not ready to let go of. Both his critique of mimesis (patho-logy) and his own implication with it (pathology) are simultaneously at work, each aspect of his thought indifferent to the other. Nietzsche, in brief, is not ready to take hold of his own patho-logical diagnosis so as to consider the mimetism that operates within his conception of the Dionysian as a sickness that needs to be overcome. Nietzsche's "attempt at self-critique" is but an attempt, and a very partial one too, at least insofar as his evaluation of the Dionysian is concerned. Yet this partiality does not prevent Nietzsche from setting his psycho-physiological insights into Dionysian histrionics to work in order to push his patho-logical critique of Wagner (and the critique of modernity it entails) further, towards unexplored theoretical territory. If Nietzsche is "grateful" to these diseases, it is because they allow him to sharpen his skills in the art of psychological dissection.

As we now shift attention from antiquity to modernity, from the Dionysian to the Wagnerian masses, from personal to collective psychology, Nietzsche's disavowed mimetic pathology turns, once again, into patho-logy, a patho-logy that diagnoses, with extreme precision, the mimetic bond that binds the actor to the crowd of spectators.

Psycho-Physiology of the Modern Soul

Nietzsche's considerations on the Wagnerian theater open up the problematic of crowd psychology, which was already beginning to haunt Plato's *Republic*, but Nietzsche gives a modern psychological twist to the Platonic critique. In fact, he transfers the psycho-physiological language of neurosis, hysteria, suggestion, and the mimetic unconscious it entails (the language of modern psycho-physiology) in order to diagnose the language Wagner uses to convince the nerves of the modern masses (the language of modernity). With this shift in mind, we can thus better understand why he says that his "objections to the music of Wagner are physiological objections" (*NW* "Where I Offer Objections"). Underlying Nietzsche's psycho-physiological critique of Wagner's success, and the means to reach it, is a heuristic model of the unconscious that, in the last years of Nietzsche's life, was gaining increasing popularity and scientific respectability: that is, the model of hypnotic suggestion.

The Language of Modernity

Nietzsche is usually still considered an original precursor of psychoanalysis, rather than an inventive inheritor of a pre-Freudian psychological tradition.[53] More recently, however, important exceptions to this trend have begun to show that Nietzsche was not an isolated thinker cut off from contemporary theoretical developments. On the contrary, he was very much aware of late nineteenth-century psycho-physiological theories, especially French theories of the unconscious predicated on the paradigm of hypnosis. Intellectual figures as diverse as the German philosopher Theodor Lipps; the French neurologist Jean-Martin Charcot of the *Salpêtrière* and his assistant, Charles Féré; Hippolyte Bernheim of the School of Nancy; and Théodule Ribot, to name a few, were all developing a conception of the unconscious, which, unlike the Freudian one, was not based on a repressive hypothesis but on what we could retrospectively call a mimetic hypothesis instead. This hypothesis was attentive to reflexes that are physiological, involuntary, contagious, and bring about a state of depersonalization characteristic of "the phantom of the ego" and of the mimetic unconscious that animates it.[54]

Starting with *Human, All Too Human* Nietzsche develops his theory of empathy on the basis of reflex, unconscious reactions, and his interests in psycho-physiology that run through the entirety of his work. But it was not only his own idiosyncratic preoccupation. The unconscious, understood in its metaphysical and physiological dimension, had been widely discussed since Eduard von Hartmann published his immensely popular *The Philosophy of the Unconscious* in 1868, a work Nietzsche had read and critiqued.[55] Closer to the mimetic tradition, the philosopher Théodule Ribot, in *Les maladies de la volonté* (1883), argues for a mimetic conception of the subject that is very much in line with Nietzsche. He writes: "If we count, in every human life, what is due to automatism, habit, passions, and, especially, imitation, we shall see that the number of acts that are purely voluntary, in the strict sense of the term, is quite small."[56] This is a mimetic conception of the unconscious that was dominant in fin de siècle Europe. And if the so-called Freudian "discovery" eclipsed it, the mimetic unconscious will continue to remain dominant among modernists with an acute psychological sensibility, influencing their works. Nietzsche, for one, in his later period, frequently returns to such unconscious phenomena. In a section titled "On the Origin of Our Evaluations" collected in *Will to Power*, he writes: "By far the greater number of motions have nothing whatever to do with consciousness; nor with sensation." And later, he adds: "We learn to think less highly of all that is conscious; we unlearn responsibility for ourselves, since we as conscious, purposive creatures, are only the smallest part of us" (*WP* 676). Well before

Freud, Nietzsche is indeed aware of the power of the unconscious in our waking, daily actions and thoughts. This psycho-physiological account of the unconscious is still in line with Nietzsche's early theory of sympathetic, automatic communication we have considered above, via the paradigm of yawning. And in his later period, Nietzsche finds in psychological research on hypnosis, psycho-physiology, and automatic reflexes ample support for his theory of unconscious communication that turns the ego into a phantom of the ego.[57]

To be sure, Nietzsche's debt to nineteenth-century psycho-physiology and the pre-Freudian unconscious it entails is far from being only theoretically salutary. Late nineteenth-century clinical obsession with hysteria (i.e., the paradigmatic example of psychic disease well before Freud) had the disturbing effect of reinforcing his already strident misogynistic tone, a tone that is pervasive in his work but constantly surfaces at those moments when the problematic of gender crosses his take on the mimetic unconscious. For instance, in *Daybreak*, in order to support his "theory of empathy," which advocates the involuntary dimension of mimesis, he writes: "one should observe especially the play on the faces of women and how they quiver and glitter in continual imitation and reflection of what is going on around them" (142; 89). And in an infamous section in *Gay Science* entitled "the problem of the actor," in one of his oscillating moves away from the phantom of the ego, Nietzsche relegates the problem of "mimicry" to "the lower classes," "Jews," and, most especially, "women." Thus, turning for support towards modern psychology he writes: "Reflect on the whole history of women: do they not *have* to be first of all and above all else actresses? Listen to physicians who have hypnotized women" (361; 317). As these passages make clear, Nietzsche is far from being original in his conception of mimetic femininity. The link between hypnosis, nervous degeneration, and femininity was a connection à la mode in the late 1880s. This is, indeed, the golden age of Charcot's highly dramatic demonstrations at the Salpêtrière where, in the famous *leçons du mardi* he used hypnosis in order to diagnose what, despite Charcot's theoretical claims to the contrary, at the time was thought to be a typically female pathological phenomenon, namely hysteria.[58] Nietzsche is more discerning than others as he recognizes that these female patients are actually *acting*, enacting the role the physician would like them to play, but his misogyny remains inexcusable. Hence, as Nietzsche defines Wagner as a "master of hypnotic tricks," he adds that his success is "success with nerves and consequently women" (*CW* 5; 166) and concludes by saying that "Wagner is bad for youth; he is calamitous for women [*das Weib*]" ("Postscript"; 185), he is clearly using the representation of women that derive from Charcot's account of la *grande hystérie* in order to support and give vent to his own anti-Wagnerian and misogynistic feelings.

And yet Nietzsche's critique of hysteria and hypnotic suggestion is not an end in itself; it is part of a larger patho-logical inquiry devoted to making sense of Wagner's power over the mass of spectators. Thus, he brings Charcot's insights to bear on a new and relatively unexplored territory: crowd psychology. The model of hypnosis underscores the totality of *The Case of Wagner*, but it is perhaps in a fragment of *Will to Power* revised from the spring to the fall of 1888 that Nietzsche makes the point with most clarity: "The Wagnerian *pur sang*" he writes, "succumbs to the elemental power of music somewhat as a woman succumbs to the will of her hypnotist" (*WP* 839). This is a problematic analogy in terms of gender, but an innovative one in terms of crowd psychology. What is at stake here, Nietzsche cautions us, is "more than a metaphor." Thus, he adds: "Consider the means for producing effects that Wagner prefers to use (—and had for the most part to invent for himself): they are strangely similar to those with which a hypnotist achieves his effect" (839). Far from sticking only to his misogynistic critique of femininity, Nietzsche turns to the model of hypnotic suggestion in order to make sense of Wagner's "will," as well as of its effect on the Wagnerian *pur sang* in the theater. Thus, he concludes by saying, "I heard an Italian woman who had just listened to the prelude [of *Lohengrin*] . . . 'Come si *dorme* con questa musica!'" relying on the stereotype of women's vulnerability to hypnosis (from Greek, *hypnos*, sleep). But we must add that for Nietzsche, the effect of Wagner's hypnotic power is not limited to "lady listeners." On the contrary, "the master of hypnotic trick," as Nietzsche calls Wagner, "manages to throw down the strongest like bulls" (*CW* 5; 166). For Nietzsche, then, hypnotic suggestion has the power to infiltrate not only women, but all kinds of masculine subjects as well.[59] This is especially true as these "bulls" are part of what Nietzsche calls a "herd" or, as he now prefers to call it, a *Masse*.

For the late Nietzsche, as for Plato before him, mass behavior and the theater cannot be dissociated. Hence he says: "We know the masses, we know the theater" (*CW* 6; 167); he defines Wagner as the "*modern artist par*

excellence" (5; 166) and his art as "mass art [*Massen-Kunst*] par excellence"
(*NW* 665). And in *Gay Science*, in the context of a discussion of theatrical
lexis he speaks of the artist's "crude artifices of persuasion, as if he addressed
a mob" (187). Lacoue-Labarthe is, thus, faithful to Nietzsche's evaluation of
Wagner, as he claims that in Bayreuth was born "*le premier art de masse.*"[60]
This equivalence between the masses and the theater amounts to saying that
for Nietzsche the *modern* characteristic of Wagner's language consists in
being a *mass* medium, in the sense that it is a language explicitly oriented to
impress the masses.

For Nietzsche, as for other modernists after him, it is precisely the power
of hypnosis or, as he also calls it, following Hippolyte Bernheim, the power of
"suggestion" (*CW* 8; 172), that accounts for Wagner's power to "persuade the
masses" (7; 171). The crucial characteristic of hypnotic suggestion, as Bernheim famously defined it, consists in "a peculiar aptitude for transforming the
idea received into an act."[61] Hypnosis, in other words, consists in a common
psychic mechanism whereby an external idea is unconsciously incorporated
by the subject and, most strikingly, is felt, experienced, lived as one's own.
Nietzsche is thus perfectly consistent with theories of hypnosis as he states:
"In the theater one is honest only in the mass; as an individual one lies, one
lies to oneself. One leaves oneself at home when one goes to the theater,
one renounces the right to one's own tongue and choice, to one's taste" (*GS*
368; 325). The problematic of affective contagion, the subject's passivity, suggestibility to suggestion, the lack of rational control over one's opinion, the
magic of hypnosis—in short, the state of mimetic indistinction between self
and other characteristic of the modern "world of phantoms"—is definitively
at work within the Wagnerian theatrocracy and the language of modernity
it prefigures. And in order to dispel any doubts as to his final diagnosis of
the "needs of the *âme moderne*" (*NW* 672), Nietzsche concludes *The Case
of Wagner* thus: "all of us have, unconsciously, involuntarily in our bodies,
values, words, formulas, moralities of *opposite* descent—we are, physiologically considered, *false.—A diagnosis of the modern soul*" ("Epilogue"; 192). In
Nietzsche's severe diagnosis, the modern subject of the crowd not only lacks
the conscious capacity of self-expression and free will (i.e., control over his
"tongue" and "choice"), but is also unconsciously informed by the physiological reflexes of the other. This dispossession takes place via what he had called
an "ancient association between movement and sensation" (*D* 142) that not

only reproduces gestures but also thoughts and, now he adds, "values" and "moralities." In short, this subject's physiological movements are not originally his own; his moral opinions are actually his neighbor's opinions; his head is his neighbor's head; his ego is a mere phantom.

We were wondering where the power of this tyrant came from. What kind of *modern* language spoke through him? Nietzsche's answer is clear: it is through the language of hypnotic suggestion and the mimetic unconscious it entails that this tyrant dispossesses the subject of the mass of its capacity to think. Indeed, an alternative genealogy of the modernist unconscious is fully at work in Nietzsche's critique of the language of modernity.

The Pathos of Will to Power

This said, we should not forget that Nietzsche's patho(-)logical thought is, as always, implicated in the pathology he denounces. When he critiques Wagner's mimetic sickness he is also reflexively turning his critique against himself. We have seen that this was true with respect to the suggestibility to suggestion at work in the Dionysian. Yet the Dionysian is just one of the manifestations of Nietzsche's protean subjectivity. There is another conception of the subject we now need to consider, a subject who is not passively overtaken by mimesis but, not unlike Wagner, is attracted to the tyrannical pathos characteristic of mimetic will to power. Absolute authoritarian power over the masses is something that, indeed, tempts that other infamous "artist" figure and "blond beast of prey" Nietzsche notoriously calls "master."

In the second essay of *On the Genealogy of Morals*, in the context of a larger discussion of the formation of bad consciousness, Nietzsche offers us an account of the formation of sociality in mimetic terms. This formation, Nietzsche tells us in a famous section, is predicated on the masters' power of "impression" over "unshaped populations" of slaves. Making clear that he understands this power of impression quite literally, he adds that the slaves (i.e., the mimetic herd) function as "raw material of common people and half animals" who are "not only thoroughly kneaded [*durchgeknetet*] and malleable [*gefügig*] but also *formed* [*geformt*]" (II, 17). According to this genealogical account of sociality, at the beginning of history was a shapeless mass of subjects waiting, like raw material in front of the artist's chisel, to be given form. The validity of this account is of course highly disputable, and Henry

Staten is thus right to point out that Nietzsche's account is "unhistorical" and should not be taken seriously in terms of a faithful description of the origins of socialization. And yet we should not conclude that "there never was nor could there ever be any such formless human matter."[62] If we consider this account from a *psychosociological* perspective, Nietzsche's description of a malleable human mass accounts for the psychological disposition characteristic of a subject who is part of a crowd.

That Nietzsche is thinking along these psychological lines is already suggested by the fact that the German adjective he uses to describe the slaves' malleability (*gefügig*) denotes exclusively *psychic* docility. This detail, which most translators slur over, indicates that Nietzsche, while not insisting on the psycho-physiological language of his Wagner books, has in mind a process of psychological impression, a "typography," as Lacoue-Labarthe calls it, that informs Nietzsche's Platonic account of the power of mimesis. The subjection of the unshaped "mass" of subjects to the masters' "shaping forces" (II, 12; 59), which are responsible for an "impression of form" (*Formen aufdrücken*) (II, 17), as Nietzsche imagines it in *illo tempore*, is not unlike the unconscious subjection of the theatrical masses to the hypnotic actor. It is, thus, perfectly consistent that Nietzsche, a few sections later, accounts for the slaves' capitulation to the "divine cult of their masters . . . through compulsion or through submissiveness and *mimicry*" (II, 20; Nietzsche's emphasis), a mimicry that in-*forms* the psychic life not only of a subject, but of an entire crowd.

But this is not all. This compulsive force is also constitutive of one of the most discussed and enigmatic Nietzschean concepts, a concept that Nietzsche did not have the time to fully articulate, but that haunts his later period nonetheless under the name of "will to power."[63] In the same essay of *Genealogy*, for instance, he accounts for the masters' force in the following terms: "a will to power has mastered something less powerful [*weniger mächtig*] than itself and impressed [*aufgeprägt*] the meaning of a function upon it in accordance with its own interests" (II, 12; 58). This is one of the clearest occurrences of Nietzsche's much-disputed theory as it appears in a text that he actually published, and in the light of the movement of mimetic patho(-)logy we have been following, the meaning of this most elusive Nietzschean concept becomes clear. The fact that he defines the will to power (the "essence of life") in terms of a "shaping force" that impresses a malleable psychic material he does not yet call *Masse* but "unshaped population" [*ungestaltete Bevölkerung*]—or more directly, *Volk*—indicates that the masters' shaping power is *mimetic* will to power. From this perspective we can equally understand why Nietzsche, later in his career, will call that "primitive form of affect" (*WP* 688) that is the will to power a "pathos": "the will to power not a being, not a becoming, but a *pathos*" (*WP* 635).[64] This term, which he also uses to define Wagner's hypnotic power of impression, implies a passive vulnerability to the sphere of affect. There is not necessarily a contradiction here. As Girard also recognized, "Nietzsche's relationship to the will to power cannot be separated from his relationship to Wagner."[65] And as we have seen, for Plato it is because the rhapsode is vulnerable to the pathos of enthusiasm that he can transmit it magnetically, that is, contagiously, mimetically, unconsciously, or as Nietzsche also says, hypnotically, to the masses of spectators, impressing thus their psychic lives along psycho-physiological lines that contemporary developments in neuroplasticity are beginning to rediscover.[66]

We begin to see how deeply mimesis operates in the general economy of Nietzsche's thought. The importance in Nietzsche's intellectual and personal development of different forms of pathos strongly suggests that the "primitive form of affect" (*WP* 688) that is the will to power cannot be fully understood if we do not take into consideration the role of affective mimesis, if only because it is through the medium of mimetic pathos that power is most effectively impressed. From Nietzsche's psycho-physiological analysis of the child's affective communication with the mother to his take on the affective power of Christian compassion, from Dionysian impersonation and artistic expression to "sovereign" forms of psychic impression, we have repeatedly seen that power, for Nietzsche, tends to be thought in terms of *mimetic* will to power. Thus, as Nietzsche shifts the focus of attention from Wagner to the master, tyrannical pathos turns into sovereign pathos, weakness turns into a sign of strength, mimetic *sickness* turns into mimetic *power*.

This, at least, is what happens as Nietzsche looks backwards, genealogically, towards the past. But with respect to mimesis, Nietzsche is always at least Janus-faced. Which also means that we should expect that he also looks forward, towards the future. Hence, despite Nietzsche's glorification of the master's power of impression, he is also ready to admit that there is a new type of master in town, a figure whose mimetic will to power is even stronger than the master. In *Gay Science*, for instance, he writes: "It is thus that the maddest and most interesting ages of history always emerge when the 'actors,' *all* kinds of actors, become the real masters" (*GS* 356; 303). Nietzsche is, of course, speaking of that "master of hypnotic tricks" who is Wagner, but also prefigures, via the case of Wagner, types of mass-mediatic political masters qua actors yet to come. The passage betrays Nietzsche's emotional ambivalence for such "ages," but it also makes his conceptual position clear concerning the value of such modern actors. Thus, Nietzsche identifies with the Platonic figure of the "great architect" *against* the figure of the actor. As he puts it, in order to "anticipate the future in plans of such scope" one must be "*a stone in a great edifice*; and to that end he must be *solid* first of all, a 'stone'—and above all not an actor!" (*GS* 356; 303).

Prophet of Nazism?

In this last section, the spiraling movement of Nietzsche's patho(-)logical thought turns, a last time, in its effort to both conjure and diagnose the phantom of the ego that haunts the modern world. Thus, he returns to consider the collective dimension of the *âme moderne* from the perspective of the physician of the soul who dissects the present in order to anticipate the future. In this last move, Nietzsche reenacts the Platonic refusal of mimesis through the language of modern psychology. But philosophy and psychology are not the only issues here. In fact, for Nietzsche, as for Lacoue-Labarthe after him, something "essential for the political is played out in the refusal of mimesis."[67] And in order to get to Nietzsche's critique of politics, we need to give a last turn of the screw to his mimetic psycho-patho-logy.

The Century of the Masses

Despite Nietzsche's insistence on linking modernity with the theater, we would be mistaken in confining the realm of these "real masters" within the theatrical walls. Let us not forget that from the outset, Nietzsche's critique of Wagner's so-called modern language—which as we know, is the language of mimesis or, to use modern terms, the language of hypnosis—immediately exceeds the limits of Bayreuth. This hysterico-, hypnotico-, mass sugges-tion is part of what Nietzsche calls "entirely modern, entirely *metropolitan* problems" (*CW* 9; 176): problems that concern the modern polis. Thus he writes that "all Europeans confound themselves with their role; they become the victims of their own 'good performance' . . . the role has actually *become* character; and art, nature" (*GS* 356; 302). Plato would have said "second nature." Clearly, Nietzsche's critique of the language of mimesis and all it entails—possession, contagion of emotions and ideas, psychic typography, hypnotic suggestion, and unconscious bodily reflexes, in short what he calls "the whole psychology of the actor" (*CW* 8; 173)—far from being limited to the theatrical sphere, is unquestionably open to the wider sociopolitical sphere. For Nietzsche, as for other modernists after him, all Europe is haunted by this mimetic phantom.

It is thus no accident that Nietzsche immediately politicizes his psycho-physiological critique of Wagner's hypnotic pathos. Thus, he says: "It is full of profound significance that the arrival of Wagner coincides in time with the arrival of the '*Reich*.' . . . Never has obedience been better, never has command-ing" (*CW* 11; 180). The cultural hero of the German people occupies the place of a "tyrant" in his theatrical autocracy, a tyrant who has the power to "hypno-tize" what Nietzsche often calls the *Volk*. Most strikingly, at times, Nietzsche even uses the German word for leader to define this new type of master—a word that, as we know, will soon become notorious. As Nietzsche puts it in *The Case of Wagner*, he sees in Wagner nothing less than a "*Führer*" ("Vorwort"), a *Führer* possessed with the hypnotic power to "move" (*bewegen*) to "persuade" (*überreden*), and finally to "win" (*gewinnen*) the masses ("Postscript"; 6, 7; 167, 171, 183). It is thus in this precise psychosociological sense that Nietzsche's insights into the workings of Wagner's mimetic will to power anticipate, at least in theory, the horrors of Nazism and the mimetic medium responsible for spreading its message. And in *Ecce Homo* he ominously concludes that "There will be wars the like of which have never yet been on earth" (1, 126). Indeed, towards the end of his career, Nietzsche is diagnosing the future forms of mimetic will to power that will soon haunt the modern period. At least, this is certainly the case if we accept Lacoue-Labarthe's definition of "fascism" as "enactment of identificatory mass emotion."[68]

Does one conclude with Nietzsche, not as a forerunner of Nazism, then, but as a prophet who condemns the very phenomena to which his name was so long connected? This thesis should not come as a surprise. After all, if we consider Nietzsche's work as a prolonged meditation on the secret workings of unconscious forms of imitative behavior, this conclusion seems nearly inevitable. Nietzsche's distaste for the mimetic herd, his profound knowledge of ancient theater in general and of Plato's critique of mimesis in particular, his own entanglement in Dionysian mimesis and the temptation to occupy the place of Wagner (i.e., the place of the master) with respect to the masses, his critical awareness of psycho-physiology, his exploration of the pre-Freudian tradition of the unconscious, and, more generally, his acute psychological sensibility are all elements that, taken together, point towards such a conclusion.

Nietzsche can see mimetic mass phenomena like Nazism coming because he is theoretically ahead of his time. But he can be ahead only because he is fully aware of the mimetic tradition that precedes him. In a way we could even say that with respect to the problematic of mimesis, Nietzsche functions as a crucial link between antiquity and modernity; Plato's ethico-political critique of mimesis on the one hand, and modern psychological theories of hypnosis on the other. In this sense, his psycho-political critique of mimesis looks back only to better see what lies ahead. In order to do so, Nietzsche blends Plato's intuitions on mimesis with the modern language of psycho-physiology, establishing a direct connection between the problematic of the mimetic actor and the problematic of hypnotic suggestion. This theoretical bridge between antiquity and modernity, the language of mimesis and the language of hypnosis, allows him to refine his psycho-patho-logy of the *âme moderne* as well as to extend its implications towards the modernist period. At stake in such a theoretical conjunction, in fact, is not only an attempt to make sense of Wagner's absolute power over the theatrical crowd, but also, and perhaps more importantly, a *theoretical* insight into the mimetic power of political leaders to communicate the same phantom to entire crowds of egos. We could even say that the Wagnerian theater functions as a microcosm that allows Nietzsche to carefully observe, analyze, and dissect the secret workings of the language of mimesis, which is also the language of modernity: the very same language that haunts the modern *Grosstädte* in a century that Nietzsche prophetically calls "the century of the *mass*" (*Jahrhundert der Masse*)" (*NW* 673).[69]

Nietzsche's neo-Platonic psycho-physiological critique of mimesis is, thus, not only historically prophetic. Insofar as he anticipates the fundamental insight of mass psychology, Nietzsche is equally theoretically prophetic.

Suggestive power over the masses via a hypnotic relationship with the figure of the leader: this is, indeed, the hypothesis that Gustave Le Bon, one of the founding fathers of crowd psychology, will reach a few years later in order to account for the irrational, contagious, and highly suggestible behavior characteristic of the crowd. Echoing Nietzsche, Le Bon proclaims that modernity is about to enter what he calls the "era of crowds" (*l'ère des foules*).[70] And like Nietzsche before him, Le Bon resorts to a mimetic analogy in order to account for the irrational, contagious, and fundamentally unconscious behavior of crowds. In his wildly popular *Psychologie des foules* (1895), he explains:

> an individual immersed for some length of time in a crowd in action soon finds himself . . . in a special state, which much resembles the state of fascination in which the hypnotized individual finds himself in the hands of the hypnotizer. The activity of the brain being paralyzed in the case of the hypnotized subject, the latter becomes the slave of all *the unconscious activities of his spinal cord, which the hypnotizer directs at will.*[71]

Freud famously proclaimed that the unconscious was a psychoanalytical discovery. Yet in Le Bon's affirmation we actually see how popular and pervasive the psycho-physiological model of the hypnotic unconscious was at the turn of the century, a pre-Freudian unconscious grounded not on a "repressive hypothesis" but on a "mimetic hypothesis" instead. This unconscious is rooted in what Nietzsche called "genuine physio-psychology" (*BGE* 23). It was thought to be associated with the spinal cord on the basis of the experimental observation that decapitated frogs still responded to external stimuli—Lawrence will later speak of "vertebral consciousness"—but it was also intimately tied to hypnosis as a paradigmatic model of unconscious behavior.

Both Le Bon's and Nietzsche's reliance on the model of hypnotic suggestion in order to analyze unconscious, mimetic phenomena that haunt modernity is directly indebted to Hippolyte Bernheim, from the School of Nancy, who, contra Charcot, argued that hypnosis is a normal and common phenomenon. Yet the theoretical sources of this hypnotic tradition are much older and, as Henri Ellenberger has shown in *The Discovery of the Unconscious*, can be traced back to Anton Mesmer's theory of animal magnetism, a theory Nietzsche also refers to, as he defines Wagner as a "*magnétiseur*" (*CW* 7; 171).[72] Of course, Nietzsche does not believe in a physical fluid that would flow from Wagner to the masses, but, like Le Bon, Bernheim, and other pre-Freudian psychologists, he recuperates the old notion of magnetism in a psychological key.[73] Nietzsche's use of French here is, thus, most appropriate and in line with this pre-Freudian psychological tradition. And yet references to magnetic tropes to account for the unconscious power of mimetic contagion are not specific to nineteenth-century psychology. Already in *Ion* Plato relied on the trope of magnetism in order to account for the contagious power of mimetic *lexis* on the theatrical crowd. The old Platonic metaphor of the "stone of Heraclea" is taken up again to account for the "will power" of the leader over the masses. But this time, that philosophical physician of (anti-)Platonic inspiration who is Nietzsche imbues this transcendental concept with the immanent language of dynamic psychology that goes from magnetism to hypnosis.

Phantom comes from Plato

The Philosophical Physician

What makes Nietzsche's modernist brand of mimetic theory, if not original, at least unique, then, is that he relies simultaneously on both ancient and modern traditions, Plato's philosophical critique of mimesis and the psychological account of hypnosis, in order to critique and diagnose the language of "modernity." The fact that Wagner is conceived as both an "enthusiastic mimomanic" and a "*magnétiseur*" endowed with an "hypnotic" will to power to deprive the masses of control over their egos suggests that Nietzsche understands modern psychological developments as extensions of the Platonic concern with affective contagion. Such a convergence of a magnetic-hypnotic-mimetic terminology in Nietzsche's account of Wagner's will to power also indicates that, despite its different historical and theoretical inflections, important continuities exist between ancient and modernist forms of mimetic theory. Not unlike Plato and, later, Le Bon, as well as more recent figures (from Girard to Lacoue-Labarthe), Nietzsche notices that "the masses are willing to submit to slavery of any kind" (*GS* 40), losing their rational control over themselves as they are carried away by the pathos of tyrannical leader figures. Whether such a leader is called *mimetes*, *meneur*, or *Führer* and the pathos they convey called mimetic, magnetic, or hypnotic, does not fundamentally alter the phenomenon involved. Nietzsche, at least, in his denomination of Wagner as "enthusiastic mimomanic," "*magnétiseur*," and "master of hypnosis" moves freely between the language of antiquity and language of modernity, philosophy and psycho-physiology, with the awareness that each term points to the same mysterious psychic phenomenon that has the power to turn the ego into a phantom of the ego. In this sense, if we follow Nietzsche, we can say that the language of hypnosis functions as a modern, psycho-physiological reformulation of the ancient language of mimesis—a language that Nietzsche, Le Bon, and a panoply of other theoretical and literary modernist figures whom we shall soon encounter are trying to decipher in order to account for the crisis of modernity.

This engagement with Nietzsche's prophetic insights into the theoretical core of psychosociology is not meant to reterritorialize Nietzsche's thought within the confines of this emerging discipline. Nietzsche is and remains the philosopher he is. Hence, he never focuses exclusively on the emotional dynamics that are responsible for the formation of mass behavior. And yet we have seen that Nietzsche is not only a philosopher. He is also an insightful psychologist, a philosophical physician who develops a critical discourse (*logos*) on the modern soul (*psyche*) and, thus, is extremely attentive to the affective, unconscious, and fundamentally mimetic dimension of both the individual and the collective ego. What was already true for the father of philosophy is even truer for Nietzsche, namely, that psychology is constitutive of his very act of philosophizing.[74] Thus, that crossroads thinker who is Nietzsche can offer theoretical contributions to the different theoretical paths that transect his writings. And as we have seen, his psychosociological theory of the modern ego leads him to align himself with Plato in order to anticipate some of Le Bon's major claims. These authors fundamentally agree (with Plato) on a crucial point: that is, they see the danger that phantoms may take the place of egos, or better that such phantoms are already *constitutive* of the modern ego. Hence, for these theorists of mimesis, the ego—especially as it is part of the crowd—is not a rational subject or *subjectum* in rational possession of its thoughts and actions. Rather, it is a fundamentally passive, malleable entity subjected to the power of unconscious affects that render it vulnerable to hypnotic manipulations. As we have seen, Nietzsche keeps returning to this suggestible conception of the subject in order to develop a critical patho-logy that anticipates both the fundamental theoretical intuition of sociopsychology and the horror of mimetic contagion that our own century of the masses will soon experience.

Finally, we might still need to assess the contemporary relevance of Nietzsche's psycho-socio-patho-logical *critique*. Of course, this critique is untimely in the sense that Nietzsche tries to understand massive outbursts of mimetic pathology like fascism and Nazism that lie ahead of him. Such precise insights are already a lot to be grateful for. But we might go even further in our expectations and ask: what does this mimetic language have to do with our own generation, a generation that did not directly witness the horrors of fascism and Nazism and the affective manipulation of the crowd they entail but is, perhaps more than ever, subjugated to the power of mimesis? To conclude this first chapter and anticipate the chapters to come, I would like to suggest that it is perhaps with respect to this last question that, as Lacoue-Labarthe writes in *L'imitation des modernes*, "[It is] urgent for philosophy to think and rethink mimesis."[75] It is true that we may not necessarily be part of a crowd in Plato's, Nietzsche's, or Le Bon's sense, getting enthusiastic over contemporary versions of Ion, Wagner, or some other mimetic tyrant—though the contemporary success of such "old magician[s]" who strive for "excitement at any price" on all kinds of platforms, screens, and interfaces should not be underestimated, most especially at decisive political times, such as election times. But who can claim not to be part of a "public"? The public, already in 1901, was defined by crowd psychologist Gabriel Tarde as a "virtual crowd" characterized by mental contagion, a contagion that works through "action at a distance of a mind over another."[76] This *actio in distans* was once channeled by those very newspapers Nietzsche could not stomach. And nowadays, it is clear that in our contemporary, mediatized, and digitalized society the modern subject's nervous system is globally channeled or, better, plugged into all kinds of new *mass* media Nietzsche would probably have stomached even less. If only because the language that speaks through these media tends to shape, mimetically, or as Nietzsche would say, hypnotically, those very opinions that all too often, the modern ego tends to mistake as its own. The language of modernity Nietzsche analyzes is still very much with us; the technical changes in the medium have not fundamentally distorted the grammar of the old, yet always actual, language of mimesis.

Nietzsche's patho(-)logy, I have argued, catches an essential glimpse of that process of mimetic communication responsible for the formation of an ego that is not one. Such a communication is characteristic of Christians and non-Christians, masters and slaves, Plato, Schopenhauer, Wagner, theatrical spectators, the crowd, the whole modern world, and, last but not least, Nietzsche himself. The communicative power of mimesis, in other words, is far from being something extraordinary, a rare pathology that affects only a few clinical "cases." On the contrary, Nietzsche has shown us that it is the most ordinary phenomenon; so ordinary that it tends to go unnoticed and, thus, unquestioned, and, thus, unthought, like the contagious dimension of a yawn. Nietzsche, the "philosophical physician" who "brings all his scientific curiosity into his illness," is warning his posthumous readers that we, along with him, may still be implicated in that strange world of phantoms he so deftly dissects.

The recovery he at times enthusiastically celebrates as something accomplished once and for all may inevitably remain a healing process, which needs always to renew itself. Even at daybreak, as the light of reason seems to return, this human, all too human imitative pathology needs to be continuously subjected to severe yet sobering forms of mimetic patho-logy. This diagnostic task, as we now turn to see, is perhaps most urgent in a period Nietzsche calls the "century of the masses"; or, as he also says, in a more Platonic mood, the "century of enthusiasm" (*Jahrhundert der Schwärmerei*) (D "Preface"; 3).

- Nietzsche talks about fascism, people who follow the crowd are sick, those who don't follow the crowd are healthy (mostly rich/ self thinkers)

- social media makes people "sick", nietzsche would be angry if alive today, it connects sick & healthy

- Lawtoo wants to create a sense of danger with mimesis,
- mimesis is a state of mind, an idea of who you should be/won't be

CHAPTER 2

Conrad and the Horror of Modernity

It is thus that the maddest and most interesting ages of history always emerge, when the "actors," *all* kinds of actors, become the real masters.
—Friedrich Nietzsche, *Gay Science*

Apocalypse Now in the Classroom

Daybreak. Captain Kilgore's squadron of helicopters ominously appears, soaring above the water, against the background of a fiery sky. "We are coming in low out of the rising sun and about a mile up we'll put on the music," shouts Kilgore (Robert Duvall) to one of the soldiers. And he adds: "I use Wagner. It scares the hell out of the slopes. My boys love it!" Then the thundering music begins, and so does the slaughtering. The cinematic pathos of this scene is tremendous. No viewer of Francis Ford Coppola's *Apocalypse Now* (1979) will ever forget its breathtaking and yet horrific impact.[1]

In his internationally acclaimed cinematic interpretation of Conrad's *Heart of Darkness*, Coppola makes Richard Wagner's musical pathos actual again. The "Ride of the Valkyries" adds a quasi-mythical dimension to the helicopters' attack, and this war mythology is made to speak again to the contemporary audience sitting in the movie theaters, at least as much as representations of the Valkyries spoke to the nineteenth century audience in the theater. The new visual medium through which Wagner's modern language is conveyed amplifies its power of suggestion and familiarizes a new generation with the tyrannical pathos of Nietzsche's "mimetic rival," as well as with the apocalyptic dangers of affective contagion.

If Nietzsche's Platonic critique of crowd behavior has taught us that Wagner's pathos is truly mimetic and has the power to "convince the nerves" (*CW* 7), the helicopter scene shows us how this pathos, conveyed by a new medium, convinces the nerves of modern subjects. This music has the hypnotic power to affect Kilgore's visibly scared "boys," fueling them with the necessary adrenaline to accomplish their slaughtering "mission" (diegetic level); it is also communicated outside the screen and reaches the nerves of the audience sitting in the movie theaters (extradiegetic level). The thrill of enthusiasm the soldiers feel going down their spines is, indeed, a contagious, magnetic, or, as Nietzsche would have also called it, "hypnotic" pathos that spreads all too easily among the public. The phantom's medium is different, yet the unconscious mimesis it generates is fundamentally the same.

Coppola's Pathos

With some distance, it is easy to see that the affective identification with the American air cavalrymen is far from being natural but is the result of specific cinematic choices. The scene is shot nearly exclusively from the American soldiers' point of view (i.e., from above); close-ups of their faces accentuate their psychological turmoil and draw viewers into their emotions, whereas the distanced, low-angle long shots, through which we see the Vietnamese soldiers, do not allow a sympathetic connection to be established. Furthermore, the grandiose, mythic dimension of the helicopter attack contrasts with the hopeless inefficiency of the victims' attempts at self-defense; the dynamism of the former contrasts with the immobility of the latter; powerful contrasts with weak, high with low; or, to use the red ink inscription that appears on Kilgore's private helicopter, "death from above" contrasts with death from below. Not surprisingly, then, these cinematographic strategies, in addition to Wagner's irresistible musical pathos, introduce a violent hierarchy that affectively and effectively works to pull us inside the perspective of the oppressor. Thus, as the commanding pilot gives orders to "make [the music] loud," boys and audience alike should better get ready for an emotional overdose.[2] And as he adds, "On a Romeo fox-trot, shall we dance," and the "Ride of the Valkyries" begins, it is difficult to resist this dance. As Nietzsche would have put it, "not only our feet follow the beat but the soul does too" (*GS* 84).[3]

And yet *Apocalypse Now* is clearly *not* a manifesto in favor of the Vietnam War. It is a movie that represents the absurdity and moral degradation that animate this conflict in particular and American imperialism in general (hence Coppola's "horror" at the public's enthusiasm for his Wagnerian scene). Even the goal of the helicopter mission is an explicit comment on the absurdity of the conflict. As critics routinely point out, what motivates Captain Kilgore's raid is simply his passion for surfing. And in order to make his moral perspective clear, during the scene preceding the Wagnerian attack, Coppola is careful to represent the innocent dimension of some of the victims, cutting from shots of the helicopters, close-ups of the American boys, the radio loudspeakers, and machine guns, to a peaceful village school where children are getting ready to run for shelter.[4]

At work in the Wagner scene, then, is a structural double-bind that violently confronts two contradictory evaluations. On the one hand, the content of the scene (Plato's *logos*) functions as a critique of this attack in particular and the war in general, a social commentary that introduces a critical distance with respect to the violence, irrationality, and hypocrisy of the war. On the other hand, the formal qualities of this cinematic language (Plato's *lexis*), such as camera angles, types of shots, sound, and so on, have the effect of conveying a feeling of enthusiasm for the military pathos the movie sets out to explicitly condemn. At the level of reception, this tension involves a structural push-pull in the heads of the public, generating a movement that is by now familiar to us: spectators are made to oscillate, pendulum-like, between an emotional, enthusiastic response on the one hand, and a rational, critical response on the other; hypnotic suggestion and resistance to it; identification with the men' war pathos and critical distance from it. We are, thus, immediately thrown back to the connecting thread of our inquiry and to what I consider to be the primary structuring characteristic of affective mimesis. This psychic mechanism whereby subjects' moral evaluations can suddenly swing from antimimetic to mimetic attitudes, from rational *logos* to irrational *pathos* is what I continue to explore in this chapter. And this time, it is to Joseph Conrad's implicit theory of mimesis and the patho(-)logies it generates, that I turn my attention to in order to push Nietzsche's epochal critique of modernity to new geographical and theoretical territories the modernist generation is increasingly confronted with. If the problematic of mimesis takes us into the horrors of colonialism and imperialism, it might also help us cast some light on the patho(-)logical problem this scene and, more generally the problematic of mimetic contagion, poses to modern and postmodern viewers.

But before turning to Conrad, a qualification is in place. This "theoretical" problem is not the result of an abstract meditation on *Apocalypse Now* but, rather, stems from a practical teaching situation that I find important to briefly relate. I became fully aware of the theoretical implications inherent in this scene as I first taught *Apocalypse Now* in conjunction with *Heart of Darkness* to a class of undergraduate students on an American campus. As everybody who has taught these two texts back-to-back knows, the movie has the power to touch students in a way that the novella (because of its difficulty as well as of its temporal and geographical distance) often does not or, at least, not so directly. In order to test the timeliness of both literary and visual texts, I asked the class a very direct and apparently simple question: namely, if they considered the "Ride of the Valkyries" scene, a celebration or, rather, a condemnation of the Vietnam War. The question was simple enough, but the responses were theoretically complex.

At first, nearly all students seemed to agree that Coppola's intention was truly critical. They pointed out the power imbalance between the two fronts, the fact that passion for surfing does not justify killing, and that the lives of innocent children are at stake. Some students also mentioned that the choice of the anti-Semite Wagner, whose music the Third Reich reappropriated, was far from being politically innocent, and gave a clear indication of Coppola's truly critical intentions. In short, I was given the appropriate response for a class of critical reading. And yet after probing a little further, the first emotional responses began to surface, responses that began to complicate the initial ethical considerations. A few outspoken (male) students began to guiltily acknowledge their identification with Kilgore's boys and the fact that they took some pleasure from this scene. Despite the problematic dimension of such an avowal, this is precisely what I had initially expected when I asked my question. I expected it because, as we have seen, the Wagner scene is formally construed in order to elicit such identifications; but also because I considered that acknowledging the emotional power of this scene, as well as one's participation in such violent affects, was the necessary *first step* to begin to gain a position of critical distance from this horrifying pathos. I still think I was right on the importance of such a first step, but hopelessly naive in my belief that such a transition from *pathos* to *logos* could be made within the scope of one class.

In the meantime, the atmosphere in the classroom was becoming increasingly tense. The consensus was broken, and a heated discussion between two opposite fields began to emerge. To the students who persevered in condemning the U.S. attack on moral grounds, students who acknowledged their emotional engagement in the helicopter raid began to find rational, textual/visual justifications for the raid. They answered, for instance, that those so-called "innocent" Vietcong are ready to kill as well— the reference being to both their self-defense and, more problematically, to a Vietnamese woman who throws a bomb into an American helicopter, blowing it to pieces. Once again, the students' discussion was making audible a tension intrinsic to the scene itself. In fact, if Coppola begins by showing us the Vietnamese schoolchildren, stressing thus the innocence of the potential victims, as the helicopter explodes he is careful to zoom in on U.S. casualties screaming in pain but tends to avoid specific representations of the suffering of innocent Vietnamese. When he does so, the victims are either dead or, as in the case of a dying man shot in the stomach, ethical responsibility is deferred to a South Vietnamese soldier. This imbalance in the *representation* of suffering is far from being politically neutral and surely contributed to inflecting the class's identificatory allegiances. But the decisive cinematic step necessary for an affective identification with the American soldiers had already been prepared before, during the mythical scene imbued with Wagner's musical pathos. We were thus feeling, with more intensity, the effects of this scene on our nerves; and as the class was speeding towards its end, textual analysis was no longer the focus of "pro-war" students' arguments. Sentences imbued with an emotional pathos that no longer seemed to pertain exclusively to the sphere of cinematic fiction began to circulate: "How can you judge?" "Have you ever been to war?" "You don't know what it's like out there!"

A most common but nonetheless troubling psychic phenomenon had just taken place. An unconscious mimesis, surely fostered by a whole tradition of (pro)war movies and—why not say it?—contemporary politics, had successfully occurred. For some students the mimetic pathos of enthusiastic emotions had taken control over the distancing power of critical reason. Indeed, mimetic infections are difficult to keep at a distance, even in contexts that train us to remain critically vigilant. Coppola's cinematic medium had the power to induce a light hypnotic-cinematic-musical suggestion that brought to the surface prowar sentiments at the heart of a class of critical reading.[5] And yet part of the class was struggling to resist this mimetic seduction. The practical effect was to swing the class back and forth, between critical distance and uncritical pathos. The simple question had, indeed, given its critical as well as affective results. I must admit that at that moment, I could find no satisfying way to articulate the conflict between critical *logos* and affective *mimesis*. And so, for the remaining sessions, we turned to Joseph Conrad, for theoretical help.[6]

Conrad's Distance

Conrad's work can be read as an attempt to cast some light on the identificatory affects (mimesis) that lurk behind linguistic expression (logos). In one of his well-known short stories, speaking of his two protagonists, Conrad makes a sweeping statement that not only applies to his fictional characters but extends to acquire a general theoretical valence:

> They believed their words. Everybody shows a respectful deference to certain sounds that he and his fellows can make. But about feelings people really know nothing. We talk with indignation or enthusiasm; we talk about oppression, cruelty, crime, devotion, self-sacrifice, virtue, and we know nothing real beyond the words.[7]

In specific passages like this one, Conrad is insistent about the fact that "we" are not only all implicated in "enthusiastic" feelings that lead us to believe "our" words, but we are also fundamentally ignorant about the affects motivating such beliefs; professional writers, critical readers, and, nowadays, spectators are to a different degree all included in this all-inclusive "we." Conrad, in fact, seems well aware that we are all, in one way or another, enthusiastically driven by the incomprehensible pathos such words (and music) mysteriously induce. To put it with the language of *Apocalypse Now*, whether we like it or not, it is unavoidable that, at times, to the rhythm of mimetic affects "we shall dance."

If Conrad affirms that "we know nothing real beyond words," a short story like "An Outpost of Progress" and, even more intensely, a celebrated modernist novella like *Heart of Darkness* involve a persistent attempt to reach, through the medium of words, that elusive "beyond" where feelings—especially "enthusiastic," mimetic feelings—innervate the mimetic unconscious of the modern ego. This, at least, is the dark, affective side of Conrad I set out to explore.

An Outpost of Regress

First published in 1896 and subsequently collected in *Tales of Unrest* (1898), "An Outpost of Progress" indicates that Conrad's "unrest" cannot be dissociated from the haunting presence of the phantom of the ego. A brief, partial look at this story, in fact, already shows both Conrad's critical awareness of, and his active engagement with, the problematic of the mimetic unconscious. It also shows us the extent of his assimilation of nineteenth-century theories of mimesis and crowd behavior—theories that, at the time he was writing, were beginning to spread contagiously all over Europe. My goal here is thus not so much to offer a detailed reading of this story as to focus on those passages that are instrumental in bringing my mimetic problematic to the surface.

"Outpost" deals with the progressive moral and psychic regress of two inexperienced and hapless colonists, Kayerts and Carlier. The goal of their mission: occupy an abandoned trading post three hundred miles up the river Congo in order to "bring light, and faith and commerce to the dark places of the earth" (94)—and, less ideally, to loot the country of its ivory. During their enactment of "the rights and duties of civilization" (94), however, both characters progressively lose their grasp on their moral ideals, their practices, and, ultimately, themselves. Like much of Conrad's fiction, this story functions as an occasion for a critical meditation on the process of psychic formation and

disintegration of the subject's moral character. Kayerts's and Carlier's progressive psychic and moral degeneration allows Conrad to critically dissect
the psychic foundations of the modern subject and, at the same time, allows
us to reset in motion the spiraling movement of mimetic patho(-)logy.

In "Outpost" Conrad makes clear that his critique of the colonizing subject must be considered against the background of the massive social forces
that inform it, so that, as was already the case with Nietzsche before him,
personal psychology is immediately open to collective psychology. Speaking
of the two protagonists, the third-person anonymous narrator says: "They
were two perfectly insignificant and incapable individuals, whose existence
is only rendered possible through the high organization of civilized crowds"
(89). And, a few pages later, he adds: "Society . . . had taken care of those two
men, forbidding them all independent thought, all initiative, all departure
from routine. . . . They could only live on condition of being machines" (91).
In such passages, Conrad uses "society" and what he calls "the high organization of organized crowds" interchangeably, indicating that for him, society is
synonymous with mass society. The crowd, for Conrad, functions as a social
"organization" whose role is to sustain the mechanical "existence" of such
individuals while, at the same time, depriving them of their status as rational,
volitional subjects altogether. Kayerts and Carlier, in short, not only function
as a Conradian *homo duplex* (as their homonymous names clearly suggest), but
also as representatives of the undifferentiated subject of the mimetic crowd.

Of course, we should not hastily conclude that Conrad's critical insights
into his two protagonists immediately apply to a critique of modern subjectivity *tout court*. After all, Conrad seems to be speaking of what appears
to be the exception, namely two perfectly "insignificant subjects" who are
"incapable of independent thought," whom the director of the trading company calls "imbeciles" (88). As Jeremy Hawthorn points out, through use of
a third-person anonymous narrator, "the characters are observed at such a
distance that there is no possibility of emotional empathy." And he adds:
"the merciless criticism of the narrator . . . forces us to observe and analyze
them."[8] These two mimetic characters are, indeed, two pathological cases for
the reader to dissect from a position of rational distance. And yet we should
be careful lest we conclude too hastily that "Carlier and Kayerts are apart
from us" and that it is "impossible for us to enter into their world."[9] In fact, if
we read a few lines further, the narrative shifts to a higher level of generality,

detaches itself from the two characters, and implicates the modern subject (and reader?) in the riddles of mimetic pathology:

> Few men realize that their life, the very essence of their character, their capabilities and their audacities, are only the expression of their belief in the safety of their surroundings. The courage, the composure, the confidence; the emotions and principles; every great and every insignificant thought belongs not to the individual but to the crowd: to the crowd that believes blindly in the irresistible force of its institutions and of its morals, in the power of its police and of its opinion. (89)

This passage makes strikingly clear that as Conrad dissects his two protagonists' psychic lives, a wider critique of modern psychology is actually at stake. Conrad, in fact, relegates the modern moral subject to the sphere of crowd psychology and the mimetic unconscious it entails. For Conrad, as for Nietzsche before him, we live in the *Jahrhundert der Masse*: the phantom has taken possession of the ego, and, as he severely adds, "few men realize it."[10]

Textual moments like this one indicate that those nineteenth-century sociopsychological theories of the crowd, which resonate so much with Nietzsche's psychosociological critique of the *âme moderne*, have not only reached Conrad's ears on the other side of the Channel, but also shaped his very understanding of modern subjectivity. In fact, as Conrad states that every thought "belongs not to the individual but to the crowd; to the crowd that believes blindly in the irresistible force of its institutions and of its morals," he echoes the essential insight of modern theories of the crowd. Here is one of Gustave Le Bon's famous affirmations:

> It is only by obtaining some sort of insight into the psychology of crowds that it can be understood how slight is the action upon them of laws and institutions, how powerless they are to hold any opinions other than those which are imposed on them [*suggérées*], and that it is not with rules based on theories of pure equity that they are to be led, but by seeking what produces an impression on them, and what seduces them.[11]

And here is Gabriel Tarde's version of the same imitative phenomenon a few years earlier: "To have only suggested ideas and to believe them to be spontaneous: this is the illusion characteristic of the somnambulist and of the social man."[12] Such striking proximity between Conrad's account of the subject of the mass and the fundamental insights of crowd psychology should begin to alert us to the fact that, at the turn of the century, ideas about the mimetic status of subjects in a crowd were circulating freely, informing the way creative writers and thinkers perceived modern subjectivity. Whether directly or indirectly, modernists like Conrad—and, as we shall later have occasion to see, Lawrence and Bataille—draw on such ideas in order to offer crucial insights into the mimetic regress of the modern ego that is part of a crowd, contributing thus to a distinguishing modernist brand of mimetic theory informed by the insights of crowd psychology.

Now, it is precisely on such sociopsychological insights that Conrad establishes a critique of modern subjectivity and ideology. Claude Maison-nat, speaking of the two protagonists, stresses the "theatrical dimension of their attitude" insofar as he sees them "as playing a role and not as com-mitted ideologists." And he adds: "they are playing at colonizing instead of being colonizer."[13] The theatrical metaphor is well taken since, as we have seen, different critics of mass behavior, from Plato to Le Bon and Nietzsche, develop their critique of mass behavior in the context of that mimetic space par excellence which is the theater. Yet the metaphysical distinction between appearance and essence, surface and depth, "playing" and "being" is exactly what Conrad's sociopsychological account of the modern subject challenges. Conrad is clear on this point. It is the "very essence of their character," as he puts it, that is informed by mass opinions. In other words, these so-called actors who are playing a role are not different from their role. Rather, they are so fundamentally possessed by their role that they are dispossessed of their proper identity. Their essence *is* the social role they are playing; playing at colonizing *is* being the colonizer. As the French saying goes: *Prends garde, à jouer au fantôme on le devient.* Conrad could not have agreed more. In fact, for him the very essence of the modern subject and all it entails ("character, emotions, principles, opinions, morals," etc.) do not stem from one's ego, but from the phantasmatic role(s) we are led to play.

Already at this early stage, it seems that for Conrad, as for Nietzsche before him, a critique of moral opinions cannot be dissociated from a severe critique of the mimetic disposition that leads the modern subject to uncriti-cally (because unconsciously) adopt such opinions. Remarking that "every great and every insignificant thought belongs not to the individual but to the crowd," Conrad makes clear that the thoughts we think, or experience to be proper to ourselves and as defining our individuality, are merely the product of a "blind belief" and submission to the irresistible force of mass opinion. Conrad's critique of ideology is predicated upon a critique of mimetic efficacy that goes to the heart of the subject's affective life. The subject of the crowd is a passive, suggestible, hypnotized individual who is completely permeable to the power of propaganda and ideological indoctrination. In passages like this one, Conrad makes clear that modern thoughts do not truly stem from an individual head, but from a multiplicity of heads instead. As a consequence, one is forever in the head of someone else; one's opinion is someone else's opinion; one's ego is someone else's ego.

The passage quoted should suffice to indicate that Conrad, independently of his knowledge of Nietzsche, can productively be aligned with Nietzsche's critique of the phantom of the ego. Yet if this phantom is partially responsible for the "unrest" at work in this tale, the context of Conrad's mimetic meditations equally indicates that he extends this line of inquiry towards new geographical and theoretical territory. If we have seen that Nietzsche's take on mimesis entails a critique of modern values and subjectivity, we shall see that a major focus of Conrad's preoccupations concerns colonial ideology and its power to infiltrate, determine, and undo the psychic life of colonial subjects. "An Outpost of Progress" already shows that Conrad's attack on colonialism involves an exposure of the mimetic status of the colonial subject and the regress it entails. In fact, Carlier and Kayerts, after a brief period of faith in "the rights and duties of civilization, of the sacredness of the civilizing work" (94), progressively fall prey to "suggestion of things vague, uncontrollable" (89). No longer sustained by what Conrad calls "the safety of their surroundings," no longer having an audience to see them play the role that *is* the essence of their character, this mechanical subject crumbles to pieces (the two protagonists, ironically, end up killing each other for a decent cup of tea). The African jungle, then, becomes a place to unmask, in a Nietzschean move, the fragility of the psychic foundations of the so-called subject of *Aufklärung* (i.e., the subject who sets out, among other things, "to bring light, and faith and commerce to the dark places of the earth" [94]). The target is different but the method of attack is fundamentally the same. Conrad's critique of mimetic pathos, in fact, focuses on forms of subjectivity that are open to the unconscious power of "suggestion" and, thus, serve as material that can be hypnotically shaped according to the dominant ideology of the moment—even if, unlike Wagnerian spectators, they are no longer *physically* part of a crowd (a point to which we shall return). In short, "Outpost" alerts us to the fact that also for Conrad, the modern subject is bound to succumb to the dark power of mimesis and to the horrors that ensue. We begin to sense, then, that Conrad's critical account of colonialism, his investigation of what makes its horrors possible in a modern world that prides itself on its progress and humanizing missions, is predicated on an inquiry into the precise modality of how, exactly, ideology penetrates mimetically the modern subject and informs its opinions, values, and practices.

While Conrad considered "Outpost" "true enough in its essentials" (ix) and went as far as celebrating it as his "best story," this "tale of unrest" is only, as he ironically called it "the lightest part of the loot [he] carried off from central Africa, the main portion being of course 'The Heart of Darkness'" (ix). It is thus to the main portion of Conrad's literary "loot" that I now turn, in order to continue to articulate his critique of the haunting power of the phantom of the ego. *Heart of Darkness* (1899), as we shall see, functions as a theoretically productive supplement not only because of the explicit continuity in content between the two tales,[14] but also because this landmark in literary modernism provides us with a mediating narrative presence that was lacking both in *Apocalypse Now* and in "An Outpost of Progress." This presence, which goes by the name of Marlow, forces us to complicate, nuance, and refine the pessimistic representation of the modern ego as a helpless unconscious figure subjected to mimetic pathos. Marlow, in fact, serves as a mediator who attempts to negotiate between distance from, and proximity to, enthusiastic forms of colonial pathos, disidentificatory and identificatory practices, critical reason and mimetic feelings. And in the process, he forces us to rethink central questions in modernist studies, such as sexism, racism, and ideology through the innovative prism of mimesis. *Heart of Darkness*, as we now turn to see, gives another spin to Conrad's patho(-)logy, contributing to opening up the door of the mimetic unconscious.

Heart of Darkness and the Horror of Mimesis

The Belgian doctor whom Marlow meets just before taking off to the heart of darkness is a minor, irrelevant character who tends to go unnoticed. He is even described as a "fool" (57). And quite rightly. In fact, the doctor's practice of measuring his patients' "crania" with a "thing like calipers [to get] the dimensions back and front and every way, taking notes carefully" (58) clearly shows that he follows, *à la lettre*, the notorious craniological theory of the Italian jurist and criminologist Cesare Lombroso.[15] Yet, at the same time, this French-speaking doctor seems to stray from Lombroso's deterministic physiognomic theory. In fact, he affirms that "the changes take place inside" (58), making clear that his true interests do not concern anatomy, but psychology instead. And he adds: "It would be . . . interesting for science to watch the mental changes of individuals on the spot" (58). What the "old doctor" says applies, of course, to his medical practice and the pathologies it confronts. Hence, as Marlow impatiently asks, "Are you an alienist?" he unequivocally answers, "Every doctor should be—a little" (58). The accuracy of this last statement in the medical field is, indeed, unquestionable; but cannot the same be said for humanistic disciplines like literary theory and criticism? After all, psychology has been a crucial component in literary studies for a while now, and, often, literary characters provide critical readers with interesting "cases" to solve. It is, thus, in this sense that I sympathize with the old alienist's project. In a way, I even intend to continue, at the literary level, his psychological research. To be honest and echo the doctor's words, "I have a little theory which you [Mesdames and] Messieurs who go out there [in that literary jungle which is *Heart of Darkness*] must help me to prove" (58).

The Little Theory

After the publication of Albert Guerard's *Conrad the Novelist* in 1958—one of the earliest influential studies to explore the psychological dimension of Conrad's *Heart of Darkness*—critics have often invoked the psychoanalytic notion of "identification" in order to define Marlow's ambivalent relationship to his "double," Mr. Kurtz. This point has been made so often that Conrad can now be referred to as "a novelist of identification." And indeed, the reference to a mimetic affect that troubles the distinction between "self" and "other(s)" seems particularly apt in accounting for Conrad's career-long fascination with the *homo duplex*. And yet Conrad himself made clear that "the homo duplex has, in [his] case, more than one meaning."[16] *Heart of Darkness* indicates what some of these meanings are. At work in Conrad's novella is, quite literally, an outbreak of unconscious phenomena: somnambulism, compassion, enthusiasm, emotional contagion, hypnosis, depersonalization, suggestion, and sacrificial violence are all fundamentally mimetic tendencies that haunt the Conradian conception of the modern ego.

What my "little theory" hopes to "prove" is that *Heart of Darkness*'s narrative struggle with colonial praxis and ideology involves a confrontation with mimetic patho(-)logies we have already encountered in Nietzsche, while at the same time extending them towards new theoretical, geographical, and ethico-political territory. Conrad's novella initially posits a pathos of *distance* between dominant and subordinate subjects. As is well known, for Marlow this distance is initially structured on the gendered and racial divide, and has given rise to the much-discussed question: is Conrad racist and sexist? Less known is that Conrad's racism and sexism cannot be fully understood if they are not considered against the background of the less visible, but fundamentally pervasive, problematic of the mimetic unconscious. In fact, we shall have occasion to notice that Marlow consistently projects irrational, mimetic tendencies onto subordinate gendered and racial others. Consequently, the debate on Conrad's sexism and racism cannot be settled without taking into consideration the problematic of mimesis. As we shall see, Conrad's "racism" should be qualified as mimetic racism, his "sexism" as mimetic sexism.

And yet Marlow's initial projection of mimetic affects onto gendered and racial others returns to haunt the white, male subject of *Aufklärung* as well as the dominant body politics this subject supports. In fact, this novella challenges positivistic representations of subjectivity understood in terms of free will, self-possession, and rationality by showing that the dominant subject *of* ideology is, quite literally, not a subject in possession of his thoughts (subjective genitive) but is possessed by such thoughts instead (objective genitive). More precisely, Conrad offers a radical critique of the process of psychic formation of the dominant subject in childhood and exposes how such a mimetic vulnerability continues to be at work in adulthood. Such a critique, I shall argue, is predicated on the realization that the modern subject who prides himself on his rationality, free will, and conscious control over his opinions continues to be in-formed by the unconscious power of affective mimesis. Finally we shall see that Conrad anticipates modern, apocalyptic forms of capitulation to charismatic leader figures—or "eloquent phantom[s]," as Marlow puts it—whose rhetorical will to power is directly responsible for the ethical and political horrors of modernity.

If the phantom of the ego continues to haunt the house of modernism, at stake in Conrad's narrative is also an attempt to make this phantom, if not tangible, at least visible for his audience and readers to *see*. As Marlow puts it, his narrative "seem[s] to throw a kind of light" (51). Hopefully, *Heart of Darkness* will help us cast some light on that elusive "shadow" or, as Marlow also calls it, on the "atrocious phantom" (133) lurking in the heart of our psychic darkness.

The Medium's Pendulum

But how can Marlow make his audience see what they have not seen, feel what they have not lived? How can he make the "phantom" and "the horror" he experiences intelligible to the "civil" audience on the *Nellie*, listening to what they perceive as one of his "inconclusive experiences" (51)? Marlow cannot hide his frustration as he says: "Do you see him? Do you see the story? Do you see anything? It seems to me that I am trying to tell you a dream—making a vain attempt, because no relation of a dream can convey the dream-sensation" (82). The narrator's frustration is evident in his repetitive interrogations. Both the content and the tonality of this passage seem to indicate that there is no way to communicate through rational language (*logos*) the raw sphere of affects "beyond words" that informs Marlow's "life sensation" (*pathos*). Thus he adds: "No, it is impossible; it is impossible to convey the life-sensation of any given epoch of one's existence, . . . We live, as we dream—alone" (82). Marlow's attempt to make the audience "see" and "feel" his quasi-oneiric experience with that "atrocious phantom" who is Kurtz, or at least to make his listeners "understand the effect of it on [him]" (51) seems from the beginning doomed to failure.

Such a communicative impossibility is even accentuated if we consider the complexity of *Heart of Darkness*'s narrative situation. Conrad's choice to filter Marlow's tale by an anonymous, framing narrator situates the reader at a twice-removed distance from the interior narrator's experience, aggravating the possibility of communicative success. It is of course well known that Conrad's multilayered narrative structure is one of his major contributions to modernist practice and is meant to thematize incommunicability, epistemological uncertainty, and radical disbelief in a transparent notion of truth. And yet if we are concerned with the political and ethical significance of Conrad's tale, as well as with its contribution to mimetic theory, it seems inevitable to ask the following questions: Is there a way for Marlow to convey something of "the horror" inherent in his unspeakable nightmare to his audience through a self-reflexive narrative that constantly underscores the impossibility of its telling? And if so, how precisely does such a communication take place?

The fact that immediately after acknowledging the impossibility of his narrative project Marlow partially nuances his pessimistic claim points towards a possible answer to this question. In fact, he tells his listeners: "Of course in this you fellows see more than I could then. You see me, whom you know" (83). The internal narrator is calling attention to his own structural positionality. His mediating narrative presence, he now suggests, places his audience in a more favorable position than he occupied himself, at the time when Kurtz was "just a word" for him as well. In fact, his listeners have access to a mediating presence, a *medium* (from Latin, *medius,* middle), who organizes the content of his experience (*logos*) within a coherent narrative form (*lexis*).

Marlow, as a protagonist and narrator, occupies a central formal and affective position. At the formal level, he functions as the locus of connection where diegetic and mimetic speech meet and intercalate each other: he talks *about* the characters he encounters as a protagonist by using the third-person narrative form (*diegesis*), but he talks about them in propria persona (*mimesis*). And, as Plato understood so well, diegetic speech implies a narrative distance, whereas mimetic speech favors the contagious transmission of an affective pathos to the audience. Moreover, Marlow functions as a mediating presence between what initially appear to be opposite spheres of experience: the listeners on the *Nellie* who now occupy key positions of power within the British Empire (a lawyer, an accountant, and a director) and are thus symbolic of "civilization," on the one hand, and that "atrocious phantom," Mr. Kurtz, who is symbolic of the incommunicable "horror" Marlow is trying to convey, on the other. To put it differently, Marlow functions as an intermediary link placed between the (rational) distance of his listeners and Kurtz's (affective) pathos, a medium who is affectively linked to both parties, as it were. In fact, the narrator not only "knows" both his audience and Kurtz. He is also emotionally tied to them: "intimacy" (143) ties him to Kurtz; "the bond of the sea" (45) links him to the listeners.[17] Such a mimetic double-bond, in short, concerns both the content of what is told and the situation of the telling: the "bonds" linking Marlow the protagonist with his double and the characters he progressively encounters, and the bonds linking Marlow the narrator with his listeners and readers.[18]

As we turn to see, and perhaps hear, Marlow's voice oscillates, like a pendulum, between rational and irrational subjects, identificatory investments with the stable egos of his listeners on the one hand, and with the mimetic subjects he progressively encounters on the other. Out of this narrative oscillation the phantom of the ego is, once again, conjured.

Sexism and Public Opinion

Despite the framing narrator's claim to the contrary, Marlow is a "teller of tales" who is very much aware "of what [his] audience would best like to hear" (51). And since he knows well enough that his listeners do not believe in "atrocious phantom[s]," he inserts, towards the opening of his tale, a punctual, yet strategically reassuring remark about his normal self: "I always went my own road and on my own legs where I had a mind to go" (53). With such a concise formula the narrator reassures his listeners that he is not a delusional dreamer of phantoms, but a rational subject who is usually in control of his thoughts and actions. Marlow's habitual self, in other words, falls neatly within normative representations of masculinity. He offers a positivistic vision of the (male) subject understood in terms of free will, self-control, and intentionality: the subject of *Aufklärung* that sustains the ethos of administrative professions such as lawyers, directors, and accountants. Hence, this statement is of rhetorical and strategic importance since it favors an identificatory bond with his listeners.[19] As long as the "legs" follow the "mind," his male listeners are reassured that they are still within the boundary of a "manly" world of intentionality and rational clarity. Further, in order to reinforce such a stable representation of the masculine subject, Marlow, able rhetorician that he is, defines masculinity over and against stereotypical representations of femininity. Significantly, three of the five female characters present in the story crop up simultaneously, in the initial pages of the narrative; and, more importantly, these women, while also involved in the colonial administration, are described in opposite terms from the rational subject of *Aufklärung*.

Conrad's characterization of femininity, as it appears in Part I, is not original. He clearly reproduces sexist, stereotypical representations of women that were common in late nineteenth-century culture, representations deeply entangled with the problematic of mimesis. Thus, he defines one of the women working for the Belgian colonial administration as a "compassionate secretary . . . full of desolation and sympathy" "wearing a compassionate expression" (56) "with an air of taking an immense part in all [his] sorrows" (57). Compassion, as we have seen in the preceding chapter, is a mimetic pathos par excellence, but Conrad's usage here is clearly characterized by ironic distance. In fact, in the context of Belgian colonialism this moral sentiment whereby one suffers with the other, feels the pain of the other, is, quite plainly, a contradiction in terms. Marlow thus conjures the widespread stereotype concerning women's over-sym-pathetic tendencies in order to deride their ideological naïveté and blindness with respect to the dominant colonial ideology.

But compassion is not the only mimetic reference Marlow invokes in the introductory pages of the novella in order to distance his position from femininity. Moving to the sphere of psychopathology, he compares the other secretary's behavior to a "somnambulist": "The slim one got up and walked straight at me—still knitting with downcast eyes—and only just as I began to think of getting out of her way, as you would for a somnambulist, stood still and looked up" (55). This may be an unusual comparison for us; but it was less so for fin de siècle readers. Somnambulism was a subject of great interest in the emerging field of psychopathology. Jean-Martin Charcot's legendary séances at the Salpêtrière, whose impression on modernist imaginations, including Nietzsche's and Freud's, should not be underestimated, relied on hypnosis in order to diagnose hysterical women. After lethargy and catalepsy, somnambulism was considered to be the third stage in what Charcot called *la grande hystérie*, and artistic representations of this state were circulating in the culture.[20] On another front, Hippolyte Bernheim, from the School of Nancy, specifies that "somnambulism is characterized, physiologically, by the exclusive exercise of the automatic activity of the brain" and by the "non-participation of the ego" in the acts accomplished.[21] Somnambulism denotes an unconscious state whereby the subject is literally not present to itself and acts automatically, on reflex, without reflecting. And as we have seen, at the end of the nineteenth century, such a disconcerting phenomenon cannot be dissociated from the modern language of mimesis—that is, the language of hypnotic suggestion and of the mimetic unconscious that pertains to it. Finally, Marlow's position with respect to these modern forms of gendered pathos is clearly one of ironic narrative distance. Both compassion and somnambulism are mimetic affects that deprive the secretaries of rational control over themselves and blind them to the horrifying reality of colonialism. Their feet do not follow their minds, but the orders of the colonial machinery; they do not have an ego, but a phantom of the ego instead.

Marlow's distance from such gendered phantoms is even accentuated if we turn to consider the third case of mimetic femininity: the enthusiastic woman. Even though Conrad affirms that during his education "he was steeped in classicism to the lips,"[22] his knowledge of Plato can in no way be compared to Nietzsche's, who started his career as a philologist specializing in classical antiquity. Hence, as Conrad defines Marlow's excellent aunt as a "dear enthusiastic soul" (53), we should not assume that such a statement is meant to echo Plato's critique of affective mimesis in *Ion* and the *Republic*. Obviously, if "enthusiasm" would be the only attribute characterizing the "excellent aunt," we should refrain from reading mimetic behavior into her. But this is not the case. In fact, Marlow makes this sweeping comment that leaves no doubts as to the imitative disposition of the "enthusiastic" aunt: "There had been a lot of such rot let loose in print and talk just about that time, and the excellent woman, living right in the rush of all that humbug, got carried off her feet. She talked about 'weaning those ignorant millions from their horrid ways'" (59). Marlow is here reiterating his critique of women's uncritical stance towards the dominant, colonial ideology; but this time, by invoking the media, he gestures towards a more general critique of mass indoctrination. This is not the first time Conrad critiques the role of mass media in the diffusion of colonial ideology. In "An Outpost of Progress" he had launched a similar attack, while making clear that his critique was not limited to femininity alone. Kayerts and Carlier, in fact, capitulate to the power of the colonialist ideology as it appears in "old copies of a home paper" (94). This paper, we are told, "discussed what it was pleased to call

'Our Colonial Expansion' in high-flown language. It spoke much of the rights and duties of civilization, of the sacredness of the civilizing work . . . bringing light, and faith and commerce to the dark places of the earth" (94). Despite their geographical distance, the enthusiastic aunt and the two hapless colonists capitulate to the same kind of "rot let loose in print."

Conrad is not the first modernist author we have encountered to critique the role of mass media in the formation of mass opinion. What is new in Conrad's account is that such a dispossession does *not* occur in the context of a physical crowd. The mimetic problematic might be similar, but Conrad confronts us with a new theoretical problem. In fact, he makes us wonder about the power of mass media to convince the masses of readers. Why are modern subjects so vulnerable to this medium's ideological indoctrination if they are sitting miles apart? Why should they be "swept off their feet" if they are not part of a physical crowd? These are, indeed, new theoretical questions that implicitly emerge from Conrad's narratives. They also puzzle social theorists who are writing at the turn of the century. Let us thus place Conrad's textual concerns in a wider theoretical context.

The French criminologist and psychosociologist Gabriel Tarde is among the first social theorists to address, in a systematic way, the psychological impact of mass media on mass opinion. In *L'opinion et la foule* (1901) Tarde realizes that the progressive development of mass media is responsible for the emergence of a new psychosociological reality that needs to be distinguished from what Gustave Le Bon calls "the crowd." As Tarde puts it: "We have done the psychology of the crowd; we still have to do the psychology of the public."[23] By this he means a psychology that focuses on a "dispersed crowd, where the influence of minds [*esprits*] on each other has turned into an action at a distance."[24] For Tarde, then, an up-to-date account of the manipulation of mass opinion characteristic of modernity can no longer be confined to a physical mass of people (or crowd) but needs to extend in order to consider those virtual masses produced by the emergence of new mass media (or publics). And given the progressive mass-mediatization of modern societies, Tarde challenges Le Bon's famous claim that "our age is the 'age of the crowds,'" arguing instead that that we are entering "the age of the public or publics."[25]

It is true that the psychic disposition of the public is essentially the same as that of the crowd. What characterizes both social groups is a lack of rational control over one's opinions, credulity, vulnerability to emotional contagion, psychic suggestibility, and, more generally, an inclination for what Tarde calls imitation.[26] And yet what distinguishes the public from the crowd is the fact that unconscious forms of imitation are no longer determined by a physical proximity to others; they are no longer a matter of being swept off one's feet by the emotional contagion a physical mass generates. As Tarde explains: "Men who are mutually suggestible in this way do not touch each other, nor do they see or hear each other: they sit, each one of them, at home, reading the same newspaper, scattered around a vast territory."[27] This everyday activity is obvious enough to a modern audience; yet Tarde is suspicious about what appears to be obvious. Hence, he wonders about the bond that ties this dispersed crowd together. Why are members of a public imitative in their opinions? How can they be mutually suggestive if they do not even see one another?

Tarde indicates that this wireless, imitative communication depends on the specific characteristic of the medium in question. What is specific to mass media is, of course, the massive number of people they reach, but for Tarde quantity is not the only issue. In fact, he specifies that this medium exposes the masses to the same message simultaneously; and it is precisely the simultaneity of the experience that, for him, is responsible for generating a mimetic communication between the members of the same public. As Tarde explains: "The bond is with the simultaneity of their conviction or their passions, the consciousness possessed by each one of them that this idea or will is shared simultaneously by a large number of people."[28] While distanced in space, then, the members of a public share the same pathos in time. And it is the unconscious assurance that their pathos is a shared pathos (i.e., a *sym-pathos*) that, for Tarde, is responsible for modern subjects' capitulation to mass opinion, ideological indoctrination, and a general consensus (from Latin, *consentire*, to feel together).

Tarde's account of imitative contagion at a distance (or *actio in distans*) provides us with a theoretical background that allows us to better understand Conrad's critique of mass media and the colonial messages they convey. Conrad is, of course, not a psychosociologist, and his remarks concerning the critique of the power of newspapers as they appear in the two narratives in question are not explicitly developed on the basis of a theory of imitation concerned with the modern public. And yet his critique of the ideological power of mass media implicitly addresses the same imitative problem Tarde is confronting. In fact, he makes clear that whether the modern subject is in a "lady's drawing-room" in Belgium or in a disheveled hut in the midst of the African jungle, as long as she or he is reading the same papers, she or he capitulates easily to the same ideological indoctrination. After reading the pamphlet "Our Colonial Expansion," "Carlier and Kayerts read, wondered and began to think better of themselves" (94–95). Why? Because despite their complete physical isolation in the African jungle, the two colonists feel psychologically connected with a public; their "civilizing mission" is no longer experienced as "theirs" but as part of "*our* colonial expansion." In short, they are no longer isolated individuals but feel the bond with the masses of other readers from a distance. We can thus better understand why Conrad writes that "every great and every insignificant thought belongs not to the individual but to the crowd: to the crowd that believes blindly in the irresistible force of its institutions and of its morals, in the power of its police and of its opinion" ("Outpost" 89). It is because the modern subject is part of what Tarde calls a "public" that its opinions are at one with public opinion; its thoughts are everyone else's thoughts; its ego is but a phantom of other egos.

Conrad's critique of colonial ideology is placed at the complex juncture of the psychic and the social insofar as it considers the process of incorporation of such social opinions in the psychic life of the subject. His work not only entails a critique of colonial ideology, but also addresses *why* the modern subject is so vulnerable to such ideology and *how* this ideology is communicated to a multitude of subjects. Not unlike Plato, Nietzsche, and Tarde, Conrad is painfully aware that dominant ideological beliefs affect, like a virus, the psychic lives of all members of the public and spread contagiously across the body politic. The reassuring knowledge that colonial ideas are, indeed, shared every morning by thousands of other readers powerfully endows delusional beliefs in the fundamental goodness of colonialism with the quasi-religious status of truth. Hence, if we return to *Heart of Darkness* we can better understand why the "excellent aunt" enthusiastically welcomes Marlow as "an emissary of light," "a lower sort of apostle," in short, a modern savior who has come to rid the world of evil. Her thoughts are, in this sense, quite literally, not her own. Another speaks through her; she is possessed, as it were, by the demon of colonial ideology.

Conrad's use of the Platonic notion of "enthusiasm" to characterize a subject's *psychic* dispossession by an ideology that is experienced in religious

terms is thus not out of place. And as we continue to follow the silent theoretical work that formally connects *Heart of Darkness*'s multiple "enthusiastic
outbreak[s]" (96), we shall have occasion to repeatedly confirm Conrad's
appropriate usage of this Platonic concept. Closer to home, Conrad's understanding of "enthusiasm" may be mediated by a more recent, Romantic literary tradition. In fact, if for Plato, "enthusiasm" is synonymous with poetic
inspiration, in the English Romantic and pre-Romantic literary tradition, as
M. H. Abrams has shown, this concept experiences a revival of interest.[29]
Kayerts, Carlier, and the aunt's enthusiastic zeal for the colonial cause is, of
course, closer to religious zealots than to inspired, original poets. But psychologically speaking their mimetic capitulation to a mass medium is not
without continuities with the state of (dis)possession already denounced
by Plato and, later, by Nietzsche, Le Bon, and Tarde in the context of their
critiques of mass behavior. In a way, their cases extend the problematic of
affective contagion, so central to mimetic theory, from the "age of crowds"
to the "age of the public." In fact, a psychosociological perspective shows
that these subjects are not in control of their thoughts, actions, and opinions
insofar as their ideological position is mimetically in-formed by the power of
mass opinion or, better, *public* opinion.

And yet we should not forget that at this stage in Marlow's narrative,
not every subject is indiscriminately (dis)possessed by the mimetic power
characteristic of mass opinion. Marlow, for one, not only affirms that his
aunt's colonial idealism and the praxis she advocates (i.e., "weaning those
ignorant millions from their horrid ways") makes him "quite uncomfort-
able"; he even opposes it on a solid, materialistic ground, "ventur[ing] to
hint that the Company was run for profit" (59). Men like Marlow, then, seem
to be able to keep their critical distance from mediatized ideological suggestions, whereas enthusiastic women, he implies, are hopelessly hypnotized by
any kind of "sentimental pretense" (51) they read in the papers. This, at least,
is the psychopolitical lesson Marlow takes home from his meeting with his
aunt. Thus, immediately after denouncing her ideological position, he gen-
eralizes his critique of femininity and says to his male listeners, tightening
his identificatory, masculine bonds: "It's queer how out of touch with truth
women are! They live in a world of their own . . . too beautiful altogether."
And he adds: "Some confounded fact we men have been living contentedly
with ever since the day of creation would start up and knock the whole thing

over" (59). Marlow's rhetorical move is clear. He contrasts women to men, relegating the former to the sphere of delusory fantasy while, at the same time, elevating the latter to a rational sphere of pure "facts" and "truth." This mimetico-misogynistic move is predicated on a "pathos of distance" between Marlow and his male, "critical" listeners on the one hand, and the female, "uncritical" characters on the other.

As Conrad swings the pendulum of Marlow's narrative away from femininity, we are clearly confronted with what Garret Stewart defines as "Marlow's often discussed view of women as cocooned dreamers whom a touch of reality would wilt."[30] Sexism, however, is not the only issue here. At stake in Marlow's complex attitude towards women is a tacit, yet funda-mental difficulty in taking hold of a mimetic conception of the subject. In the initial pages of *Heart of Darkness*, mimesis is not only disavowed but is also projected onto gendered others. In fact, if we sum up his considerations on women as they appear condensed in a few pages, the following, crude evaluation ensues: For Marlow, women are somnambulistic-compassionate-enthusiastic creatures who are not in control of their thoughts, actions, and opinions. Consequently, they are conveniently exploited by the dominant colonial administration in order to perpetuate atrocities in the name of what they believe to be a deeply moral, civilizing mission. Finally, women are inev-itably predisposed to easily get carried off their feet by all forms of ideologi-cal "rot" that appears in print, while men's feet continue to diligently tread the path of facts and truth. In short, Marlow's sexism should be qualified as *mimetic* sexism.

Such a mimetic misogyny is, of course, far from being Marlow's original idea. The stereotypical connection between femininity and vulnerability to pathos is pervasive in Western culture.[31] But it is especially strong at the end of the nineteenth century, a historical period when representations of the hysterical, suggestible woman were à la mode. Marlow, in fact, is formulating in his own language a mimetic prejudice that haunts late nineteenth-century humanistic disciplines as a whole, a prejudice that tends to relegate the *common* burden of mimesis to a single side of the gender divide. As we have seen, this theoretical bias is fully at work in Nietzsche, a brilliant psycholo-gist, but also a notoriously misogynist thinker who, in his worst moments, relies on his critical awareness of the power of mimetic pathos (or patho-logy) to denounce female hysterical outbreaks in the Wagnerian theater (or pathology). Moreover, this bias equally informs those crowd psychologists who rely on the model of hypnotic suggestion in order to account for the irrationality characteristic of crowd/public behavior. Hence, before proceeding any further, let us cast a retrospective critical glance upon the theories of mimesis we relied on in order to purge our approach of the historically contingent sexist pathology these theories entail.

The Laws of Imitation

Fine psychologists like Nietzsche, Le Bon, Tarde, and, we can now add, Conrad, not only provide us with a critical insight into the mechanism responsible for the modern subject's capitulation to the unconscious power of mimesis (patho-logy), but they also diffuse the stereotypical connection between feminine behavior and different forms of mimetic sickness (pathology). In fact, if they critically adopt the model of hypnotic suggestion developed in the field of psychopathology to make sense of crowd behavior and massive forms of emotional contagion, they also uncritically incorporate the suggestible-somnambulistic-hysterical representation of women this model entails. We have seen that for Nietzsche, femininity and hysterical suggestibility are practically synonymous. Thus, he speaks of Wagner's "success with nerves and consequently women" (CW 5). Along similar lines, Le Bon, considered women as "the most suggestible beings" and confidently claimed that "crowds are everywhere distinguished by feminine characteristics."[32] Tarde puts it even more succinctly as he states that the "crowd is a woman."[33] Such statements suffice to indicate that among theorists invested in analyzing the mimetic disposition of the modern ego, there is a disturbing, misogynist tendency to let women carry the heavy burden of psychic dispossession. Implicit in these accounts is the patriarchal belief that women tend to be naturally more imitative than men; that their vulnerability to suggestion is ingrained in their nature; that the mimetic unconscious is above all visible on their faces; and that, as a consequence, they are more vulnerable to different forms of mimetic pathology.[34]

Is mimetic theory, then, essentially sexist? Are psychologists of mimesis necessarily blind to the patriarchal and historically contingent ideologies that inflect their accounts of human vulnerability to mimetic behavior? At the turn of the century this seems certainly to be the rule. Yet, as always, one can find exceptions to such rules. For instance, we have seen that Hippolyte Bernheim did much (with Charcot) to lend credibility to the theory of hypnotic suggestion, while at the same time (contra Charcot) refusing to confine hypnosis to the sphere of mental psychopathology. Bernheim also makes clear that the connection between femininity and mimesis is far from being essential to the development of mimetic theory. Instead, he argues that "the proportions of subjects that can be hypnotized are about the same in men as in women."[35] Of course, the sexist prejudice that connects femininity to mimetic pathology has no value whatsoever for contemporary theory. As such, this connection should be unmasked as being the product of nineteenth-century patriarchal culture and dismissed as a historically determined ideological contingency that distorts a common, transgendered vulnerability to the power of psychic suggestion.

And yet the spiraling movement of mimetic patho(-)logy has taught us to be cautious with such clear-cut gestures. Hence, I would like to suggest that a theoretical perspective that is aware of *both* feminist *and* mimetic theory should go beyond this important and still necessary condemnation of mimetic sexism in order to probe further the patho(-)logical reasons that are responsible for such a misogynist connection. This involves abandoning the safe path of the common theoretical consensus in order to ask what might initially sound like a gauche question. Namely, is it possible that stereotypical *representations* of the mimetic woman, while obviously biased and in no way excusable, actually pointed to a mimetic "reality"? More precisely, couldn't it be that late nineteenth-century women *acted* more mimetically than men, *played the role* of mimetic pathology (the somnambulist woman, the hysteric patient, etc.) precisely as a consequence of being constrained within a dominant, patriarchal culture that violently imposed such mimetic roles on them? If we acknowledge that the subject, independently of gender distinctions, is, indeed, vulnerable to the molding power of mimesis, then it should follow that dominant pathological representations of mimetic femininity circulating in a public must have informed the "feminine" roles women were supposed to perform, shaping, to a certain degree, their gendered personae.

This theoretical possibility is in line with recent developments in gender studies that acknowledge the role played by imitation in the subordination of gendered subjects,[36] but this tradition has an old genealogy. In fact, in a different, embryonic form this psychological realization is already present in the Platonic tradition we are pursuing. Plato had already observed that "imitations, if continued from youth far into life, settle down into habits and second nature in the body, the speech and the thought" (*Rep.* 640; 395d). Does this mean that women's nature is essentially different from men's nature, naturally more mimetic? For Plato this is generally, but not always, the case. In the *Republic* for instance, Plato mentions that "the natural capacities are distributed alike among both creatures, and women naturally share in all pursuits and men in all" (694; 455e). Perhaps, modernist thinkers like Nietzsche, Le Bon, and Tarde are not as discerning as Plato here. In fact, these writers systematically fail to introduce a fundamental distinction that was at the center of Plato's discussion of mimesis in the *Republic*. Namely, they fail to distinguish between the human subject's inherent malleability and its subsequent, typographic impressions, the mimetic human material and its culturally determined seal, or to use Plato's distinction, "nature" and "second nature." In short, even from a Platonic perspective or, better, especially from a Platonic perspective, the mimetic sexism that informs their accounts of the subject should be subjected to a severe patho-logical critique.

More recently, the Canadian philosopher Ian Hacking implicitly has recuperated this Platonic realization in the context of a discussion concerning nineteenth-century gender-laden accounts of hysteria that allows us to conclude our critical diagnostic of the mimetic sexism under scrutiny. In *Rewriting the Soul* Hacking notices that "the easiest thing is to behave as you are supposed to"; and translating Plato into a contemporary theoretical language he adds, "[This behavior] becomes second nature. That is a traditional suggestion of labeling theory: people adapt their natures to the labels assigned to them by authority."[37] Hacking also gives an interesting new spin to this Platonic realization. Narrowing down his focus to the level of the intersubjective dynamic interaction at work between doctor and patient, he notices that the power of mimesis is not unidirectional, moving vertically from top to bottom, but is part of a retroactive movement whereby the effect returns to act upon the cause. Hacking calls this "the looping effects of human kinds."[38] In the context of psychopathology, for instance, he explains that "the patients were different because the doctors' expectations were different," but as he also notices, "The doctor's vision was different because the patients were different.[39] In a way such a looping effect sounds familiar to us. As we have repeatedly had occasion to see, a variation of this spiraling movement is constantly at work in thinkers *of* mimesis (reading the genitive both ways) we have encountered. Namely, thinkers who critique mimetic sickness (pathology) on the basis of their own vulnerability to the sickness they denounce (pathology). Yet, at the same time, the result of the looping effect Hacking is describing is precisely the opposite of the one we have been pursuing. In fact, if we have seen that this spiraling movement can function as an effective tool for a psychic and social diagnostic that goes deeper and deeper into the problematic of mimetic contagion, Hacking cautions us against the possibility that such a looping, mimetic effect can be a source not only of diagnostic insight but of mutual blindness.[40]

If we move the logic inherent in this mimetic loop to the level of Nietzsche's, Le Bon's, Tarde's, and Conrad's psychosocial diagnostic of femininity, we could specify that their accounts of women are different from ours. But perhaps they are also different because women forced to shape their identities on the models of oppressive patriarchal social roles *acted* differently, *played* different roles—which does not mean that this role-playing was fully determined, but that it partially in-*formed* (gave form to) their characters. With the benefits of both feminist and mimetic theory behind us, we are thus in a better position to critique modernist theorists of mimesis who shared the patriarchal bias of their culture. Figures like Nietzsche, Le Bon, Conrad, and Tarde should be critiqued not only because they uncritically reproduce stereotypical ideological connections between femininity and mimetic behavior, but because they fail to distinguish between nature and second nature, a psychological human constant and the historically contingent social mask or persona. Their theoretical accounts of mimetic femininity should also be critiqued for their potentially pathological *performative* effects on the audience. In fact, once they reach a public (in Tarde's sense), the sexist ideas male theorists uncritically reproduce actively contribute to spreading, by imitative contagion, the sexist pathology they are supposed merely to represent. In short, their critical discourse on mimetic pathos (or patho-logy) is not only a tool for a social diagnostic that relegates women to the status of compassionate-suggestible-hysterical-somnambulistic subjects; it also contributes to spreading the mimetic disease (or pathology) it is supposed to describe. The modernist laws of imitation diagnose modern subjects as mimetic, but not in the simple, realist sense that they reproduce "original" external phantoms that preexist representation. Rather, they are mimetic in the performative, creative, and much more disquieting sense that they contribute to bringing such phantoms into being.

The Hypnotic Snake

After this detour via the loops of imitation let us return to Conrad's *Heart of Darkness*. This text obviously falls within the same misogynist fallacy as the theories of mimesis encountered thus far. In fact, we have seen that Marlow sets up a pathos of *distance* in order to divide femininity from masculinity, mimetic from nonmimetic subjects. This move is in line with the expectations of a typical nineteenth-century male audience (the "we men" Marlow is addressing) and is thus instrumental in reinforcing the identificatory bonds that tie Marlow to his listeners (i.e., the bonds upon which the success of his narrative depends). Hence, the narrator's exclusion of mimesis from his manly group does not go without producing some mimetic effects: distance from mimetic women has the potential to establish a sympathetic bond with his male listeners. And yet this is the moment to stress that Marlow's pathos of distance is not without its necessary countermovement that swings the conception of the subject he promotes towards the pathos he initially distances himself from. In fact, after condemning "feminine" forms of mimetic pathologies, Marlow proceeds to expose, in a more patho-logical mood, the mimetic disposition of the male, dominant subject. Both such an (uncritical) essentialist connection between femininity and mimesis and (critical) insights into the subject's mimetic tendencies continue to unfold if we do not let go of the pendulum of Marlow's narrative voice.

While defining himself over and against mimetic women, the narrator is well aware that his adventure, as well as his psychic attitude towards it, puts him in a position of proximity to the feminine/mimetic world he explicitly repudiates. Thus he says, in a confessional tone: "Then—would you believe it?—I tried the women. I, Charlie Marlow, set the women to work—to get a job. Heavens! Well, you see, the notion drove me" (53). The tone as well as the rhetorical emphasis on disbelief that informs this passage is, again, meant to solicit sympathy from his audience. But this time, we cannot fail to notice a certain anxiety in his tone of voice—an anxiety that compels him to give linguistic substance to his feeling of selfhood (notice the string of three signifiers "I, Charlie Marlow") in opposition to the anonymous other ("women"). This passage, in fact, indicates that Marlow is painfully aware of his dependency upon the world of "women" we saw him vehemently repudiate. Further, the idea that the "notion" to participate in a colonial adventure "drives" the mind of the colonizing subject (rather than being the product of the "mind") contrasts with Marlow's earlier emphasis on free will and intentionality (i.e., legs following the mind). The masculine subject is here in a position of passivity (both grammatical and psychic) that resonates with the kind of passive docility Marlow consistently denounces in women. We begin to sense that despite the initial distance Marlow posits between women and men, suggestible and nonsuggestible subjects, the subject of *Aufklärung* and the subject of mimesis, he is nonetheless tacitly aware that such a distance is not as absolute as he would like to think.

Distance for Marlow, as for Nietzsche before him, functions as a defensive reaction from mimetic pathos that is already internal to the kind of subject he embodies. Marlow's own colonial journey, in fact, is rooted in an unconscious disposition that not only approximates but far exceeds his mimetic representation of women. Here is a thorough explanation of the psychic origins of his colonial adventure:

> Now when I was a little chap I had a passion for maps. I would look for hours at South America, or Africa, or Australia and lose myself in all the glories of exploration. . . . I would put my finger on it and say, When I grow up I will go there. . . . True, by this time it was not a blank space any more. . . . It had ceased to be a blank space of delightful mystery—a white patch for a boy to dream gloriously over. It had become a place of darkness. But there was in it one river especially, a mighty big river, that you could see on the map, resembling an immense snake uncoiled, with its head in the sea, its body at rest curving afar over a vast country, and its tail lost in the depths of the land. And as I looked at the map of it in a shop-window it fascinated me as a snake would a bird—a silly little bird. . . . I went on along Fleet Street, but could not shake off the idea. The snake had charmed me. (52–53)

The fact that Marlow claims not be influenced by colonial "humbug" does not mean that he has always been immune to it. As this passage makes clear, his childish "passion for maps" (the colonial instrument par excellence) is predicated on a mimetic pathos that totally deprives him of his critical presence to selfhood. The "blank space" is, in fact, endowed with a kind of hypnotic magnetism that does not let go of Marlow the "little chap." Thus, as a child, he is literally compelled to turn this "white patch" into a mental landscape where he can "lose himself" for hours in an altered state of consciousness characteristic of the mimetic unconscious. Or, to put it in Platonic language, a capitulation to the power of colonial suggestion has already taken place, as Marlow was a "young and tender" creature that is "best molded and takes the impression that one wishes to stamp upon it" (*Rep.* 624; 377b)— the impression of a colonial type, as it were.

It is true that, with time, Marlow the "little chap" turns into a self-reliant "seaman" and "wanderer" (48), and that the "white patch for a boy to dream gloriously over" turns into a "place of darkness." And yet both the map's hypnotic power of suggestion and Marlow's suggestibility to it remain essentially the same. In fact, the suggestive tropes of the "snake" and the "charmed" "bird" unable to "shake off the idea" of colonial "exploration" (and the "glories" that go with it) do *not* apply to the "little chap" but, rather, to the adult "wanderer" looking at "shop-window[s]" in a street in central London (Fleet Street) that is metonymic of the British press.[41] Needless to say that the trope of the fascinated bird, immobilized by what is known, technically, as a hypnosis of fright (a paradigmatic example of reflex, unconscious reaction), perfectly captures the state of psychic passivity, docility, and dispossession so characteristic of the mimetic unconscious that concerns us. As it was already the case with Nietzsche, this unconscious has nothing to do with the hypothesis of repression but, rather, with automatic, psychophysiological reflexes that deprive the subject of its rational presence to selfhood, of its conscious control of an ego that is no longer one—since it has been turned into phantom of the ego instead.[42]

Indeed, Marlow the adult is quite literally hypnotized and deprived of mastery over his feet and thoughts. And as he is in such a dreamy-hypnotic-mimetic state, he is, once again, affected by his childish dreams concerning the "glories of exploration." It is, thus, no accident that precisely as he glances at the map, Marlow "remember[s] there was a big concern, a Company for trade on that river" (52). The sight of the map, in other words, triggers the narrator's urge to actualize the colonial "dream" (or imperative) he first experienced as a child to "go there." The theoretical insight implicit in this passage is as clear as it is fundamental. Conrad is perfectly aware that the child's initial psychic impressions, if invested with emotional energy, are extremely difficult to erase and, thus, continue to inform the psychic life of the adult subject, his actions, and his choices. In short, the colonial ethos is thus typographically impressed, as Lacoue-Labarthe would say, in-forming the neurological channels of what Conrad calls his "still plastic character"[43] (from Greek, *kharassein*, to engrave, stamp).

At work in this passage is a critical genealogy of the colonial subject of theoretical import insofar as it traces the history of the colonizer's subjection to the dominant ideology back to childhood. The affective repetition at work in this quote, whereby an adult compulsorily reenacts a passionate attachment to the ideological objects (i.e., maps) that fascinated him in childhood, unmercifully exposes the limits of the humanist notion of free will and confirms the Conradian subject's passive-suggestible-malleable-hypnotic—that is, mimetic—status. Moreover, the fact that Conrad immediately places the subject in a sociopolitical field (i.e., a field that has the power to inform and conform citizens by inducing in them the beliefs that dominate a given society) indicates that his critique of the subject does not stop at the psychological/personal level, but involves an ethico-political dimension as well. The radicalism of Conrad's critique of the subject of ideology stems from a dual realization. First, a hypnotic state of dispossession characterizes the dominant subject (i.e., his choices, values, and aspirations), and, thus, the unconscious power of mimetic pathos cannot easily be placed on the side of femininity alone. Second, that psychic state of dispossession is far from being something extraordinary. As the "case of Marlow" suggests, it is such an ordinary everyday experience that, especially in childhood (though not only), can be triggered by any ideologically charged commodity, such as a map in the old days, or videogames and war films in more recent times, as my classroom experience suggested. In a way, we could even say that *Heart of Darkness* invites us to look deep into the map of our psychic life: that is, that "blank space" which, since early childhood, is mimetically informed by the dominant ideology of the moment. And what Conrad shows us is that the dominant subject is not only the subject of *Aufklärung* (the rational man) but also the subject of mimesis (the "silly little bird").

If we now return to critically reevaluate Marlow's considerations on gender, we notice that a countermovement swings him *towards* the mimetic conception of the subject he denounces in women. This second, less visible, but more insidious textual oscillation undermines the distance he previously set up. In fact, the "charmed" Marlow finds himself in a psychic position that not only approximates, but even exceeds, the mimetic pathos he denounces in women; his childish "dream" concerning the "glories of exploration" relegates him to what we could call, using his sexist language against him, "a world of [his] own . . . too beautiful altogether." Moreover, Marlow's manly colonialist project is not only compared to a childish fantasy but, more radically, is shown to be founded and motivated by a hypnotic dispossession. To sum it up, this passage swings a representation of male subjectivity understood in terms of rational self-control towards a dangerous region of suggestibility, passivity, depersonalization, and psychic vulnerability. To put it figuratively, the pendulum of Marlow's narrative is set in motion, and the phantom of the ego that haunts modernity as a whole is, once again, conjured.[44]

We are now in a position to see that Marlow's patho-logy is not as stable as it first appears to be; the affective mimesis he tends to foreclose is inevitably constitutive of his own psychic life. What cultural critic Jonathan Dollimore says of *Heart of Darkness*'s treatment of race is equally true of gender: "in the very process of defining itself over and against the primitive, the civilized is invaded by the other whose history and proximity it requires yet disavows."[45] And if Marlow's take on femininity cannot be dissociated from his take on mimesis, the same thing can be said with respect to Marlow's equally problematic take on race. Hence, I now let go of Marlow's mimetic sexism in order to pick up his mimetic racism.

The Rhetoric of Racism

Marlow's understanding of racial differences in Part II is predicated upon a violent hierarchy reminiscent of his earlier considerations on gender. The link is all the more clear since, in a notorious passage, Marlow introduces a distinction between subjects who are in possession of themselves (white men) and subjects who are not ("prehistoric men"); and once again the notion of "enthusiasm" pops up in order to mark a difference between mimetic and nonmimetic subjects. Here is how Marlow describes his encounter with an African group of Fang people on the shores of the river Congo:

> a burst of yells, a whirl of black limbs, a mass of hands clapping, of feet stamping, of bodies swaying, of eyes rolling, under the droop of heavy

and motionless foliage. The steamer toiled along slowly on the edge of a
black and incomprehensible frenzy. The prehistoric man was cursing us,
praying to us, welcoming us—who could tell? We were cut off from the
comprehension of our surroundings; we glided past like phantoms, wondering and secretly appalled, as sane men would be before an enthusiastic
outbreak in a madhouse. (96)

As it was already the case with Marlow's "enthusiastic" aunt, the Africans'
"enthusiastic outbreak" deprives racial subjects of rational control over
themselves.[46] But here, the mimetic degree of such subjects is much more
accentuated and acquires a bodily dimension that was lacking in the somnambulistic-compassionate-enthusiastic Belgian women. If the aunt was part
of a *psychic* mass (i.e., a public), the Africans are part of a *physical* mass (i.e.,
a crowd). Moreover, if the aunt was only metaphorically "swept off her feet,"
the Africans are literally so. In fact, Conrad's detailed physical description ("a
mass of hands clapping, of feet stamping, of bodies swaying, of eyes rolling")
makes clear that he has in mind a ritualistic dance endowed with the affective power to induce in its members a state of unconscious (dis)possession.
Such a state of "frenzy" has tended to puzzle critics. But readers familiar with
the mimetic tradition will recognize it as a well-known phenomenon, both
in ancient and modern times. Plato calls it "enthusiasm," Nietzsche calls it
"Dionysian," Girard calls it a "crisis of differences," modern anthropology
calls it a "possession trance."[47]

   While Marlow's *description* clearly accounts for a mimetic phenomenon
par excellence, his *evaluation* of it lacks the impartiality of recent anthropological observations that consider trance independently of racial distinctions.
Marlow's anthropology, at this stage, is based on the naive, because fundamentally ethnocentric, idea that the mimetic, unconscious subject is always
the other. This view was quite pervasive at the time: if Freud notoriously
spoke of female sexuality in terms of the "dark continent" and compared the
"content of the unconscious . . . with a primitive population in the mental
kingdom,"[48] Jean Paul Richter had already compared the "unconscious" to a
"genuine inner Africa."[49] Needless to say that such a racist description rein-
forces the violent hierarchy between "blackness" and "whiteness," "savagery"
and "civilization." Marlow's theoretical premises, in other words, fall neatly
within nineteenth-century evolutionary anthropology.[50] This is why Marlow

says that "going up that river was like travelling back to the earliest beginnings of the world, when vegetation rioted on the earth and the big trees
were kings" (92–93). From an evolutionary perspective, traveling in space
involved a temporal return to prehistoric times. This "theoretical" move is
instrumental in introducing a cultural, temporal, and biological distance
between colonizers and colonized. Such a distance is also physical (they are
"cut off"), as well as moral (they are "appalled"). And finally, the only way for
Marlow to make sense of such a disconcerting mimetic phenomenon (disconcerting for people educated in Victorian England) is to relegate it to the
"madhouse." In our language, at this stage, Marlow's racist pathos of distance
confines mimesis on the side of pathology.

And yet, while contemptuously dismissing this state as a sort of mental
derangement, Marlow's pendulum begins to tentatively swing in the opposite direction.

> Well, you know that was the worst of it—this suspicion of their not being
> inhuman. It would come slowly to one. They howled and leaped, and spun,
> and made horrid faces; but what thrilled you was just the thought of their
> humanity—like yours—the thought of your remote kinship with this wild
> and passionate uproar. Ugly. Yes, it was ugly enough; but if you were man
> enough you would admit to yourself that there was in you just the faintest
> trace of a response to the terrible frankness of that noise, a dim suspicion
> of there being a meaning in it which you—you so remote from the night
> of the first ages—could comprehend. And why not? The mind of man is
> capable of anything—because everything is in it, all the past as well as all
> the future. (96)

At stake in this passage is a complex intertwinement of contradictory
thematic and rhetorical movements that we need to carefully disentangle
because they go to the heart of the mimetic dilemma that informs the tale
as a whole. Marlow's narrative oscillates madly, back and forth, between racist injunctions that dehumanize racial others ("they howled and leaped, and
spun, and made horrid faces") and repeated attempts to nuance such racist
distinctions in order to communicate the Africans' human status ("their
humanity—like yours"). Marlow's statements are, indeed, paradoxical. In
fact, he seems intent in conveying *both* a feeling of distance *and* a feeling

of proximity to racial others. "Racism," in other words, is clearly part of his rhetoric, but so are his persistent attempts to establish a connection between his white "civilized" listeners and the "prehistoric" Africans; between rational, nonmimetic subjects and enthusiastic, mimetic subjects. It is, thus, not surprising that over the past thirty years, after the publication of Chinua Achebe's influential attack on Conrad, considerable critical attention has been given to the racist or nonracist aspect of these lines.

The underlying tension that underscores the racist/antiracist debate emerges from the way Achebe and his critics have interpreted this passage. On the one hand, as Achebe considers these specific lines, he repeatedly ends his discussion with Marlow's affirmation, "ugly," using this expression as a rhetorical trope to shift the emphasis in the oxymoronic phrase "distant kinship" towards Conrad's anxious need for distance.[51] This hermeneutical choice is, of course, part of Achebe's general move, which consists in proving that Conrad is "a thoroughgoing racist," but is also instrumental in exposing the underlying "anxiety" responsible for such dehumanizing representations of Africans. What Achebe says of Conrad's comparison of the Thames to the Congo River equally applies to his reading of the above-quoted passage: what "worries Conrad," as he puts it, is "the lurking hint of kinship."[52] Conrad's racism, for Achebe, is thus part of a larger, anxious need of Europeans to compare themselves to such debased images of Africans in order to reassure themselves about their so-called "civilized" status. Racist distance, in brief, is instrumental in diminishing the anxiety of kinship.[53] On the other hand, C. P. Sarvan, one of many critics to have taken up the challenge to respond to Achebe, resituates the debate within the European perspective. In fact, he claims that *Heart of Darkness* is referring to "the condition of European man; not to a black people but to colonialism."[54] Considering the novel as a critique of the inhuman aspect of colonialism allows Sarvan to conclude that the narrative is about "continuity" and the "fundamental oneness of man and his nature."[55] In short, if Achebe's Africanist perspective underscores discontinuity and racist *distance*, the opposite pole stresses continuity and human *kinship*.

Now, before continuing to argue, we should ask ourselves a more specific, formal question: namely, what exactly motivates such contradictory, oscillating movements towards / away from racial others? In order to answer this question we must move beyond binary arguments and reveal what critics across both sides of the postcolonial fence have so far failed to see: namely that this passage is not only about race; it is also about mimesis. And it is only if we consider the problematic of race in conjunction with the problematic of mimesis that the affective as well as rational logic that motivates such contradictory, oscillating movements towards /away from racial others progressively emerges.

A reading attentive to the movement of mimetic patho(-)logy makes clear that at this stage in the narrative, Marlow not only uncritically displaces the mimetic conception of the subject onto subordinate others, but also acknowledges that mimesis is *constitutive* of the modern subject of *Aufklärung*. For this reason, he now claims that a "kinship" exists between his listeners and the "wild and passionate uproar" the Africans give voice and body to. And, for the same reason, he insists that at work in such an "enthusiastic outbreak" is a "meaning" that the modern "civilized" subject can still "comprehend." Marlow supposes that his listeners can still "comprehend" enthusiastic affects because according to the nineteenth-century evolutionary anthropology he uncritically adopts, traces of prehistoric psychology are still present, albeit in a sedimented form, in the psychic life of modern, "civilized" men. Thus, he says: "The mind of man is capable of anything—because everything is in it, all the past as well as all the future."

The evolutionary model upon which Marlow's considerations repose cuts both ways. We have seen that the idea that the colonizers are traveling back in time, that geographical displacement parallels temporal displacement (traveling to the "earliest beginnings of the world"), involves a representation of so-called "primitive" cultures as temporally preceding Western culture (primitive, from Latin *primus*, first). According to this perspective, the racial subject is totally other, incomprehensible. And yet despite its violent hierarchical dimension, evolutionary theory acknowledges an underling unity of mankind—what E. B. Tylor called "the general likeness of human nature."[56] Within this typically nineteenth-century evolutionary paradigm, mimetic behavior, reflexes, and responses are inevitably found once the surface of civilized behavior is scratched away, insofar as the nervous system of subjects who come "after" is supposed to carry the traces of these "primitive" forms of behavior. The scientific validity of such hierarchical paradigms has long been put into question: Not only did anthropology cast the notion of racial superiority into disrepute, but also the notion of biological race has been shown to be a fiction. With respect to the problematic of mimesis, however, the question that immediately ensues is the following: is a mimetic conception of the other as antiquated as a racist conception of the "primitive," or are mimetic affects indifferent to arbitrary racial/racist distinctions? Despite its evolutionary bias and racial ambivalence, *Heart of Darkness* is very clear on this point.

This passage leaves no doubts as to Marlow's primary concern: he is struggling to convey a feeling of proximity to forms of enthusiastic pathos to his skeptical listeners on the *Nellie*—just as Conrad is doing with respect to his (skeptical?) readers. In our language, both narrator and writer struggle to conjure the phantom of mimesis and to prove its uncanny actuality. And yet this apparently linear project to bring mimesis back home, on the side of "modernity" and "civilization," entangles Marlow's narrative in an impossibly paradoxical situation. In fact, he attempts to convey the mimetic status of modern subjectivity to his "civil" Victorian listeners via the example of the "prehistoric" Africans—that is, those very subjects Marlow seems to repudiate on a racist ground. A contradictory push-pull between racist and mimetic imperatives is, thus, at work in the narrative structure of this complex paragraph: if a racist conception of the subject introduced a distance, such a distance is nonetheless immediately challenged by the frenzied pathos that, according to Marlow, emotionally connects African and European subjects. In short, if half of the passage is about racism, the other half is about mimesis. And Marlow's dialectical narrative trajectory (i.e., affirmations of racial distance followed by a "but" that immediately negates distance and affirms a common mimesis) indicates that his focus is less on a disjunctive, racial distance than on a conjunctive mimetic pathos.

So much at the level of content (*logos*). But what about the formal, rhetorical strategies Marlow uses to convey the mimetic status of the modern subject (*lexis*)? Marlow finds himself in an extremely delicate narrative situation. In fact, his attempt to expose the mimetic status of the modern subject via the example of the "enthusiastic" Africans in a state of "frenzy" threatens to disrupt the identificatory connection with his (racist) listeners. That Marlow is stretching such identificatory bonds too thin is exemplified by interruptions in the narrative like this one: "Who's that grunting? You wonder I didn't go ashore for a howl or a dance? Well, no—I didn't" (97). Griffith points out that passages where Marlow maintains a certain distance from the Africans (and the mimetic pathos they convey) must be read against the background of a "common fear that degeneration unleashes primitivistic and atavistic desires in Europeans."[57] What we must add is that passages like this one suggest that the fear of going native (degeneration) cannot be dissociated from anxieties about the contagious dimension of outbreaks of enthusiastic pathology (mimesis). Gustave Le Bon supports this hypothesis. In fact, in a passage imbued with mimetic racism he makes clear that for him the imitative behavior of the crowd and "going native" are one and the same thing. As he puts it, a subject who is part of a crowd is endowed with "the spontaneity, violence, ferocity, and also the enthusiasm and heroism of primitive beings."[58] Both Le Bon and Conrad seem to agree that mimetic contagion is, at least in part, responsible for spreading the germ of atavistic degeneration.

Within this impossible narrative situation, Marlow's offensive characterization of the Africans occupies a paradoxical rhetorical function. We have seen that racist injunctions like "the worst of it," or "ugly" are instrumental in introducing a distance between the dominant and the subordinate; antimimetic and mimetic subjects. Less obvious, however, is the fact that such a racist distance is precisely what his listeners expect to hear. If we reread the passage under consideration by paying careful attention to the rhetorical dimension informing the narrative as a whole, it is, indeed, not even certain that these racist judgments stem directly from Marlow's perspective. Marlow's narrative is not that uninterrupted monologue it is often thought to be, but is interactive and extremely attuned to his readers' emotional responses.[59] Such affective interactions usually take place at moments of maximum tension between the content of Marlow's tale and his listeners' "civil" expectations and often involve a shift from diegetic to mimetic speech. Importantly, at such moments, Marlow tends to repeat, with indignation, the listeners' intrusive ejaculations (ejaculations we do not always get to hear). Here are a few examples: "Yes; I looked at them [i.e., the African cannibals] as you would on any human being, with a curiosity of their impulses . . . when brought to the test of an inexorable physical necessity. Restraint! What possible restraint?" (105). Or, "[A man] must meet that truth [i.e., mimetic truth] with his own true stuff—with his own inborn strengths. Principles? Principles won't do."[60] And again: "Who's that grunting? You wonder I didn't go ashore for a howl or a dance? Well, no—I didn't. Fine sentiments you say? Fine sentiments be hanged!" (97). Marlow's rhetorical pattern indicates that words like "restraint," "principles," and "fine sentiments" are, indeed, not originally his own. He simply restates, for rhetorical effect, what a listener has been saying. With this formal point in mind, the following messages resonate differently: "[The earth] was unearthly and the men were . . . No they were not inhuman." And again, "the thought of your remote kinship with this wild and passionate uproar. Ugly. Yes, it was ugly enough, but . . ." The rhetorical movements at work in Marlow's voice seem to indicate that racist injunctions like the unvoiced "inhuman" and the voiced "ugly" do not stem directly from the internal narrator, let alone from Conrad, but from his listeners instead. This point is crucial in order to take hold of the interactive, affective dimension of the narrative, as well as to critically reevaluate Conrad's problematic take on race.

Marlow's racist narrative moves, while in no way excusable, acquire a strategic rhetorical function: they serve to reassure his audience that Marlow is still one of them, after all, and thus are instrumental in maintaining the identificatory ties with his listeners—ties that are indeed necessary for a successful communication of the content of his tale. Hence, Marlow is now relying on this identificatory bond predicated on a common racism, which is conveyed in a mimetic narrative speech, in order to paradoxically bring home the mimetic affects the Africans incorporate. This is a communication of mimetic *pathos* by mimetic *lexis*, of a mimetic *message* by a mimetic *medium*. And yet, in order to carry out this message, Marlow is compelled, at the same time, to constantly give nuance to his racist injunctions. In fact, if racial "otherness" is exaggerated, the mimetic "sameness" that interests Marlow can no longer be conveyed. In other words, in this impossibly paradoxical narrative situation, racism functions both as a rhetorical communicative strategy and, at the same time, as an impediment to the communication of the mimetic content of Marlow's narrative. Structurally speaking, this passage entails a conjunctive-disjunction, a double bind that swings Marlow's narrative back and forth between contradictory poles. And it is precisely through this maddening oscillation that the narrator desperately attempts to make his skeptical listeners recognize and acknowledge their affective vulnerability to such enthusiastic outbreaks.

Marlow goes even further in order to bring mimesis back on the side of the cultural hegemony. Not satisfied with his racist rhetorical strategy, he equally recurs to masculinist rhetoric. Thus, he incites his listeners to be "at least . . . as much of a man as these on the shore" (97). And in a similar mood he adds: "if you were man enough you would admit to yourself that there was in you just the faintest trace of a response to the terrible frankness of that noise" (96). Not only racist but also macho rhetoric is here invoked in order to tickle the masculine pride of his listeners and challenge them to confront and acknowledge, once and for all, their vulnerability to mimetic affects—affects that lead the modern subject to respond to the "frankness of that noise" by "hands clapping," "feet stamping," "eyes rolling," and so on.

We are now in a better position to see that the heated controversy concerning racism and sexism in *Heart of Darkness* is heavily inflected by the less visible but more fundamental—in the sense that it tacitly informs *both* racism *and* sexism—problematic of mimesis. In fact, what we have said of sexism can equally be said of the racism characteristic of this much-discussed modernist text: Inherent in Marlow's gendered/racial pathos of distance is not only a sexist/racist distance from frenzied pathos, but also, and more fundamentally, an attempt to acknowledge that the mimetic conception of the subject he initially disavows and displaces onto racial/gendered others equally informs the modern, male, "civilized" subject. *Heart of Darkness* insistently tells us that, often, where there is racism and sexism, also lurks the disavowed phantom of mimesis—a phantom endowed with a kind of affective, rhythmic power to sweep not only women and Africans, but also white male colonialists, off their feet.

But why is Marlow so insistent about it? Why is it so terribly important that his modern listeners acknowledge that they too, are still vulnerable to states of ritual dispossession? In order to address these questions, which go to the bottom of *Heart of Darkness*, let us consider first what kind of "noise," exactly, Marlow is referring to as he speaks of the "terrible frankness of that noise" modern man can still "comprehend." If we consider the final version of the text, it is clear that Marlow is alluding to the mimetic "burst of yells" that characterizes the African ritual. Modern readers who ever set foot in a disco know exactly what Marlow is talking about.[61] But his Victorian listeners on the *Nellie*, "in the holy terror of scandal and gallows and lunatic asylums" (116) as Marlow puts it, still have a hard time establishing a connection with such an enthusiastic outbreak. Their "grunting"—a prelinguistic, primitive mode of expression that ironically reveals the fragility of their so-called "civil" status—clearly indicates that Marlow's listeners, to put it mildly, are not inclined to find in themselves even *"the faintest* trace of a response to the terrible frankness of that noise" (my emphasis). Marlow's rhetorical tricks, in other words, fail to convey the ordinariness of mimetic behavior.

The situation may be a little different for modern readers, not only because we should be more open to acknowledging the traces of Dionysian frenzy in ourselves than Victorians were (affective reasons), but also because the footnotes in the Norton Critical Edition of *Heart of Darkness* give us access to a manuscript passage Conrad decided not to include in the final version (scholarly reasons). This passage makes strikingly clear what kind of "noise" Conrad is referring to. It also makes clear why, for Conrad/Marlow, it is urgent that the modern subject of *Aufklärung* realizes its vulnerability to mimetic pathos:

> You know how it is when we hear the band of a regiment. A martial noise—and you pacific father, mild guardian of a domestic heart-stone [*sic*] suddenly find yourself thinking of carnage. The joy of killing—hey? Or did you never, when listening to another kind of music, did you never dream yourself capable of becoming a saint—if—if. Aha! Another noise, another appeal, another response. All true. All there—in you.[62]

In this instance, Conrad's anthropology is, indeed, far from being naive. In fact, Conrad anticipates a contemporary understanding of this discipline in terms of translation of cultures: a discipline that studies distant traditional societies in order to cast some light on the workings of the more familiar (and, thus, also less visible) modern societies. More precisely, this manuscript passage shows that for Conrad, the "enthusiastic outbreak" in the jungle is not any different from a modern response to the pathos of musical rhythm within a given social institution (in this case, the army). Hence, this example is clearly instrumental in displacing the mimetic-suggestible-unconscious status of the modern subject from Africa to Europe, from blackness to whiteness, from a ritual dance in the middle of the jungle to a ritual march parading to the rhythm of a "martial noise" in the street of our own "monstrous town[s]" (48). We should also specify that, for Conrad, modern man's mimetic tendencies are far more worrisome. In fact, if some kind of music can provoke the noblest responses in modern subjects, other kinds can as easily provoke the basest reactions; if the Africans' enthusiasm culminates in

a ritual dance whose consequence is to reinforce the feeling of social community, the enthusiasm of "pacific father[s]," as they abandon their living rooms
and newspapers in order to march to the rhythm of military parades, can
potentially culminate in the "joy of killing." We can now better understand
why, once back in Europe, Marlow, speaking of the "bearing of commonplace
individuals" says: "[It] was offensive to me like the outrageous flauntings of
folly in the face of a danger it is unable to comprehend" (152).

Conrad's description of the power of musical rhythm to emotionally
overtake the modern subject is directly in line with the mimetic tradition
that concerns us, a tradition that casts some light on the obscure language of
feelings that, conveyed through both ancient and modern media, have the
power to take possession of the subject's ego. Nietzsche would add that this
pathos also surfaces in the theater among the enthusiastic crowd of spectators
whose feet and souls follow the rhythm of Wagner's music. Thus, speaking of
antiquity, but with Wagner not too far from his argument, Nietzsche writes
in *Gay Science*: "Above all, men desired the utility of the elemental and over-
powering effect that we experience in ourselves as we listen to music: rhythm
is a compulsion; it engenders an unconquerable urge to yield and join in; not
only our feet follow the beat but the soul does too" (86). And in *Daybreak*
Nietzsche explains this "unconquerable urge to join in" by establishing a
firm connection between music and mimesis: "It is music which reveals to us
most clearly what masters we are in the rapid and subtle divination of feelings
and in empathizing: for, though music is an imitation of an imitation of feelings, it nonetheless . . . often enough makes us participants in these feelings"
(142). Further, in *Gay Science* he warns us that "the wisest among us are still
occasionally fooled by rhythm—if only insofar as we sometimes consider an
idea truer simply because it has a metrical form and presents itself with a
divine skip and jump" (84).

Mimetic art may be far removed from ideal reality; but precisely for this
reason it is close to the immanence of bodily affects. Clearly, as Nietzsche
writes about mimesis, Plato is always inevitably at the back of his mind. And
if the *ontology* of this passage is anti-Platonic, its *psychology* is not so. In the
Republic, in the context of Socrates's condemnation of affective mimesis, a
discussion of the dangerous, affective impact of music ensues. There Socrates
says: "more than anything else rhythm and harmony find their way to the
inmost soul and take strongest hold upon it" (646; 401d).[63] In short, both

Conrad's and Nietzsche's critical awareness of the compulsive power of musical rhythm, as well as its power to unleash the most noble as well as violent affects, is directly in line with the Platonic critique of mimesis that traverses the modernist period. And yet Nietzsche and Conrad never simply repeat a Platonic point without managing to make the critique of mimesis written in ancient Greece new and relevant for their contemporary historical situation, thus anticipating contemporary developments in mimetic theory. As it was already the case with Nietzsche, Conrad's considerations of the mimetic status of the modern subject acquire a quasi-prophetic status. History, unfortunately, will prove Conrad's insights into the horrific results of contagious, collective behavior prophetic: in the Europe of the first half of the twentieth century, martial parades will soon stimulate the "joy of killing" in usually "pacific fathers." Mimesis and the "crisis of difference" it entails, as René Girard importantly insisted, can lead to apocalyptic forms of sacrificial violence. As Philippe Lacoue-Labarthe also recognized, in a groundbreaking philosophical reading of *Heart of Darkness*, this *is* "the horror of the West" Conrad attempts to make us see.[64] The modernist brand of mimetic theory I am unearthing is in line with these foundational realizations.

The mimetic, affective side of *Heart of Darkness* I am struggling to make visible and audible indirectly warns us that, from a position of safe geographical and historical distance, it is easy for modern readers to "grunt" at the idea that a proximity could potentially exist between ourselves and such extreme forms of horrific historical events. In a way, we could even say that it is as easy for us to relegate such epidemic outbreaks of enthusiastic ritual behavior to the devastating historical situations that appeared in Nazi Germany, as it is for Marlow's listeners to relegate mimetic behavior to ladies' drawing rooms, the African jungle, or the madhouse. I am, of course, not suggesting that Nazi, racial, and gendered "others" occupy the same status. They obviously do not. If the former were radically empowered criminal subjects, the latter were/are victims, deprived of power; if the former's mimetism is there for all to see and to condemn in historical documentaries like Leni Riefenstahl *Triumph of the Will* (1935), recording the martial parades Conrad foresees, the latter are, at least in part, the product of dominant projections and disavowals. What I am suggesting is, rather, that each epoch has its favorite "mimetic others" (whether radically guilty or fundamentally innocent) ready at hand in order to let them carry the *common* burden of mimesis. Deferring mimetic affects all too hastily to such "scapegoats," as Girard would say, implies recurring to the naive belief that the mimetic subject is always and only the "other" or the "enemy," and prevents us from thinking through our own implications in mindless imitative behavior and the horrors that directly or, more commonly, indirectly ensue. Finally, it may be tempting to answer this critical point by referring to our "civil" status and the moral principles that go with it. Here is Marlow's uncompromising response: "Principles? Principles won't do. Acquisition, clothes, pretty rags—rags that would fly off at the first good shake."[65] The cover of civilization with its "policeman," "kind neighbours," and especially, "public opinion" (116), as Marlow says, is but an artificial veil cast over the modern ego.[66]

Marlow's narrative makes clear that it is always tempting to repeat the naive, anthropological gesture to project the phantom of mimesis onto "others" of some sorts. This is not only a narrative problem that concerns Marlow's listeners. It is also a political problem that concerns modern audiences. In fact, what is difficult for listeners, readers, and spectators alike is to see our own affective entanglement in contemporary versions of the same imitative phenomenon we are so quick to spot and denounce in others. For instance, it is difficult to recognize what Marlow calls the "trace of a response" we may still continue to feel today as we sit in the darkness of a movie theater, watching and listening to scenes like Captain Kilgore's helicopter attack in *Apocalypse Now*. Indeed, the mimetic patho(-)logy at work in *Heart of Darkness* is beginning to cast some light on the pathos of distance generated by horrifying, apocalyptic scenes with which we started this chapter. If modernist texts have the power to generate uncritical responses to mimetic pathos, they equally stimulate critical and affective faculties that put us at some distance from the mimetic pathologies we are inevitably caught in. Marlow, at the end of his considerations on the Africans' "enthusiastic outbreak" says: "mine is the speech that cannot be silenced" (97). If we listen carefully to his voice, we realize that it attempts, with urgent insistence, to expose the modern subject's vulnerability to horrific forms of mimetic pathos. It is a voice that shows us that all kinds of mimetic "responses" are potentially there, in all of us; it is also a voice that confronts both listeners and readers with the theoretical and political implications that ensue as the dominant subject of ideology gives way to the "horrorism" that, according to the Italian philosopher Adriana Cavarero, is endemic to the mutilating and disfiguring dimension of contemporary violence.[67] As we now turn to see, Marlow's mimetic challenge to his listeners and readers to acknowledge their vulnerability to the horror of modernity continues to retain its full validity.

The Horror of Modernity

As Marlow and his men follow the meandering course of that hypnotic snake which is the river Congo, the haunting presence of the phantom of mimesis progressively intensifies. As the narrative unfolds, mimetic affects not only appear in relation to gendered subjects (Part I), nor do they exclusively qualify racial subjects (Part II), but also characterize, with increasing insistence, that "troupe of mimes" who are the white male colonizers (Part III). In this last part, the underlying mimetic politics of *Heart of Darkness* progressively comes to light.[68] If Conrad is still our contemporary, it is because he reveals the horror of mimesis that emerges from a psychosociological dissection of the status of the modern subject. To put it in the diagnostic language of the old Belgian doctor, I continue to be interested in the analysis of the changes that "take place inside," especially as the power of rhetorical pathos infiltrates the psychic life of the colonial subject. Mimesis and all it entails (suggestibility, hypnotic (dis)possession, depersonalization, contagion, power of words, violence, unconscious reflexes, etc.) characterizes "enthusiastic" figures like the Harlequin, but also rational figures like Marlow and, last but not least, that "atrocious phantom" (133) and charismatic leader figure who haunts the heart of darkness: Mr. Kurtz. Such a critical diagnostic, then, concerns the dominant subject of ideology, his vulnerability to tyrannical leader figures, and his complicity with the horrors of modernity.

Marlow's pathos of distance involves an oscillation towards / away from the phantom of mimesis, a phantom that becomes more clearly visible if we turn to consider the Harlequin's ego. The Harlequin embodies the most extreme version of the subject's suggestibility, enthusiasm, and mimetic dispossession that Marlow and his listeners and readers with him have encountered thus far. The narrator first introduces him as a subject totally devoid of individuality, a "beardless, boyish face, . . . no features to speak of" (122) and compares him to a "baby" (124), and he soon makes clear that this man without *physical* qualities is also deprived of all kinds of *psychic* qualities. In fact, Marlow adds that he lacked "all thought of self" and that "even when he was talking to you, you forgot that it was he—the man before your eyes—who had gone through these things (126–127). The Harlequin is, indeed, a mimetic nobody who has lost all sense of proper selfhood; even though he speaks in his proper name, he has no name to speak from. He is a "be-patched youth" (126), a character of the commedia dell'arte whose patched costume matches the fragmentation of his psychic life. Thus, Marlow says: "There he was before me in motley as though he had absconded from a troupe of mimes, enthusiastic, fabulous" (126).

Insofar as Conrad couples the notion of "mimesis" with that of "enthusiasm" in order to account for a disconcerting psychic phenomenon that deprives the subject of his presence to selfhood, he continues to operate within the Platonic and Nietzschean tradition that concerns us. In Nietzsche's critique of Wagner as "the most enthusiastic mimomanic of all times," we have seen that such a psychic dispossession does not concern one individual alone but, rather, is always a matter of an affective communication between two or more subjects. In *Heart of Darkness* the context is radically different. Yet the unconscious phenomenon under consideration—what Marlow calls "an insoluble problem" (126)—is fundamentally the same. If the Wagnerian crowd rejoices in Wagner's cult, the Harlequin participates in Kurtz's cult; if the former is affected by Wagner's musical pathos, the latter is overwhelmed by Kurtz's rhetorical pathos. What we must add now is that the relationship between the Harlequin and Kurtz can be characterized in terms of a relationship between the mimetic, impersonal subject of the crowd and his hypnotic leader. "Kurtz's last disciple," as Marlow calls him, is filled with a religious awe as he tentatively describes his colonial idol. "It was curious to see his mingled eagerness and reluctance to speak of Kurtz," says Marlow; and he immediately adds: "The man filled his life, occupied his thoughts, swayed his emotions" (126). The "fabulous" "admirer of Mr. Kurtz" (131) is not simply under the influence of another subject. He is possessed by that other in such a fundamental way that the distinction between self and other no longer holds. This subject is but the "shadow" of another subject; his ego is but the "phantom" of another ego.[69]

As it was already the case in previous encounters with mimetic sexism and mimetic racism, Marlow's attitude towards the Harlequin's mimetic dispossession is fundamentally ambivalent. While being clearly ironic throughout his entire portrayal of "Kurtz's last disciple" (132), the narrator is equally forced to admit that he "was seduced into something like admiration—like envy" (126). Thus, he specifies:

> I almost envied him the possession of this modest and clear flame. It seemed
> to have consumed all thought of self so completely, that even when he was
> talking to you, you forgot that it was he—the man before your eyes—who
> had gone through these things. (127)

Despite his ironic distance, Marlow is, indeed, drawn to this "flame" and the psychic consumption it entails. Such a psychic lack of critical presence to selfhood, Conrad warns us, has a fascinating, hypnotic drive. Perhaps because, like sleep—and, nowadays, TV or a videogame at the end of a hard day—it frees the modern subject of the burden of consciousness and the ethico-political responsibilities it entails. What is sure is that even the critically vigilant Marlow is fascinated by this state of unconscious depersonalization: he is drawn to it, as a moth is drawn to a candle flame; or, if you prefer Conrad's earlier trope, as a charmed bird is attracted to a snake.

And yet this time Marlow manages to pull himself together and to retain enough lucidity to keep at bay the unconscious mimesis that animates this enthusiastic colonial figure. Abruptly changing his tone of voice, he sets himself at a safe critical distance from the Harlequin's hypnotic flame and retrospectively comments:

> I did not envy him his devotion to Kurtz, though. He had not meditated
> over it. It came to him, and he accepted it with a sort of eager fatalism. I
> must say that to me it appeared about the most dangerous thing in every
> way he had come upon so far. (127)

Nonmediated "devotion" to a leader and to the ideological flame he carries, Marlow now realizes, is "the most dangerous thing in every way," insofar as it deprives the subject of ideology of a rational ground on which to make ethical and political choices. Significantly, after his meeting with the Harlequin, Marlow adds: "never, never before, did this land, this river, this jungle, the very arch of this blazing sky, appear to me so hopeless and so dark, so impenetrable to human thought, so pitiless to human weakness" (127). Conrad, via the intermediary of Marlow, makes clear that the darkness pervading his novella is first and foremost an ethico-political darkness that follows from a psychic capitulation to the power of mimesis and the sacrificial violence it tends to generate. The horror of mimesis appears in all its devastating dimension in the "amazing tale that was not so much told as suggested" to Marlow" by the "admirer of Mr. Kurtz" (131). Such a tale suggests that the power of affective mimesis leads directly to Kurtz's "inconceivable ceremonies of some devilish initiation" (115). And as Marlow soon realizes, these "midnight dances" do not culminate in a quite harmless, enthusiastic "frenzy" but, rather, in "unspeakable rites" (118) that terminate with "heads drying on the stakes under Mr. Kurtz's windows" (132).[70] As Marlow puts it, the Harlequin's tale "transported [him] into some lightless region of subtle horrors" (132): Kurtz's sacrificial horrors and the terrors of colonialism they symbolize.[71]

The moral darkness of colonialism Conrad wants to bring home is inextricably tied to the mimetic status of the colonial subject. In a way, we could even say that *Heart of Darkness* repeats, in a different way, what Gabriel Tarde had already pointed out: namely, that for the imitative subject "there is no middle way between horror and enthusiasm."[72] Enthusiasm can easily turn into horrors, while horrors generate enthusiasm, because in a state of possession there is no ego left to judge. Conrad, in fact, shows that enthusiastic followers like the Harlequin, convinced of their leader's divine power—"he came to them with thunder and lightning" (128), says the disciple—are totally incapable of moral judgment. Thus, the hapless victim of Kurtz's will to power exclaims: "You can't judge Mr. Kurtz as you would an ordinary man. No, no, no!" (128). As Marlow severely puts it: "you may be . . . too dull even to know you are being assaulted by the powers of darkness" (116–117). This darkness and the horrors that ensue, it should become progressively clear, cannot be dissociated from the threat of mimetic dispossession and the contagious violence that ensues. The phantom that haunts *Heart of Darkness* is the phantom of mimesis; the horror of mimesis *is* the heart of darkness.

Still, Conrad's hero seems here to maintain his critical distance and moral judgment intact with respect to Kurtz's mimetic will to power and the horrors it entails. The fact that he "hadn't heard any of these splendid monologues" helps him to proclaim that "Mr. Kurtz was no idol of [his]" (132). Thus, before meeting Kurtz, Marlow goes on to ironically condemn his "less material aspirations" (130) from a distance. And by uncompromisingly affirming, "'he is mad!'" (129), Marlow relegates that "poor chap" to the

loony bin. From the narrator's distanced critical perspective, the heads on the
stakes are not only food "for vultures" but also "food for thought" (130): that
is, an occasion to meditate on the horrific effects of mimetic affects. Unlike
"An Outpost of Progress," then, *Heart of Darkness* suggests that the subject is
not always a hapless victim of the power of suggestion but at times (especially
with the benefit of temporal distance provided by retrospection) manages
to withstand its (almost) irresistible pathos. In short, Marlow's pathos of
distance intervenes in order to keep mimetic horrors at bay, as the phantom
of the ego all too visibly takes possession of the modern subject.

And yet, alongside this confident Marlow who *judges* from a position
of temporal, patho-logical distance, there is another Marlow who *feels* his
own pathological entanglement in the horrors of mimesis he critically condemns. This Marlow is, indeed, an interesting case for the alienist who considers it "interesting for science to watch the mental changes of individuals
on the spot." As Marlow himself recognizes, remembering the old doctor's
warning, he "was becoming scientifically interesting" (72). For instance, a
passage of the Harlequin's suggestive tale manages to throw our hero into
a state of rage, and we, along with Marlow, are left to wonder where his
sudden pathos comes from. The Harlequin says: "the chiefs came everyday
to see him. They would crawl." At this point Marlow loses control over his
nerves and bursts out:

> "I don't want to know anything of the ceremonies used when approaching
> Mr. Kurtz," I shouted. Curious, this feeling that came over me that such
> details would be more intolerable than those heads drying on the stakes
> under Mr. Kurtz's windows. (131–132)

This is one of the many "curious" but revealing moments in Marlow's narrative when his emotions take over his rational control; affective pathos takes
over critical distance. At such moments, Conrad would probably agree with
Nietzsche that "thoughts are the shadows of our feelings—always darker,
emptier, and simpler" (*GS* 179). But what exactly are these dark and empty
thoughts that cover up the complex reality of feelings? Marlow the narrator,
even with the benefit of hindsight, is not in a position to explain what is
affectively going on here. But if we attend carefully to the formal qualities of
the narrative, as well as to the affective dimension of Marlow's narrative voice

(i.e., its *lexis*) and compare this curious emotional moment to similar ones, some light can be shed on Marlow's puzzling affective reaction.

An often-quoted passage gives us a possible key to the narrator's emotional outburst. Toward the beginning of the narrative Marlow enthusiastically celebrates his idealist conception of colonialism in these terms:

> "What redeems it is the idea only. An idea at the back of it; not a sentimental pretence but an idea; and an unselfish belief in the idea—something you can set up, and bow down before, and offer a sacrifice to . . . ." He broke off. (51)

This is the first abrupt and unexplained interruption in the telling, occurring at a moment of rhetorical and emotional enthusiasm. Something quite unexplainable happens in this shift of tonality and subject matter. Marlow's voice seems to be suddenly inspired with a sort of colonial fervor that manages to "redeem" what he had just dismissed as "conquest." A certain feeling or *pathos* (what Conrad says "people really know nothing" about) gets the better of the rationalistic discourse or *logos* characteristic of Marlow's usual self. Now, if we pay close attention to his shifts of linguistic register, a disconcerting development—which is truly a *tour de force*—emerges: Marlow's sober materialism (colonialism as "conquest") ascends into a quasi-Platonic ideal sphere (colonialism as "idea"), hovers in the high spheres, metamorphosed into a kind of religious faith (colonialism as "belief"), before degenerating into a sort of ritualistic praxis (colonialism as "sacrifice"); finally, his inspiration fails him, and he breaks off. Why? What is the *pathos* that interrupts his *logos*?

If we compare these two textual moments it seems that formally and affectively speaking we are confronted with a repetition of a pattern. Both passages, in fact, are clearly imbued with religious terminology: Marlow's colonial idealism (his "unselfish belief"), the Harlequin's psychic dispossession (his selfless "devotion"), and Kurtz's colonial practices (the "ceremonies" Marlow does not want to hear anything about) are, indeed, thematically linked. And significantly, each time this religious language is conjured, it triggers an unexplained emotional response that causes an abrupt interruption in the narrative. Now, if we consider these passages vibrating with emotional pathos as structurally linked, Marlow's "curious feeling"—as was

already the case with his "queer feeling" about his aunt—gestures towards
what Marlow's thoughts cannot fully take hold of and make explicit: namely,
that inherent in his sudden and unexplained emotionally charged interruptions is an affective (rather than rational) intuition of psychological,
political, and ethical import. An unexplained "feeling" senses proximity to
disruptive forms of mimetic violence where "thought" explicitly introduces
an idealizing distance. At work in Marlow's silences and interruptions is a
tacit emotional realization of the potential consequence of colonial *idealism* when put into praxis: ideological "sacrifice" turns into ritual "sacrifice;"
"bowing" to an idea turns into "crawling" towards Kurtz; "unselfish belief"
turns into "the horror."

Phantom of a Phantom

Conrad insistently shows that while Marlow consciously struggles to distance
himself from this psychic dispossession and the horror that ensues from it,
he nonetheless repeatedly avows his proximity and vulnerability to mimetic
affects. This vulnerability is especially apparent as Marlow, at the "culminating point of [his] experience," finally manages to directly confront the will to
power of that charismatic leader who is Kurtz: An "eloquent phantom" (160),
as the narrator aptly calls him, who, not unlike the snake of colonialism that
hypnotized the narrator, has "the power to *charm* or frighten rudimentary
souls into an aggravated witch-dance in his honour" (119, my emphasis).
And Marlow adds, in a confessional tone: "he had conquered one soul in the
world that was neither rudimentary nor tainted with self-seeking" (119).[73]

   At stake in Marlow's narrative, then, is not only a personal avowal of his
own suggestibility to Kurtz's rhetorical will to power, but also a realization
of this phantom's political impact on the dominant body politic. That Conrad has politics in mind is clear. Towards the end of the novella a journalist
tells Marlow that "Kurtz's proper sphere ought to have been politics," and
he adds, "on the popular side" (154). Although he does not say so explicitly,
Marlow implicitly agrees. In fact, from the very beginning, he imagines that
Kurtz is endowed with the essential characteristic for a charismatic leader: a
"gorgeous eloquence" (155). Well before encountering him, the narrator says:
"I had never imagined him as doing, you know, but as discoursing. . . . The
man presented himself as a voice" (113). And as he finally meets Mr. Kurtz,

his intuition is confirmed: "A voice! a voice! It was grave, profound, vibrating, while the man did not seem capable of a whisper" (135). The essence of
Kurtz's being is not located in his actions, nor in his mind or body, but in a
voice that addresses other subjects. It is thus not surprising that this voice,
as Marlow puts it, "wanted an audience" (127). Like Wagner or any other
leader figure, Kurtz, who, we are told, is also "essentially a great musician"
(153), likes to test his pathos over the mimetic crowd. In Africa, where "his
ascendancy was extraordinary" (131), he addresses himself to what Marlow
calls a "wild mob" (146) or a "wild crowd of obedient worshippers" (155).[74]

   Marlow is, once again, conjuring racist representations of the mimetic
Africans, but this time he does so in order to underscore Kurtz's power over
the masses. As we have seen, stereotypical notions about the psychic malleability of the African subject, whether alone or as part of a crowd, were
widespread in late nineteenth-century crowd psychology. And as the Abbé
Demanet already put it in the eighteenth century, the African's psychic life is
"similar to a soft wax [*cire molle*] that can be shaped in the figure desired."[75]
The Africans, however, are not the only subjects to capitulate to the imprint
of Kurtz's mimetic rhetoric. The Harlequin, to be sure, is precisely such a *cire
molle* who is impressed by the typographic (will to) power of what Lacoue-
Labarthe calls Kurtz's "all-powerful [*toute puissante*]" voice.[76] But even Conrad's self-reliant, ironic, skeptical hero is not immune to the pathos inherent
in Kurtz's "magnificent eloquence." As Marlow says, Kurtz's voice has "the
terrific suggestiveness of words heard in dreams" (144). It is a voice through
which the phantom of mimesis speaks. Thus, Marlow feels entitled to say that

> of all his gifts the one that stood out preëminently, that carried with it a
> sense of real presence, was his ability to talk, his words—the gift of expres-
> sion, the bewildering, the illuminating, the most exalted and the most
> contemptible, the pulsating stream of light, or the deceitful flow from the
> heart of an impenetrable darkness. (113–114)

The heart of darkness and the phantom of mimesis are, once again, tightly
strung together. And, once again, Marlow's evaluation of this phantom oscillates between opposite poles. With one of his narrative voices, the narrator
openly condemns the mimetic suggestion at work in Kurtz's "gift of expression" in terms of the "most contemptible" "deceitful flow"—a flow that

springs directly from "the heart of an impenetrable darkness." And yet, at the same time, another voice enthusiastically celebrates it as an "illuminating," "pulsating stream of light." For Marlow, Kurtz's hypnotic, rhetorical gifts entail an untidy intermixture of light and darkness, unbounded good and unrestrained evil. He is both attracted to and repelled by what he defines as "something altogether without a substance" (113), a "shadow ... draped nobly in the folds of gorgeous eloquence" (155). In our language, the pendulum of Marlow's pathos of distance makes him oscillate towards /away from the phantom of the ego.

What is true with respect to Kurtz's oral gifts is equally true with respect to his written skills. Marlow tells us that "he had been writing for the papers and meant to do so again: 'for the furthering of my ideas. It's a duty'" (148–149), says the leader figure. Kurtz is, indeed, very much aware that ideologies spread contagiously if they are conveyed via the mass media to that "virtual crowd" (Tarde's term) which is the modern public. Even in the jungle, the charismatic leader continues to write with a public in mind. And as his rhetoric reaches a reader, it seems to have a certain effect. Marlow at first seems to resist the power of Kurtz's words. Thus, as he evaluates the "report" Kurtz wrote for the "International Society for the Suppression of Savage Customs," he critically notes that it was "too high-strung" and that the opening paragraph—with its claim that whites "must necessarily appear to them [savages] in the nature of supernatural beings"—"in the light of later information, strikes [him], now as ominous" (118). As he retrospectively meditates on this report, Marlow *the narrator* can maintain a critical/ironic distance from Kurtz's rhetorical pathos. Yet at the moment Marlow *the character* first reads the "pamphlet," his critical distance vacillates. After recognizing that "it was a beautiful piece of writing," "eloquent, vibrating with eloquence" (117), he quotes a passage of Kurtz's pamphlet affirming, "'By the simple exercise of our will we can exert a power for good practically unbounded,' etc. etc." And at this stage, Marlow confesses his capitulation to Kurtz's "magic current of phrases" (118): "From that point he soared and took me with him. . . . It gave me the notion of an exotic Immensity ruled by an august Benevolence. It made me tingle with enthusiasm" (118).

Now, why, we may ask, is Marlow subjected to an ideological position that he earlier vehemently denounced as enthusiastic "devotion" (Harlequin) or "sentimental pretence" (women)? It is tempting to say that his capitulation to the phantom of the ego is caused by the fact that he is in the jungle, lacking what he calls a "solid pavement under [his] feet" (116), and has often "'a little fever,' or a little touch of other things" (105) since all this is clearly part of the diagnosis. And yet Conrad does not allow such easy pathological resolutions. The phantom of mimesis that Marlow's narrative pendulum conjures clearly shows that for Conrad, the modern ego, with a temperature or without, is equally affected by the "unbounded power of eloquence—of words—of burning noble words" (118).[77] Conrad's narrative makes clear that the power of mimesis is indifferent to human, all too human racial, gendered, and cultural categorizations. In fact, this kind of "magnificent eloquence" not only has the same effect on Marlow as on his aunt, but affects Europeans as it does Africans. Once Marlow is back in the sepulchral city, a journalist tells him, "'heavens! How that man could talk. He electrified large meetings. . . . He would have been a splendid leader of an extreme party'" (154). The leader figure may move around the world, but his electrifying-magnetic-hypnotic-mimetic power, as well as the predisposition of crowds to be magnetized by his pathos, remains fundamentally the same. Whether "the magic current of phrases" appears in "print" or "pamphlets," in speeches in the jungle or "at large meetings" in Europe, such words, and the propaganda they convey, have the power to "electrify" subjects and dispossess them of rational control over their opinions, moral beliefs, and eventually their own ego.[78]

For Conrad then, as for Nietzsche before him, the contagious effect of mimetic words does not even depend primarily on content but, rather, on the rhetoric used in conveying them. The "magic" of these words lies in their power to convince independently of, or even despite, their meaning. Significantly, not even the leader is seriously concerned with the content of his own speeches. As Marlow asks, "what party" Kurtz was presiding, the visitor answers: "Any party. . . . He was an extremist" (154). This striking affirmation indicates that the charismatic leader is not devoted to a cause, to an idea, or a belief, but to the power of mimesis itself, a power that he thinks himself to possess, but that actually dispossesses his ego instead. This also means that Mr. Kurtz, not unlike the Harlequin, is not really a subject in control of his thoughts, values, and opinions. His suggestibility parallels that of a most innocent child. We are told that "he could get himself to believe anything—anything" (154). Thus understood, the charismatic leader appears paradoxically to be the most tragic victim of the power of suggestion: he is represented as a "Shadow" (65), a "phantom" (133), "something altogether without a substance" (113), an essentially void, selfless subject who is "hollow at the core" (131). *Heart of Darkness* teaches us that the ordinary and the extraordinary man, the hypnotized and the hypnotist, the suggestible subject in the crowd and his leader, the readers of newspapers and those who write them, share a distinctive psychic feature: like children, they are both essentially the same in their depersonalization, in their suggestibility to hypnosis, in their vulnerability to the mimetic unconscious. In short, Conrad agrees with the modernist figures I examine that a phantom haunts the modern ego—the phantom of mimesis.

Finally, Conrad's inquiry in the heart of the ego's mimetic darkness suggests that we would be seriously mistaken in locating the power of mimesis exclusively in such specific pathological "cases." If Conrad fundamentally agrees that the phantom of mimesis takes possession of Mr. Kurtz, he equally reminds us that "all Europe contributed to the making of Kurtz" (117). As Plato would put it, Kurtz is but a ring in the chain of mimesis; a magnetic ring through which the phantom of mimesis that is haunting modern Europe is made to speak. Significantly, even at the moment of death, as Kurtz is uttering his last words, it is not clear whether the charismatic leader is the subject of discourse or simply an empty shell through which we hear the echo of the dominant mass-mediatized ideology. In fact, we are left to wonder with Marlow: "Was he rehearsing some speech in his sleep, or was it a fragment of a phrase of newspaper article?" (148). The fact that the question is asked at all seems an indication that, for Conrad, the leader's opinion and mass opinion, even in the case of so-called makers of opinion, cannot easily be disentangled. Conrad seems to imply that extremist leaders are not original figures who master theirs and others' opinions but are themselves the product of public opinions instead.[79] He certainly makes us wonder whether the success of extremist political leaders relies on the reproduction of ideologically charged opinions that already inform subjects who live in what that insightful criminologist and social psychologist Gabriel Tarde in 1901 aptly diagnosed as the "era of the public."[80]

The alienist's theory was a mimetic theory, after all. His hypothesis that "the changes take place inside" (58) is confirmed by the multiple enthusiastic outbreaks that haunt Conrad's tale. And what he shows us is that this phantom is not a shadow that disappears when the light of reason returns. It is not only a psychological reality, but also a fundamentally political and ethical one. Conrad, in fact, makes us see that this phantom haunts the psychic lives of individual egos, as well as the entire dominant mass-culture that shapes such egos in the first place. And if he reminds us that in our mass-mediatized societies haunted by simulacra of the real, this mimetic dispossession can be effectively induced by impressive cinematic spectacles like *Apocalypse Now*, he equally shows us that this pathos can be diagnosed from a distance by looking through the lenses of mimetic patho(-)logy.

After this diagnostic textual evaluation of the doctor's theoretical affirmation, we should be in a better position to reevaluate *Heart of Darkness*'s timeliness. Marlow's oscillating narrative functions as a persistent effort to conjure the phantom of mimesis in front of his listeners, to make it visible and intelligible and, thus, to cast some light on the obscure process whereby mimetic affects continue to have the power to dispossess and inform the modern ego, whether through rhetorical speeches, the press, or mass-mediatized visual media. Conrad reminds us that affective mimesis is responsible for the incorporation of dominant ideological imperatives, for putting them into practice, and for the horrors that all too often still ensue. Further, implicit in *Heart of Darkness* is a critique of totalitarian politics that alerts us to the fact that the modern subject of *Aufklärung* is not immune to the massive influence of such tyrannical figures that have access to all too powerful mass media. In this sense, Conrad's novella functions as a penetrating psychological exploration of the horror of mimesis that still haunts the modern ego. According to Marlow, acknowledging such insights is already a "moral victory" (151). More moderately, it is perhaps the first step towards a critical reevaluation of our own ideological, mass-mediatized beliefs.

Joseph Conrad does not propose easy resolutions that would dissipate, once and for all, the dark shadow of the phantom of mimesis. Still, *Heart of Darkness* "seemed somehow to throw a kind of light. . . . Not very clear. And yet it seemed to throw a kind of light" on that phantom of the ego, which both defines us and constantly eludes us.

CHAPTER 3

D. H. Lawrence and the Dissolution of the Ego

We all seem to be haunted by some specters of ourselves that we daren't face.

—D. H. Lawrence *Phoenix*

It is not a question of Lawrence imitating Nietzsche. Rather, he picks up an arrow, the one of Nietzsche, and shoots it elsewhere, with a different tension.

—Gilles Deleuze, *Critique et Clinique*

Ghostly Reappearances

After Joseph Conrad, perhaps no modernist writer more than D. H. Lawrence invests the notion of "darkness" with mimetic affects that have the power to dissolve the unity of the ego. In *The Plumed Serpent* (1926),[1] his last and most infamous leadership novel, Lawrence picks up Conrad's investigation into the dark power of mimesis. Ramón Carrasco, a Spanish aristocrat, anthropologist, and charismatic leader figure, functions as Kurtz's mimetic counterpart. Kurtz's "ceremonies" are prolonged by Ramón's "rites," the

former's "grave, profound, vibrating" voice reechoes in the "solemn, powerful voice of Ramón" (337), and in a passage that suggests the reappearance
of the mimetic phantom we have been tracking within Lawrence's narrative
universe, we read:

> With his words, Ramón was able to put the power of his heavy, strong will
> over the people. The crowd began to fuse under his influence. As he gazed
> back at all the black eyes, his eyes seemed to have no expression, save that
> they seemed to be seeing the heart of all darkness in front of him. (337)

The context has changed from the Congo to Mexico, from the historical
reality of colonial exploitation to the mythical sphere of the cult of Quetzal-
coatl; but the psychic phenomenon at stake remains essentially the same. The
"power" of Ramón's "words" to "fuse" the "crowd" of "black" subjects in the
context of a religious ritual with ethical and political implications strikingly
resonates with Kurtz's will to power over both African and European crowds.
And in order to make clear that he intuits the fundamental link we traced in
the preceding chapter, Lawrence specifies that as the leader's expressionless
eyes turn towards the hypnotized crowd, he faces "the heart of all darkness."
Indeed, Lawrence read Conrad's novella attentively; or, at least, he read it
closely enough to see—or, as he would prefer to say, to *feel*—that the "heart
of darkness," for Conrad, is tightly intertwined with the unconscious power
of mimetic (dis)possession.[2]

But if Lawrence succeeds in identifying the fundamental theoretical
connection that functions as the driving telos of *Heart of Darkness*, this
passage also indicates that he fails to take hold of Conrad's ethico-political
critique of authoritarian uses of mimetic will to power. Far from condemning the horror of mimesis on moral and political grounds, Lawrence seems
to think that the spiritual liberation of the Mexican people and, eventually,
of the whole world lies in yet another hypnotic capitulation to a European
leader figure who does not hesitate to reenact sacrificial "horrors" (51) in
order to impose his ascendancy over the indigenous crowd.[3] To be sure, Lawrence is not only situating his narrative project in relationship to Conrad's
tale; he is also marking his philosophical proximity to the tyrannical bent
we have already critiqued in Nietzsche's mimetic thought. Ramón's "strong
will" over the masses is, in fact, a manifestation of that infecting "pathos"

which, as we have seen, corresponds to Nietzsche's characterization of the master's will to power. Among British modernists, Lawrence is probably the writer whose thought is most indebted to the German philosopher.[4] As is well known, he often indulges in Nietzschean distinctions between "masters" and "slaves," "superior" and "inferior" or, as he also puts it in *Fantasia of the Unconscious* (1922), those who have the "power" and "responsibility" to lead and those who have the docility and "freedom" to be led (120). In short, as Lawrence enthusiastically exclaims "leaders—this is what mankind is craving for" (120), it is clear that what he calls "the shadow of power" (*K* 300) has fallen upon his ego.

We are thus back again to the circuit of mimetic patho(-)logy that serves as the structuring component of this book. On the one hand, Lawrence manifests a characteristic modernist attraction towards tyrannical forms of mimetic pathos that have the power to dispossess the ego of its presence to selfhood. Hence, in his leadership novels, he goes as far as dramatizing heroes endowed with the willpower to mesmerize the masses and bring about a cultural revolution based on authoritarian methods—methods that, as critics have noticed, border on fascist psychology.[5] On the other hand, Lawrence is fundamentally aware of the theoretical connection that we have been patiently following thus far, implicitly linking the Nietzschean notion of (will to) "power" and the Conradian trope of (heart of) "darkness" to the "phantom" of (unconscious) mimesis. Consequently, we shall see that in the context of postwar Europe, he develops a strong critique of totalitarian forms of hypnotic capitulation to leader figures and of the ethical and political consequences that ensue from massive mimetic contagion, a contagion that Lawrence denounces as a modern "disease" (*AR* 153). There is thus a sense in which Lawrence not only is a victim of the infective power of affective pathology, but also strives to play what he calls, following Nietzsche, the role of "the surgeon the modern soul needs so badly" (*STH* 213). This fundamental ambivalence in Lawrence's critical diagnostic, the interdisciplinary dimension of his take on mimesis, and his profound awareness of the mimetic tradition I am exploring—from Plato to Nietzsche to more recent developments in mimetic theory—make Lawrence the most promising candidate to pursue into the central modernist period and the era of world wars. Therein a mimetic patho(-)logy confronts us with what he calls the "specters of ourselves that we daren't face" (*P* 736).

Following the movement of Lawrence's mimetic thought will lead me to engage with the dark, often problematic, but always stimulating side of Lawrence that emerges from his writings of the 1920s, including the so-called leadership novels (*Aaron's Rod*, *Kangaroo*, *The Plumed Serpent*), autobiographical narratives (*Mornings in Mexico* and other essays on Native Americans), his books on the unconscious (*Fantasia of the Unconscious* and *Psychoanalysis of the Unconscious*), as well as a wide range of critical essays collected in the two volumes of *Phoenix*. These writings lack the canonical status of the major novels of the middle period,[6] yet they allow us to bring to light a little-discussed, mimetic side of Lawrence that informs his modernist Weltanschauung. They also have the merit of illustrating the crucial role the mimetic unconscious plays in Lawrence's conception of Western subjectivity in general, and in his critique of what he calls "the old stable ego" in particular.

Critics often quote the passage in the famous 1914 letter to Edward Garnett where Lawrence writes, "you mustn't look in my novel for the old stable *ego*—of the character," but it is important to remember that Lawrence qualifies this claim. Thus, he adds that "there is another *ego*, according to whose actions the individual is unrecognizable and passes through, as it were, allotropic states which it needs in a deeper sense than any we've been used to exercise," and that these states represent "some greater human will."[7] It is well known that the problematic of desire proves to be the main door to understanding Lawrence's critique of the ego in his early and middle period; let us say, schematically, until the end of World War I. Much less known, however, is the fact that in the postwar period, as Lawrence continues to sharpen his critical lenses to dissect and diagnose the modern ego, he does so on a different ground. His writings of the 1920s mark a theoretical turn in Lawrence's theory of subjectivity, a turn that swings his preoccupations from the much-discussed problematic of *desire* to an engagement with the thus far unrecognized problematic of *mimesis*. Obvious continuities exist between these two periods in Lawrence's career, as well as between the two affects in question.[8] Yet in order to take hold of the conception of the ego that emerges from the last full decade of Lawrence's creative life (i.e., his mature period) we can no longer rely on a pious, and for our postmodern age, rather quaint, representation of Lawrence as a "priest of sex." Nor can we limit our approach to a homogeneous perspective that would frame

Lawrence within a single "great tradition." Rather, we need to enlarge the spectrum of our theoretical lenses in order to include a wide range of transnational and transdisciplinary mimetic theories that are constitutive of Lawrence's conception of the ego. As Anne Fernihough reminds us, Lawrence is characterized by a "refusal to respect lines or boundaries."[9] This refusal of disciplinary submission is in line with current tendencies in mimetic theory and new modernist studies to integrate the human sciences, and leads him to engage with areas of thought as diverse as religious anthropology, ontology, aesthetics, and different psychological perspectives, such as crowd psychology, psychoanalysis, and psychophysiology. From Plato to Nietzsche, James Frazer to Jane Harrison, Freud to Trigant Burrow, the Lawrentian conception of the ego remains incomprehensible if we do not take into consideration the theories that already inform his struggle with the old, yet always new problematic of mimesis.

It is not that critics have not paid enough attention to the heterogeneous dimension of Lawrence's conception of subjectivity, or that critical accounts of specific disciplinary perspectives are lacking. On the contrary, excellent studies exist for each theoretical aspect of Lawrence's thought I have just mentioned, and in what follows I rely on them.[10] Yet no study exists as yet that maps the *mimetic logic* (or patho-logy) that underlies and organically connects the different disciplinary perspectives that inform Lawrence's account of the modern ego. One of the goals of this chapter is to fill this gap in Lawrence studies. More broadly, we shall see that Lawrence, whose anti-Freudian stance is well known, is one of the foremost advocates of the mimetic unconscious, as well as one of the pioneering analysts and critics of a culture increasingly dominated by visual representations and simulacra. I suggest that his thought remains important today for at least three reasons. First, his brand of mimetic theory takes into consideration not just the violent forms of affective contagion emphasized by his modernist predecessors (bad mimesis), but also focuses on the positive, vitalizing forms of mimetic communication that have a unifying, social effect (good mimesis). If René Girard's mimetic theory has tended to emphasize "bad" mimesis, he also recognizes that "the 'good' one is of course even more important. There would be no human mind, no education, no transmission of culture without mimesis."[11] Lawrence contributes to mimetic theory by helping us think through the theoretical implications of "good" mimesis. Second, among modernists,

Lawrence is one of the first *literary* writers to explicitly quarrel with Freud in order to propose an alternative conception of the unconscious that challenges the foundations of the modern ego. His critique of the idealist underpinnings of psychoanalysis remains timely not only because it paves the way for subsequent anti-Oedipal critiques of Freud, but also because it expands the Romantic problematic of mimetic *desire* in order to include the broader modernist concern with mimetic *pathos*. And third, we shall see that in both his theoretical impasses and critical insights, Lawrence's mimetic patho(-)logy helps us clarify why, exactly, the modern subject of *Aufklärung* informed by an idealist tradition that privileges the eye over the body, *representational* mimesis over *affective* mimesis, continues to be vulnerable to massive forms of sacrificial horrors that turn the ego into a phantom of the ego.

One of the fundamental assumptions that guides Lawrence's thought is that knowledge emerges out of the marriage between the sensuous and the rational or, better, between an affective participation in the sphere of feelings and a critical distance from them, so that *pathos* needs to be complemented by *logos*, and vice versa. As he puts it, speaking of the emotional and rational side of man: "You've got to marry the pair of them. Apart, they are no good. The emotions that have not the approval and inspiration of the mind are just hysterics. The mind without the approval and inspiration of the emotions is just a dry stick" (*P* II 625). Lawrence's work testifies to a tremendous ability to be affected by the psychic life of others, to be absorbed in their perspective and to account for it from within.[12] Yet, at the same time, it also testifies to a deeply felt wish to preserve his boundaries of individuation and to dissect from a critical distance what he calls, thinking of imitative feelings, the "strange dark continent we do not explore" (*STH* 203).

As we follow the spiraling movement of Lawrence's mimetic patho(-)logy, we shall focus on aspects of Lawrence's conception of subjectivity that are usually treated in isolation, exposing the mimetic undercurrent that traverses his heterogeneous work. I argue that Lawrence's dissolution of the "old stable ego" and the fluid, communicative subject that emerges, phoenix-like, from its ashes, can only be fully understood in the light of Lawrence's larger anthropological, metaphysical, and psychological research, whose mimetic roots I now set out to progressively unearth.

Primitivist Participation

Perhaps less famously than Conrad, but equally fundamentally, Lawrence has been severely critiqued for his account of "primitive" cultures. These critiques concern his anthropological generalizations, his complicity with evolutionary anthropology, and his more general endorsement of a characteristically modernist fascination with "primitivism" that renders him unable to apprehend "the other" on its own terms.[13] Although such critiques are indisputably correct, they do not take into consideration what Neil Roberts calls "the empathy that often characterizes Lawrence's writing about native people."[14] Moreover, they tend to neglect the role mimetic affects and theories of sympathetic magic occupy in his writings about Native Americans with respect to both the content of his inquiry and his method of approach, and, thus, miss the specificity of Lawrence's modernist take on the "primitive" other. A mimetic perspective brings to the fore Lawrence's affective method of inquiry, accounts for his ambivalent oscillation towards / away from what he calls "the pathos of the religion" (*MM* 181), and assesses both his debt and contribution to anthropological theories of sympathetic magic. Michael Taussig is right to say that "something insightful can be learned about mimesis . . . by taking up the issue of sympathetic magic."[15] Among modernists, Lawrence is an ideal figure through whom to approach mimesis from this angle: he was not only familiar with anthropological accounts of sympathetic magic, but he also had the experience of witnessing ritual, magical dances firsthand. He is thus in a privileged position to extend the anthropological line of inquiry into "primitive cultures" we have already encountered in Conrad, to evaluate the positive, vitalizing function of ritual mimesis in forms of ritual "participation," and, finally, to root sympathetic magic in the immanence of a bodily, mimetic unconscious.

The affective dimension of Lawrence's account of ritual mimesis (or pathos) cannot be dissociated from its theoretical potential (or distance), insofar as his work is predicated on the dynamic interplay between the two (pathos of distance). For the sake of clarity, however, I shall consider Lawrence's affective implication in ritual mimesis first, before turning to the anthropological theories that are internal to his account.

The Sympathy of Religious Pathos

That Lawrence relies on an emotional, experiential approach in order to establish a living contact with ritual dances is most clearly indicated in his essay devoted to his first encounter with Native American culture, "Indians and an Englishman." This essay, written in September 1922 upon his arrival in New Mexico and collected in *Phoenix*,[16] has the advantage of clarifying Lawrence's methodological position and theoretical focus at the outset: "I am no ethnologist," he writes; "the point is, what is the feeling that passes from an Indian to me, when we meet? We are both men, but how do we feel together?" (*P* 95). This passage makes clear that Lawrence is not interested in an impartial, objective ethnographic description of ritual dances per se.[17] Instead, he consciously relies on his sensitivity in order to analyze the lived, affective communication between self and other. Anticipating Georges Bataille's emphasis on the cognitive dimension of *l'expérience vécue*, Lawrence adopts the perspective, if not of the active participant, at least of the moved bystander, and sets out to analyze the affects that transgress the boundaries that divide "self" and "other," "Englishman" and "Indians." His approach is thus sympathetic in the literal sense that he attempts to share the pathos of the other: "Sympathy," he reminds us, "means feeling with, not feeling for" (*SCAL* 158).

Lawrence's "subjectivist" approach to cultural "otherness" has been seen as problematic insofar as it can quickly disregard the otherness of the other in favor of a reduction of the other to an aspect of the self. As Marianna Torgovnick puts it in *Gone Primitive*, "any 'intuitive' response . . . projects onto the object beheld the deepest, most tangled concerns of the viewer."[18] For Torgovnick, in so-called intuitive modernists such as Conrad and Lawrence, "the conditions for a genuine receptiveness to the primitive Other do not exist" insofar as "the primitive Other, like all others, must be processed and reprocessed as a potential sign and symbol of the self."[19] Such a subjectivist-modernist-primitivist fallacy is definitively present in Conrad's representations of the entranced Africans: that is, the cultural "others" serving as a reflecting mirror re-presenting the mimetic pathos "civil" Westerners tend to disavow. It is certainly also present in Lawrence, who, at the end of the essay, ends up identifying the ancestral figure of the Indian with his own working-class father.[20] Lawrence's "receptiveness to the primitive Other" is, indeed, not "genuine" in the sense that it does not offer an impartial, objective evaluation of "primitive cultures" purged from his own personal, emotional concerns. Torgovnick's warnings are, therefore, perfectly justified, and we should be careful not to take Lawrence's account of ritual as a transparent mirror of the "feelings" of Native Americans when they dance. And yet in the context of Lawrence's project, an affective implication may not be without cognitive value. Especially given that his object of inquiry is precisely the elusive "dark continent of feelings" that escapes, by definition, an external, impartial consideration. As Bataille will also stress, "there is a contagiousness that rules out the possibility of dispassionate observation."[21] Before proceeding any further, we should thus consider the precise dynamic responsible for causing such a contagious, nonverbal communication to flow between self and other.

In the context of his anthropological descriptions, Lawrence does not elaborate on the conditions necessary for such an intuitive understanding of the feelings of others, but in *Kangaroo*, a novel written over the summer of 1922, shortly before arriving in New Mexico, he gives us a clue to this riddle as he suggests that his emotional receptivity to others is rooted in his working-class origins. What Lawrence says of Somers's "power of intuitive communication with others" (37) is a thinly disguised description of himself. Despite the fact that "he had the speech and the clear definiteness of a gentleman," we read:

> Somers was of the people himself, and he had the alert *instinct* of the common people, the instinctive knowledge of what his neighbour was wanting and thinking, and the instinctive necessity to answer. . . . He was different because, when he looked at you, he knew you more or less in your own terms, not as an outsider. (36, 37)

Lawrence is not the first modernist to connect the capacity to enter mimetically into the perspective of the other with class disadvantage, implying that such an "instinct"—as he misleadingly calls it—is socially conditioned.[22] Nietzsche, in a famous passage from *Gay Science*, dissects the social "pressures" that are responsible for the accentuation of what he derogatorily calls "mimicry" among the lower classes:

> Such an instinct will have developed most easily in families of the lower classes who had to survive under changing pressures and coercions, in deep

dependency, who had to cut their coat according to the cloth, always adapting themselves again to new circumstances, who always had to change their
mien and posture. (*GS* 361)

Mimetic "instinct," Lawrence and Nietzsche agree, is enhanced by social
disadvantage and the "dependency" on the perspective of the other it entails.
Class subordination enforces an external adaptation in cloth, mien, and posture that a person from a subordinate class requires in order to survive in an
ongoing class dependency, or to fit "higher" social circumstances for which
working-class subjects had not been prepared in childhood. This agreement, however, leads to opposite diagnoses. Nietzsche stresses the negative,
debilitating (or pathological) consequences of the necessity of continuous
adaptation, making this violent social "pressure" responsible for the loss of
proper identity. Thus, he adds, "they learned gradually to turn their coat with
every wind and thus virtually to *become* a coat" (361). Lawrence, on the other
hand, stresses the positive, cognitive (or patho-*logical*) value of such socially
enhanced "mimicry." Hence, he specifies that it allows the subordinate class
subject to develop an "instinctive knowledge" that sees through the perspective of the other.

　　Lawrence is commenting on the elusive sphere of feelings and intuition
that tends to be understood in terms of "projection" of the self onto the
other. But projection, while always a danger, is strictly speaking not what is
described here. Insofar as such a passage troubles common understanding of
"objective" and "subjective" knowledge, we should take these notions with
a grain of salt, so as not to let preconceived connotations cloud the unconscious *dynamic* Lawrence is pointing to. It is clear that this cognitive process
is not "objective" in the usual sense of involving an external consideration of
a quantifiable object that can be empirically verified by others. This approach
is, indeed, "subjective," in the sense that attention to interiority involves
the self in an affective participation in the psychic life of the other. And yet
Lawrence insists that this subjective, intuitive approach does not absorb the
other into the self, reducing otherness to selfhood, difference to sameness,
but rather is triggered by an "instinctive necessity to answer . . . [to] what
his neighbour was wanting and thinking." This formulation indicates that
for Lawrence the access to the psychic life of the other—who is not just any
other, but already a known other, a neighbor—is not predicated on a violent

mapping of the thoughts and wants of the self onto the other (*projection*). Nor does it involve a desire to be the other, to enter willingly the perspective of the other or, as the saying goes, to put oneself in somebody's shoes, on the basis of an active, volitional effort on the part of the self (*imitation*). Instead, what is at stake in this silent communication is a social "instinct" enhanced by class disadvantage whereby the subject is affectively, involuntarily, and automatically absorbed in the psychic life of the other (*mimesis*). For Lawrence, then, it is precisely this passive, affective disposition, this mimetic pathos that allows an active understanding of the other "more or less in his own terms." In short, for Lawrence, at least in theory, there is a sense in which a deep-seated imitative disposition leads to an intuitive understanding of the other *as* other.

If we now return to the ritual context of "Indians and an Englishman," we are in a better position, if not to blindly trust, at least to recognize the mimetic mechanism that implicitly underscores Lawrence's account of Native Americans' ritual "feelings." This mechanism operates at the level of Lawrence's mode of communication with the Indians, (i.e., his response to the "feeling that passes between the Indian and [him]"), but is also inextricably intertwined with the content of what is communicated, and with his translation of this content in writing, for his readers to feel. At the first, formal level of communication, Neil Roberts, one of the most informed critics to recently reconsider Lawrence's anthropological thought, rightly stresses that his writings on the Pueblo ceremonial dance involve "an attempt not only to understand it but to sympathize with it."[23] In the light of what we have just said, we should specify this claim by saying that it is *through* sympathy as Lawrence understands it—that is, as an affective *participation* in the pathos of the other—that his attempt at understanding takes place.[24]

This sympathetic participation is central to Lawrence's project, given that the specific content of his experiential encounter with Native Americans deals directly with the elusive sphere of feelings: something that eludes the gaze of an exterior, objectifying perspective, but can be communicated, quite directly, via affective contagion. Like Nietzsche and Conrad before him, Lawrence considers that mimetic pathos—what he calls the "deep pathos" of the Indian (*MM* 119) or, alternatively, the "pathos of the religion" (181)—is triggered by the affecting rhythm of the drum. And in order to define the psychic state of dispossession that results from the ritual dance, Lawrence, again like Nietzsche and Conrad, draws a connection between the religious/ anthropological language of "ecstasy" (115) and the psychophysiological language of "somnambulism" (118). What is new in his account is that he notices yet another affect that spreads contagiously among the ritual crowd, an affect that will be tremendously important for Georges Bataille's understanding of communication and for the modernist brand of mimetic theory this book promotes, namely "laughter."

Speaking of the "chuckle" Native Americans produce "from the deeps of the stomach" (116), Lawrence makes clear that this sympathetic communication does not stem from a volitional choice but overtakes the self involuntarily (i.e., unconsciously) from within the body and establishes a direct, nonlinguistic psychophysiological communication that flows like a current from the other to the self. Lawrence's receptiveness to the feelings of Native Americans, whether he wants it or not, is indeed quite genuine—at least in the sense of what Nietzsche called "genuine physio-psychology." The chuckle that "surprise[s] [him] in [his] very tissue" (116) testifies that an affective flow between self and other, the "Indians" and the "Englishman," is effectively taking place through an unconscious, sympathetic communication. Lawrence is thus suggesting that in order to account for the "pathos of the religion," this pathos must be shared in the first place, so that "sympathy," as he understands it, is the most direct way to be receptive to mimetic feelings. What is ultimately at stake in Lawrence's affective, sympathetic relation with the other, then, is a communication of mimetic pathos via mimetic contagion; a communication *of* mimesis *through* mimesis where the medium *is* the message.

But if this communication is purely affective and nonlinguistic and can be mediated directly by mimetic contagion, we may now ask, how can it be effectively communicated to the reader through discursive language? How can the immediacy of religious *pathos* be conveyed through a *logos* that mediates the experience it describes? More than any modernist concerned with primitivism, Lawrence goes out of his way to communicate the power of mimesis to his readers, bending the rules of discourse in an effort to reproduce, onomatopoetically, the feelings that overtake him from within his stomach. Thus, with respect to the dance, he speaks of the "pát-pat, pát-pat quick beat on flat feet" that follows the "thud-thud of the drum" (115); for singing he reproduces the "Hie! Hie! Hie! Hy-a! Hy-a! Hy-a! Hie! Hie! Hie! Ay-away-away!!" (115); as for the chuckle in the war whoop he compares it with "a turkey giving a startled shriek and then gobble-gobbling with laugh-ter—Ugh!" (116). To be sure, language pushed to this imitative degree does not communicate any meaningful message; nor does it simply reproduce sounds in an effort to offer a well-documented ethnographic representation of the "other." Instead, this mimetic speech—in the Platonic sense whereby the speaker "assimilates . . . his own diction as far as possible to that of the person whom he announces as about to speak" (*Rep.* 638; 393c)—involves an attempt to communicate the *effect* of the Indians' religious pathos to the reader who re-presents it from a distance.[25] This translation of contagious affects geared towards reawakening a mimetic echo in the soul of modern readers is, of course, impossible on paper. No matter how hard Lawrence tries to give voice to such "feelings" in onomatopoetic speech, this written (mimetic) medium is *not* the (mimetic) message. The shift from an oral to a written culture, from the ritual to the page, *pathos* to *logos* renders imitative affects less ticklish, as it were. These rather awkward reproductions of sounds on paper may make us smile, but they definitely do not make us laugh. Hence, they fail to communicate the reflex unconscious "chuckle" that "surprise[s]" Lawrence "in his very tissue" and reduces, for an instant, the gap that divides self and other.

This failure of communication, however, may not only be a consequence of the limits of mimetic representation. In fact, despite Lawrence's enthusi-astic attempt to share his experience of religious pathos with his readers, this essay does not mark an unconditional celebration of ritual mimesis. Abruptly changing his tone of voice, he adds: "The voice out of the far-off time was not for my ears. Its language was unknown to me. And I did not wish to know. . . . It was not for me, and I knew it. Nor had I any curiosity to understand" (119–120). This disavowal of the affective language of mimesis in a writer who has just attempted to represent it is, indeed, strange, and critics have commented on the multilayered, biographical, emotional, and cultural rea-sons that motivate Lawrence's initial resistance to Native American culture.[26] What we can add is that Lawrence's inability to "understand" the language of affective mimesis with what he calls "his *conscious* mind" is paralleled by a profound receptivity to it by his *unconscious* mind. As he makes clear at the beginning of "Indians," this first encounter was an overwhelming experience for which his "soul" was not fully prepared: "It was not what I had thought it would be. It was something of a shock. Again something in my soul broke down, letting in a bitterer dark, a pungent awakening to the lost past, old darkness, new terror" (116). Moreover, invoking the language of pathology we have already found at work in Nietzsche, he writes: "a sickness of the soul came over me" (116); "it brings a sick sort of feeling over me, always, to get into the Indian vibration" (126).[27] And relying on the evolutionary bias we already encountered in Conrad, he concludes, "I don't want to go back to them, ah, never . . . there is no going back. Always onward, still forward" (130). At such moments, we sense that Lawrence's take on the ecstatic power of "darkness," even in ritual, organic contexts, betrays an underlying anxiety concerning the power of affective contagion to penetrate the boundaries of his modern soul, threatening to dissolve his permeable, adaptable, working-class ego in the mimetic darkness of blood consciousness he so often celebrates.

In sum, Lawrence's first account of Native Americans is torn between the contradictory imperatives of a pathos of distance that swings his ego towards/away from the religious pathos of the other. On the one hand, his receptive, working-class instinct is attuned to the affective vibration triggered by the Indian pathos. On the other hand, his vulnerability to mimetic infection leads him to disavow his understanding of this sympathetic language and to set up a distance that denigrates racial others as the source of a "sick sort of feeling." In "Indians," Lawrence does not resolve this fundamental ambivalence towards primitivism. Thus, in the concluding sentences of the essay, he multiplies dialectical "buts" (six in two paragraphs) in order to account for his simultaneous investment in religious pathos and the need for distance: "Neither denied nor accepted," Lawrence concludes that he "can't cluster at the drum anymore" (130). This intermediate, liminal position situated on the exclusive line of the "neither/nor" prevents him from aligning himself with *either* the "Indians" he observes *or* the "Englishman" he represents. At such moments, the spiraling movement of Lawrence's mimetic patho(-)logy breaks down, revealing an impasse that is not unusual among modernists who are both attracted to and repelled by the contagious outbreaks they encounter. Pathos of distance, as we have already seen in previous chapters, is not always a source of critical insight and theoretical illuminations; it can also lead to contradictions where the inquiring subject is, quite literally, mastered by the *sym-pathos* he struggles to conquer.

And yet this does not mean that in subsequent writings this uneasy site of affective disjunction cannot function as a locus of theoretical conjunction,

so that like the "and" of the essay's title, Lawrence continues to mediate, via
a more discursive anthropology, the pathos of the religion of the Indians for
his readers. In fact, after sensing the pathological danger of affective contagion, Lawrence's patho-logy reveals the positive, nonviolent, and ultimately
vitalizing dimension of archaic forms of communication as well as the affective mechanism that gives life to them. Lawrence's contribution to mimetic
theory consists in emphasizing *both* the violent, pathological dimension of
ritual mimesis *and* its beneficial, patho-*logical* counterpart.[28]

The Magic of Participation

The collection of travel essays entitled *Mornings in Mexico*, written in 1924,
at a time Lawrence was finalizing the second version of *The Plumed Serpent*,
and published in 1927, is one of the least read and discussed of his works. Yet
perhaps better than any other of his anthropological texts, it testifies to his
critical insights into rituals of sympathetic magic. His account of the Pueblo
Indians' "Dance of the Sprouting Corn," for instance, adds a layer of complexity to his previous descriptions of ritual mimesis:

> Take the song to make the corn grow. The dark faces stoop forward, in a
> strange race darkness. The eyelids droop a little in the dark, ageless, vulner-
> able faces. The drum is a heart beating with insistent thuds. And the spirits
> of the men go out on the ether, vibrating in waves from the hot, dark, inten-
> tional blood, seeking the creative presence that hovers forever in the ether,
> seeking the identification following on down the mysterious rhythmus of
> the creative pulse, on and on and on into the germinating quick of the maize
> that lies under the ground, there, with the throbbing, pulsing, clapping
> rhythm that comes from the dark, creative blood in men, to stimulate the
> tremendous, pulsating protoplasm in the seed-germ, till it throws forth its
> rhythms of the creative energy into rising blades of leaf and stem. (63)

Lawrence's personal, sympathetic response to the sprouting corn dance
still provides him with the affective basis to comprehend the function of
ritual from an internal, experiential perspective. And yet this is not only
a description based on a personal communication of "religious pathos"; it
is also an interpretation of the function of a ritual that implicitly relies on

anthropological theories of sympathetic magic that informed the modernist generation.[29]

Theories of magic were dominant at the time Lawrence was writing and had an enormous impact on literary accounts of "primitivism" in general and Lawrence in particular. John Vickery, for instance, argues that James Frazer "is the most convenient touchstone for gauging Lawrence's interest in anthropology and comparative religion."[30] We can, indeed, see how Frazer's theory of sympathetic magic—as it appears in chapter 3 of the abridged version of his monumental work *The Golden Bough* (1890–1915)—provides Lawrence with the underlying principles to understand magical rituals. Frazer, in fact, famously posits two laws at the center of his understanding of primitive magic: the "law of contagion" (or contagious magic) whereby "things that have been in contact with each other continue to act on each other," and the "law of imitation" (or imitative magic) predicated on the belief that "like produces like."[31] What these principles have in common, Frazer writes, is the belief that a "secret sympathy" flows through what he calls an "invisible ether" and is responsible for the fact that things "act on each other at a distance."[32] It thus appears that Lawrence's repeated references to the notion of "ether," and his realization that the human, emotional energy triggered by the dance acts at a distance on the corn, awakening the natural creative energy within the seed-germ, is a typical case of magic predicated on the law of imitation whereby "like produces like."

And yet Lawrence's divergence from Frazer is as significant as his debt to him, and we should be careful in bringing their respective accounts of "contagion," "sympathy," and "imitation" too close. In fact, Frazer understands "contagion" in terms of *physical* contagion, a law of contact in the sense that objects that have been in physical proximity with a person or a thing (such as clothes) carry the properties of the person they belong to. Similarly, for Frazer, imitation is predicated on a representational notion of mimesis concerned with an *external* "similarity" between ritual action and the effect wished. For instance, the gesture of pouring water on the ground is based on the magician's assumption that "he can produce any effect he desires merely by imitating it," in this case a mimetic reproduction of the natural coming of rain.[33] Thus understood, "imitation" and "contagion" are deprived of the raw (internal) stuff of sacred affect in order to become (external) abstract principles or, as Frazer calls them, "laws."[34]

In the passage just quoted, but also consistently in his writings, Lawrence's emphasis is clearly less on the external logic that governs ritual magic than on the state of emotional participation that animates such imitative, contagious frenzy from within, what he also calls the "wild inward delight, participating in the natural mysteries" or, alternatively, "the mystery of participation" (*MM* 65). The notion of "participation" is important in Lawrence's take on religious magic; it accounts for the sympathetic communication between men and the natural world that is at the center of his primitivist preoccupations. In this sense, his position is reminiscent of that other, long-neglected, yet equally central figure in the field of comparative anthropology, a figure responsible for what Michael Bell calls "a new conception of the primitive":[35] the French philosopher and anthropologist Lucien Lévy-Bruhl.[36]

Closer to Lawrence in sensibility, Lévy-Bruhl questioned the foundations of a Western, rationalist, Cartesian culture and explored other modalities of thought as they appeared among archaic cultures. Thus, in his most influential work, *La mentalité primitive* (1922),[37] he focused on the emotional dimension (or *participation mystique*) responsible for the belief in a mimetic permeability between the human, the animal, and the (super)natural spheres. "Participation," as Lévy-Bruhl understands it, is predicated on a mode of thinking that, at the logical level, transgresses the rule of noncontradiction. For instance, he explains that a state of participation "establishes a relation between the sorcerer and the crocodile whereby the sorcerer becomes the crocodile, without confusing himself with it."[38] Furthermore, he specifies that what is at stake in this mimetic confusion of identities is an *affective* rather than *logical* confusion: participations, he writes, "are felt and lived rather than thought."[39] In short, Lévy-Bruhl's emphasis is not so much on a default logic, and definitively not on a rationalist critique of this logic, but rather on understanding the affective dynamic that leads the "primitive" subject to transgress the boundaries of individuation.[40]

In a subsequent study, titled *Le surnaturel et la nature dans la mentalité primitive* (1931), Lévy-Bruhl devotes an entire chapter to the affective dimension at work in ceremonial dances, coming to conclusions similar to those implicit in Lawrence's account.[41] Focusing on the ritual dimension that generates states of collective participation, he identifies the drum as the "essential element" of magical rituals.[42] This instrument, for the French anthropologist, is indispensable for sympathetic magic to work insofar as it stimulates "the movements and gestures of actors . . . , of rhythm, dance, music and songs" and generates what he calls an "intense emotion" that, in turn, induces a state of collective participation.[43] More precisely, Lévy-Bruhl stresses the importance of the psychophysiological effect of the rhythm of the drum on the affective system of the participants for magical participation to take place: "Such methods of collective hypnosis," he writes, "are very apt to determine those often-described states of ecstasy or *trance* where ecstatic [*hors d'eux mêmes*] subjects live solely in a world of intense mystical emotion."[44] Hypnotic forms of dispossession, for both Lévy-Bruhl and Lawrence, are the door to access religious forms of participation; mimesis turns out to be the privileged medium of the sacred.

This striking isomorphism between Lévy-Bruhl's and Lawrence's accounts of the psychic effects of ritual dance indicates that for both authors imitative magic is not a logical mistake. Nor is it predicated on the naive belief that laws of similarity and contiguity can be mechanically applied in order for magical results to emerge. Instead, they both insist that belief in the efficacy of magic is the product of a collective, ritual experience responsible for establishing an experiential continuity between the gesture accomplished and the result expected. More precisely, for Lawrence, as for Lévy-Bruhl, it is the *hypnotic* power of the drum that dispossesses the dancing subjects of their "spirit" and allows them to "seek the creative energy," establishing thus an identificatory, sympathetic connection between the world of man and the world of nature at large. This affective rapport is, in turn, instrumental in actively taking possession of the impersonal forces of nature (or "ether") and in reactivating their creative energies (or "protoplasm"). For Lawrence, then, like produces like and the rhythmic "pulsing" of the drum activates the rhythmic "throbbing" of nature only insofar as the participants experience a "wild inward delight, participating in the natural mysteries." Figuratively put, for Lawrence, mimetic participation is nothing less and nothing more than the living sap that flows through the channels of sympathetic magic.

This is an important and rather innovative anthropological point. It not only corrects widespread modernist tendencies to devalue magic on a rationalist ground (i.e., as a "mistaken association of ideas" characteristic of cultures that are still in the infancy of thought),[45] but it also anticipates more recent anthropological definitions of magic that are aware of the vitalizing power of imitative affects. In fact, for Lawrence, sympathetic magic can be experienced as effective only insofar as it is predicated on what the French anthropologist Edgar Morin, extending Lévy-Bruhl's thought, calls "mimesis." As he puts it, "Man mimes everything; he is the mimetic animal par excellence." And he adds: "Mimetism is the faculty of resonating with the environment, the openness to the world, participation itself, the possibility of confusion with the other."[46] Lawrence's account of sympathetic magic is predicated on a desire to get back in touch with the power of mimetic impersonation in order to open the boundaries of the ego to its human, animal, and natural outside. This archaic, ritual mimesis is, for Lawrence, the source of an interpersonal (or "mystical") participation that roots the subject in the fluid affectivity of the mimetic unconscious (or "blood consciousness") and, as such, is repeatedly invoked as a site of idealized authenticity that is radically opposed to a Western emphasis on the mind (or "mind consciousness"). For Lawrence, then, mimesis not only functions as an instrument of will to power and psychic subjugation of people to charismatic leader figures—although *The Plumed Serpent* is certainly a warning against the violence of sacrificial forms of "bad mimesis," as Girard would call it; it is also a medium that establishes an affective, sympathetic connection with individual others, the community, and nature at large and, by doing so, illustrates the vitalizing, cohesive dimension of affective forms of participation. Perhaps part of Lawrence's attraction to primitivism stems from his fascination with a form of mimetic participation that goes beyond the rivalry and violence of modernity, and that opens up the ego to the potentially vitalizing affects of communal effervescence.

In sum, Lawrence's celebration of magical dances in the context of leadership novels like *The Plumed Serpent* that celebrate authoritarian politics remains problematic and should be critiqued as a mimetic pathology characteristic of a tyrannical bent in literary modernism Lawrence uncritically partakes in. And yet the detour via anthropology also allowed us to see that Lawrence's fascination with ritual dances is not deprived of patho-*logical* insights, if only because his anthropological writings reveal an affective mechanism at the heart of "primitive" cultures that has escaped mainstream rationalist accounts of sympathetic magic and that explains why, exactly, mimetic forms of participation have the power to bring man back in touch with the living sap that flows through the human, animal, and natural world.

What we must add now is that Lawrence, in his later period, not only offers a backward-oriented anthropological account of a "good" ritual mimesis in order to celebrate a bodily, sympathetic ego characteristic of "primitive" cultures, but also offers a forward-oriented philosophical account of Western culture via the focus on "bad" representational mimesis in order to critique a mental, ideal ego that haunts modernity as a whole. If thus far we have seen that mimesis understood as *affective participation* is central in Lawrence's *celebration* of the ritual affects that open up the boundaries of individuation ("good" mimesis), we now turn to see that mimesis understood as *visual representation* is also at the center of his philosophical and psychological critique of Western culture and subjectivity ("bad" mimesis).

In this shift from the *pathos* of archaic rituals to the *logos* of Western spectacles, participation to representation, Lawrence's anthropology turns into a philosophical critique of mimesis, a critical patho-*logy* that diagnoses a process that gives birth to an ego that is but a phantom, or shadow of the ego.

The Birth of the Ideal Ego

Lawrence considered it "the greatest pity in the world, when philosophy and fiction got split" (*P* 520). And since this split occurred on the basis of an ancient quarrel over the value of mimetic art, it is appropriate that Lawrence's modernist engagement with *both* art *and* philosophy concerns precisely the cause of such an unfortunate quarrel: that is, mimesis. This is indeed a classical theoretical move that has both ancient and modern antecedents. Like Nietzsche before him, Lawrence is, of course, anti-Platonic in his attempt to reconcile philosophy and literature via the question of mimesis. And yet, again like Nietzsche, he is also Platonic in considering that the ego is essentially the product of the dramatic spectacles that inform it. This section is devoted to an analysis of Lawrence's genealogy of the phantom of the ego, a genealogy that considers the process whereby Western consciousness, or, as Lawrence also calls it, "phantasmal self-consciousness," is given form by the power of mimetic representation and the idealist metaphysics it entails. As we shall see, Lawrence's critique of a Western, ideal consciousness (or ego) is predicated on an inquiry into the mimetic forms (or ideas) that bring this ego into being. It is my contention that by showing us how this ego is born, Lawrence tells us something essential about why its phantom continues to haunt the modern world.

Lawrence's engagement with representational mimesis takes place at different moments in his writings of the 1920s, but is already present in his anthropological accounts of rituals we have considered thus far. For instance, in one of the essays collected in *Mourning and Mexico* entitled "Indians and Entertainment" (1924), Lawrence transgresses the limits of the title and sets out to offer a theoretical comparison between Indian and Western forms of "entertainment" in the context of a critique of mimetic art—as it originates in Greek drama.[47] The underlying theoretical tension that structures the entire chapter (as well as Lawrence's take on mimesis) surfaces in the opening lines, as Lawrence says: "We go to the theater to be entertained." And he adds: "We want to be taken out of ourselves. Or not entirely that. We want to become spectators at our own show" (*MM* 59). Lawrence is here relying on an ecstatic notion of "entertainment" whose theoretical roots, as we know, go as far back as Plato's account of theatrical "enthusiasm," understood as a state of possession by a god. Yet he immediately feels the need to qualify this statement by introducing a visual distance from a bodily pathos. In this introductory oscillation from possession to spectacle, from ritual to entertainment, from mimesis understood as *participation* to mimesis understood as *representation*, we have in a nutshell the origins of Lawrence's fundamental distinction between Indian and Western egos.

The Dionysian "Upflow"

Thus far we have seen that Lawrence's description of the Indians' mystical fusion in the mystery of participation is in line with anthropological accounts of ritual magic, but magic is not the only source of Lawrence's inspiration. Dissolution of selfhood in the impersonal mystery of Being through the intoxicating rhythm of the drum in the context of a ritual dance with ecstatic effects: this is, indeed, also a transplantation of Nietzsche's account of the Dionysian into Mexican soil.[48] That Nietzsche's thought looms large in Lawrence's account of subjectivity is well known, and critics have called attention to this Dionysian undercurrent that traverses literary modernism in general and Lawrence's thought in particular.[49] Both Conrad and Lawrence are, indeed, "heirs to Dionysus" who inherit Nietzsche's concern with the affective, intoxicating dimension of mimesis. But despite this general awareness of the importance of Nietzsche's Dionysian thought

for Lawrence, rarely, if ever, is Nietzsche discussed in the context of Lawrence's anthropological writings. This compartmentalization of Lawrence's
heterogeneous thought according to prepackaged disciplinary boundaries
is unfortunate; it prevents a full understanding of the general scope of
Lawrence's critique of Western culture and entertainment, as well as of the
larger philosophical, aesthetic, and psychological implications that inform
his account of the birth of the ego.

Nietzsche's early concerns with what, in *The Birth of Tragedy*, he calls the
"mystic feeling of oneness" (1) can be felt throughout Lawrence's account of
ritual mimesis; yet it is with respect to the underlying conceptual polarity that
informs Nietzsche's argument that Lawrence's debt is most fully revealed. In
fact, Lawrence explicitly relies on Nietzsche's thesis of the birth of tragedy in
order to articulate a connection between ritual magical dances and Western
dramatic spectacles. Thus, he says: "Drama, we are told, has developed out of
these ceremonial dances. Greek drama arose this way" (*MM* 66). This Nietzschean echo, which considers Greek drama as an offshoot of Dionysian rituals,
allows Lawrence to ground the theoretical distinction between Indian and
Western entertainment, ritual possession and visual spectacle, on the basis of
Nietzsche's fundamental distinction between Apollonian (mimetic) representation and Dionysian (mimetic) intoxication. Contrasting Western to Indian
entertainment, Lawrence writes that in the latter "there is no spectacle, no
spectator" (63), "no division between actor and audience" (65). "There is none
of the hardness of representation. They are not representing something, not
even playing. It is a soft, subtle *being* something" (65). "Representation" versus
"being," mind versus body, distance versus pathos or, to put it in Nietzschean
terms, Apollonian *Rausch* predicated on a "visual stimulation" and Dionysian
Rausch involving "a complete affectation of the nervous system" (*TI* 10; 519).[50]
Lawrence is, indeed, implicitly relying on Nietzsche's artistic metaphysics in
order to structure his account of the birth of Western "consciousness"—out
of the womb of "entertainment."

And yet once this comparison is made, a series of questions immediately
emerge. For instance, if Lawrence agrees with the Nietzschean thesis that
Greek drama arose out of these ceremonial dances and goes as far as relying
on the distinction between Dionysian fusion and Apollonian representation, why then should he insist on marking an absolute, incommensurable
difference between ritual ecstatic dance and theatrical spectacle, Indian

entertainment and Western entertainment? Why should he write that "the two ways, the two streams are never to be united. They are not even to be reconciled. There is no bridge, no canal of connection" (*MM* 61)? Should he not rather say that Western and Indian entertainment are complementary principles, just as Dionysian mimesis and Apollonian mimesis complete each other in *The Birth of Tragedy*? After all, this would have been a position much more faithful to Nietzsche's thesis. Despite Nietzsche's celebration of Dionysian forms of mimetic intoxication, he never dispenses with the need for Apollonian "representation." On the contrary, he considers representation a necessary condition for the birth of Greek tragedy to take place; a necessary filter through which the Dionysian One is mediated and given form on the theatrical stage. It is in this sense that Nietzsche speaks of "redemption through illusion" (*BT* 4; 45). If there is no appearance, no theatrical representation, we might have what Nietzsche calls that "witches brew" which, for him, is the "Dionysian barbarian," but not *"Dionysian Greek"* (2; 39), and definitely not that *aesthetic* phenomenon par excellence which is Greek tragedy. Lawrence, in short, absorbs the Nietzschean thesis and the theoretical polarity that sustains it, but where Nietzsche posits a complex continuity and a fruitful interchange between Apollonian and Dionysian mimesis, Lawrence posits a radical discontinuity and stresses the deadly danger of cross-fertilization. Hence he says that "the consciousness of one branch of humanity is the annihilation of the consciousness of another branch" (*MM* 61). I wonder why.

Lawrence addresses this question as he continues to ground his genealogy of Western consciousness in Greek drama. Here is how he articulates the implications of the fundamental conflict between ritual participation and visual representation in the formation of what he now calls Western "Mind":[51]

> And here finally you see the difference between Indian entertainment and even the earliest form of Greek drama. Right at the beginning of Old World dramatic presentation there was the onlooker, if only in the shape of the God Himself, or the Goddess Herself, to whom the dramatic offering was made. And this God or Goddess resolves, at last, into a Mind occupied by some particular thought or idea. And in the long course of evolution, we ourselves become the gods of our own drama. The spectacle is offered to us.

And we sit aloft, enthroned in the Mind, dominated by some one exclusive idea, and we judge the show. (*MM* 67)

This is a key, yet obscure and elliptical, passage in Lawrence's genealogical account of the birth of the ego.[52] It is thus difficult for the reader to follow the intermediary steps that justify the abrupt slides from "God" to "mind," or from the "onlooker" to the "idea"—slides loosely connected by a string of "ands." More generally, it is difficult to see how Lawrence moves from the origins of Western "entertainment" to the birth of Western "consciousness," and what role mimesis plays in this process. In order to reconstruct the intermediary steps of Lawrence's elliptical account of the process whereby visual spectacles are responsible for the formation of a "phantasmal con-sciousness," it is necessary to consider more closely the theoretical sources on which he relies.

The emphasis on the primacy of Apollonian representation—what Lawrence calls the "God as onlooker"—in the earliest form of tragedy is still recognizably Nietzschean, but this influence is also mediated by Jane Harrison's account of the origins of Greek drama in *Ancient Art and Ritual* (1913).[53] One of the first influential female classicists in England and a central figure of the so-called Cambridge Ritualists,[54] Harrison lends support to the Nietzschean thesis that drama originated out of Dionysian rituals. In oppo-sition to the Platonic critique of art as mimetic representation, Harrison emphasizes the role of affective mimesis in the birth of Greek art. Thus, she writes that "the origin of art is not mimesis, but mimesis springs up out of art, out of an emotional expression." And she adds: "We translate mimesis by 'imitation,' and we do very wrongly. The word mimesis means the action or doing of a person called a *mime*."[55] Harrison, however, is not only repeating Nietzsche's thesis. She also relies on anthropological theories of sympathetic magic (mostly Frazer, but also Lévy-Bruhl and Durkheim) in order to give her own account of the birth of tragedy. Thus, she accentuates the *magical* over the *musical* dimension of art, linking Greek tragedy with primitive fertility dances whose goal is to awaken the coming of spring. In her view, the "dithyramb was, to begin with, a leaping, inspired dance" to celebrate the birth of Dionysus in the spring and thus magically stimulate the coming of spring and the growth of corn.[56] We can thus already see that as Lawrence offers an account of the dance of the sprouting corn, while at the same time linking it with Western drama, he is inverting a move that is at the center of Harrison's Nietzschean/anthropological thesis concerning the transition from ritual to art in Western culture. It is thus only if we situate Lawrence's "elliptical" account of entertainment against the background of Harrison's reading of ritual that we can understand the underlying *philosophical* logic that sustains his account of the birth of an ego that is but a phantom.

The theoretical core of Harrison's thesis on the origins of Western drama concerns precisely the intermediary steps that lead from a ritual based on physical participation (or impersonation) to "art" understood as a visual spectacle (or representation). Thus, she writes that "the merely emotional dance develops from an undifferentiated chorus into a spectacle performed by actors and watched by spectators."[57] This point is still in line with Nietzsche's *The Birth of Tragedy*, but Harrison adds a psychological dimension to his argument. Well-read in what she calls "contemporary psychology,"[58] she specifies that the primitive subject is characterized by a reflex tendency to mimic, so that "whatever interests primitive man," "whatever makes him feel strongly he tends to re-enact."[59] Such a reflex, mimetic participation springs, in her view, from a bodily urge that overtakes subjects unconsciously and leaves no space/time for conscious reflections from a distance. Subjects who physically participate in the dance are not thinking about the dance, they are dancing; spectators who see a representation, on the contrary, do not experience the dance but can evaluate it from a distance.

This pathos of distance whereby mimetic participation turns into mimetic representation is, in Harrison's view, the hinge between ritual and art: "out of representation *repeated*," she writes, "there grows up a kind of *abstraction* which helps the transition from ritual to art." And later, she adds that the transition from participation to observation introduces a "space between an impulse and a reaction" or, alternatively, an "image conceived, 'presented,' what we call an *idea*."[60] If representation introduces a distance from the unconscious reflex to participate, its repetition or re-presentation allows the process of abstraction to take place. "Ideas," for Harrison, are therefore initially visual images that crystallize in thought as the subject is no longer a direct participant in bodily pathos, but is situated at a visual distance instead. Finally, for the Cambridge Ritualist, this shift from participation to representation equally affects the Greek conception of divinity. The god, Harrison tells us, is no longer a living immanent presence that is felt while dancing. On the contrary, "he is gradually detached from the rite and as soon as he gets a life and being of his own, apart from the rite, he is a first stage in art, a work of art existing in the mind."[61]

We should now be in a better position to see that despite the highly elliptical dimension of Lawrence's account of the origin of Western entertainment and Mind, he faithfully follows Harrison's anthropological and psychological elaboration of the Nietzschean account of the transition from ritual to art. As Lawrence speaks of the transition from Indian ritual to Western entertainment, (Dionysian) participation to (Apollonian) representation, via the transition of "God as onlooker," which in turn generates spectators who are "enthroned in the mind" and informed by "ideas," he is not saying anything truly original, but he aligns himself with a mimetic tradition instead. Thus, he condenses Harrison's complex argument to the major steps responsible for what she considers to be the Western cultural shift from ritual to visual art, mimetic participation to mimetic representation.

And yet this does not mean that Lawrence is simply recapitulating Harrison's (early Nietzschean) thesis of the birth of art out of ritual. As often with Lawrence, exterior sources are incorporated in his own theoretical agenda, an agenda that, in this case, is predicated on the *opposed driving telos* from his two theoretical sources. If both Harrison's and Nietzsche's objective is to give an account of the birth of Western *drama*, Lawrence's primary concern is to give an account of the birth of Western *consciousness* that emerges from such dramas. This change of focus entails a 180-degree shift of evaluation of the birth of tragedy, a shift that, far from supporting Nietzsche's and Harrison's thesis, counters the drive that motivates it. In fact, the two classicists' attempts to recuperate the bodily dimension of Greek drama lead them to establish a *continuity* between Dionysian pathos and Apollonian distance, bodily impersonation and visual representation; Nietzsche speaks of "marriage" and "reconciliation," Harrison of "transition" and "development." Lawrence, by contrast, emphasizes the radical *discontinuity* between Dionysian mimesis and Apollonian mimesis, Indian pathos and Western distance, in order to severely condemn the formation of a type of Western ego rooted in a transcendental mind rather than in the immanence of bodily reflexes.

Lawrence's proximity to Nietzsche as well as other intellectual models is often marked by an anxious need to differentiate his position from his predecessors. This Romantic "anxiety of influence" and the "mimetic rivalry" that ensues are certainly still present in Lawrence's thought, a writer who often absorbs his models' thoughts into his own, while at the same time overturning their conclusions.[62] Schematically put, Nietzsche celebrates the reconciliation between Dionysian and Apollonian as "the most important moment in the history of Greek religion" (*BT* 2; 39). Lawrence, on the other hand, considers the necessity to posit an Apollonian distance responsible not only for the death of a truly "religious pathos" and of the fluid, Dionysian "blood consciousness" it entails, but also for the birth of a static ego "enthroned in the mind" and identified with the "idea." For Lawrence, then, Nietzsche's early thesis of "the birth of tragedy" turns out to be complicit with the idealism he sets out to undermine—a point Nietzsche's attempt at self-criticism partially confirms. This is probably why, in one of his other essays devoted to Native American rituals, Lawrence goes as far as lumping together the Dionysian and Christianity, defining the Native American ecstasy as "the very reverse of the upflow of Dionysiac or Christian ecstasy" (*MM* 179). For Lawrence, it is because this ecstasy is mediated by the need of Apollonian representation that it flows upwards, towards an ideal transcendental sphere, rather than downwards, towards a bodily immanent ground. In short, what emerges from these considerations is that, for Lawrence, the birth of tragedy is necessarily a partial miscarriage: the birth of Apollonian distance brings about the abortion of Dionysian pathos.

The Shadow of the Ideal (Plato to Lacan)

We have learned from Nietzsche that mimetic relationships with intellectual models are always ambivalent and that gratitude for them can be detected at a more profound level of thought. This is clearly also the case with Lawrence, who, despite his implicit critique of the *early* Nietzsche, continues to heavily rely on Nietzsche's *later* critique of idealism in order to complete his genealogical critique of Western "phantasmal consciousness." This is especially clear as Lawrence shifts from the root of the problem as it appears in Greek theaters to that modern form of entertainment which is the movie theater.[63] In this shift from antiquity to modernity, from Greek theater to modern cinema, Lawrence's critique of entertainment continues to turn around the question of Apollonian, representational mimesis. But this time the onto-psychological dimension of his argument comes directly to the fore insofar as Lawrence sets out to critique the idealist metaphysics that gives form to the modern ego.

In order to denounce modern forms of mimetic entertainment Lawrence does not proceed according to a strictly logical, explicit argumentation. Instead he relies on an associative, tropological dynamic, which is not fully articulated, leaving the task of translating the theoretical import of his poetic language to his interpreters. For instance, still in "Indians and Entertainment," he writes:

> In the moving pictures he [the modern subject] has detached himself even further from the solid stuff of earth. There, the people are truly shadows: the shadow-pictures are thinkings of his mind. They live in the rapid and kaleidoscopic realm of the abstract. (*MM* 60)

These lines make clear that as Lawrence moves from antiquity to modernity, from Greek entertainment to modern entertainment, he remains fundamentally indebted to Nietzsche's thought. Not unlike Nietzsche's critique of the Wagnerian theater, Lawrence's critique of the movie theater does not explicitly mention his theoretical sources, but assumes that his readers are familiar with the philosophical tradition he is engaging with. And again like Nietzsche, Lawrence's agonistic confrontation with this tradition reproduces the theoretical perspective of his models/opponents in order to turn his critique against them. Now what is at stake in Lawrence's account of cinema is a reenactment of the Platonic critique of mimetic art characterized by a Nietzschean spin that turns this Platonic gesture, boomerang-like, back on Plato. For the sake of clarity, let us artificially divide the synchronic Platonic/Nietzschean double movement that informs Lawrence's critique of the seventh art.

The initial vector of Lawrence's narrative movement is in line with Plato's ontological critique of representational mimesis. In fact, as Lawrence describes the cinematic images appearing in the darkness of the theater as "shadows," he is alluding to what Plato in Book VII of the *Republic* calls the "shadows cast from the fire on the wall of the cave" (747; 515a). The connection between cinema and the Platonic myth of the cave, which Lawrence already intuited in the 1920s, is now commonly made in the field of cinema studies.[64] Yet unlike cinema scholars, and in line with Plato, Lawrence stresses the *ontological*, rather than *aesthetic* implications of cinematographic mimesis in order to discredit a Western form of modern art. In fact, if Plato in Book X of *Republic* famously critiques mimetic arts such as poetry and painting for producing mere "copies," or "phantoms" "three times removed from nature" (882; 597e), Lawrence makes a similar move as he critiques "moving pictures" on the basis that their representations are "even further" detached from reality. Cinema, for Lawrence, is thus but a devalued copy of that other mimetic art which is the theater; an imitation of yet another artistic imitation. The Platonic language of shadows is, thus, most appropriate to designate this ontological critique based on a representational notion of mimesis: the modern spectators, not unlike the subjects tied at the bottom of the Platonic cave, are exposed to "shadows" or "phantoms" of reality. Or, as Lawrence puts it in *St. Mawr*, in a discussion devoted to what he calls "film psychology," in the cinema, as spectators follow the moving pictures on the screen, one moves "from phantasm to phantasm" (131). The Platonic notion of *phantasma* that we have already encountered in Nietzsche's critique of the modern ego appears again. But this time it is used in its original, ontological sense, as a devalued representational copy of the real. Lawrence, in short, agrees with Plato that these subjects do not see reality, but an imitation of what Plato would call a "phantom of reality" instead.

But then, if Lawrence's critique of cinematic art replicates a Platonic move, the ontological hierarchy that sustains his critique is fundamentally anti-Platonic; Lawrence only reenacts Plato's metaphysical gesture in order to better overturn its logic. In fact, he argues that "being is *not* ideal as Plato would have it" (*P* II 470), and he roots reality in what he calls "the solid stuff of earth." This is an apparently straightforward move, clearly indebted to Nietzsche's inversion of metaphysics. Yet the double reliance on *both* Plato's critique of mimesis *and* Nietzsche's ontological inversion allows Lawrence to formulate, in the same breath, a critique that cuts both ways. If it cuts with Plato against cinematic mimesis on the basis of a critique of art as imitation of reality, it also cuts with Nietzsche against Plato, on the basis of an ontological critique of idealism. Notice in fact that Lawrence defines cinematic forms as "shadows" or "phantasms" not because they belong to the sphere of "becoming" as Plato understands it (i.e., the *changing* sphere of immanence), but precisely because these images are *not* rooted in reality as Lawrence understands it (i.e., the *solid* sphere of immanence). They are dismissed as mere copies that lack ontological value. These cinematic forms, as he also puts it in *St. Mawr*, are "flat shapes . . . without any substance of reality" (131). The result of this inversion is to turn the Platonic myth of the cave and the metaphysics that sustains it inside out. In fact, insofar as cinematic forms are defined as "thinkings of the mind," they turn out to be practically isomorphous with the Platonic forms and the abstract idealism that produces them. Hence, Lawrence's nonargumentative, associative method allows him, in a single move, to conflate *Platonic* forms with *cinematic* forms and relegate both to what he calls the "kaleidoscopic realm of the abstract." For Lawrence, then, Platonic *Being* turns out to be as ephemeral as those twenty-four images per second that move shadow-like on the cinematic screen. Ideal reality, as Plato understands it, turns out to be a mere phantom of a phantom.

Now, Lawrence's inversion of Platonic metaphysics predicated on a (reversed) critique of representational mimesis is not an end in itself but is instrumental in completing the genealogical critique of consciousness that has been the driving telos of this section. In fact, if we agree with Michael Bell that for Lawrence "the psychic and the ontological are inseparable aspects of the same process,"[65] we should add that the problematic of mimesis functions as the hinge that allows Lawrence to make the shift from ontology to psychology necessary to complete his genealogy of consciousness. Lawrence, in fact, relies on the ontological critique of cinematic mimesis (what he calls "shadow" or, alternatively, "phantasm") in order to offer a psychological critique of the formation of mimetic consciousness (what he calls "ideal-consciousness," or, alternatively, "phantasmal self-consciousness" [*STM* 131]).

The causal connection between Lawrence's critique of representational mimesis and the birth of the Western ego underscores the entire discussion of "Indian and Entertainment," but it is in "Art and Morality," written in 1925, while still in New Mexico, that Lawrence articulates it most clearly and succinctly. Continuing his argument against Western entertainment, he writes:

> This has been the development of the conscious ego in man, through
> several thousand years: since Greece first broke the spell of "darkness."
> Man has learnt to *see* himself. So now, he *is* what he sees. He makes
> himself in his own image. . . . We behave as if we had got to the bot
> tom of the sack, and seen the Platonic Idea with our own eyes, in all its

photographically-developed perfection, lying in the bottom of the sack of
the universe. Our own ego! (STH 165)

The fact that Lawrence posits the identity of being and seeing as the essence
of the Western subject is consistent with his critique of Western entertainment predicated on the Apollonian subject of representation, a subject characterized by visual rather than bodily mimesis; *"das Auge erregt"* rather than
"das gesamte Affekt-System erregt," as Nietzsche would put it later in his career
(*TI* 10). But now the reference to the "Platonic idea" brings to the fore the
ontological dimension of Lawrence's argument that was only implicit before.
The modern ego who *"is* what he sees" is uprooted from the "darkness" characteristic of the affective, Dionysian mimesis we have seen at work in Native
American immanent dances ("solid reality") and is posited as a derivative of
an abstract Platonic form ("shadow-pictures" of reality). Thus understood,
the modern ego is isomorphous with what Lawrence calls, thinking of
photography but with cinema not far from his mind—the "kodak idea of
himself" (*STH* 164), a phrase that joins his critique of mimetic representation
with his critique of the idealist ontology that sustains it. Western consciousness, for Lawrence, is thus "phantasmal" insofar as it incorporates, through
vision, the shadowy forms represented on the screen as the very essence of its
being. In a deft, subversive move, Lawrence turns the Platonic myth of the
cave into the womb—or as he ironically calls it the "sack"—out of which not
an ego, but a mere phantom of the ego, is born.

With Lawrence, then, the concept of "phantom" recuperates its original
Platonic meaning insofar as it is tied to a critique of *representational* mimesis
and the metaphysical hierarchy it entails. Yet at the same time he links, in a
causal way, this critique of the phantom of representation to a psychological critique of the phantasmal ego. This crucial point is worth repeating in
a study titled *The Phantom of the Ego*. In fact, we understand nothing of the
modernist critique of the "old stable ego" if we do not grasp the ontological
foundations that are responsible for its formation and subsequent stabiliza-
tion. In order to make this point absolutely clear, Lawrence does not hesitate
to reiterate it in other writings. For instance, in *Introduction to these Paintings*,
written in 1929, one year before his death, he stubbornly returns to critique
the Western emphasis on mimetic representation and the idealist metaphysics that sustains it in the context of an account of modern painting. Speaking

of Paul Cézanne's attempt to liberate himself from a representational (i.e., Platonic) conception of art, he writes:

> All we know is shadows, even of apples. Shadows of everything, of the whole world, shadows even of ourselves. We are inside the tomb, and the tomb is wide and shadowy like hell . . . our world is a wide tomb full of ghosts, replicas. We are all specters, we have not been able to touch even so much as an apple. Specters we are to one another. . . . Shadow you are even to yourself. And by shadow I mean idea, concept, the abstracted reality, the ego. (P 569–570)

Like Nietzsche before him, Lawrence links Plato's ontological critique of mimesis to a psychological critique of mimetic subjectivity: the shadows of the world we know and live in (or the phantom of reality) and the shadows of the self we are (or the phantom of the ego). But Lawrence's Nietzschean critique makes explicit what was only implicit and not fully articulated in Nietzsche's critique of subjectivity: namely, that the phantom of the ego is not the product of a psychic dispossession that should be traced in a bodily (Dionysian) mimesis and the immanent ontology it entails. On the contrary, · it is the product of an idealist, abstract philosophical tradition that privileges seeing over feeling, representation over impersonation.[66] This ontological point is Nietzschean in spirit, of course, but Nietzsche does not actually frame his critique of the phantom of the ego within a critique of *representation*. It is Lawrence who puts us in a position to see that it is because the Western ego is formed by mimetic representations rather than mimetic impersonations, visual consciousness rather than bodily consciousness, that it turns out to be an "abstract," "ideal," or, as he also says, "ghostly" ego. In short, the phantom of the ego, for Lawrence, comes into being thorough what he calls "the tomb" of idealism and the mimetic "replicas" and "ghosts" it entails.

Now if we turn a last time the screw of Lawrence's interdisciplinary mimetic patho-logy we realize that in addition to the already complex theoretical intertwinement of anthropology and ontology we have disentangled, Lawrence does not hesitate to add psychology to the mix in order to complete his genealogy of the birth of the ego. And he does so by relying on the anti-Oedipal insights of the American psychologist and psychoanalyst Trigant Burrow.

Burrow's anti-Freudian stance did not make him a fashionable figure in a Freudian century, but Lawrence was enthusiastic about Burrow's first book, *The Social Basis of Consciousness* (1927).[67] He positively reviewed it the year it appeared and advised "every man interested in the human consciousness to read [it] carefully" and to "assimilate" it (*P* 377, 382). That Lawrence had assimilated it is clear. The elements that inform Lawrence's account of entertainment are central to Burrow's argument concerning the social origins of consciousness. These include, among other things, the critique of what Burrow calls "the detached spectator of a merely static *aspect* of life," the condemnation of the "flat or reflected mental image of the world about us," as well as his objections to the "mechanical bidimension" of cinema.[68] Further, in his review Lawrence writes that the "most interesting part of Dr. Burrow's book is his examination of normality" (379). Here is a passage from Burrow's thesis quoted by Lawrence that illustrates this "normal" process:

> It would appear that in his separativeness man has inadvertently fallen a victim to the developmental exigencies of his own consciousness. Captivated by the phylogenetically new and unwonted spectacle of his own image, it would seem he has been irresistibly arrested before the mirror of his own likeness and that in the present self-conscious phase of his mental evolution he is still standing spell-bound before it. (378)

As David Ellis recognized, this passage "has a curious modern ring for anyone interested in psychoanalysis." And he adds: it "might be compared with *somewhat* similar thoughts in Jacques Lacan's 'Le stade du miroir comme formation de la function du Je.'"[69] Burrow is not primarily concerned with the imaginary formation of the ego in pre-Oedipal childhood, but Ellis's comparison with Lacan is well-taken and is worth exploring further, especially since it is directly in line with the ontological and psychological foundations of Lawrence's genealogy of "phantasmal consciousness."

Let us recall that Lacan considers a specular identification with what Burrow calls "the spectacle of his own image" to be absolutely essential in the process of ego formation. What is at stake in the child's confrontation with this image (or *imago*) is a clash between the living but disorganized sphere of bodily affects, on the one hand, and a visual, static representation, on the other. This image, as Lacan puts it, is "in contrast with the turbulent movements that the subject feels are animating him," a contrast that, at the moment of the child's self-recognition, sets in motion the dialectic between these two opposing poles out of which the ego, according to Lacan, is formed.[70] More precisely, we are told that this image is assumed into the ego via a process of "identification" that, while alienating the subject outside of itself, gives coherence, stability, and boundaries to what was just a bungle of disorganized chaotic affects without unity. The ego, in Lacan's interpretation, is thus brought into being as it mimetically assumes the imprint of a boundary. This boundary gives the chaos of the "turbulent movement" the subject "feels" inside its body a solid external structure (*un relief de stature*) that frames the ego in what Lacan calls a "form."[71] Hence the child's triumphant cry of "jubilation" at the moment of self-recognition in what Lacan calls the "ideal unity" (*unité idéale*) or, alternatively, "phantom" (*fantôme*) represented in a mirror: I am that form, I am that idea, I am that phantom! And as this phantom goes through the looking glass, an ego is born.[72]

Burrow's book, as well as Lawrence's review of it, appeared in 1927, nine years prior to the first version of Lacan's much-celebrated article (subsequently rewritten in 1949), and in a sense, anticipates his claim concerning the formative power of identificatory images. Lawrence and Burrow not only address the same mimetic phenomenon whereby "the soul of man stood divided against itself,"[73] but also agree with Lacan on the potentially pathological consequences that are at stake in the process of identification with an *alienating* imago of the self. Yet in a deeper sense, Burrow's and Lawrence's theoretical premises are fundamentally opposed to the underlying "Platonism" (Borch-Jacobsen's term) that underscores Lacan's account of the birth of the ego (out of a phantom in a mirror), an account that, in its generalizing tendency, is perhaps more prescriptive than it is descriptive. Far from accepting the primacy given to visual mimesis as a spectacular "ontological structure of the human world," as Lacan calls it,[74] Burrow and Lawrence take a step back from this idealist ontology in order to challenge the cultural, psychological, and philosophical primacy given to vision over the body, excitation of the eye over the excitation of the whole affective system, the subject of *Aufklärung* and the subject of mimesis.

A psychoanalyst of Freudian training but of Jungian and Nietzschean inspiration, Burrow became progressively dissatisfied with the yawning gap he experienced between orthodox psychoanalytical theory and his daily practice with his patients.[75] Burrow was convinced that the study of mental pathology cannot be limited to the individual or even the family. Giving psychological substance to future Marxist critiques of "one-dimensional," mimetic men,[76] he argued that a study of the formative power of mimesis must stretch beyond the ego in order to take into consideration the wider social field that shapes the subject. His perspective is, thus, not narrowly psychologistic, nor is it rooted in a theory of neurosis based on sexual repression but, rather, takes into account the complex articulation between the spontaneous fluxes of affects that animate the child's psychosomatic life (or "organic consciousness") and the larger cultural forces responsible for the formation of a public persona (or "social consciousness"). According to Burrow's post-Freudian view, in modern Western culture the subject from childhood on must progressively forsake a bodily and affective spontaneity in order to conform to given social models, roles, and images that are considered "good" by dominant social standards. At the same time, like Nietzsche before him, Burrow is fundamentally aware of the constructed dimension of what society considers "good" and "evil" and is deeply suspicious of the value of these values. Hence, he sets out to unmask the individualistic interests of self-affirmation, self-promotion, and opportunism responsible for the "spell-bound" capitulation to one's visual image. The model of the mimetic unconscious Lawrence and Burrow convoke in order to unmask, in a Nietzschean move, the modern subject's hypnotic fascination in front of what Burrow calls "the mirror of his own likeness" as a symptom of a culture that, from childhood on, encourages the development of the subject's "own egoistic advantage"—what Burrow calls "perceptual relationship to life."[77] In this culture, he argues, the subject progressively loses touch with the spontaneity of its psychic and somatic life in order to con-*form* to the external representation of itself, to the role it needs to play in order to be socially acceptable. As a consequence, he writes, in a formula that we have seen Lawrence reproduce, "we have unconsciously become artificially detached spectators of a merely static aspect of life."[78] In Burrow's view, modern subjects, as they are forced to adopt a rigid social mask imposed from without, progressively lose touch with the living, affective "flow" that animates the organism from within. Or, as he also puts it, using another Nietzschean insight, the psychic formation of the modern ego is not "spontaneous or from within out," but "necessarily adaptive or from without in."[79] Notice that according to this view, the subject is not inherently suffering from an "organic insufficiency" that leads the ego to anticipate its precipitation in a totalizing, unitary form, as Lacan would have it. On the contrary, for Burrow, such a *manque à être* is not originary but is the direct result of a dominant cultural primacy given to exterior images of selfhood over the turbulent fluxes of bodily affects, visual mimesis over bodily mimesis. For Burrow, then, the subject's spellbound fascination in the mirror scene is not the solution to the riddle of ego formation but the problematic source of its deformation.

Affective flow, organic life, participation in life, and a violent critique of the modern emphasis on mimetic representations: we begin to understand why Lawrence was enthusiastic about Burrow's book. His position is one of such striking affinity with the American psychologist that it is often difficult to draw a clear line between their perspectives.[80] What is clear, however, is that Lawrence adds a philosophical dimension that is only implicit in Burrow's critique. Lawrence's attention to the bodily, living affects that animate what he calls the "unspeakable inner chaos of which we are composed" (*STH* 70) renders him allergic to the idealist underpinnings of what he calls, following Burrow, "liv[ing] from the picture; that is from without inwards" (*P* 381). Such a picture, he says, addressing the reader, is "your *idea* of yourself" (381), it is a "philosophic or geometric idea" (458) "superimposed from the above" (713) and gives form, *in*-forms, *de*-forms and ultimately *con*-forms the modern ego. As Lawrence also puts it: "The self that is begotten and born from the idea, this is the ideal self. . . . This is man created from his own Logos. This is man born out of his own head. This is the self-conscious ego" (711). And we may add: This is the Lacanian ego.

According to Lawrence, in modern individuals subjected from childhood onwards to the primacy of visual representation, the difference between the ego and its imago is progressively blurred, so that the ego turns out to be identical with its specular reproduction. If the ego "*is* what he sees" (*STH* 165) in front of the mirror, if the subject feels itself in that disembodied shadow reflected on a flat surface, it follows that this phantom *is* the ego. For Lawrence, then, the modern ego—in its increasingly laborious morning toilette, as it experiences itself visually in front of the mirror or, later during the day, models itself on fashionable representations, abundantly available in the public and virtual sphere—is still operating within what is ultimately a Platonic, idealist tradition that is inimical to bodily, mimetic affects. We can thus better understand why, for Lawrence, idealism is "the real enemy today" (P 711). His objections do not concern abstract ontological speculations per se. Rather, they unmask the everyday pathological effects of this metaphysics as it absorbs the ego in the ethereal sphere of ideal, phantasmal reality. Lawrence's target is thus a representational (static) ego that has turned into a (dead) phantom insofar as it has lost touch with the (living) pathos that animates its (mimetic) body. Hence, he concludes his review of *The Social Basis of Consciousness* thus: "Men must get back in *touch*"; and he immediately specifies that in order to do so, we must first "shatter that mirror in which we all live grimacing" (P 382).

Now, despite the theoretical anticipation of Lacan's account of ego formation, Lawrence's opposition to the "fictional ontology" (Lacoue-Labarthe's term) that informs such a specular and speculative account is clear and concerns a series of interrelated reasons. First, for Lacan, the child's specular mimesis with the image of itself sets in motion a dialectical process whereby a synthetic *conjunction* between the subject and the world can be achieved.[81] Lawrence, on the other hand, following Burrow, considers such a specular identification a locus of *disjunction* between the living reality of the bodily organism on the one hand, and its idealized, narcissistic image on the other. Second, Lacan acknowledges that the precipitation of the ego into the "rigid structure" that is its ideal form is responsible for the formation of an "alienating identity." But we should not forget that the mirror stage, for Lacan, forms the ego as much as it alienates it; or, better, forms the ego in the very process of alienating it. And if it is true that Lacan stresses the pathological dimension of this "alienating destination," it is equally true that he repeatedly defines this ideal form "symboliz[ing] the mental permanence of the I in terms of 'health.'"[82] Third, if Lacan thinks that this specular process functions as a necessary "stage" in the *formation* of the ego, something that takes place universally, in pre-Oedipal childhood, Lawrence and Burrow stress the socially enforced identificatory pressures that are eventually responsible for a violent *de*-formation of the bodily, affective dimension of the ego. Finally, the French psychologist (or should we rather say, idealist philosopher?) speculates that the primacy given to representations is rooted in an atemporal "ontological structure of the human world" that informs the ego "before its social determination."[83] On the other hand, the British novelist (or should we rather say, empirical psychologist?), following both Nietzsche and Burrow (and anticipating Bataille), considers it the arbitrary product of a particular philosophical tradition that has its roots in Platonism and, thus, as being culturally, historically and theoretically enforced.

Does this mean that the phantom of the ego that emerges from the idealist, Platonic tradition—"this is man born out of his own head," as Lawrence calls it—is fundamentally more reasonable and conscious than the affective, unconscious phantom we have been chasing? Is the phantasmal self-consciousness understood in terms of representation a more rational version of the phantom of ego understood in terms of impersonation? Given the rationalist, mental dimension characteristic of the idealist, Platonic tradition that pertains to it, this would seem to be the case. And indeed, Lawrence specifies that "the self that is begotten and born from the *idea*" is "created from his own Logos" and is thus "quite reasonable" (*P* 711). And yet the move is clearly ironic. We should not forget that Lawrence is writing in the 1920s, in the aftermath of a universal carnage that reveals the fictional foundations of the subject of *Aufklärung*. No wonder that he insists that such a phantasmal self-consciousness is by no means less vulnerable to the unconscious pathos of affective mimesis.

As a cultural critic *avant la lettre*, Lawrence is concerned with a critique of the power of impression of the social mold and its pathological influences on the Western ego. This also means that like Plato, Nietzsche, Conrad, and Burrow before him, and Lacoue-Labarthe after him, he is aware that the typographic stamp of a mimetic will to power that deprives the modern subject of control over its ego is particularly effective if such an ego is part of a crowd. Thus, he extends Burrow's critique of social consciousness to mass consciousness, inflecting the latter's insights in the direction of crowd psychology: "The mass, the great mass," Lawrence writes "goes on worshipping the idol, and behaving according to the picture: and this is normal" (*P* 380). Writing after World War I, both authors share the same disillusionment with modern politics and the type of modern ego that makes such a politics possible.[84] But Lawrence pursues Burrow's line of inquiry by relegating the "normal" masses that form the modern body politic to the sphere of mental pathology. As he puts it, "the normal betray their utter abnormality in a crisis like the late war. There, there indeed the uneasy individual can look into the abysmal insanity of the normal masses" (*P* 380–381). And in another essay he confirms this diagnosis as he says that "the modern masses are rapidly going insane" (*P* 771).

Lawrence's genealogy of consciousness and the mimetic patho-logy that kept it moving have thus taken us full circle, back to the question of mass psychology with which we started. And yet the diagnosis is now radically reversed: from an enthusiastic *celebration* of Dionysian mimesis in the context of Indian rituals in terms of organic health, we have reached—via a genealogy of the Western ego out of the spirit of idealism—a radical *critique* of the Western masses in terms of mental sickness. In the shift from Indian entertainment to Western entertainment, "primitive" consciousness to "modern" consciousness, mass behavior is no longer celebrated under the rubric of "religious pathos." Instead, the "the surgeon of the modern soul" in Lawrence diagnoses it as a pathology that needs to be cured.

Mass Patho(-)logy Reloaded

If we move, via a somewhat backward chronology, to the leadership novels that immediately precede the Mexican writings and the essays we have considered so far, we notice that Lawrence is forced to admit that despite the representational distance characteristic of Western entertainment, Western consciousness continues to be particularly vulnerable to forms of enthusiastic pathos. In this respect, the Western theater is not only a manifestation of the idealist tradition he denounces, but also serves—as was already the case with Plato, Nietzsche, and Le Bon—as a microcosm through which to continue analyzing the affective and infecting dynamic of mimetic contagion.

The Apollonian Crowd

A typical manifestation of Lawrence's critical stance towards contagious forms of mass-behavior occurs towards the beginning of *Aaron's Rod*, published in 1922, but written in the midst of, and as a reaction to, the horrors of World War I. In an introductory chapter entitled "At the Opera" Lawrence writes that it "is impossible to be there [at the opera] without some feeling of horror at the sight the stage presents" (47), and then he adds:

> The curtain rose, the opera wound its slow length along. The audience loved it. They cheered with mad enthusiasm. . . . What a curious multiple

object a theater-audience was! It seemed to have a million heads, a million
hands, and one monstrous, unnatural consciousness. (*AR* 47)

Lawrence's characterization of the mad, enthusiastic spectators as a single,
protean consciousness is strikingly reminiscent of the Dionysian affective
con-fusion we have repeatedly encountered. At these moments, Lawrence
seems much closer to Plato's condemnation of the "mob assembled in the
theater," to Nietzsche's castigation of the confusion of "heads" among the
Massen of Wagnerian spectators, and to Conrad's condemnation of "the horror" of mimesis than to his enthusiastic celebration of "fusion," "dark blood
consciousness," and ritual "possession" as a cure for mental pathologies.
Furthermore, Lawrence's critical take on forms of enthusiastic manias, again
like his predecessors, is not confined to the sphere of Western entertainment,
but is representative of the massive outbreaks of "pathological" forms of
dispossession at work in the body politic at large. As he puts it later in the
novel, his protagonist, Aaron, "had no eye for the horrible sameness that was
spreading, like a disease over Italy from England and the north" (153), a point
he reiterates in *Twilight in Italy* as he states: "Northern Europe, whether it
hates Nietzsche or not, is crying out for the Dionysiac ecstasy, practicing on
itself the Dionysian ecstasy" (200). Dionysian mimesis and the return to the
ecstatic blood-consciousness it entails are no longer the object of an enthusiastic celebration. They are now denounced as the infecting germ that spreads
like a horrifying mimetic disease.

Lawrence's awareness of the political consequences inherent in epidemic
forms of psychic dispossession on European soil leads him to recuperate the
filter of Apollonian clarity in order to set up the necessary *distance* to resist
the pathological consequences of psychic pathos. In *Kangaroo* (1923), for
instance, he offers one of his many scathing accounts of crowd psychology, as
they occur in the context of the postwar period:

> The terrible, unnatural war, made so indecent because in every country
> practically every man lost his head, and lost his own centrality, his own
> manly isolation in his own integrity, which alone keeps life real. Practically
> every man being caught away from himself, as in some horrible flood, and
> swept away with the ghastly masses of other men, disinclined to speak, or
> feel for himself, or stand on his own feet. (213)[85]

Again, if we compare such moments with his writings on Mexico that temporally succeed his Australian novel, the contrast could not be more striking. In *Mornings in Mexico* we have seen him celebrate the dissolution of the subject in one single flux under the rubric of "blood consciousness"; now he condemns this loss of conscious control as part of a "horrible flood." In *The Plumed Serpent* we have seen him celebrate the masses' capitulation to the leader figure and the fusion of heads it entails under the rubric of "heart of darkness"; now he claims the need to preserve the boundaries of individuation and concludes that "a true man should not lose his head" (213).

Like his modernist predecessors, Lawrence is fundamentally ambivalent about the power of affective mimesis, oscillating pendulum-like, from an affective fascination for mimetic pathos to a diagnostic distance from it. Schematically put, if Lawrence celebrates states of affective intoxication on a *religious* ground in "primitive" cultures, it is clear that now he stresses the debilitating *ethical* and *political* consequences of crowd psychology. Thus he makes explicit the connection between collective dispossession and the political "horrors" that ensue at the heart of "modern" cultures. Gilles Deleuze, one of the few philosophers who has explored the continuities between Nietzsche and Lawrence and taken seriously the conceptual value of Lawrence's writings (especially his writings of 1920s), writes in *Essays Critical and Clinical*, "For Nietzsche and Lawrence, war is the lowest degree of the will to power, its sickness."[86] But then, we may ask, if Lawrence now posits a radical distance from the infecting pathos of mimesis and the phantom of the ego that more than ever haunts modern Europe, why does he end up celebrating the tyrannical authoritarian aspect of mimetic will to power? Shouldn't the "surgeon of the modern soul" speaking in him diagnose *all* mindless forms of dispossession as a sickness that needs to be overcome?

Since we have witnessed this countermovement before in Nietzsche, this "contradiction," as Girard would call it, should not come as a surprise in an author whose affinities with the German philosopher run so deep. As for Nietzsche before him, Lawrence's pathos of distance from modern mass-behavior functions not only as a *defensive* move away from what he considers culturally "sick" forms of mimetic dispossession (Nietzsche's "becoming hedgehog"); it also entails an *aggressive* and rather desperate attempt to fight off the dangers of infection on the basis of a celebration of strong individuals endowed with the power to subjugate the masses (Nietzsche's "blond beasts of prey"). Lawrence's ambition, in other words, is not only to passively resist the contagion characteristic of the "century of the masses" and the horrors it fosters, but also to actively propose his fictional dreams of utopian political solutions based on tyrannical forms of mimetic will to power. This also means that for Lawrence, it is by no means inconsistent that the same character (Lilly) who wants to distance himself from the masses and "get [him]self out of their horrible heap" plaintively exclaims: "why can't they submit to a bit of healthy individual authority?" (*AR* 97).

Jonathan Dollimore rightly notices that "Lawrence, like other Modernists, was attracted to *potency* in proportion to his conviction that the energies of the modern world were failing."[87] And Gilles Deleuze adds: "there is always the risk that a diseased state . . . push[es] literature toward a larval fascism, the disease against which it fights—even if this means diagnosing the fascism within itself and fighting against itself."[88] What we should add is that for Lawrence, as for Nietzsche before him, both potency and fascism are intertwined with the pathos of identificatory affects, affects they consider a healthy manifestation of Dionysian mimesis. Lawrence is, indeed, aware that his clinical diagnosis can boomerang against himself. Hence, he is anxious to multiply conceptual distinctions in order to wrest apart "salutary" and "decadent" forms of *Schwärmerei*: Health versus sickness, strong versus weak, organic versus mechanical, primitive versus modern, leading versus bullying, and blood consciousness versus mob consciousness are but some of the most often invoked dichotomies Lawrence continuously sets up in order to maintain the stability of his Manichaean Weltanschauung. Yet, as Nietzsche already taught us, such conceptual distinctions are less stable than they initially appear to be, if only because mimetic *pathos* flows freely through the boundaries of philosophical *logos*. In this sense, Lawrence is vulnerable to the same problems we found at the heart of Nietzsche's Dionysian thought; his position comes, at different levels, extremely close to the mimetic pathology he attempts to distance himself from.

What is specific to Lawrence's patho(-)logical account of the masses, however, is that his implication in mimetic sickness does not prevent him from developing a critical patho-logy that remains theoretically consistent with both the metaphysical and psychological foundations of his thought. And more importantly, this patho-logy offers us a different etiology of the same unconscious phenomenon that concerns us. In *Aaron's Rod*, for instance, following his critique of theatrical entertainment, Rawdon Lilly swings away from the modern masses and gives expression to his ethical indignation against the war:

> I want to get myself awake, out of it all—all that mass-consciousness, all that mass-activity—it's the most horrible nightmare to me. No man is awake and himself. No man who was awake and in possession of himself would use poison gases: no man. His own awake self would scorn such a thing. It's only when the ghastly mob-sleep, the dream helplessness of the mass-psyche overcomes him, that he becomes completely base and obscene. (*AR* 119)

This is an instance of Lawrence's well-known celebration of individual self-affirmation against modern, degenerative forms of mass psychology that can be understood in both personal and ethico-political terms: personal because Lawrence privileges the individual over the masses as a locus of resistance to the mechanical forces of modernity, and ethico-political because he considers the democratic masses responsible for the horrors of the Great War, mimetic horrors that have shaken the ethico-political foundations of modernity. Furthermore, if we retain the Nietzschean categories that structure Lawrence's genealogy of the birth of the ego, we notice that the modern masses are, in fact, not as Dionysian as they initially appear to be. Their irrationality and dispossession are not predicated on the bodily, unconscious affects that entrance archaic cultures. On the contrary, insofar as they are characterized by "sleep" and "dream" (or "nightmare"), the modern masses are implicitly relegated to a mental alienation that takes place in the sphere of Apollonian representation, a representation that imprisons the ego within a ghastly ideal form disconnected from bodily pathos. As Deleuze, speaking of both Nietzsche's and Lawrence's inimical relation vis-à-vis Apollo, the god of dreams, also recognized, "it is the dream that imprisons life within these forms," and he adds, "The dream erects walls . . . creates shadows, shadows of all things and of the world, shadows of ourselves."[89]

Lawrence is, thus, once again, operating within the boundaries of the Nietzschean (Platonic) condemnation of the phantom of the ego and the "arbitrary" evaluations it conveys. But we must now add that in his critique of the crowd and the "mob-sleep" that ensues, Lawrence's mass patho(-)logy is perhaps more discerning than Nietzsche's. In fact, Nietzsche's Platonic critique of Wagner's will to power over the masses implicates, *volens nolens*, the Dionysian neurosis he celebrates to the very end of his career. And as we have seen, this is the reason Nietzsche is careful never to invoke the Dionysian in the context of his late critique of Wagner, treating the "Wagnerian pathos" as if it were completely external to Dionysian pathos. Lawrence, on the other hand, makes a conceptual distinction that is absent in Nietzsche and is in line with the foundations of his own (Nietzschean) thought. In fact, while celebrating a ritual, *Dionysian* mimesis among archaic cultures and the immanent psychology it entails, Lawrence condemns the modern masses on the basis of a critique of representational, *Apollonian* mimesis and the idealist ontology it presupposes. For Lawrence, in other words, the egos of the Western masses remain prisoners within the walls of a visual/mental *representation*. Rather than being rooted in forms of bodily/affective *participation*, the ego turns into a mere shadow (or phantom) of the ego. Hence ethical horrors of the war can occur. Nietzsche's theoretical dilemma, that is, how to critique modern forms of tyrannical pathos without implicating his main philosophical categories (the Dionysian, the master, will to power, etc.) is thus resolved, at least in theory, as Lawrence attributes the ethico-political degeneration of the modern masses to the triumph of Apollonian representation over Dionysian impersonation.

Lawrence is not only resolving an abstract, conceptual problem here; he is also offering us a new diagnostic of the etiology of massive forms of mimetic dispossession responsible for the ethical and political horrors that continue to haunt the modern world. At first sight, there appears to be nothing radically new in Lawrence's critique of the masses. Like all the authors considered thus far, Lawrence is critical of Western forms of mass entertainment (theater, cinema, newspapers) for ethical and political reasons. And like them, he is aware that dominant representations (and the ideologies they convey), as they are typographically imprinted, from childhood on, in the mind of the modern public, are responsible for informing and conforming the ethical foundations of the modern ego. And yet, if we look more closely, we notice that Lawrence inverts his predecessors' critical diagnostic, suggesting an alternative theoretical foundation for his critique of mimetic information. The authors considered thus far, from Plato to Lacoue-Labarthe, via Nietzsche and Girard, in fact, tended to agree that the ethical horrors of modernity are the product of massive forms of blind capitulation to a bodily, *affective* mimesis (pathos) that deprives the subject of the capacity to *see* clearly, and thus to *think* critically. Lawrence, on the other hand, argues that the same horrors stem from a tradition where *representational* mimesis (distance) informs, via these media, the modern, Western ego and prevents it from *feeling* the pathos of the other and thus *acting* ethically. This is a crucial theoretical point. In fact, for Lawrence, the Western emphasis on visual, representational distance is far from being a guarantee for *clarity* of thought, feeling, and action. On the contrary, in his view a subject continuously bombarded by mimetic representations remains all the more vulnerable to the power of dominant ideologies—such as the *logos* about the *idea* of war—and to the imperative of putting such ideas into practice.[90]

Why? Because for Lawrence, the ideal, phantasmal ego that is continuously in-formed by such ideo-logies is progressively disconnected from a basic sense of sym-*pathos* for the other, and is encouraged to act mechanically as "a sort of deliberate reaction of the *accepted* ideal" (*P* 630). Or, as he also puts it, addressing his readers of the future: "as a ghastly simulacrum of life you may be firing bombs into men who are neither your enemies nor your friends, but just things you are dead to" (*STH* 197). To contemporary readers these lines have a postmodern ring. Somewhat surprisingly, Lawrence opens up the problematic of mimetic contagion to the question of simulation and simulacra.

Is Lawrence Postmodern?

Lawrence's definition of the modern subject as a "simulacrum of life" not only signals his preoccupations with the alienating psychic effects of mimesis (the phantom of the ego), but also recuperates his metaphysical concerns with the question of representations of reality (the phantom of reality). In the midst of the critique of the modern masses, Aaron and Lilly have a fascinating discussion concerning the reality of the Great War. Both characters share a disgust with its horrific ethical consequences, but they disagree on its "reality." Aaron's position could be defined as objectivist, insofar as he insists that the war was "real enough" and that it actually happened independently of the status of the subject that perceives it: "'the war did happen, right enough,' smiled Aaron palely." Lilly, on the other hand, adopts a radical subjectivist view that makes reality a function of the perceiving subject: "No, it didn't. Not to me or to any man, in his own self. It took place in the automatic sphere, like dreams do" (*AR* 118). Aaron's position seems reasonable enough, given the undeniable historical reality of the war, and Lawrence's critical stance would incline us to think that he would side with this perspective. Yet it is Lilly's scandalous claim about the war that seems more invested with the narrative voice.[91]

Is D. H. Lawrence suggesting that the Great War did not take place? Is this often marginalized modernist anticipating postmodern concerns about the dissolution of reality? After all, the claim about the unreality of war is strikingly reminiscent of Jean Baudrillard's more recent, and equally scandalous, statement that the Vietnam War, as well as the Gulf War, "did not take place."[92] These statements should of course not be confused; they refer to different historical periods, types of conflicts, and technological forms of mediatization. And yet, theoretically speaking, both Lawrence and Baudrillard ground their critique of simulacra in the same philosophical tradition. In fact, they not only share a common ontological concern with a "reality" threatened by the emergence of representational forms of Western entertainment but, more fundamentally, they both continue to be informed by the Platonic tradition that haunts the ontology of modernism and, per-haps, of postmodernism as well.[93] A brief theoretical comparison between these seemingly incompatible partners can thus help us further specify the untimeliness of Lawrence's theoretical position concerning what he calls "simulacrum of life."

At the most fundamental level, which is the mimetic level that concerns us, Baudrillard's postmodern critique of virtual reality is no longer predicated on an ontological hierarchy kept in place by the logic of representation. For the French theorist, in fact, postmodern media bring into being a totally new phenomenon, which he calls "real without origin or reality: a hyperreal."[94] This means that the media, for Baudrillard, are not concerned with copying a reality already present prior to its re-presentation. This phantom no longer functions as a devalued and derivative copy of the real. In the postmodern world, the sphere of hyperreal phantoms (or simulacra) can no longer be con-tained within the logic of mimesis. It is "no longer a question of imitation," Baudrillard writes, but "rather a question of substituting signs of the real for the real itself."[95] Hence, as he claims that the "Gulf War did not take place,"

Baudrillard is pushing this antimimetic logic to the extreme. His goal is not so much to deny the ethical consequences of the war but, rather, to expose what he calls the "programmed and melodramatic version of what was the drama of war," a melodrama that is mistaken for a truthful representation of the real.[96] Thus, in Baudrillard's view, this simulacrum of war displays "no images of the field of battle, but images of masks, of blind and defeated faces, images of falsification."[97] Clearly, Baudrillard's critique of what he calls "the specter raised by simulation" must be understood as both an extension of, as well as break with, the Platonic metaphysics based on the phantom of representation. It is an extension because he aligns this critique with Plato's metaphysical concerns with "specters," denounces such "images of falsification," and relies on previous inversions, most notably Nietzsche's, whose abolition of the "true" Platonic world implies the abolition of the "apparent" one as well.[98] It is a disruption because simulacra cannot be contained within the logic of imitation understood as representation. If Nietzsche's anti-Platonic account of the "'True World,'" as he says in a famous section of *Twilight of the Idols*, represents "noon," the moment of "briefest shadow" (486) and the abolition of the "true," ideal world, Baudrillard's postmodern thought moves beyond the dualistic metaphysics of mimesis in order to abolish the notion of "shadow" altogether. What haunts the postmodern world is not the shadow of the real, nor the reality of the shadow, but the desert of hyperreality itself.

To be sure, the degree of media coverage in World War I can in no way be compared to our postmodern, "hyperreal" wars. Yet the Great War marked a turning point, not only in the scope of the conflict, technological innovations, and the number of casualties, but also in introducing for the first time mass-mediatized representations of war scenes. There is thus a sense in which Lawrence/Lilly is expressing, in embryo, the same doubts about the reality of war on the basis of an ontological critique of mimetic representation we are now familiar with. As Anne Fernihough puts it, commenting on Lawrence's critique of the modern subject's desire to watch "shadows on a screen" rather than confronting flesh and blood people" (*P* II 590): "Our world has, according to Lawrence, become a world in which nothing is itself, everything is simulacrum."[99] In this sense, Lawrence's modernist position can appear to anticipate Baudrillard's postmodern critique of the dissolution of the real by the hyperreal sphere of virtual entertainment. But as I have said, despite the continuities in the mimetic tradition that concerns us, we must be careful to not confuse a modernist for a postmodernist claim. It would be a gross mistake to associate the two critiques too closely. In fact, if Lawrence senses in advance the postmodern dissolution of reality triggered by the media, his metaphysics never lets go of the ground of referentiality. On the contrary, the Nietzschean inversion of Platonism we have seen at work in his critique of cinema is an attempt to remain rooted in what he calls the "solid stuff of earth" that, for him, is Reality itself. In this sense, Lawrence's metaphysical inversion still operates within the mimetic logic Baudrillard's postmodern theory is moving away from.

In light of the real enough effects of hyperreal wars, we should resist the temptation to dismiss this Nietzschean faithfulness to the earth as a theoretical anachronism. Lawrence is, in fact, sensing a danger that already haunted the mind of modernism and is more than ever evident in postmodern culture. What is ultimately at stake in Aaron and Lilly's discussion is not the reality of mediatized wars and the horrors they entail per se (on both the ontological and ethical points they fundamentally agree) but, rather, the failure of the modern ego to both *perceive* and *feel* these horrors as such. Once again, Lawrence ties, in an apparently casual move, a critique of representational mimesis with an ethical critique of psychic mimesis, the phantom of reality with the phantom of the ego. In his view, it is because the modern ego is a passive victim of the power of visual representations and is imprisoned in a "reality" dominated by the Apollonian sphere of illusory dreams, or nightmares, that the horrors of the war, while represented on the screen and perceived by the eyes, are not experienced and felt as such. As Lilly insists: the war "never happened to me . . . [n]ot to me, or to any man *in his own self.* It took place in the automatic sphere, like dreams do" (*AR* 118; my emphasis).

Lawrence's contribution to mimetic theory consists in calling our attention to the fact that a civilization of the image continuously exposed to a stream of visual representations remains, perhaps more than ever, dangerously vulnerable to massive forms of mimetic dispossession, and for at least two reasons. First, because representations that stimulate the eyes have the power to locate the ego in the mind and disconnect it from its affective, sympathetic system—from its capacity to feel and be in touch with the pathos of the other. And second, representations, for Lawrence, induce a state of hypnotic dispossession that renders the modern ego an easy, docile prey to dominant ideologies. Lawrence's critique of mimesis, in this sense, can be seen to give Baudrillard's critique of the hyperreal an ethical and political spin that is often perceived as lacking among postmodern quarters. It reminds us that the primacy modern culture gives to representations—in traditional forms of mimetic entertainment such as theater and cinema, to be sure, but how can we *not* think of TV, the Internet, video games, and other avatars of postmodern entertainment?—does not involve only the substitution of reality with simulacra of reality. It also entails the substitution of real human beings for what he calls "*simulacrum* of a man" (*P* 770), a man who, in a state of light-hypnotic sleep, does not act on the basis of individual consciousness, but on the basis of the mimetic unconscious.

This critique of the pathological effects of massive doses of *Apollonian* mimesis on the modern ego is typically Lawrentian. But like the literary and theoretical modernists we have already encountered, Lawrence thinks such a form of psychic dispossession in the language of modernity: the language of mimesis, or as it is still called at the time Lawrence writes, the language of hypnosis. Here is how the discussion about the War continues:

> "That's a fact" said Aaron. "They [the masses] are hypnotized by it!"
>
> "And they want to hypnotize me. And I won't be hypnotized. The war was a lie and is a lie and will go on being a lie till somebody busts it."
>
> ". . . It never happened to me. No more than my dreams happen. My dreams don't happen: they only seem." (*AR* 118).

In such references to the illusory dimension of dreams, we find an echo of Lawrence's metaphysical speculations concerning the sphere of Apollonian entertainment, but it is clear that here the *ontological* concern with the war as simulacrum of reality is a function of a *psychological* concern with hypnosis and the mimetic unconscious it entails. Given this reference to the language of hypnosis, we can now better understand the apparent contradiction between Lilly's statement about the war not being real, and his concern with the real effects of the war. As he says that "no man who was awake and in possession of himself would use poison gases," he understands sleep as synonym of hypnotic sleep, a liminal psychic state whereby the subject fails to experience reality as fully "real," yet can still effectively carry out orders that have real enough effects. Lawrence, in other words, is following *à la lettre* Hippolyte Bernheim's definition of hypnotic suggestibility understood as "a peculiar aptitude for transforming the idea received into an act."[100] Bernheim, as we have seen, had already commented on the everyday, non-pathological, psychic dimension of light hypnosis, and the facility whereby not only hysterical patients, but also normal, intelligent subjects, are prey to the unconscious reflex of suggestions. Lawrence, as a coda to his critique of a culture dominated by what Baudrillard calls "contagious hyperreality,"[101] unmasks the pathological, ethical, and political consequences that ensue from massive forms of capitulation to the power of hypnotic dispossession.

The critique of the phantom of reality swings us, once again, back to an analysis of the phantom of the ego, an ego characterized by a type of consciousness that acts on hypnotic reflexes and is thus in line with what we called the mimetic unconscious. If we follow, one last time, Lawrence's spiraling movement *towards* mimetic pathos, his patho(-)logy reveals an unconscious that animates his notion of the ego, which is not one. And here is where the quarrel with Freud starts.

Lawrence contra Freud

Addressing the question of the Lawrentian unconscious and the fluid, relational ego that emerges from it immediately opens up the larger, much-discussed question of Lawrence's discontent with psychoanalysis. Given Lawrence's early fascination for triangular, Oedipal patterns of desire (most notably in *Sons and Lovers*) and his later, rather violent critique of psychoanalysts in terms of "priests" whose "church" postulates "the serpent of sex coiled around the root of all our actions" (*PU* 7), it is not surprising that Lawrence's discontent has tended to be read through Freudian lenses: that is, as a typical case of repression of an Oedipal truth too hard for the novelist to face and work through. More recently, however, developments of Nietzschean and anti-Oedipal inspiration have pointed out that Lawrence's critical reaction goes beyond personal affects and ultimately concerns his theoretical opposition to the idealist foundations that, in his view, inform "psychoanalysis as the advance-guard of science" (*PU* 15).[102] What we must add now is that Lawrence's critique of psychoanalysis, and the ambivalences that emerge from it, must be reframed in the wider context of the mimetic patho(-)logies that traverse his work. Lawrence's stance contra Freudian idealism, as we turn to see, is inextricably intertwined with his critique of visual representations that form the ego as an ideal image of itself. Consequently, his anti-Freudianism turns out to be an anti-Platonism; his anti-Oedipus an antimimesis—at least if one understands mimesis as simple representation. And yet this does not mean that Lawrence's celebration of a fluid, dynamic, polarized, and, as he often says, "magnetic" unconscious has nothing to do with the power of affective mimesis—at least if we understand mimesis in the modernist tradition of the mimetic unconscious. But let us proceed in order.

Freudian Symptom, Anti-Oedipal Diagnosis

It is well known that Lawrence relegates psychoanalysis to the Cartesian, rationalist tradition; less known is that his specific challenge to the Freudian unconscious relies on a more general critique of representational mimesis and the Platonic metaphysics it presupposes. The Platonic overtones, as well as the metaphysical inversion we have already confronted in his account of the birth of the ego, are especially clear in *Psychoanalysis and the Unconscious* (1921):

> [W]e watched Freud disappearing into the cavern of darkness, which is sleep and unconsciousness to us, darkness which issues in the foam of all our day's consciousness. He was making for the origins. We watched his ideal candle flutter and go small. Then we waited, as men do wait, always expecting the wonder of wonders. He came back with dreams to sell. (9)

Lawrence is once again playing with the Platonic myth of the cave in order to challenge his opponent's ontological foundations and unmask the idealism that underscores psychoanalysis. The initial vector of Lawrence's narrative move suggests that Freud functions as a heroic candidate opposing the rationalist, philosophical tradition of the Enlightenment and the emphasis on a purely conscious subject that pertains to it. Lawrence agrees with Freud that man's "origins" must be searched for in the darkness of the unconscious, rather than in the light of "day's consciousness." In this sense, Freud's attempt to reach the bottom of the "cavern of darkness" indicates a return to the sphere of "sensual immanence" that, in Plato's idealist philosophy, is but a phantom of reality. Yet insofar as Freud is said to venture into this cave with an "ideal candle" and finds the origins of the unconscious in "dreams," Lawrence's figurative language suggests that Freud's project is compromised by the very idealist, "enlightened" tradition he sets out to critique. [103] The conflict could not be more sharply delineated. If in Freud's (Platonic) meta-psychology "affects," as he himself puts it, "even in the unconscious, . . . can only be represented by the idea,"[104] in Lawrence's (Nietzschean) metaphysics, dreams are but devalued (Apollonian) re-presentations of real (Dionysian) bodily affects. Lawrence, then, denounces the Freudian unconscious in terms similar to those in which he denounced Western entertainment: as a purely abstract theoretical projection or, as he also calls it, a "shadow cast from the mind" (*PU* 15). Freud is thus aligned with the Platonic, idealist tradition his exploration of the unconscious sets out to undermine—via a Platonic myth.

Indeed, the language of "shadows" as it appears in the context of the image of the "cavern of darkness" strongly suggests that Lawrence's critique of representational mimesis, and the idealism it entails, continues to implic-itly frame his critique of psychoanalysis.[105] This hypothesis is confirmed if we consider Lawrence's fundamental objection to Freud. Of course, this objection does not concern the importance Freud gives to sexual desire per se[106]—though Lawrence, like Burrow and Jung, thinks that Freud overem-phasizes this importance for speculative reasons. Nor does it disavow what Lawrence calls "incest-craving" (10) tendencies in men—though he is skepti-cal that the Oedipus complex would vanish once it is brought to the surface of consciousness: "why should it?" (10), he asks, ironically. Rather, his objec-tion concerns the idealist, metaphysical underpinnings that underscore the Freudian unconscious and the repressive hypothesis that informs it. Relying on Burrow's critique of Freud, which he considers "brilliantly true," Lawrence writes: "Burrow says that it is knowledge of sex that constitutes sin, and not sex itself. It is when the mind turns to consider and know the great affective-passional functions and emotions that sin enters" (*PU* 11). Lawrence agrees with Burrow that it is the "repressed idea of sex" (11), as he puts it, rather than the sexual *drive* itself that is at the source of neurosis. Thus, he continues: "the incest-craving is propagated in the pristine unconscious by the mind itself, even though unconsciously. . . . The mind, that is, transfers the idea of incest into the affective-passional psyche, and keeps it there as a repressed motive" (11–12). Repression not as a barrier to the psychoanalytic cure, but as a consequence of the cure itself! This is no minor critique: it implicates the theory and praxis based on the *idea* of sexual repression (psychoanalysis) in the process of formation of the *symptom* that it attempts to cure (neurosis). No wonder that Lawrence, paving the way for anti-Oedipal theorists yet to come, compares psychoanalysts to "priests" who attempt to build a "church" (7) on a theory predicated on the (idealist) belief that the unconscious is structured like an (Oedipal) theatrical representation, staged at the bottom of a (Platonic) cavern.

A mimetic approach to Lawrence's critique of the Freudian unconscious reveals the extent to which this often marginalized modernist serves as a major theoretical source of inspiration for Gilles Deleuze's and Félix Guattari's influential critique of psychoanalysis. In *Anti-Oedipus*, not only do the French theorists borrow Lawrence's notion of psychoanalysts as "the last priests," but they also rely on Lawrence's critique of repression to unmask the psychoanalytic "cure" as being the source of the "disease." As Deleuze and Guattari put it:

> The law tells us: You will not marry your mother, and you will not kill your father. And we docile subjects say to ourselves: so *that*'s what I wanted! . . . Such is the nature of Oedipus—the sham image. . . . It is not a question of the return of the repressed. Oedipus is a factitious product of psychic repression. It is only the represented, insofar as it is induced by repression.[107]

And revealing their source of theoretical inspiration, they immediately add: "D. H. Lawrence . . . has a foreboding of this operation of displacement, and protests with all his might: no, Oedipus is not a state of desire and the drives, it is an *idea*, nothing but an idea that repression inspires in us concerning desire."[108] Here we see that if literary critics, with few exceptions, have tended to be skeptical of Lawrence's anti-Oedipal stance, dismissing it, in a much used and abused Freudian move, as the product of Lawrence's repressed Oedipal issues, high theorists of the caliber of Deleuze and Guattari evaluate Lawrence's untimely critique differently, and encourage a new generation of post-Freudian critics to "keep D. H. Lawrence's reaction to psychoanalysis in mind, and never forget it."[109] Thus, they directly rely on Lawrence's critique of Apollonian representation in order to undermine the idealist foundations of the Freudian conception of the Oedipal unconscious.

If Lawrence, as Deleuze puts it, picks up Nietzsche's arrow in order to propel it further in a new direction, his arrow arrived—and these anti-Oedipal, postmodern effects have indeed pierced the foundations of psychoanalysis and permanently unmasked the so-called science of the unconscious as being the product of a "Freudian legend."[110] Clearly, in light of the influence of Deleuze and Guattari's anti-Oedipal critique of Freud and of contemporary developments in the history of psychoanalysis, Lawrence can no longer be confined to the role of outdated modernist but needs to be reevaluated as an important source of inspiration for postmodern critiques of new forms of idealism of the psyche yet to come.

This does not mean that Lawrence is ready to dispense with the notion of the unconscious as such but, rather, that his own model of the unconscious is predicated on theoretical foundations that are radically opposed to the idealism that underlies the Freudian schema. And given what we have said so far, we should not be surprised to see that the Lawrentian unconscious is much closer to Nietzsche's mimetic hypothesis than to Freud's repressive hypothesis. Lawrence, in fact, relies on a psychophysiological model that roots the ego in the immanent sphere of bodily, Dionysian affects. Critics attentive to the theoretical underpinnings of Lawrence's conception of the unconscious have noticed the link to Nietzsche before.[111] They have usefully pointed out that Lawrence's debt is not only to Nietzsche but to a much larger late nineteenth-century psychophysiological tradition that includes figures like Marshall Hall and William James, and that considered the unconscious in psychophysiological, reflex terms.[112] More recently, anti-Oedipal critics have argued that Lawrence's "view of the unconscious or consciousness as a flow is a typically modernist trope that extends to a writing technique [i.e., stream of consciousness]."[113] What we must add is that Lawrence's assimilation of this pre-Freudian tradition leads him to develop a conception of the unconscious ego that is mimetic in the sense that it is radically vulnerable to Dionysian states of the sort we have already encountered in the Nietzschean, modernist tradition—states such as affective contagion, hypnotic suggestion, automatic reactions, and reflex forms of psychic depersonalization characteristic of what I call the mimetic unconscious.

Acknowledging Lawrence's debt to, and extension of, this much-neglected pre-Freudian tradition is important for at least two reasons. First, it allows us to take the last step in our understanding of that which is "psychic" in Lawrence's positive conception of the ego, what he calls, in the same letter to Garnett, "another ego, according to whose action the individual is unrecognizable, and passes through as it were, allotropic states." And, second, it gives us an insight into the affective relation, "sympathetic communion" (*PU* 142), or, as Lawrence also calls it, following the terminology of the ancient magnetists, the affective *rapport* that allows fluxes of nonlinguistic, direct communication between self and other to flow and dissolve the boundaries of the ideal ego. If Lawrence, then, builds his critique of the old stable ego on the basis of a more general critique of *representational* mimesis, his positive conception of the allotropic ego emerges out of a celebration of a *psychophysiological* mimesis. This bodily, affective mimesis continues to be rooted in Dionysian affects (and the "blood consciousness" it entails), but Lawrence now explicitly aligns it with the pre-Freudian unconscious (and the "vertebral consciousness" it entails).

Lawrence and the Unconscious

Traditionally, the most obvious way to continue addressing the problematic of the Lawrentian unconscious would be to pursue our reading of *Psychoanalysis and the Unconscious* as well as *Fantasia of the Unconscious*. Such works have the advantage of positing the unconscious at the center of their investigation, of articulating the polarized dynamic that informs the "mysterious stream of consciousness" (*PU* 8) that ties self to others, and are interesting in their own terms. And yet they have the disadvantage of entangling the reader in the specific details of Lawrence's psychophysiology and the jargon thereof: that is, the infamous "ganglia" and "plexuses" that have tended to throw off commentators. Hence, we could perhaps take an alternative, less-explored route into the Lawrentian unconscious—a route in line with the main thread of our investigation and instrumental in exposing the more general psychological assumptions Lawrence relies on in order to "trace the unconscious to its source" (16).

In a chapter of *Kangaroo* devoted to crowd psychology entitled "A Row in Town," Lawrence returns to consider what he calls "the mode of communication of the herd instinct" (298) and the collective, imitative behavior that characterizes it. This time, however, he takes the notion of "herd" literally and starts to inquire into animal forms of unconscious communication thus:

> Why does a flock of birds rise suddenly from the tree-tops, all at once, in
> one spring, and swirl round in one cloud towards the water? There was
> no visible sign or communication given. It was a telepathic communica-
> tion. They sat and waited, and waited, and let the individual mind merge
> into a kind of collective trance. Then click!—the unison was complete, the
> knowledge or suggestion was one suggestion all through, the action was
> one action. This so-called telepathy is the clue to all herd-instinct. . . . It is a
> complex interplay of vibrations from the big nerve centers of the vertebral
> system in all the individuals in the flock. (299)

"Collective trance," "telepathic communication," "vertebral consciousness,"
"suggestion": this passage clearly shows that Lawrence was completely
soaked in the mimetic terminology that permeates the modernist period.
Thus, in order to give an account of these contagious reflexes in the herd
instinct—which, for Lawrence, is as much an animal as a human instinct—he
transgresses disciplinary boundaries and relies on concepts that come from
traditions as diverse as religious anthropology (trance), dynamic psychology (suggestion), psychophysiology (vertebral consciousness), and psychic
research (telepathy).

   In order to catch a last glimpse of the Lawrentian conception of the allotropic transformation of the ego, let us identify, as schematically as possible,
four main theoretical sources that are internal to his account of unconscious
communication. First, the comparison between animal and human "herd
instinct" on which Lawrence relies is Nietzschean, of course, but it is also
in line with British collective psychology. Wilfred Trotter, the author of
Instincts of the Herd in Peace and War (1916)—a book Lawrence had read
in the year it came out—appears to be his most direct source of inspiration
here. Trotter not only speaks of the herd instinct in terms of "desire for
completion, for mystical union, for incorporation with the infinite" (what
Lawrence calls "God-urge"). He equally adds that "this yearning in us . . . is
identical with the mechanism that binds the wolf to the pack, the sheep to
the flock," drawing a connection between animal herd instincts and human
group instincts that Lawrence endorses.[114] Second, the notion of "suggestion," as we know, stems from the French psychologist Hippolyte Bernheim,
who defined hypnosis as "a state of enforced suggestibility induced by suggestion." But Lawrence, like Le Bon and British crowd psychologists such

as Trotter and McDougall before him, extends this notion to account for collective behavior *tout court*.[115] Third, the now esoteric-sounding notion of "telepathy" stems from inquiries into the supernatural carried out by Frederic Meyers and his team in the context of the Society for Psychical Research devoted to the study of spiritism.[116] This research was primarily concerned with inquiring into the possibility of communication with spirits (what they called, "phantoms of the living"). Yet crowd psychologists such as McDougall cautiously considered the notions of telepathy in order to account for an affective communication within the group mind and the psychic dispossession that ensues (what I call "phantom of the ego").[117] Similarly, Lawrence's use of the notion of "telepathy" in the context of a discussion of an entranced "unison" indicates that he understands it in the same psychological sense: that is, he understands it literally, as an affective vibration (*pathos*) transmitted, nonlinguistically, from a distance (*tele*). Finally, this point is supported by the fact that Lawrence speaks of "vertebral telepathy" and thus relies on a vertebral model of consciousness rooted in what he calls the "big nerve centers of the vertebral system": a consciousness that, once opened up and attuned to the instincts of the group, involuntarily reacts to external stimuli and movements, on the basis of mimetic, involuntary reflexes that are not consciously controlled and are, in this sense, unconscious.

The theoretical sources that inform Lawrence's account of crowd psychology are vertiginously eclectic; they come from different fields of research, and at first sight it is difficult to see what these traditions could possibly have in common, or in which way Lawrence's incorporation and adaptation of these theories can possibly achieve organic cohesion. What is clear, however, is that the link between the psychophysiological tradition, the vertebral emphasis on automatic reflexes, and the focus on states of dispossession such as "trance," "suggestion," "rapport," and "telepathy" is consistent with the conception of the mimetic unconscious we consider central to the Nietzschean axis of modernism. This "cerebral unconscious," as the historian of psychoanalysis Marcel Gauchet calls it, is not based on the hypothesis of repression, nor is it situated in the ideal sphere of a topography of the mind. Rather, it is based on a mimetic hypothesis that is clinically attentive to the psychophysiological, relational, and interpersonal reflexes that escape the control of consciousness and whose origin was thought to be in the spinal cord.[118] Indeed, Nietzsche, Conrad, and Lawrence, along with figures like Bernheim, Le Bon, Tarde, Harrison, and Burrow, partake of the same tradition, a pre-Freudian psychological tradition where, as Henri Ellenberger reminds us in *The Discovery of the Unconscious*, hypnosis, rather than dreams, functions as the *"via regia* to the unconscious."[119] According to this model, subjects who are under the influence of significant others (such as parents, models, friends, or leaders) yawn, empathize, dance, and, in extreme situations such as war, even go as far as to pull the trigger on the basis of automatic, mirroring reflexes. Further, the authors I consider also agree that the power of such mimetic reactions is amplified if the subject is part of a "mass"; they circulate freely from one subject to another through a wireless communication responsible for collective entities (flocks of birds, to be sure, but also human herds) to act in unison. Hence, when Lawrence says, for instance, that "the so-called telepathy is the clue to all herd instinct," he understands it on the basis of a psychophysiological model of the mimetic unconscious that has automatic, hypnotic reflexes as its main door. If neuroscientists are currently beginning to discover that such imitative reflexes are triggered by the mirroring structure of our neurons, then, it is time to realize that this is a rediscovery of preoccupations with automatic forms of imitation that already haunted the modernist imagination.

This realization, then, brings us back to the forms of authoritarian communication with which we started, but with a mimetic, unconscious principle to explain it. Lawrence agrees with the thinkers of mimesis considered thus far that this mimetic principle not only informs communication at the horizontal level, but also vertically ties the members of the group to the leader figure. In *The Plumed Serpent*, for instance, we have an account of Don Cipriano— Ramón's less-articulate Mexican double and military leader figure—that illustrates the political efficacy of the mimetic unconscious, opening up the question of mirroring reflexes neuroscientists study within the confines of the lab to the cultural sphere of politics. At the culminating point of a ritual dance, we read that Cipriano feels "surcharged with extraordinary power" (365):

> [H]e felt his limbs and his whole body immense with power, he felt the black mystery of power go out of him over all his soldiers. And he sat there imperturbable, in silence, holding all those black-eyed men in the splendour of his own, silent self. His own dark consciousness seemed to radiate through their flesh and their bones; they were conscious, not through

themselves but through him. And as a man's instinct is to shield his own head, so that instinct was to shield Cipriano, for he was the most precious part of themselves to them. It was in him they were supreme. They got their splendour from his power and their greatest consciousness was his consciousness diffusing them. (365)

This is a fictional representation of those ritual dances Lawrence witnessed in Mexico, with a political, authoritarian spin. It is predicated on a Dionysian, "primitivist" mimesis of which the hypnotized "modern" counterpart is but a pale, Apollonian copy. And yet despite the difference in evaluation, the model of the unconscious that underscores these two forms of mimesis is basically the same. Cipriano's power is communicated directly, without the intermediate of any *logos*, through an immediate bodily *pathos*, which spreads contagiously from the leader to the crowd. The affective result is that the soldiers' identification with the leader is so complete that not only their "consciousness," but also their "instincts," are no longer in their own control, but are stirred by the latter's willpower. In such a state, Lawrence suggests, even an involuntary reflex like "shielding [one's] own head" is converted, by the mimetic unconscious, into a shielding of the leader's head. Indeed, as it was also the case in Nietzsche's and Conrad's account of the crowd, these subjects' heads are no longer under the control of the ego, but of the phantom of the ego instead.

But if Lawrence reenacts Nietzsche's and Conrad's mimetic patho(-)logies, he also adds a personal touch to their understanding of the leader's will to power. Even in his worst authoritarian moments, Lawrence does not think that mimetic *power* is the only affect responsible for this wireless communication between the leader and the masses to flow. For Lawrence, that *tele-pathos* which is the will to power is Janus-faced: it can be achieved as effectively via hypnotic impression, as via "love" or "sympathy." Thus he writes:

> Man, whether in a savage tribe or in a complex modern society, is held in unison by these two great vibrations emitted unconsciously from the leader, the leaders, the governing classes, the authorities. First, the great influence or shadow of power, causing trust, fear, and obedience: second, the great influence of protective love, causing productivity and the sense of safety. (*K* 300)

Lawrence's double take on unconscious "vibrations" begs the following theoretical questions: Are "the shadow of power" and "protective love" mutually exclusive affects that flow across different channels? Is love or desire as he understands it different from tyrannical forms of mimetic will to power? Freud will ask the same questions and will answer affirmatively, as we shall see in the next chapter. As for Lawrence, Terry Eagleton argues that in his leadership period, he "rejects the 'female' principle of compassion and sexual intimacy for the 'male' principle of power," reminding us that a similar distinction between affects is at work in Lawrence's thought.[120] This is certainly true at the conceptual level of Lawrence's gendered polarized and essentialist metaphysics; hence his influence on "two" vibrations, one male the other female. Yet no matter how important this abstract, *metaphysical* distinction is for the stability of Lawrence's dualistic Weltanschauung, this passage also indicates that at the immanent *psychophysiological* level where the dissolution of the ego actually takes place, this distinction is much less stable than it appears to be. The fact that *both* power *and* love are part of what Lawrence calls "telepathic communication" or, alternatively, *rapport*, suggests that the mechanism that informs both (hypnotic) power and (sympathetic) love is predicated on different aspects of the same (mimetic) flux.

What emerges from this account is the hypothesis that, for Lawrence, desire, or what he also calls "the greater sex," is not essentially different from those affective states (trance, hypnosis, contagion, etc.) that we have grouped under the rubric of "mimesis." If this hypothesis is correct, then we could still speak, with Girard, of "mimetic desire" since the two affects are intimately related in Lawrence's account, but we would have to give this concept a different inflection. Lawrence would agree with Girard that these subjects do not desire "spontaneously," that their desires are "mediated," and that a figure of a "model" is necessary to "direct" their desire.[121] And yet Lawrence's emphasis is not on the fact that mimesis directs the subject's desires, that the subjects of the leader desire the desire of the model (though this mechanism certainly remains true). Rather, he suggests that mimesis and desire or, as Freud would call them, identification and object cathexis, are not neatly divided but are part of a pathos that flows through the channel of the mimetic unconscious. If this hypothesis is correct, then it would perhaps be useful to speak of *mimetic pathos* in order to designate a variety of contagious affects (including but not limited to desire) that have

the power to dissolve the modern ego in a river of psychic depersonalization. Such a concept, as we shall see in the conclusion, provides a possible
immanent alternative to models of the psyche that tend to frame affects in
ideal triangular forms. But let us consider the flows of mimetic pathos more
closely by zooming in on other unconscious communication that dissolves
the ideal boundaries of the old stable ego.

In Lawrence's fictional writings, intense moments of psychic dispossession and depersonalization occur, as a rule, at the climax of a dramatic resolution where the communicating, desiring subjects enter into an altered state
of consciousness that we would qualify as contagious, hypnotic, entranced,
or, more generally, mimetic. In *The Plumed Serpent*, for instance, Kate's first
contact with her bodily, sexual self (or soul) occurs in the context of those
ritual dances that turn men into "dark, collective men, non-individual" (131).
These individual dances have the power to dispossess subjects of control over
their ego and to cast a "spell on the mind" (120). Thus, we are told that as she
danced, "She was not herself, she was gone, and her own desires were gone in
the ocean of the great desire" (131). The great desire Kate experiences is not
confined to libido (though it is certainly libidinal), nor can it be read solely
in terms of mimetic desire (though it is certainly mimetic), but involves a
bodily, Corybantic, Dionysian pathos that, at least since Plato, is conjoined
with forms of mimetic dispossession.[122] Along similar lines, but via a different
technique, Ramón mesmerizes Cipriano by touching different centers of his
body and by asking trance-like, repetitive questions that have the effect of
plunging Cipriano in "bottomless deeps, like sleep": "Is it dark?" "Is the darkness alive?" "Is it dark in your heart?" (367–368). This is, indeed, a variation
of the hypnotic method to reach that state of psychic dissolution of the ego
which Lawrence, following Conrad, calls "the heart of darkness."

But then again, Lawrence adds a physical touch to this mimetic darkness. Thus, he specifies that after applying pressures on the eyes, breast, and
navel Ramón reaches the waist:

> Ramón knelt and pressed his arms close round Cipriano's waist, pressing
> his black head against his side. And Cipriano began to feel as if his mind,
> his head were melting away in the darkness . . . he was a man without a
> head, moving like a dark wind over the dark waters. . . . Who lives? Who—!
> Cipriano no longer knew. (368)

Who, then, is this ego, and what does he desire? Consciousness no longer knows, but the mimetic unconscious does. This scene, in fact, is shot through with libidinal, homoerotic affects and has explicit postorgasmic overtones: we are told that at the climax of this experience Ramón presses his body against Cipriano's waist and that thereafter "both men passed into perfect unconsciousness" (369). Ramón is here relying on a physical technique to establish a magnetic connection between self and other that Anton Mesmer and later practitioners of hypnosis called *rapport*.[123] Unsurprisingly, Lawrence will also speak of a "long, strange rapport" (*FU* 77), as well as of "hypnotic massage" (*WRA* 577) in order to make clear that he is operating within the tradition of the mimetic unconscious. While being mimetic, this unconscious state whereby the subject no longer knows "who lives" is not, strictly speaking, based on mimetic *desire* as Girard understands it—no matter how contagious the relation between the two men actually is. Rather, the magnetic, hypnotic, impersonal *rapport* Lawrence is describing entails a form of mimetic *pathos* that blurs the distinction between mimesis and desire. In sum, the Lawrentian unconscious is not founded on the idea of repression, nor is it structured like a language but is based on a mimetic hypothesis that looms large in the modern period and that posits the impersonal current of affective and infective pathos at the source of the modernist dissolution of the old stable ego.

Lawrence's early fascination for triangular structures of desire in early texts of Romantic inspiration such as *Sons and Lovers* is well known, has been abundantly discussed, and has gained him the Freudian title of "priest of sex." And yet as he enters deeper into the modernist period, the problematic of mimetic contagion—as it traverses his entire account of primitive cultures, modern cultures, the unconscious, and the dissolution of the ego it entails—while more central than ever, can no longer be contained within a single triangular structure but flows freely along the channels of mimetic pathos. To be sure, references to impersonal electric flows, magnetic rapport, and hypnotic currents are pervasive in Lawrence's psychological account of intersubjective forms of nonlinguistic communication. Thus, he speaks of the "long, strange rapport" that connects members of a family (*FU* 77), the child's "dynamic rapport with the objects of the outer universe" (121), and of the "great forces of magnetism and electricity" (172) that, he insists, are not only characteristic of sex but always flowing. Lawrence did not believe in an actual physical, magnetic fluid (or ether) connecting subjects; he uses these terms metaphorically, for lack of better terms. It is thus true, as Torgovnick puts it, that Lawrence "had no adequate vocabulary for expressing his [psychological] ideals"; yet this is not so much because he was "filled with the language and ideas of Freudian psychology"[124] but, rather, because he relies on a psychological language that is no longer familiar to a generation of Freudian literary critics.[125] From Nietzsche to Conrad, via crowd psychology, religious anthropology, and psychophysiology, we have repeatedly seen that thinkers of mimesis are forced to rely on the old Platonic metaphor of magnetism in order to account for such affective rapports that break down the distinction between self and other(s). The terminology is, indeed, loose, and the precise dynamic of this nonlinguistic communication continues to escape us. Yet these authors agree that an affective communication that induces a psychic dissolution of the boundaries of individuation—whether we call it trance, possession, rapport, hypnosis, or mimesis—cannot be relegated to archaic, primitive, or pathological subjects, but is constitutive of modernist accounts of the mimetic unconscious.

I find it astonishing that so much has been said about Lawrence as a priest of love and sex, while the mimetic affects that all too obviously inform his conception of communication are hardly ever mentioned as belonging to his conception of the modern ego, let alone analyzed in detail. John Vickery is, to my knowledge, the only critic who stresses that "Lawrence probably describes more characters as 'spell-bound' and does so more repeatedly than any other writer of recent times."[126] Vickery sees this fascination with "spells" and "swoons" as part of Lawrence's debt to Frazer's theory of magic. Magic, as we have seen, is indeed important in Lawrence's conception of the spellbound ego, but religious anthropology is not the only door that gives access to Lawrence's account of the fluid, allotropic, suggestible ego or, as he prefers to call it, "soul." In fact, as the vertebral conception of the unconscious he relies on and the states of hypnotic communication and dispossession that ensue clearly indicate, it is because Lawrence is in line with the long-neglected tradition of the mimetic unconscious that his conception of the ego is vulnerable to spellbound states. And given the pervasiveness of these states in Lawrence's works, I think it is safe to say that the mimetic unconscious functions as the *via regia* to the Lawrentian dissolution of the ego.

In addition to what we have already seen, it would be easy to multiply examples where the main characters in Lawrence's fiction fall prey to different sorts of hypnotic spells that induce trance, possession, somnambulism, and other mesmerized states. Most often Lawrence's heroes are endowed with the power to cast hypnotic spells over weaker, suggestible egos. Examples of this category, which always verge on the didactic, pervade all the political novels and late theoretical texts we have analyzed, but also *The Fox* and, to different degrees, short stories such as "The Lady Who Rode Away," "You Touched Me," and "None of That." In such texts, usually the male character induces in female subjects a state analogous to sleep that deprives the latter of control over her ego in order to achieve his own egotistic, patriarchal, and often phallocentirc ends. Here we find, at the micro-level, an actualization of the authoritarian mimetic will to power we have condemned as ethically and politically *pathological*. The second case concerns Lawrence's *critique* of characteristically modern forms of hypnotic will to power that deprive subjects of the ability to think, paradoxically, by locating consciousness exclusively in the mind. In addition to *Aaron's Rod*, "Mother and Daughter," and "The Princess," perhaps the best example of a mentally induced hypnotic/telepathic state geared towards the materialist ends Lawrence condemns is "The Rocking-Horse Winner," a short story where hypnotic dispossession induced mechanically by the rocking movement of a wooden horse is responsible for the development of a telepathic, materialistic ethos that leads directly to the subject's demise. This is part of Lawrence's patho-*logical* critique of modern forms of mimetic dispossession. Finally, Lawrence's work continuously strives towards an intersubjective dissolution of the self predicated on a more consensual, yet never fully egalitarian, mimetic relation. *Lady Chatterley's Lover*, "The Blind Man," "The Horse-Dealer's Daughter," and *The Ladybird* can be seen as examples of this rapport. In the latter, for instance, despite Lawrence's insistence on the need for totalitarian leader figures, the protagonist's narrative perspective (all too obviously called Dionys) gives us an insight into the process that leads his "ladybird" to "relax" and "open out the dark depths, the dark, dilated pupil" (*Fox* 182). Dionys's song, in the end, succeeds in calling his ladybird "out of herself" and inducing a state of "bewitched sleep," throwing a "kind of swoon upon her" (214) that eventually engulfs both in "the darkness inside the room which seemed alive like blood" (215). In such states, the pathos of mimesis affects the communicating subjects so deeply that there is no longer an "ego" left to communicate with an "other" who is *perceived* as other. Instead, what we have is a dark, affective vibration whereby the whole organism is, indeed, *erregt*, and which allows the communicating subjects to *experience* the current of affects that flow freely from one body to the other—contagious affects that dissolve the ego in a darkness that is no longer the source of horror, but of ecstasy instead.

From a transdisciplinary, patho-*logical* perspective this Lawrentian insistence on a dissolution of the ego into a more fluid entity that he calls "soul" should not come as a surprise. These allotropic transformations whereby the solid form of the ego is dissolved in a river of blood consciousness are perfectly in line with a mimetic conception of the unconscious that considers the "subject" vulnerable to psychic forms of depersonalization. As we have repeatedly seen, for Lawrence the soul, whether it is part of anthropological rituals, modern crowds, or truly intersubjective rapports, is not a monadic, self-enclosed unity but rather is a permeable, affective, relational, and extremely sensitive entity that, for better or worse, is open to the pathos of the other. Gilles Deleuze is thus right to say that Lawrence's immanent conception of the soul is part of a "physics of relations."[127] And René Girard is equally right to speak of the "quasiosmotic immediacy" of mimesis.[128] What we can add is that this osmotic, mimetic physics is not "pure and simple sexuality" (Deleuze), nor can it be channeled in the "universal structure" of desire (Girard) but rather is animated by the immanent, spiraling patho(-)logical movement of mimetic pathos that composes, decomposes, and recomposes the vibration of mimetic relations in the modernist period (Lawrence).

As we have seen and perhaps felt too, subjectivity for Lawrence is a fluid, dynamic, magnetic, hypnotic, and above all contagious pathos that crosses, like a current, the boundaries of individuation, opening up the possibility of becoming other. His work constantly reminds us of the ethical and political dangers of such an opening, as well as of the ontological and psychological implications of its closure. It also reminds us of the liberating potential of the current of mimetic pathos that traverses the old stable ego and, like a solvent, opens its boundaries to the outside. Whether this ego has its intimate being interior to the self, in its exterior, or in the moment of communication between interior and exterior is a question that, if addressed by Lawrence's work, is not fully answered. Instead, he openly acknowledges that there is "an infinite range of subtle communication which we know nothing about" (*P*

193), encouraging us to pursue our investigation in the heterogeneous work of our last thinker of mimesis, a transgressive and affective thinker whose take on intersubjective forms of unconscious communication has the power to turn the celebrated postmodern death of the linguistic subject into an untimely modernist rebirth of a mimetic ego: the French writer and theorist Georges Bataille.

CHAPTER 4

Bataille's Mimetic Communication

[Y]ou ought to learn how to laugh, my young friends. . . . Then, perhaps, as laughers, you may some day dispatch all metaphysical comforts to the devil—metaphysics in front.

—Friedrich Nietzsche, *The Birth of Tragedy*

Phantom Matador

The opening chapter of D. H. Lawrence's *The Plumed Serpent* (1926), entitled "Beginnings of a Bull-fight," stages a repellent, yet disturbingly fascinating spectacle. Newly arrived in Mexico City, the novel's protagonist, Kate Leslie, finds herself attending a bullfight in the company of Owen, an American acquaintance who is convinced he will find in such "native" spectacles the roots of "Life" itself. Lawrence describes the climax of this dramatic scene in cinematic detail. In an instant of lacerating violence, the bull's horns hit one of the horses from below:

> Down went the horse, collapsing in front, but his rear was still heaved up, with the bull's horn working vigorously up and down inside him, while he

lay on his neck all twisted. And a huge heap of bowels coming out. And a
nauseous stench. And the cries of pleased amusement among the crowd.
. . . When [Kate] looked again, it was to see the horse feebly and dazedly
walking out of the ring, with a great ball of its own entrails hanging out of
its abdomen and swinging reddish against its own legs as it automatically
moved. (*ps* 18; 16)

The pathos of such a horrifying spectacle communicates itself contagiously to
the spectators and triggers the most contradictory emotional reactions. We
read that the "shock of amazement almost made [Kate] lose consciousness"
(16). And indeed, Lawrence makes clear that it is not only a visual "shock"
that she is confronted with: "the smell of blood, a nauseous whiff of bursten
bowels" infiltrates her being, so that the European lady is not only forced
to "turn her face away" (16), but also to leave, in disgust, lest she throw up.
"Good bye! I can't smell anymore of this stink," she exclaims, out of an intimately felt repugnance, and sets out to put herself at a maximum distance
from the pathetic spectacle, fighting her way through the enthusiastic crowd
which, we are told, is "surging in in waves (20). Owen, on the other hand, does
not budge. Emotionally at one with the collective movement composed of the
"mongrel men of Mexico city," he finds himself "like a guilty boy spellbound"
by what he considers a "delightful spectacle" (19). The contrast in emotional
responses with respect to this abject scene could not be more sharply delineated: if Kate is convinced that participating in such a show is like enjoying
"somebody else's diarrhoea" (19), Owen, while being "as nearly in hysterics as
Kate . . . was convinced that this was life. He was seeing LIFE" (19).

Sacrificial blood, stinking bowels, diarrhea, hysteria, collective effervescence, mob behavior, instants of spellbound fascination, and shocks of disgust,
all this in the context of a novel invested in recuperating the sacred aspect of
life via the will to power of authoritarian leaders. Indeed, Lawrence's dramatization of the affective forces at stake in this violent spectacle would have found
Georges Bataille's theoretical and emotional approval. Not only the base
subject matter, but also the structural and emotional oscillations that drive
Lawrence's characters towards/away from sacred forms of mimetic horrors,
constitute the raw material upon which Bataille never ceased to meditate.[1]

Throughout his polymorphous career as an emotional philosopher, sacred
anthropologist, and pathological psychologist, Bataille persistently attempts

to get as close as possible to the sacred dimension of "Life," which for him, as for Owen, is most tangible in such bloody and stinking spectacles. From his early literary and theoretical fascination with heterology, to his later meditations on sacrifice, erotism, and transgression, there is, indeed, a lot in Bataille's corpus that is reminiscent of a "spellbound boy" irresistibly attracted to the pathos of the sacred. And yet throughout his writings we also find something of Kate's intimately felt disgust; a kind of repulsion and need for distance, which is as visceral as it is critical, and forces Bataille to recognize that the spectacle of "Life" is, after all, nothing but the horror of death. This movement of "attraction and repulsion" (1, 347), as he calls it, is yet another variation of that modernist pathos of distance that swings the mimetic ego towards / away from the heterogeneous power of mimesis. But then again, Bataille specifies that he cannot rest content with the position of an ambivalent spectator, situated on the safe side of visual representation, coke and popcorn in his hands, ready to be horrified or thrilled by all kinds of tragic shows. What is at stake in his writings stems from the affective turmoil located at the heart of what he calls his "lived *affective* experience" (1, 348). In this sense, we could say that Bataille's subject position is, metaphorically speaking, also similar to that of the bull. "A bull in the bullfight," as he himself puts it in *Inner Experience* (1943), that "seized with rage, . . . rushes forth upon the void which a phantom matador [*matador fantôme*] opens before it without respite" (*IE* 92).

The boy, the lady, and the bull are all *en jeu* in Bataille's communicative thought—a thought set in motion by an unconscious, spellbound attraction to violent forms of mimetic *pathos* (the boy), the counterbalancing critical *distance* that ensues (the lady), and is kept going, back and forth, animated by an automatic repetition of the same gesture, which Bataille is compelled to reenact ad infinitum (the bull). Whether Bataille finds himself among heterogeneous crowds, in tragic and comic dramas, laughter, tears, in erotism, ecstasy, drunkenness, trance, or at the instant of sacrificial death, he persistently confronts a different manifestation of the same *matador fantôme*: a mimetic, sacrificial phantom that has the force to penetrate and lacerate the boundaries of the ego, to deprive it of a sense of proper identity, and to expose it to that impersonal, metaphysical ground which, for Bataille, is real Life, death, or Being itself.

Bataille's thought on contagious, affective and infective forces runs along his entire oeuvre insofar as he never ceased to meditate on the power of

sovereign forms of communication to transgress the boundaries of individuation.[2] Animated by a theoretical ambition that supplements both his own and
Lawrence's dramatic representations, Bataille turns to consider such different
(*hetero*) materials via a theoretical discourse (*logos*) that is directly concerned
with the question of mimetic affects (*pathos*). It is true that Bataille, like Lawrence before him, is not usually considered a thinker of mimesis, but a thinker
of erotism instead. But it is equally true that erotism, as Bataille understands
it, is far from being indifferent to the unconscious power of mimetic pathos.
Like Lawrence, Bataille is a cultural theorist concerned with the power of
charismatic leader figures, massive phenomena of mimetic contagion, and
various states of psychic depersonalization characteristic of the phantom of
the ego. In this sense, Bataille confirms the Girardian realization that mimesis
is contagious and leads to forms of sacrificial violence such as those we have
just seen Lawrence dramatize. Moreover, he also offers us a characteristically
modernist insight into the affective reasons (or patho-logies) responsible for
the contagiousness of mimesis itself (or pathology), and he does so along
patho(-)logical lines that anticipate contemporary developments in mimetic
theory. Continuing a transdisciplinary line of investigation characteristic of
the Nietzschean current in modernism I follow, Bataille explicitly engages
with disciplines as diverse as philosophy, religious anthropology, crowd
psychology, psychoanalysis, psychophysiology, and, last but not least, Pierre
Janet's psychological analysis in order to account for the unconscious reflexes
at work in mimetic forms of communication.

Unearthing the heterogeneous foundations of Bataille's account of
sovereign communication will not only help us clarify this voluntarily disor-
dered thought. It will also force us to realize that even this much-discussed
precursor of the so-called postmodern death of the subject (the subject of
the signifier) is a faithful descendant of a Nietzschean tradition concerned
with the modernist birth to the ego, out of the reflex of unconscious communications (the subject of mimesis). This point aligns Bataille with current
realizations that mimesis is more formative of the ego than previous psychoanalytical accounts had realized. As we will see, the French theorist *avant
la lettre* who is Georges Bataille extends the modernist diagnostic of the
mimetic unconscious to the postmodern insight that the ego can no longer
be contained within a single, homogeneous, and quite unitary mirror frame,
but shatters this mirror, and the metaphysics it entails, with a contagious

outburst of laughter. But before turning to this gay effusion we need to diagnose the infected side of Bataille's mimetic patho(-)logy.

Enlightening Fascist Psychology

In the early 1930s, Bataille turns to consider those aspects of human life that are
"excluded" by the principle of capitalist production (i.e., the "homogeneous"),
insofar as they are utterly useless, involve an excess of irrational, violent energy
that is mindlessly wasted, and generate feelings of attraction and repulsion
that cannot be accounted for in rational terms (i.e., the "heterogeneous").
Bataille includes in this category those abject, mimetic elements Lawrence
dramatized in the bullfight scene, as well as other heterogeneous matters
that, for him, are "the object of every affective reaction" (1, 346–347). The
reader of the early texts on heterology is, indeed, not spared any of Bataille's
theoretical and affective patho(-)logies. These include sacrificial animals,
blood, defecation, urination, menstruation, sperm, rotting bodies, cannibal-
ism, but also sobbing, dreams, neurosis, madness, and laughter. Despite the
theoretical frame he attempts to construe, the reader often has the impression
that Bataille, at this early stage in his career, is not in a position to control his
base subject matter. He vomits it out, in unstructured, amorphous lists, which
seem to betray a need for cathartic purgation, an expulsion through writing of
pathological unconscious forces that, at this time, were threatening to undo
the homogeneity of his psychic life. This is, indeed, the diagnosis of André
Breton, the champion of surrealism and Bataille's main rival at the time. In his
Second Manifesto of Surrealism (1929), in fact, Breton, relying on his medical
training, diagnoses Bataille's obsessions as "pathological" and implicitly suggests that he was in need of a cure[3]—a suggestion that Bataille did not actually
need, as he had already come to the same conclusion.

Story of the I

It is thus possible to trace Bataille's theory of heterology back to a personal
psychic pathology. This direction of inquiry is encouraged by certain biographical confessions in his (according to Breton) "pathological" literary
writings. For instance, in a postscript to his first literary work, *Histoire de l'œil*

(1928), written while he was undergoing a psychoanalysis with Dr. Adrien Borel, Bataille (under the pseudonym of Lord Auch) gives an account of a familial drama that he does not hesitate to qualify as "the most loaded event of [his] childhood" (176). The passage is worth quoting at length, for both its affective content and the structure that informs it:

> During puberty, the affection for my father turned into an unconscious aversion. I suffered less from his screams caused by the pain of tabes. . . . The dirty, stinking state to which he was frequently reduced by his incapacities (he often shat in his underpants) was not as unpleasant to me. I adopted in all things opposed attitudes and opinions to his.
>
> One night, my mother and I were woken by a speech of the poxy invalid who was quite literally screaming words of inordinate violence in his room. He had suddenly gone insane. I went to fetch the doctor, who came immediately. . . . The doctor had gone into the next room with my mother when the madman bawled out, in a booming voice: "Tell me, Doctor when you have finished fucking my wife!" He was laughing. This sentence destroyed all the effects of a strict upbringing and left me in a horrible, hilarious state, the constant obligation to find in my life and my thoughts its equivalences. (176–177)

Lacerating pain, the stench of human feces and urine, but also madness, proximity to death, sexuality, unconscious reflexes, the breaking of taboos, and laughter! Bataille will, indeed, remain faithful to his project of finding, in his life and thought, the affective and theoretical "equivalence" of the heterogeneous forces at work in this primal scene. But thematic obsessions are not the only issue here. What this scene seems to stage is also the psychic, personal origin of a structural mechanism of attraction and repulsion that will continue to animate Bataille's corpus. Bataille's attitude towards the heterogenous elements embodied by his father figure pulls the subject between contradictory imperatives: Affection and aversion, spellbound fascination and disgusted repulsion, or as he will later put it, "transgression" and "taboo," are clearly linked to the heterogeneous father figure. Not only the content, then, but also the structural movement of the forces characteristic of heterology seem clearly based on a personal mimetic pathology.

This should come as no surprise. Modernist authors of Nietzschean

Interesting [handwritten marginal note]

inspiration have already alerted us to the fact that the boundaries between personal and collective psychology tend to be permeable to the infectious power of mimetic sickness. As the "cases" of Nietzsche, Conrad, and Lawrence already taught us, mimetic pathologies tend to transgress familial boundaries in order to infect these thinkers' social and political considerations. Nietzsche's celebration of the master's will to power, Marlow's enthusiastic fascination with the charismatic Kurtz, and Lawrence's dramatization of leader figures can all be rooted in a personal vulnerability to the affective power of mimesis, which, in turn, bleeds into their respective accounts of sociality. Such a permeability between the personal and the collective, experience and theory, is even clearer in Bataille's case: a thinker who, from the very beginning, explicitly relies on what he calls "lived, *affective* experience" (1, 348) in order to directly account for his spellbound relation to the heterogeneous power of fascist leader figures. In "The Psychological Structure of Fascism" (1933/1934), for instance, Bataille makes clear that he is still concerned with the heterogeneous matters that preoccupied him during adolescence. "The waste product of the human body and certain analogous matter" (1, 346), "delirium," and "madness" are still the source of ambivalence insofar as they generate "as much attraction as repulsion" (1, 347). However, if he previously connected these heterogeneous elements to his personal father figure, he now associates them with political father figures. Thus, he writes that "fascist leaders are incontestably part of heterogeneous existence." And he adds: "Opposed to democratic politicians, who represent in different countries the platitude inherent in homogenous society, Mussolini and Hitler stand out as something *totally other* [*tout autres*]" (1, 348). Such statements make clear that as Bataille shifts his consideration of heterology from the familial to the political sphere, from personal to collective psychology, his personal pathology bleeds into his critical patho-logy and risks compromising, from the beginning, both his political stance and his status as a critical thinker.[4]

Given Bataille's personal implication in the heterogeneous forces he struggles to analyze, he often fails to preserve the critical distance necessary for an impartial investigation of fascist psychology. In fact, as he pitches the squandering "heterogeneous" force of fascist leaders against the "homogenous," productive dimension of capitalism, "Mussolini and Hitler" against "democratic politicians," it is clear that the former are the source of fascination, while democracy is deemed by him "peaceful but fastidious" (1, 348).

In 1933, while no longer a boy, Bataille is indeed spellbound by the power of attraction inherent in such heterogeneous father figures who dominate the public arena; and, at least in part, he capitulates to the emotional forces he struggles to dissect. The phantom of fascism, it would be useless to deny, does indeed cast a shadow on Bataille's early career.[5]

The Seduction of Mimesis

In a way, Bataille only makes explicit an epistemological danger that we have been facing all along. As it was already the case with Lawrence, Conrad, and before them, Nietzsche, these modernist writers fall within the category of what Jean-Michel Besnier, thinking of Bataille, calls "the emotive intellectual": that is, a writer who "pursues every occasion which facilitates pathos" and as a consequence "lets himself be possessed by all the situations offered to [the] experience of limitlessness" such a pathos opens up.[6] Since Bataille is the last link in the chain of mimetic thinkers I consider, his direct implication in fascist psychology is problematic: it threatens not only to obscure at the outset his patho-*logical* insights into the workings of collective contagion, but also to cast a retrospective shadow that risks compromising the entire mimetic tradition I have been struggling with throughout this study. Insofar as modernist writers succumb, at some point, to the seduction of mimesis, they inevitably make themselves vulnerable to the accusation of "irrationalists" who are easily led astray by the seductive power of unreason. This, at least, is the critical position expressed by advocates of the philosophical tradition of the Enlightenment.

Jürgen Habermas, one of the most influential opponents of the modern philosophical tradition of which Bataille is one of the most influential recent representatives, rightly denounces the latter's "fascinated excitement" and "admiration" for the power of fascist leader figures.[7] Habermas's critique focuses on Bataille, but he is careful to situate the French thinker in a wider theoretical context. Thus, he observes that "there was no theory of contemporaneity not affected to its core by the penetrating force of fascism." And he adds, "this holds true especially of the theories that were in the formative period in the 1920s and early 1930s."[8] What is at stake in his account of modernity is, thus, not only a critique of individual thinkers, singular "cases" in the history of philosophy, but also, and more fundamentally, a severe evaluation of the underlying theoretical tradition that informs these thinkers. And in the opening paragraph of his chapter on Bataille, Habermas clearly indicates what is, for him, the root of the problem. As he puts it, his critique is explicitly directed at those theorists who have taken up what he calls "the impossible heritage of Nietzsche as a critic of ideology."[9]

It should be clear by now that this study is far from being inimical to these critiques of Bataille in particular and of the Nietzschean tradition in general. Throughout previous chapters, we have repeatedly seen that insofar as thinkers of the irrational succumb to the mimetic affects they struggle to dissect, a severe critique is definitively in order. This task, I have argued, is particularly urgent at those moments when modernist authors seem to promote the cause of authoritarian politics. A spellbound, affective fascination for the will to power of charismatic leaders, whether among enthusiastic crowds or enthusiastic thinkers, must be the object of a careful patho-*logical* dissection that does not refrain from drawing severe diagnostic evaluations. Thus, insofar as the authors I examine have capitulated to the power of (mimetic) unreason, I have tried not only to unmask their authoritarian tendencies, but also, and perhaps more importantly, to account for the affective/conceptual logic—or mimetic patho(-)logy—responsible for their capitulation. In short, the study at hand promotes the necessity for a rational critique of the weak, infected, or "distasteful political debilities" at work in the Nietzschean tradition of Counter-Enlightenment.[10]

And yet there is another side to this heritage that proponents of an enlightened critique of the Nietzschean tradition fail take into consideration. Namely, that thinkers of the irrational are not only victims of the power of mimesis—"irrationalist" thinkers who are passively carried away by the "seduction of unreason." They are also part of a much older critical tradition that actively struggles to rigorously understand and evaluate, with all the tools of critical and extracritical reason, the process of mimetic seduction in which they are affectively implicated. As we have seen, this patho-*logical* countermovement involves a critique of unconscious forms of mimesis that anticipates the horrors of fascism and Nazism. And if we consider that the theoretical origins of this modern critique of mimetic contagion can be traced back to the beginning of philosophy in Plato's *Republic* and stretches ahead so as to include contemporary discoveries in the neurosciences, then, perhaps, dismissing this project as "impossible critique of ideology" is not only a hasty, uncritical move but also risks compromising the theoretical foundations and destination of the tradition of Enlightenment itself.

It is true that Habermas is willing to acknowledge the role of mimesis in the problematic of fascism. In the context of his critique of Bataille, for instance, he writes that "fascism uses the mimetic behavior (eliminated by civilization) for its own purpose."[11] Habermas is here implicitly following Horkheimer and Adorno's claim in *The Dialectic of the Enlightenment* (1944) that "all pretexts over which the Führer and his followers reach agreement, imply surrender to the mimetic attraction."[12] And indeed, both critical theorists consider "civilization" an attempt to outlaw uncontrolled forms of mimetic behavior—this is part of what they call the "program of the Enlightenment." Yet Adorno and Horkheimer's point is that historical reality deviated from the program. In the context of their critique of fascism, for instance, they recognize that "the mimetic impulse can never be completely destroyed."[13] And for this reason, like Nietzsche before them, they take very seriously the mythic dimension of fascist mimesis. The founders of critical theory, then, agree that what appears at first sight to be irrational has not lost its magical effectiveness. Habermas, on the other hand, is much more confident that mimetic behavior is, as he puts it, "eliminated by civilization." Hence, not only does he refuse to account for the affective, irrational power generated by fascist rituals and propaganda, but he also dismisses this aspect as the superficial manifestation of fascism. For Habermas, in fact, "the cultic honouring of leaders as sacral personages, the artfully staged mass rituals, the manifestly violent and hypnotic elements" are nothing but "the show aspect of Fascist leadership" or, as he also puts it, "the psychological surface of fascism."[14] The affective power of mimesis we have been struggling with throughout is, thus, excluded by Habermas's account; or, at best, it is treated as a puppet show of no real significance.

This is where Bataille radically disagrees. In fact, he makes clear that the refusal to acknowledge the potential of violent (heterogeneous) affects at the heart of civilization marks the limit of an objective (homogenous) science that situates itself at a safe distance from the contagious power of mimetic affects. As Bataille puts it, "the *heterogeneous* elements that are excluded from the latter [i.e., homogeneity] are equally excluded from the field of scientific investigation: as a rule, science cannot know *heterogeneous* elements as such" (1, 344). If Habermas's rationalist perspective neatly falls within the boundaries of homogeneous science, Bataille sides with the mimetic tradition that concerns us—from Plato to Girard, via Nietzsche and Lacoue-Labarthe—and argues that the mimetic contagion at work in modern crowds does not magically disappear as we turn our back to it. As he puts in *On Nietzsche* (1945), "at the moment I write, to transcend the crowd is like spitting in the air" (VI, 173). Thus, he cautions us against the temptation of positing a clear-cut distinction between "civilization and barbarism." As he puts it in *Erotism* (1957): "the use of these words is misleading, for they imply that there are barbarians on the one hand and civilized men on the other." And he goes on to remind us of the basic yet fundamental fact that "all civilized men are capable of savagery" (*E* 86). Moreover, in one of the lectures at the Collège de Sociologie (1937–1939) he already is aware of the disturbing effects of mimesis. Thus, he observes in dismay that "Adolf Hitler was chosen among 75 millions of his fellow men" (*Soc.* 22). Bataille does not offer easy answers to such a disconcerting fact. Yet he observes that fascist rituals generate "currents of an extreme intensity" that have the power to dilute the average subject (what Bataille calls "the man among thousand") in an impersonal mass where the individual (from Latin, *individuus*, indivisible) "does not count more than a molecule of water projected from within a powerful wave" (30–31). With the benefit of historical hindsight on the horrors of the twentieth century, Bataille's following request should sound quite reasonable: "what I ask here with insistence, is that these currents be studied" (23).[15]

Insofar as Bataille is a thinker who consciously exploits his unconscious vulnerability to mimetic contagion as a diagnostic lens to unmask the affects that overtake him as well as others, he is working within the modernist tradition of mimetic theory that concerns us. Far from being based on "an aversion to reason,"[16] Bataille's analysis of violent, heterogeneous affects is located precisely in that spiraling, patho(-)logical movement where an affective implication in the phenomenon observed serves as the necessary condition for a critical logos on pathos to emerge. This methodological principle is clearly expressed in the opening paragraph of "The Psychological Structure of Fascism" as he makes clear that his method of analysis reposes on both "lived states" (*états vécus*) and "rigorous representation" (*représentation rigoureuse*) (1, 339), affective pathos and critical distance. Or, as he will later put it: "I have personally felt it necessary to accept the difficulties of both paths, the path of transgression as well as the path of work" (*E* 261).

Bataille's active critique of the modern subject of *Aufklärung* involves a direct confrontation with the irrational force that ties the masses to fascist leaders and vice versa in the Europe of the 1920s, 1930s, and 1940s. His account of the "mysterious force" (1, 345) that haunts the house of modernism transgresses neat distinctions between modern and primitive people, personal and social pathologies, as well as disciplinary boundaries between philosophy, sociology, anthropology, psychoanalysis, and crowd psychology. Bataille's transdisciplinary perspective is, thus, in line with the increasingly heterogeneous world in which modernists live, write, and think. It also offers us new and valuable insights into the unconscious process that turns the ego into a phantom of the ego in a world where sacred outbreaks of ritual effervescence can no longer be relegated to the jungle, or the madhouse, but literally take possession of the European body politic itself.

Anthropological Effervescence

It is common for the modernist writers I examine to refer to cultural, gendered, and racial "otherness" in order to account for the effect of the mimetic will to power of charismatic leader figures on the modern ego. Nietzsche's approach to "hysteria" remains gender biased; and both Conrad and Lawrence partake of an evolutionary anthropological model that tends to initially displace irrational, contagious affects onto racial others, stressing the natives' vulnerability to the "religious pathos" of European leader figures. And yet we have equally seen that for these writers, sexist and racist ethnocentric moves, which consider the mimetic subject always to be the "other," boomerang against the modern subject of *Aufklärung*—a subject who despite its "civilized" status, "restraint," and "ideal beliefs" proves to be no less vulnerable to the contagious force of violence. Bataille continues this modernist line of investigation as he turns his anthropological lenses toward the reemergence of enthusiastic outbursts of mimetic pathos at the heart of Europe.

Well before founding the Collège de Sociologie with Roger Caillois and Michel Leiris in 1937, intended to promote the study of the sacred in contemporary societies, Bataille, not unlike Girard after him, considered that the insights of the French school of anthropology into "primitive" cultures could be used to frame his understanding of the emergence of fascist psychology in "modern" culture. Thus, in "The Psychological Structure of Fascism" (1933/1934) he relies on Émile Durkheim's seminal distinction between the "sacred" and the "profane" in order to distinguish between two radically opposed spheres: the "homogenous," characterized by work, productivity, and rationality, on the one hand, and the "heterogeneous," defined by expenditure, violence, irrational affects, and collective effervescence, on the other. Bataille thus agrees with Girard that "there is a lot to learn . . . from Durkheim's idea of a collective *effervescence*."[17] Moreover, in order to account for what he calls the "mysterious force" characteristic of fascist leader figures (*meneurs fascistes*), Bataille also follows Henri Hubert and Marcel Mauss's accounts of magic in general and of the Polynesian notion of *mana* in particular.[18] As Bataille explains: "*Mana* designates a mysterious and impersonal force possessed by certain individuals such as kings and sorcerers" (1, 345). And he adds: "the heterogeneous element is assumed to be charged with an unknown and dangerous force (recalling the Polynesian mana)" (1, 346). If "primitive" cultures relied on their kings and magicians to turn the homogeneous sphere of work into the heterogeneous sphere of collective effervescence, Bataille realizes that "modern" societies rely on their fascist leaders. Like "mana personalities," he writes, the latter are "manifestly treated by their followers as sacred persons" (1, 349). And in order to make clear that these figures are "totally other" and that magical forces can no longer be confined to archaic societies, he adds: "it is impossible not to be conscious of the force that situates them above men, parties, and even laws" (1, 348).

The Force of Mana

What, then, is this mysterious, magical force that, for Bataille, is responsible for the leader's affective power over the modern masses? Why should it be considered "immanent," given its apparent transcendent, religious character? And, more crucially, what is its importance for the general economy of Bataille's thought and for the modernist take on mimetic theory? Reading Bataille's scattered references to Hubert and Mauss, one cannot help but wondering if he does not rely on the notion of *mana* for lack of a more precise terminology to account for the contagious power of the leader, using the language of "the natives" to mask a theoretical failure to account for this language in more precise, anthropological terms.[19] After all, *mana* is as elusive a term as one can find in anthropological literature. Mauss and Hubert, in the context of their theory of magic, had been discontented with what they called the "obscure and vague" status of this notion, characterized by a grammatical instability that opens up multiple semantic possibilities.[20] Functioning as an adjective, noun, and verb, the signifier *mana* has different signifieds including "power of the magician, magical quality of a thing, magical thing, magical being, to possess magical power, being charmed, acting magically."[21] The Polynesian *mana*, as Claude Lévi-Strauss will later say in his influential introduction to Mauss, is similar to the French *truc* or *machin*: a signifier that can signify virtually everything and that, as a consequence, means nothing in particular, a "floating signifier" endowed with "zero symbolic value."[22]

This said, Bataille's reading of Mauss's theory of *mana* is not mediated by Lévi-Strauss's structural/linguistic approach, but is guided by his own heterogeneous interest in the affective and contagious dimension of such a force. This also means that Bataille is less likely to focus on the linguistic *formal* indeterminacy of this elusive signifier (what Lévi-Strauss's calls "simple form") than on the immediate emotional *referent* of Hubert and Mauss's account of ritual (what Bataille calls "affective unification"). In this sense, Girard's interest in what he calls the *immédiateté du vécu* that structuralism disavowed in favor of discontinuity and differentiation[23] is directly in line with Bataille's ritual focus on what he calls "l'expérience vécue *affective*" and the "continuity of being" it entails. From this immanent perspective, a second look at Hubert and Mauss's definitions of *mana* shows that this notion, while elusive, is not as vague as it initially appears to be. Here are some of the defining characteristics of *mana* as the two French anthropologists understand it:

> It is a spiritual force, that is, a force that does not act mechanically and that produces effects from a distance. Mana is the force of the magician. . . . It is because the magician and the rite have *mana* that they can act on the mana-spirits, conjure them, command them, and possess them.[24]

This force is "transferable and contagious," and they add that

> it legitimizes the power of the magician, it justifies the necessity of formal acts, the creative virtue of words, sympathetic connections, transfers of

qualities and influences. . . . In sum, mana is first of all an action of a certain type. *It is a spiritual action at a distance that is produced between sympathetic beings. It is equally a sort of ether, imponderable and communicable.*[25]

In their attempt to pin down the magical referents of *mana*, Hubert and Mauss are directly echoing accounts of sympathetic magic we are by now familiar with.[26] While refraining from situating their theory within this tradition, the two anthropologists find themselves aligned with the mimetic terminology that is so pervasive at the turn of the century. From Nietzsche to Le Bon, Conrad to Tarde, D. H. Lawrence to Burrow, Bataille to Mauss, this terminology emerges to account for that contagious phenomenon of psychic dispossession which Plato already called mimesis.[27]

I hasten to add that if I consider mimetic affects to be constitutive of ancient, primitive, and now modern cultures, my intention is not to conflate different cultural manifestations of such affects, nor to treat the theoretical discourses in which such affects are framed as interchangeable. Rather, my goal is to articulate the continuities and discontinuities between different mimetic traditions in order to reach a better understanding of Bataille's account of the "mysterious force" of fascist leaders in particular, and sovereign forms of communication in general. In order to continue to do so, let us recall that, in the first chapter, we shifted from the ancient notion of *mimesis* to the modern notion of *hypnosis* on the basis of the Nietzschean recognition that the two concepts can be treated as complementary, if not as synonymous. I now operate a similar theoretical shift from *mana* to *mimesis* on the basis of yet another authoritative figure for Bataille's understanding of fascist psychology in general and anthropological accounts of mimesis in particular.

In *The Elementary Forms of Religious Life* (1912), Émile Durkheim, the founder of the French school of sociology, returns to consider Hubert and Mauss's account of *mana* in the context of a discussion of Australian totemism. "In Melanesia and in Polynesia," Durkheim writes, "people say that an influential man has *mana*, and impute his influence to this."[28] And in order to explain the origins of this "anonymous and impersonal force" and the process whereby the "psychic energy immanent in the idea we have of [a] person [who] makes us bend our will and incline our compliance," Durkheim takes the example of "the special attitude of the man who speaks in a crowd." As he puts it:

His language has a kind of grandiloquence that would be absurd in ordinary circumstances; his gestures are overbearing; his thought itself is impatient with order and easily becomes carried away in all sorts of extreme pronouncements. He feels filled to overflowing with an over-abundance of forces that spill out around him. Sometimes he even feels dominated by a moral power that is larger than he is, for which he is merely the interpreter. This quality marks what is often called the demon of oratorical inspiration.[29]

These observations occur as part of a larger discussion of the idea of force or *mana* at work in Australian totemism, but it is clear from this example that for Durkheim a continuity does indeed exist between so-called primitive cultures and Western cultures. The "moral authority" or "psychic energy" we find at work in *mana* personalities who speak with "grandiloquence" and "overbearing gestures" is, for Durkheim, a manifestation of that state of mimetic "inspiration" which Plato, speaking of the rhapsode, called "enthusiasm." This subject is, indeed, no longer itself because it has been taken outside of itself. Or, as Durkheim says, it is "carried away" by a "power that is larger than he is," of which he is but an "interpreter." If we follow Durkheim, then, it appears that in the shift from the "primitives" to the Greeks, from a ritual context to a theatrical context, from what the Polynesians call *mana* to what Plato called *mimesis*, the psychic force in question has not fundamentally changed. In fact, Durkheim appears implicitly to agree with Plato, the Nietzschean modernists, and even with his rivals, the crowd psychologists, that "within a crowd moved by a common passion, we become susceptible to feelings and actions of which we are incapable on our own."[30] And in a language once again reminiscent of Plato's magnetic trope—but also of nineteenth-century magnetism and, closer to Durkheim's positivist spirit, the natural sciences—he adds that this contagious, impersonal force hits the masses with the force of a "shock that can be compared to an electric charge."[31] For Durkheim, contrary to, say, Plato, there is an important sense in which mimesis is not inevitably the source of irrational violence and of social dissolution but also of organic cohesion and collective regeneration. His modernist brand of mimetic theory reminds us that mimesis, like electricity, can have *both* positive *and* negative charges: contagion is always potentially dangerous, yet it also has the power to magnetize the entire social body and to bring about its revitalization. This is why Durkheim speaks of the "moral unity" generated by contagion, while at the same time specifying that the "result is a general effervescence characteristic of revolutionary or creative epochs."[32]

It is primarily for the potentially galvanizing, unifying, and revolutionary effects of mimetic contagion among primitive cultures that Bataille turns to study mass phenomena in modern culture. His account of fascist psychology, for instance, is concerned with the very same process of affective contagion that electrifies modern subjects who are part of a crowd assembled around a leader endowed with the power of *mana*. The same tropes are invoked to account for this phenomenon; the same suggestible conception of the subject is present in his descriptions. Bataille writes, for instance, that the "*heterogeneous* reality [such as a crowd] is that of a force or a shock. It presents itself as a charge, as a value, passing from one object to another" (1, 347). The effect of this force, he continues, is that "in a disconcerting way, the subject has the opportunity to displace the exciting value of one element onto an analogous or neighboring one" (1, 347). Along similar lines, in one of the articles for *Contre-attaque*, written in May 1936, he speaks of "the contagious emotion that, from house to house, suburb to suburb, suddenly turns a hesitant man into one who is no longer himself [*hors de soi*]" (1, 403). And he adds: "we remain certain that this force results less from strategy than from collective exaltation, and that this exaltation can only come from words that touch not reason so much as the passions of the crowd [*les passions des masses*]" (1, 411). The theoretical sources of this disconcerting phenomenon of affective contagion triggered by the magic of words go back to Plato. But it is clear that Bataille finds its most recent articulation in the French school of anthropology in general, and in Durkheim's notion of collective "effervescence" in particular. As Michèle Richman recognized, Bataille's analysis of fascism as well as his later project at the Collège de Sociologie must be reconsidered from what she calls a "Durkheimian perspective."[33] And in her theoretical focus and evaluation, Richman shares my concern to treat Bataille's theory of the pathos of fascist "affective effervescence" (1, 348) seriously, while at the same time urging us to engage with what she calls "a brilliant innovation in cultural theory."[34]

Beyond Good and Evil Mimesis

Pursuing this Durkheimian line of investigation from a mimetic perspective, we notice that already in "Structure" Bataille is particularly attentive to the contagious dimension of the leader's force. For him, the leader's "affective flux" is responsible for a collective state of psychic union that animates the crowd as it assembles around him. Bataille thus stresses the sacred dimension of the "*chef-dieu*" endowed with a "force that places him above men" (1, 348). And later he adds that "the religious value of the leader [*chef*] is really the fundamental (if not formal) value of fascism" (1, 363). Mimetic effervescence, for Bataille, is thus generated by the presence of a charismatic leader whose religious status has the power to deprive the masses of rational control over themselves. We can thus see that in a general sense Bataille is still in line with the Platonic tradition we are engaging with. In this tradition, the transcendental power of mimesis is mediated by heterogeneous individuals such as "madmen, *meneurs*, and poets" (1, 346) who stand above the crowd and communicate the electric current that traverses them magnetically, mimetically, that is, tyrannically, to the enthusiastic crowd from the top down.

And yet, despite this general, underlying continuity between Bataille's anthropological account of the leader and the modernist variations of the Platonic tradition, significant differences emerge, at the levels of both the moral evaluation and the theoretical articulation of mimesis. For instance, we have repeatedly stressed that for Plato, as for Girard and Lacoue-Labarthe after him, affective mimesis is the source of a *disruption* of the social bond, an irrational, violent affect that needs to be controlled insofar as it constitutes a threat to the moral and political stability of the just Republic ("bad mimesis"). Bataille, on the other hand, as Durkheim before him, pursues an alternative line of thought we found at work in both Lawrence and Nietzsche. This line considers this social effervescence essential for social *cohesion* and regeneration of the communal bond ("good mimesis"). For Bataille, then, the presence of a figure who "demands not only passion, but ecstasy from its participants" (1, 363) is experienced not always as a threat to social stability but also as vital to social cohesion. Hence, his insistence on what he calls "the inexhaustible richness of forms characteristic of affective life" (1, 371), as well as the activist, engaged tone that characterizes Bataille's prewar writings concerned with the problematic of affective contagion. In sum, for Bataille affective mimesis is not only a problem for the stability of the (French) Republic, but also a possible solution—Bataille also says a "weapon" (I, 371)—that has the power to trigger social revolution and transformation.

Furthermore, Bataille's Durkheimian inversion of *moral* evaluation of the mimetic phenomenon observed has its correlate in an inversion of the *theoretical* perspective adopted with respect to the precise affective dynamic that ties the leader to the masses. We have seen that Bataille's emphasis on the heterogeneous force of a divine leader who is "totally other" and has the power to "electrify" the masses initially appears to be in line with the vertical flow of mimetic affects we have repeatedly encountered, from Plato to Nietzsche, Conrad to Lawrence. And yet a closer look at Bataille's account allows us to see that his perspective does not fit easily within this still Platonic schema that privileges the individual over the crowd, verticality over horizontality. As Bataille puts it, speaking of the leader's will to power:

> The affective flux that unites him to his followers . . . is a function of the common consciousness of increasingly *violent* and excessive energies and powers that accumulate in the person of the leader and, through him, become widely available. (I, 348)

Despite his use of a religious, transcendental terminology, Bataille, following Durkheim, attempts to offer an immanent, down-to-earth social perspective on the process of generation of mimetic pathos. Here we see that the leader's force does not have its source in a transcendental principle alone (God, muses), nor does it originate in a mimetic individual who conveys it vertically, down to the masses (poet, leader). Instead, Bataille argues that this "mysterious force" is placed within a circular dynamic that ties the leader to the masses and vice versa, and gains momentum in the *affective circulation* between these two poles. Thus understood, the leader figure functions as an energetic catalyst that accumulates the heterogeneous "energies" generated from the crowd—what he calls "affective effervescence [that] leads to unity" (I, 348)—and redirects this effervescence back to them, in a spiraling, cumulative move. The source of this force, in other words, is in the spiraling flux that ties the (horizontal) social body to the (vertical) head that is the leader figure and vice versa. The emphasis is, thus, not on verticality alone but on the articulation between verticality and horizontality; not on individuality alone but on the interaction between individuality and collectivity; not on the linearity of the mimetic flux but on its spiraling, cumulative movement. Here we can catch a more precise glimpse of the affective dynamic responsible for the process of mimetic unification that troubles the modernist imagination. And what we find out is that, contrary to the Platonic, idealist model of enthusiastic contagion, the modernist, anthropological model offers an immanent, anti-Platonic solution to the riddle of group formation.

Notice that it is once again Durkheim, whose take on effervescence both Richman and Girard urged us to reconsider, who paves the way for Bataille's back-looping articulation between the individual and the collective, the *mana* of the fascist leader and the affective *force* it generates. As he continues his account of the "demon of oratorical inspiration," Durkheim says that "the feelings provoked by his speech return to him inflated and amplified, reinforcing his own. The passionate energies he arouses echo back to him and increase his vitality."[35] Moreover, the father of French sociology makes clear that in this affective circulation what is decisive is not the individual but the group. Thus, he specifies that "this unusual surplus of forces [of the man who addresses a crowd] is quite real: it comes to him from the very group he is addressing." And he adds: "religious force is nothing but the collective and anonymous force of the clan."[36] In this sense, we can see how charismatic leaders, for Durkheim, function like Australian totems: their sacred force, or *mana*, does not originate from them but from society instead. More precisely, the collective awareness of the impersonal, psychic state that envelops the masses is responsible for generating the "impersonal" mysterious force, a mimetic, contagious force the masses mistakenly attribute to the leaders/totems. From this sociological perspective, locating the source of the psychic energy in an individual leader is a misrecognition similar to the one Australians make in the context of totemism. "The primitive," writes Durkheim, "does not even see that these feelings come to him from the group."[37] Thus, when Bataille states that the "force" that ties the fascist leader to the masses "is a function of a common conscience" of violent "power," he endorses the Durkheimian perspective whereby the collective, rather than the individual, is the source of the effervescence that energizes the leaders' will to power. As Bataille puts it: "The leader as such is in fact only the emanation of a principle which is none other than that of the glorious existence of a nation raised to the value of a divine force" (1, 363).

Considering Bataille against the anthropological background on which he relies puts us in a position to give nuance to those literary critics who claim that his notion of "force" is "vague," based on "anthropological abstractions" and that his theoretical debt to this tradition is steeped in "wishful thinking."[38] In his understanding of the leader's force, Bataille articulates the invisible, yet quite effective affective dynamic that ties the leader to the masses and is responsible for the generation of mimetic effervescence and contagion along lines that are congruent with the French school of anthropology. Bataille, in this sense, shifts the perspective from the individual to the collective source of affects, rooting mimesis in what Mauss and Durkheim call an "immanent," social dimension. In this sense, my reading concurs with Michèle Richman's injunction not "to discredit thoroughly intellectual efforts to understand the functioning [of effervescent energies], thereby effectively discouraging future speculations on the role of collective thought and action in relationship to politics in the modern period."[39] And yet if my reading of Bataille's notion of force supports a Durkheimian perspective, I cannot follow Richman's theoretical efforts to root Bataille's account of the social bond *uniquely* in an anthropological perspective, a perspective that she posits over and against the emergence of another discipline intent in offering a contribution to mimetic theory: that is, crowd psychology. Since the theoretical stakes of this point are relevant for the entire mimetic tradition that traverses this study, a brief explanation is in place.

Richman not only offers a scathing account of the insights of this discipline, but also launches a passionate appeal to "break the stranglehold on the development of social psychology effected by the early crowd psychologies."[40] Her objections concern primarily Le Bon, but stretch in order to include Tarde and Freud. Thus, she axiomatically states it as a "fact" that, contrary to Durkheim "neither Le Bon nor Freud arrived at a genuinely collective psychology."[41] Such a severe hierarchical distinction between sociology and crowd psychology, while reminiscent of turn-of-the-century disciplinary quarrels, is not only foreign to contemporary mimetic theory, but also distorts Bataille's take on what he calls, after all, "psychology of fascism" or, alternatively, "social psychology" (1, 344). Furthermore, Richman does not hesitate to dismiss, in a casual gesture, the entire tradition of the mimetic unconscious that informs all modernist writers we have encountered so far. Thus, she claims that "recent scholarship has revealed the extent to which

French psychology at the close of the nineteenth century was dominated by a model of the unconscious derided by one historian of psychoanalysis in France as *'l'inconscient à la française.'*[42] The rhetorical strength of this critique should not mask two facts, one relating to the history of psychology, the other to Bataille. First, the historian she refers to (Elisabeth Roudinesco), who is Richman's final authority on the question of the unconscious, is writing from within the bastions of a Freudian/Lacanian perspective. It is thus not surprising that her take on the unconscious favors the tradition of which she is a disciple. A panoply of other, less partial, historical accounts have taught us to look around, beyond the dominant orthodoxy; and what we discovered is that at the turn of the century, hypnosis still functions as the *via regia* to the modernist unconscious, and not only in France but across Europe as a whole.[43] Second, the critique of what Richman calls the "pseudo-scientific model of suggestive influence" is fashionable and routinely made in a Freudian century in which the concept of the "unconscious" (at least in literary studies) is still synonymous with psychoanalysis. Yet such a categorical rejection in the context of a discussion of Bataille is problematic, to say the least. This is so not only because Bataille's conception of fascist "force" that informs his prewar writings is inextricably intertwined with the notion of hypnosis, but also because the central concept of "communication" that runs through the entirety of the Bataillean corpus, as we shall have occasion to confirm, is based precisely on the conception of the unconscious Richman derides. Laughter will, indeed, be our final concern.

Richman's second and, for her most important, angle of attack upon psychosociology and its characteristic suspicion of the power of mimesis, concerns politics. Thus she notices that both Tarde's and Le Bon's "explicit political message was the denunciation of socialism as a manifestation of mass hysteria."[44] In her view, then, crowd psychologists' accounts of the disruptive aspect of mass behavior are but a consequence of their political agenda. Contrary to this tendency, she stresses Durkheim's democratic approach in order to emphasize the "potentially revolutionary explosiveness of effervescence," an explosiveness whose paradigmatic model is, for Richman, May '68.[45] The agon is, thus, neatly drawn: in order to promote revolutionary forms of effervescence (good mimesis), the psychosociological reminders of the dangers of hypnotic manipulation (bad mimesis) need to be silenced, and the theorists' respective *political* orientations provide a way to favor their *theoretical* evaluation. While I agree with Richman's political evaluation, the fundamental ambivalence characteristic of mimesis has taught us to be extremely suspicious of clear-cut theoretical oppositions between "good" and "bad" mimesis, especially when what is at stake is the politics of mimesis. Mimesis itself, as we have repeatedly seen, goes beyond good and evil and can be appropriated for both liberating and destructive purposes. Thus, I would refrain from dismissing the theoretical insights of crowd psychology as a whole on the basis of Le Bon's political stance. Notice that this move contradicts Richman's injunction *not* to discredit Bataille's thought on fascism on the basis of his enthusiastic fascination for fascist politicians. More important, according to the diagnostic perspective that I follow, it is precisely because of politics that both Tarde's and Le Bon's theory of the mimetic crowd should not be too hastily dismissed. In fact, it is true that in the late nineteenth century, crowds are still associated with what Marx called "the specter of socialism," and Le Bon's thought (but not Tarde's) is tainted by his political conservatism. Yet in the 1930s, it is no longer the specter of socialism that is haunting modern Europe, but the specter of fascism instead. And Bataille, for one, will become increasingly aware of the unpredictable nature of the power of mimesis. Thus, in one of his articles of *Contre-attaque* written in 1936 he asks: "How can one know whether a movement that initially designates itself as anti-fascist, will not turn, more or less rapidly, towards fascism?" (1, 424–5). This fundamental doubt at the heart of Bataille's early thought makes us realize that so-called weapons designed for social revolution on the basis of explosions of mimetic effervescence might unexpectedly backfire, turning a theoretical patho-logy into a social pathology.

My point, then, is that in the context of a discussion of the unconscious, mimetic forces that haunt the modern body politic, Le Bon's reactionary critique of the masses' collective irrationalism, mimetic violence, and suggestibility to charismatic leader figures can be turned to *both* fascist *and* critical use. The fact that Mussolini directly benefited from Le Bon's advice and used it as a fascist weapon rather than as a tool for social diagnosis, unquestionably discredits Le Bon's political stance, but unfortunately does not invalidate his theory. On the contrary, in the light of disastrously effective applications of what he calls "leaders' means of action," which include "affirmation, repetition, and contagion,"[46] it is not only theoretically anachronistic, but also politically dangerous to continue to dismiss Le Bon's theory as "sensationalistic crowd psychology."[47] In *The Age of the Crowd*, Serge Moscovici, one of the leading contemporary sociologists concerned with mass behavior, "find[s] it astonishing that even today we believe that we can ignore [crowd psychology's] concepts and dispense with them."[48] That such a claim is made by a leftist, Jewish sociologist writing in the aftermath of the Holocaust should give us pause for thought. It clearly indicates that political orientations should not preclude an appropriation of crowd psychology's diagnostics of mimetic irrationality characteristic of mass behavior and the horrors that continue to ensue.[49]

In a way this is precisely Bataille's position as he sets out to develop what he calls "a system of knowledge allowing us to predict affective, social reactions" (1, 371). Quite indifferent to fin de siècle disciplinary skirmishes between sociology and crowd psychology, Bataille recognizes that in order to account for the mechanism that ties the leader to the masses, his reliance on Durkheim's "exterior," sociological perspective needs to be supplemented by an "interior," psychological perspective. This perspective should account for the fact that the "man among thousand" is characterized by what Bataille calls the "need to place oneself under the direction of a single person" (1, 351). It should also account for "the unconscious structure [*structure inconsciente*]" that is responsible for his vulnerability to violent, contagious emotions, psychic depersonalization, and unconscious, collective behavior.[50] We should thus not be surprised if Bataille does not hesitate to rely on Le Bon's fundamental thesis in order to account for the force of the leader or, as he calls it, *meneur*. Echoing Le Bon, he writes: "Considered not in regard to its external action but in regard to its source, the *force* of the leader is analogous to that exerted in hypnosis" (1, 348).[51] Once again, as was already the case for Nietzsche, Conrad, and Lawrence, the model of hypnotic dispossession, which defines the operator's suggestive power over the patient, is invoked in order to account for the leader's affective will to power "directed, as an authority, against men" (1, 348). Despite Bataille's and Le Bon's political opposition and divergent evaluations of crowd behavior, they share similar *theoretical* assumptions with respect to the psychology of the crowd. These include the importance given to the figure of the prestigious *meneur*, the willpower of the latter over the masses, the violent dimension of contagious emotions, the attention given to an interior, unconscious perspective, and the reliance on the model of hypnosis in order to account for the masses' unconscious behavior. In short, Le Bon's thesis concerning the leader's hypnotic power provides Bataille with an interior, psychological perspective to confront the mysterious force (*mana*) of the leader (*meneur*).

This does not mean, however, that Bataille is firmly writing within a Le Bonian or psychosociological perspective. *Hetero*-logy, as the term clearly says and the content of Bataille's work confirms, constantly transgresses homogeneous disciplinary discourses, so that any attempt to confine Bataille to a homogeneous perspective inevitably does violence to the interdisciplinary spirit that keeps his thought in motion. What we must add now is that Bataille does not borrow the model of hypnosis directly from the French psychological tradition. Rather, he relies on a more recent modernist theory that is beginning to be à la mode in France, as well as elsewhere, at least among avant-garde groups and so-called pathological cases. Bataille's understanding of the "hypnotic" force of the leader in particular and "the structure of the unconscious" in general finds yet another source of inspiration in a figure Serge Moscovici calls "the best disciple of Le Bon and Tarde: Sigmund Freud."[52]

The Freudian Triangle

The detour via Bataille's religious anthropology was instrumental in clarifying his understanding of the mysterious notion of "force" that transects his early writings, as well as the affective dynamic responsible for group formation. It also allowed us to articulate the continuities and discontinuities between the anthropological perspective on which Bataille relies and the larger mimetic tradition we are concerned with, to engage with some of the critics of this tradition, and to continue to open up the problematic of mimesis to an interdisciplinary perspective that transgresses disciplinary barriers. And yet, by focusing on the theoretical aspect that sustains Bataille's patho-*logical* account of fascist psychology, we have tended to lose sight of the affective and infective foundations of his mimetic pathology. Our focus was more on Bataille's exterior, anthropological distance than on his interior, personal engagement with the pathos he dissects. We should not forget, however, that Bataille's mimetic patho(-)logy is predicated on what he calls "lived states" (1, 339) or, alternatively, "lived *affective* experience" (1, 348). And as we noticed, this experience is linked to a primal, familial scene characterized by an ambivalent relationship to the heterogeneous father figure. This is the moment to return to this scene.

Story of the I Revisited

As we first encountered Bataille's account of what he calls "the most loaded event of [his] childhood" in *Story of the Eye*, we were concerned with moving from personal to collective psychology, and we refrained from asking the quintessential Freudian question: is this familial scene Oedipal? Indeed, the fact that Bataille says that during puberty the "affection for [his] father turned into an unconscious aversion" and that this account involves an explicit sexual reference to the mother makes it possible to answer affirmatively. More precisely, Bataille's ambivalent relationship with the heterogeneous father figure appears to be motivated by the play of identifications that, for Freud, is at the heart of the Oedipal complex. Freud, in fact, in *Group Psychology and the Analysis of the Ego* (1921) reminds us that "identification is ambivalent from the very first"; and in *The Ego and the Id* (1923) he famously roots this ambivalence in a contradictory imperative that structures the Oedipal psyche: "'You ought to be like this (like your father).' . . . You may not be like this (like your father)—that is, you may not do all that he does; some things are his prerogative.'"[53] According to this view, the (male) Oedipal child is subjected to a contradictory, mimetic imperative whereby a positive identification with the father with respect to the moral values he represents contrasts with a rivalrous identification with the father with respect to the possession of the maternal object of desire.[54] This is, indeed, the paradoxical problem the adolescent Bataille seems to inherit from his Oedipal past—a past that continues to inform the contradictory push-pulls of "attraction and repulsion" we have seen at work in his account of the heterogeneous fascist leader.

And yet if we take a closer look at Bataille's primal scene, we notice that it might be less Oedipal than it initially appears to be. The subject, in fact, is not fixated on the figure of the mother at all. He does not seem to be driven by an instinctual object cathexis that, for Freud, sets in motion the Oedipal triangulation. The status of the mother as an object of desire is mediated by the perverse imagination of the father. We could thus say, with Girard, that it is only after identifying with the father, after imitating the desire of the model, that the subject desires to possess the mother. This hypothesis is certainly more plausible insofar as the father's sexual imagination seems to be stimulated by the presence of yet another mediator, namely the doctor. And yet when it comes to the "I" of this narrative, from this passage it is not even clear that he wants "to have" his mother, that mimesis informs, directs, and even creates desire, as Girard's inversion of the Oedipal structure suggests. What this account makes clear, on the other hand, is that the "I" is fixated on the heterogeneous elements the father embodies. His stench, violent state of pain, obscenity, madness, and laughter are, *in themselves*, the source of the most contradictory feelings: repulsion and attraction, disgust and laughter, fascination and horror seem to originate in the abject father figure, leaving desire in the background along with the mother, as it were. In other words, "this primal scene of Bataille's writing" indicates the possibility that the central question for Bataille is not structured around an Oedipal triangle where desire for the object precedes identification (Freud), nor on a deft and rather brilliant overturning of such a triangle where mimesis generates a desire for the desire of the other (Girard), but, rather, on a heterogeneous form of affective mimesis that transgresses the boundaries of this structure and privileges the contagion of *mimetic pathos* as a subject of heterological investigation (Bataille).

This mimetic hypothesis can only be inferred but not tested at the level of Bataille's personal psychology; yet it can be pursued further if we turn to consider Bataille's explicit reliance on Freud at the level of collective psychology, a reliance that allows him to continue to unfold his account of the force of that surrogate father figure who is the fascist leader and to further his insights into the unconscious foundations of the modern ego.[55]

While already steeped in an array of anthropological and psychological theories, Bataille, at the time he writes "Structure," makes clear that he finds in Freud's science of the unconscious a valuable tool for developing his unlikely "science" of heterology. Not only is psychoanalysis concerned with many of the unconscious phenomena that are at the heart of heterology (madness, dreams, neurosis) and thus confronted with the same epistemological difficulties, but Freud's fundamental hypothesis seems also in line with the one that structures Bataille's conception of the heterogeneous. "The exclusion of *heterogeneous* elements from the *homogeneous* realm of consciousness" writes Bataille, "formally recalls the exclusion of the elements described (by psychoanalysis) as *unconscious*, which censorship excludes from

the conscious ego [*moi conscient*]" (1, 344). With this formula, Bataille seems
to indicate that, as he speaks of the unconscious, he is indeed adopting the
Freudian, Oedipal model based on the repressive hypothesis. But we need to
look at it more closely. Despite Bataille's reference to the sphere of personal
pathology, his interest in Freud is basically limited to *Group Psychology and
the Analysis of the Ego*, a work where Freud is addressing the same sociological
"riddle" Bataille is trying to resolve. In fact, of all the Freudian texts, *Group
Psychology* deals most directly with crowd psychology in general, and the
mimetic force of the leader in particular. As Bataille readily acknowledges
in a note, "if one refers to the whole of the elements brought together in
the present study, that work, published in German in 19[21], appears as an
essential introduction to the understanding of fascism" (1, 356).

If we read this affirmation in the context of the general economy of
Bataille's mimetology, it is clear that he attaches so much importance to
Freud's account because *Group Psychology* is predicated on two examples that
have paradigmatic value for Bataille's account of fascist psychology. Bataille
continues in the same note: "Freud, in *Group Psychology and the Analysis of
the 'Ego*,' studied precisely the two functions, military (army) and religious
(church) in relation to the imperative form (unconscious) of individual psychology" (1, 356). Despite his Durkheimian interest in the collective, Bataille
agrees with Freud and, thus, with Le Bon, that an understanding of crowd
psychology also needs to focus on the individual figure of the leader and the
collective, unconscious dynamic it generates. This is why he devotes a section of his essay to "the army" and one to "religious power," drawing on the
Freudian realization that "the most interesting examples of such structures
[groups characterized by the presence of a leader] are Churches—communities of believers—and armies" (*GP* 25). Similarly, for Bataille "fascist power is
characterized first of all by the fact that its foundation is both religious and
military" (1, 362). Bataille is aware that invoking the army and especially the
church in our "postsacred" societies in order to account for the emergence of
fascism is a tricky move that risks anachronism. As he anticipates, it might
be easily dismissed as "an agitation of apparently anachronistic phantoms" (1,
362)—an idealist move that disconnects fascist psychology from the immanence of heterogeneous affects.[56]

And yet if we place these examples in the context of Bataille's larger recuperation of the sacred in modern societies, it is clear why these institutional

"phantoms" are essential for his understanding of the phantom of the ego. If Durkheim's distinction between the sacred and the profane underscores Bataille's distinction between the heterogeneous and the homogeneous, Freud's reliance on the church and the army allows Bataille to operate a smooth transition from archaic rituals to modern institutions; from the *mana* of Australian totems to the force of fascist leaders. Bataille is thus quick to recognize the continuity between religion and politics, sacred and modern societies. Modern subjects who are enthused with the power of charismatic leaders in postsacred societies are, for him, in no way less religious than "primitive" subject entranced by totemic figures.[57] It is thus not surprising that Bataille finds Freud's reliance on these *social structures* central for the general movement inherent in his project. But, we may now ask, what about Freud's specific understanding of the *psychological structure* of fascism that concerns us here? Surely Freud's inquiry into the field of psychosociology has more to say to Bataille about psychological structures than social structures. This, at least, is what Bataille seems to suggest as he writes that "the unity of fascism is located in its proper psychological structure" (I, 367) and goes on to rely on the Freudian notion of "identification" in order to account for the unconscious force of the leader. As he puts it in "Essai de définition du fascisme," the relation between the masses and the fascist leader is characterized by what he calls "affective relations [*rapports*] determined so that each follower, under the power of an irrational attraction, identifies with this leader." As a result, he adds, "the will and the thoughts of this leader must turn into the follower's proper will and thoughts" (II, 215).[58] A confrontation with what Mikkel Borch-Jacobsen calls "*the* fundamental concept, the *Grundbegriff* of psychoanalysis" (identification), and the "trial of magic" it entails can, at this stage, no longer be postponed.[59]

The Trial of Magic

A glance at the table of contents of *Group Psychology and the Analysis of the Ego* makes clear that the father of psychoanalysis openly acknowledges his theoretical debt to those advocates of crowd psychology (a better translation of Freud's *Massenpsychologie*). In the introductory chapters, Freud summarizes Le Bon's theory, endorsing his analysis of the irrational dimension of the crowd, its feeling of power, as well as the importance given to affective contagion and unconscious behavior. As he puts it, Le Bon's account is "deservedly famous," "fits in so well with our own psychology in the emphasis it lays upon unconscious mental life," and entails a "brilliant psychological character sketch of the group mind" (GP 4, 14, 61). Recognizing the insights of Le Bon, as well as other crowd psychologists such as McDougall and Tarde, Freud affirms that "there is no doubt that something exists in us which, when we become aware of signs of an emotion in someone else, tends to make us fall into the same emotion" (21). Previous crowd psychologists were already dealing with the importance of the unconscious in social life, and, at the general level, Freud agrees with the tradition that precedes him on the irrational, contagious, and imitative status of the subject who is part of a *Masse*.

And yet the father of psychoanalysis is not only a faithful inheritor but also an ambitious innovator who challenges the main assumptions of the mimetic tradition on which he initially relies. His main theoretical objections to previous psychosociological theories concern precisely their account of the force tying the followers to the leader on the basis of the model of hypnotic suggestion. Freud, in fact, recognizes that accounts of this "mysterious power" have a long prehistory he needs to confront in order to propose his own resolution:

> The hypnotist asserts that he is in possession of a mysterious power that robs the subject of his own will; or, which is the same thing, the subject believes it of him. This mysterious power (which is even now often described popularly as "animal magnetism") must be the same power that is looked upon by primitive people as the source of taboo, the same that emanates from kings and chieftains and makes it dangerous to approach them (*mana*). (GP 57)

Magnetism, hypnosis, suggestion: Freud agrees that these are but modern signifiers that attempt to account for that mysterious, magical power Polynesians call *mana*. And Freud acknowledges this thematic/theoretical continuity we have been following as the *fil rouge* into the labyrinthine question of the unconscious. Thus, in "The Unconscious" (1915) he is ready to admit that "hypnotic experiments, and especially post-hypnotic suggestion, had demonstrated tangibly even before the time of psycho-analysis the existence and mode of operation of the unconscious in the mind."[60] And yet despite this avowal, Freud has no intentions of aligning psychoanalysis with the magnetic/hypnotic/magical tradition that precedes him. The "mysterious power" might be the same, Freud agrees, but this does not mean that for him the *accounts* of this power are equivalent. Or better, the equivalence, for Freud, stretches from the anthropological account of *mana* to the psychological account of hypnosis. But it stops with the birth of what he considers to be a truly scientific account of mimesis: psychoanalysis. We can thus see how Freud's analogy with *mana* cuts both ways. On the one hand, it establishes a thematic continuity emphasizing that the fundamental nature of the *riddle* of mimetic contagion remains the same. On the other hand, the relegation of the tradition of the unconscious that precedes him to the sphere of magic allows him to cut all links with past *solutions* of the riddle.

Freud notices that previous crowd psychologists' accounts of the social bond are predicated on a mimetic principle that cannot be further explained, "an irreducible, primitive phenomenon, a fundamental fact in the mental life of man" (*GP* 21). As he puts it, summarizing the views of Tarde, McDougall, and Le Bon: "what compels us to obey this tendency is imitation, and what induces the emotion in us is the group's suggestive influence" (21). According to this tradition, imitation functions as the *via regia* to the unconscious. For pre-Freudian thinkers, mimesis is thus a fundamental fact that is not reducible to other interpretations and this fact is constitutive of the mimetic unconscious. The genealogy of this tradition ultimately goes back to Plato but also stretches ahead—via the missing link of modernism—to include recent discoveries in the neurosciences. Freud, however, does not align himself with this genealogy. For the father of psychoanalysis, in fact, the theory of "suggestion" (advocated by Bernheim), far from offering a scientific explanation for the problem of imitation and group formation, is but a modern version of the Polynesian *mana*, a "magical word" that, as he shrewdly puts it, "explains everything [but is] itself to be exempt from explanation" (21). Freud, in fact, cannot accept this psychophysiological conception of the ego, which considers that unconscious mimetic tendencies are directly wired into our nervous system, a "normal property of our brain," as Bernheim, anticipating the discovery of mirror neurons, puts it. For Freud, hypnotic suggestion is not a final "answer" but just another "riddle"; it is not a "fundamental fact" but an interpretation—and a dated or, as he implies, "primitive" interpretation at best. It is thus clear that Freud does not intend to refer to yet other magical concepts—such as "mana," "participation mystique," or "suggestion"—in order to solve the "riddle of group formation." His goal is, rather, to provide us with a truly "scientific" analysis of the power of the leader. And in order to do so he attempts to recuperate the affective forces that tie followers to leaders within the structural passages already explored by his so-called science of the unconscious.

Freud considers that his essential contribution to the understanding of group formation concerns his reinscription of the social bond within the theory of libidinal drives that are already familiar to psychoanalysis from its account of the child's psychic formation. Surprisingly, however, in order to make the move from suggestion to libido, crowd psychology to individual psychology, and, thus, extend the psychosociological tradition that precedes him, Freud relies on the authority of a field he usually tends to dismiss for its rationalistic blindness to unconscious phenomena, namely philosophy. In fact, it is on the authority of Plato that Freud introduces the libido theory into his account of the social bond: "the 'Eros' of the philosopher Plato," he says, "coincides exactly with the love-force, the libido of psychoanalysis" (*GP* 23). Invoking the androgynous myth in the *Symposium*, the father of psychoanalysis relies on the father of philosophy in order to claim that it is "Eros which holds everything together in the world" (24). A modernist theory of the unconscious is, thus, once again, tied back to Plato. And this theoretical tie allows Freud to introduce the primacy of libido in his account of the social bond. In crowds characterized by the presence of a leader, Freud writes, "each individual is bound by libidinal ties on the one hand to the leader (Christ, the Commander-in-Chief) and on the other hand to the other members of the group" (27). In short, it is because followers invest the leader figure with a libidinal energy that they are ready to blindly follow his orders and capitulate to his force: Love, then, turns out to be the key to what Freud calls "the riddle of group formation."

And yet it is not so simple. Having said this, Freud immediately complicates his account of the social bond by introducing another "emotional tie" in his account. Thus, he recognizes that "there do exist other mechanisms for emotional ties, the so-called *identifications*" (36). Members of a group are not only held together by "what one would like to *have*" (Eros or libido) but also by "what one would like to *be*" (38) (mimesis or identification). Now, if Freud's reliance on Eros is explicitly in line with Plato, we might expect that this debt would be even more pronounced with respect to that emotional tie par excellence that Plato calls *mimesis*. After all, this connection would have been much more straightforward because Plato's account of affective mimesis, as we have seen, already entails an embryonic theory of crowd psychology. Surprisingly, however, Freud never makes this theoretical link. Perhaps this silence is for lack of specific knowledge of Books III and X of the *Republic*, but more probably because at this stage in his argument he is no longer concerned with finding allegiances with influential past theories of mimesis but, rather, with developing his original theoretical contribution to the emerging field of psychosociology. Once again, Freud is leaving the mythic past behind and is looking forward to his "science" of the unconscious.

The "Science" of the Unconscious

In his account of identification, Freud attempts to map his dynamic account of the psychic formation of the child, as developed in his second topography, onto the social body. Toward the beginning of the chapter devoted to identification, Freud reminds us that the Oedipal structure of the psyche is predicated on what he calls "a straightforward sexual object-cathexis towards his mother and an identification with his father which takes him as his model" (37). We have seen that the tradition that precedes him did not introduce a radical break between these emotional ties. Plato, for instance, in the *Phaedrus* situates Eros in a relationship of continuity with other kinds of mimetic madness (e.g., Dionysian trance and Apollonian divinatory possession), and Lawrence considers eroticism in terms of psychic "possession" or "trance," states that are not strictly distinguished from what I call mimesis. Freud, on the other hand, breaks with this mimetico-erotic tradition. Thus, in a clear-cut theoretical move, he speaks of "two psychologically distinct ties," dividing the affective stream responsible for the emotional force that ties the followers to the leader into two mutually exclusive channels: object cathexis and identification, or, as he also puts it, the desire "to have" the other and the desire "to be" the other. Needless to say that this perspective is perfectly in line with the Oedipal/triangular structure of the psyche, if only because two emotional ties are necessary to compose a triangle. Now, at the level of personal psychology, it is clear how the child manages to undo the knot of contradictory ties that structure the Oedipal complex: that is, he must give up the maternal object and identify with the father, in order to (later) have access to a substitute mother.[61]

So far so good. But how does this dynamic apply to Freud's collective psychology? If Freud's account of the social bond follows an Oedipal structure, how, we may ask, is the riddle of group formation to be resolved in the absence of a clear familial triangle? Simply put, if the followers already love that father figure who is the leader, whom should they identify with?

Insofar as Freud attempts to solve the riddle of group formation by articulating the dynamic relationship that ties libido to identification with a parental figure in absentia, he is inevitably confronted with a fundamental structural difficulty. And it is precisely in order to resolve this problem that Freud finds an alternative paradigmatic example outside the family triangle, taken from the field of psychopathology. Here is the decisive example that allows Freud to move from an individual to a social dynamic: A boarding school girl has "fits of hysterics" upon receiving a letter from her lover that arouses her jealousy, and this fit spreads contagiously to affect the other girls. And here is the riddle: How is this mental infection communicated? Freud insists that this contagion does not stem from a direct sympathetic/identificatory bond with the hysterical girl. The other girls, in his view, do not feel directly the pathos of hysteria as their own; they do not respond on the basis of the mirroring reflexes characteristic of the mimetic unconscious. As he puts it, "it would be wrong to suppose that they take on the symptom out of sympathy" (39). If we keep in mind the general aim of Freud's project (to provide us with a "scientific," that is, psychoanalytic, account of group formation), it is clear why he rejects sympathy: such a direct mimetic communication would do away with the need of object cathexis altogether. We would then be confronted with a direct affective, sympathetic contagion of the sort we are already familiar with from the tradition we have been considering—a "magical" tradition Freud wants to distance himself from. Freud's ambition is, however, to preserve the Oedipal (libidinal) structure central to his "science," even without a clear triangle in sight. His solution to this intellectual riddle is, indeed, astute. Notice in fact that, in this example, we can still construe a triangular structure, albeit a more abstract, speculative one (hysterical girl—lover's letter—other girls) and that the pole of this triangle is open to a plurality of subjects (hysterical outbreak). We can thus see the structural interest of an example located at the intersection between personal and collective psychology—a familial triangle open to the social body, as it were.

This structure is taking a more subtle, purer, more ideal form, but an additional speculative step is still needed. Freud now argues that what is at stake in this hysterical outbreak in the boarding school is not a direct mimetic bond between girls but an identification with a common emotion instead. As he puts it:

> One ego has perceived a significant analogy with another upon one point—in our example upon openness to a similar emotion [love]; an identification is thereupon constructed on this point, and, under the influence of the pathogenic situation, is displaced on to the symptom [hysteria] which the one ego has produced. (GP 39)

Things are clearly getting less embodied, more abstract: identification is not an emotional tie with other bodies but with a "point" in the ego where a certain idea of love is shared. And it is only insofar as girls are characterized by a preexisting openness to a similar emotion (i.e., libido) that they can catch in a contagious way the mimetic pathology (i.e., hysteria). The object cathexis, in other words, is not directed to the mimetic object (the hysterical girl), nor to the same male lover in absentia (the romantic author of the letter). But insofar as, for Freud, all girls would like to be in love, it is precisely this common libidinal "point" in the ego—what Freud calls "the point of coincidence between the two egos"—that opens up one ego to the other and allows mimetic affects to flow. In short, identification with the other(s) takes place through the medium of libido; desire is the source of mimesis.

Now that the structure is clearly in place, the solution to the riddle follows. We can thus see how Freud manages to account for a social case of mimetic contagion that does not explicitly repose on a triangular familial structure, while at the same time implicitly preserving the solid, ideal, triangular form that lies at the theoretical foundations of psychoanalysis. Having cracked this riddle, Freud is in a position to make a transition from the sphere of psychopathology back to psychosociology and thus to extend psychoanalysis to the analysis of the social. The psychic mechanism responsible for mimetic contagion in the case of the irrational dimension of subjects in a crowd, for Freud, is isomorphous with the one at work in a pathological hysterical outbreak in a boarding school. As he puts it, "the mutual ties between members of a group is in the nature of an identification of this kind, based on an important emotional common quality; and we may suspect that this common quality lies in the nature of the tie with the leader" (*GP* 40). In sum, after introducing two incompatible emotional ties in his account of sociality, Freud manages to give them a canonical Oedipal articulation: it is a shared (vertical) libidinal tie with the leader (Christ or the commander), he says, that is responsible for the mutual (horizontal) identificatory tie between members of the group and the con-fusion of egos that ensues. Identification is, therefore, but a function of libido; mimesis follows the path indicated by Eros.

The Return of Mimesis

Here we reach the theoretical core of Freud's account of the *psychological structure* of group formation as well as what he considered to be his essential contribution to the field of psychosociology. His argument can be schemati-cally summarized by saying that the force of the leader cannot be explained by the model of hypnotic suggestion, nor by the crowd's direct identification with such a political father figure. Rather, it is predicated on a prior verti-cal libidinal tie with the leader, which in turn determines a horizontal, identificatory tie with members of the group. This is, to be sure, a sophisticated theoretical account of group formation that is not foreign to the idealism of the Platonic conception of Eros it convokes. It also adds a layer of complexity to the mimetic psychologies we have been considering thus far, promoting an Oedipal account of the unconscious that still informs modernist studies. And yet Freud is far from thinking that he has solved, once and for all, the riddle of group formation. And surprisingly, in a move that runs against his explicit argument concerning the primacy of libido over mimesis, verticality over horizontality, ideal love over bodily mimesis, he opens an alternative line of investigation concerning the question of mimetic identification.

Recognizing that "we are far from having exhausted the problem of identification," Freud adds that "we are faced by the process which psychol-ogy calls 'empathy [*Einfühlung*]' and which plays the largest part in our understanding of what is inherently foreign to our ego in other people" (40). And in a footnote that concludes the chapter on identification, he reiterates the same point, explicitly locating the key to the riddle of suggestion in imitation, rather than libido:

> [W]e are very well aware that we have not exhausted the nature of identification with these examples taken from pathology, and that we have consequently left part of the riddle of group formation untouched. *A far more comprehensive psychological analysis would have to intervene at this point. A path leads from identification by way of imitation to empathy,* that is, to the comprehension of the mechanism by means of which we are enabled to take up any attitude at all toward another mental life. (GP 42; emphasis added)

With Freud, then, we seem to have reached a theoretical loop. At the moment of extending the theory of the social bond towards new theoretical horizons opened up by the "science" of psychoanalysis by moving from mimesis to libido, his account folds upon itself, as it were, pointing backwards towards the "magical" theories of the unconscious he initially discarded. The new path he opened by moving away from the riddle of suggestion by means of libido and, finally, identification, ultimately returns us to the old nineteenth-century problems of empathy. Eros, in short, redirects us back to mimesis.

This realization is central to the development of mimetic theory. It is, in a sense, the cornerstone of Girard's claim that mimesis directs desire and of his own incisive reading of Freud; more recently, figures of Girardian inspiration have drawn different conclusions from this mimetic hypothesis.[62] The study at hand is in line with this effort to allow for a return of mimesis in psychoanalytical theory and modernist studies. So we must ask: what about Bataille? How does he situate himself with respect to this "essential introduction" to the psychology of fascism? And if he follows the path opened up by Freud, in which direction does he follow him? Forward towards idealizing dreams constitutive of psychoanalysis? Or backward towards empirical mimetic reflexes and the tradition of the mimetic unconscious that pertains to them? Let us restate Bataille's account of the leader's force in its entirety:

> The *force* of a leader [*meneur*] is analogous to the one exerted in hypnosis. The affective flux that unites him to his followers—which takes the form of a moral identification of the latter with the one they follow (and vice

versa)—is a function of the common consciousness of increasingly *violent* and excessive energies and powers that accumulate in the person of the leader and, through him, become widely available. (1, 348)

If we have seen that Bataille's understanding of force is clearly indebted to Durkheim's anthropological account, we are now in a position to see that, like Freud before him, Bataille begins by shifting from the analogy with the psychological notion of "hypnosis" to the psychoanalytical notion of "identification."[63] Moreover, Bataille agrees with Freud that the identificatory flux does not tie the subjects directly to an object (in this case the leader) but is dependent on—or as he puts it, is "a function of"—a prior "common consciousness" (Freud says "common quality") that traverses the crowd. And when he will later say that his approach "presupposes that a revelation of what had been unconscious is possible," he does so in a relation of continuity with the "psychoanalytical experience" (11, 321).[64] And yet despite these suggestive analogies, we would be grossly mistaken in recuperating Bataille's account of mimesis within the Freudian schema. The differences, in fact, are much more important than the similarities and touch on the essential elements that are constitutive of psychoanalysis. Not only does Bataille refuse to distinguish between "two psychologically distinct ties," leaving libido completely out of the picture of his account of the social bond, but he also refrains from introducing a strict break between the model of hypnosis and the identificatory model, treating so-called "magical" notions as synonymous with their "scientific" counterpart. Most strikingly, as Bataille positively invokes the analogy with hypnosis in order to account for the leader's force, he does so by relying on the authority of Freud.[65]

Did Bataille fundamentally misread Freud? Could he miss Freud's essential innovation? Or could it be that Bataille intuited that despite Freud's explicit rejection of hypnosis, the latter continues to implicitly rely on the "magical" model he disavows? Bataille does not say. What is clear, however, is that in his exploration of the unconscious fluxes at work in the identificatory/ hypnotic force of the sovereign, he does not follow the royal road opened up by Freud—a road that goes from suggestion to libido, mimesis to Eros. Given the primacy he gives to mimesis, Bataille is closer to Girard, and, indeed, striking continuities exist between these two figures. Yet he does not operate the Girardian inversion of the Freudian model by taking the road that goes from mimesis to desire either. Could it be, then, that Bataille pursues the path indicated but not followed by Freud? That is, the path that "leads from identification by way of imitation, to empathy"? As we now turn to see, Bataille's understanding of the leader's "force," and the conception of "communication" it presupposes, is situated within the theoretical loop that goes from identification to *Einfühlung*. This loop swings us back to the reflex conception of the unconscious we have been following all along, a bodily, mimetic unconscious that leads us to reconsider the patho-*logical* foundations of the Bataillean conception of "sovereign communication."

Sovereign Communication, Unconscious Imitation

"Sovereign communication" is perhaps the central concept of Bataille's heterogeneous thought. It is certainly one of the most discussed topoi in Bataille studies insofar as it encompasses most of his theoretical obsessions. From sacrifice to inner experience, eroticism to death, dramatization to trance, tears to laughter, the movement of Bataille's thought continuously interrogates contagious experiences that have the power to transgress the limits of individuation. Yet if critics tend to agree that the concept of "communication" is at the center of Bataille's "single mythic thought" (Baudrillard's term), disagreement reigns with respect to the specific theory of the subject that informs and underlies this thought.[66] Subjected to a number of influential readings, Bataille is now mostly remembered as a precursor of the poststructuralist "death of the subject," an unrecognized giant who, in an untimely fashion, prepared the ground for the burial of a reassuring notion of "subject" always centered on itself, always present to itself, never different from itself. And yet despite the tremendous importance of such readings and the productive "occasions for misunderstanding" they have generated, the question remains: is Bataille's thought, despite its emphasis on the impossibility of communicating interior experiences, really centered on a linguistic decentering whereby the subject slides (*glisse*) along an endless chain of signifiers?

Recent critical developments have begun to suggest otherwise, stressing that, throughout his career, Bataille never ceased to meditate on experiences that are firmly rooted in the immediacy of bodily affects, affects that are impossible to convey through language but that can be "communicated" quite directly through affective contagion.[67] Extending this emergent line of inquiry, I now turn to reconsider the precise contagious dynamic that informs, at the fundamental level, Bataille's understanding of sovereign communication. If we fundamentally agree that communication *is*, indeed, contagious, and that communicative affects flow in a nonmediated way through the boundaries of subjectivity, then we may ask: Which conception of the ego allows itself to be so easily traversed and overtaken by an affective flux? And if this affectivity is, indeed, "without a subject," then we may wonder: what is the underlying affective mechanism that allows communication to flow and dissolve the boundaries of individuation? Answering these fundamental questions involves going at the affective and theoretical foundations of Bataille's engagement with what he continues to call, in his later period, "contagious subjectivity" (*subjectivité contagieuse*) (VIII, 288).

My claim is that it is only if we unearth the psychological, or better, psychophysiological roots of Bataille's early account of the sovereign's "force" that we can understand how contagious forms of sovereign communication continue to operate within the Bataillean corpus as a whole. Rather than being based on a Freudian hypothesis, his thought is predicated on what he calls, following the French philosopher, psychologist, and founder of "psychological analysis," Pierre Janet, a "psychology of the socius" (II, 287). This psychology considers the other with whom I communicate as already interior to myself, already constitutive of my ego—in short, already a *socius*. While demonstrating this hypothesis, we shall confirm that Bataille's theory of subjectivity is less Freudian than it initially appeared; nor is it primarily concerned with the postmodern death of a linguistic subject (the subject of the signifier), but remains a Nietzschean, modernist thought that advocates the birth of an affective subject (the subject of mimesis). Bataille's account of the birth of the ego (out of the womb of the mimetic unconscious) is thus in line with the modernist figures we have considered. And like them, he anticipates contemporary theoretical developments in the neurosciences (such as the discovery of "mirror neurons") that demonstrate the mimetic foundations of the subject. In this sense, Bataille turns out to be an acute theorist of mimetic intersubjectivity, a theorist who allows us to finally unmask, if not the phantom itself, at least the communicative mechanism that brings the ego into being as a phantom. In doing so, Bataille's mimetic account of the birth of the ego may even offer us a provisional answer to the much-discussed question, "who comes after subject?"[68]

Mimetic Communication

Let us recall that in "The Psychological Structure of Fascism" Bataille's understanding of the psychology of fascism is predicated on a process of affective contagion that, for the first time, he calls "communication." His focus is still on the leader's magnetic force, but the language, this time, is more recognizably Bataillean. Thus, he wonders how "a mode of sovereign being [*manière d'être souveraine*], which is both linked to domination and to the imperative and separate character of the chief," can be "communicated [*communiqué*] to his soldiers" (I, 359). At this stage in his argument, Bataille is no longer referring to the anthropological notions of *mana* or "participation." Nor does he rely on the psychological notion of "hypnosis" or "identification" in order to account for this "mysterious," elusive "force." His language has changed, once again. Yet the problem is fundamentally the same. Bataille, in fact, is still relying on his previous anthropological and psychological investigations in order to push his understanding of sovereign force further, towards new theoretical territory. And in order to do so he joins, for the first time, the notion of "sovereignty" with the notion of "communication," coupling two terms that will remain central to his thought throughout his career.

Of course, we should be careful here. The fact that Bataille joins these two terms does not mean that we are already confronted with the well-known Bataillean concept of "sovereign communication." Sovereignty, at this stage, refers to a political category (from Latin *superaneus*, which means *superior*), and even though Bataille alludes to the Hegelian language of negativity as well as to the Nietzschean language of expenditure, this notion still lacks the Hegelian/Nietzschean theoretical implications it will later assume (such as the readiness to confront death, to live in the instant, outside the realm of project, work, time, etc.). The same appears to be true for the notion of "communication," a term that does not directly account for those well-known communicative instances that will continue to preoccupy Bataille (such as erotism, tears, sacrifice, dramatization, inner experience, and laughter). And yet we cannot help but wonder whether we are simply confronted with a mere linguistic coincidence. The fact that Bataille uses the notion of "communication" to designate the transmission of a "mysterious force," which spreads contagiously from one subject to others, in a ritual context that has the characteristics of a dramatic spectacle, should at least alert us to the possibility that this may not be an incidental linguistic association, but a conceptual emergence instead.

As Bataille further specifies the dynamic responsible for the process of affective contagion, he makes clear that he is not thinking along the official Freudian parameters, but, rather, extends his own inquiry into a territory left unexplored by Freud. The crowd, he writes,

> has ceased to be itself in order to become affectively ("affectively" refers here to simple psychological behaviors, such as *standing at attention* [*garde-à-vous*] or *marching in step* [*pas cadencé*]) the chief's thing and like a part of the chief itself. A troop standing at attention is in a sense absorbed by the existence of command. (I, 359)

The difference between Freud's and Bataille's choices of paradigmatic examples to account for the leaders' will to power over the masses could not be more striking and exposes the implicit theoretical *différend* with respect to their take on mimetic identification. We have seen that Freud finds his paradigmatic model in a school for girls (a choice that introduces a qualification in both age and gender). Freud is, thus, clearly relying on the malleable status of youth as well as on the patriarchal stereotype of the female hysteric in order to construe his theory of the social bond. Bataille, on the other hand, focuses on a military parade, indicating that mimesis can effectively be theorized via the paradigmatic example of male, adult subjects. Freud starts from a phenomenon of mental psychopathology (a fit of hysteria) already contained within a normalizing institution (a boarding school). Bataille starts with what is usually considered to be a normal phenomenon (a military parade) and posits this mimetic ritual at the heart of the modern public sphere (in the streets). If Freud's example indicates that his theory is firmly located in a personal, psychopathological perspective, Bataille makes clear that his account is located in the field of crowd psychology proper. Finally, the former considers a phenomenon from a position of clinical *distance* where the observer is not directly implicated in what he observes, while the latter is dealing with a mimetic *pathos* that he has himself lived, experienced.[69]

We have seen that this implicated method of analysis has the obvious danger of infecting the observer with the pathology he is trying to dissect; yet it is also instrumental in developing a critical patho-logical discourse that considers such a pathos from a critical distance. And as was already the case with the authors considered thus far, the spiraling movement of mimetic patho(-)logy that ensues manages to anticipate modern horrors yet to come. In the concluding pages of *Blue of the Noon* (1935), for instance, Henry Troppmann, walking in the streets of Frankfurt, bumps into what he calls an "obscene" and "terrifying" spectacle: a Nazi musical parade in a state of "trance" that foreshadows the massive psychic dispossession responsible for the horror of mimesis. "All these Nazi children" he says, "seemed prey, like stiff sticks, to a cataclysmic exaltation." "In the night, every musical explosion, was an incantation that called to war and murder." And speaking of the impact of the infecting rhythm of the drums [*rafale de tambour*] he recognizes that it has the power to turn such children into impersonal, "mechanical entities" (*haineuses mécaniques*) (BC 183–184). These lines confirm Andrew Hussey's claim that "Troppmann . . . like Nietzsche, offers a pathological account of the insufficiency of politics."[70] Both thinkers are, indeed, philosophical physicians who do not hesitate to extend the language of pathology to the social, political, and ethical sphere. Furthermore, Bataille exposes the disconcerting efficacy of the power of mimesis as it is used at the heart of fascist politics. As previous modernist theorists had equally stressed, such an affective/bodily dispossession where "the mind follows the feet" is most effectively triggered by the affective power of musical rhythm.[71] Echoing his predecessors, Bataille will later say that "a man enters a dance because the dance makes him dance" (E 115). As for the type of thinker who can account for such mimetic phenomena, Bataille, following Nietzsche, will call it a "bacchant philosopher" (IE 28) or, alternatively, *Dionysos philosophos*. Clearly, mimesis, in the intrawar period, continues to be an affective, immanent, Dionysian affair—and it is precisely in this respect that Bataille's account of the ego differs from Freud's.

In *The Ego and the Id,* Freud affirms that "the ego is first and foremost a bodily ego" (20), and throughout his investigations he places much attention on the libidinal formation of the subject, following the Nietzschean imperative to root what is considered lofty in humans in what happens underneath the belt. Yet, in his account of crowd psychology, Freud never lingers too long on the importance of instinctual, bodily reflexes. As we have seen, his main focus consists in developing a speculative theory of the social bond, predicated on the articulation of two distinct emotional ties, that is consistent with his mental topography of the Oedipal psyche and the meta-psychology that accompanies it. Compared to previous crowd psychologies, the theoretical sophistication of such a model is, indeed, impressive; but in order to develop it, Freud leaves out of the picture those instinctual, bodily reflexes that for the modernist theorists of mimesis are central to the mecha-nism of affective contagion. We can thus see why Lawrence, in a moment of impatience towards Freud's speculations, boldly affirms that "men with a theory, don't know anything about their own inward experiences" (P 377). This statement may well be one of Lawrence's overstatements. Men with a theory do after all have the ability to situate their mimetic patho(-)logies within a solid frame that not only allows them to avoid dispersion, but also to cast new light on phenomena that would have remained invisible without such a frame. And yet, as always, there is an element of truth in Lawrence's exaggerations, namely, that men with a theory not only tend to apply their frame to the phenomena they are dissecting, leaving out of the picture ele-ments that do not fit within the frame, but also run the risk of mistaking the frame for the phenomenon itself. Bataille is less agonistic towards Freud than Lawrence, perhaps having outgrown the latter's still partially romantic need of differentiation; yet he also denounces psychoanalysis as a "*pensée abstraite*" (VIII, 18), reinforcing Lawrence's suspicion that Freud's project is fundamentally an idealist, metaphysical project that leads him to downplay the importance of immediate physical affects in favor of what recent critics of psychoanalysis skeptically call "higher Truth."[72]

Contrary to this idealizing, Platonic tendency, Bataille is not trying to fit the flow of mimetic affects within an ideal topography of the mind. Thus, at the opening of "Structure," he specifies that "the psychological method adopted excludes any recourse to abstraction" (1, 339). This does not mean that his account of fascist psychology lacks theoretical sophistication; nor that it refuses to situate the affective fluxes that traverse the masses within a larger theoretical picture. Rather, Bataille's suspicion of abstraction stems from his effort to remain faithful to the immanent dimension of affective, mimetic reflexes, reflexes that have the power to lead the feet and wills of egos who are part of a mass. As the examples of "standing at attention," "marching in step," and the state of "trance" induced by the rhythm of drums make clear, for Bataille, it is through a coordinated, rhythmic, and mindless physical movement that the mass of children and soldiers alike become completely "absorbed," body and soul or, better, *from* body *to* soul, in the monocephalic figure of the fascist leader. Faithful to the Nietzschean tradition of thought, Bataille continues to bring this identificatory process back in touch with its immediate bodily dimension—a dimension that is suspicious of "abstract," theoretical distinctions and is attentive to what he calls "immediate understanding of life" (1, 410).

Now, it is precisely because Bataille's communicative thought is not confined within the limits of a theoretical structure that he is in a position to pursue the path Freud indicated but was unable to follow: the path that "leads from identification by way of imitation, to empathy," bringing us back to the pre-Freudian conception of the mimetic unconscious we have been tracking all along.

Bataille makes clear that the unconscious mechanism that informs the sovereign's communication with the soldiers is not only at work at the level of collective psychology, but also operates at the level of intersubjective psychology. In one of the articles collected in "Essais de sociologie," for instance, in a telling theoretical gesture, he switches parental figures as he moves from the leader's communication to the masses, to the mother's communication to the child. Speaking of the maternal attempt to convey a feeling of disgust for the child's own stools—which attract children as much as they repel adults—Bataille writes: "During the formation of behavioral attitudes in childhood, the act of exclusion is not directly assumed. It is communicated from the mother to the child through the medium of funny faces [*grimaces*] and expressive exclamations" (II, 220). Bataille makes clear that, from the very beginning, even what may seem the most natural response is not dependent on the object itself (no matter how abject the object is). Nor does it originate within the subject, from the depth of an original interiority (no matter how interior the experience is). Rather, affects for Bataille emerge through a relation of mimetic communication itself, a relationship with a significant other, in this case, the mother. The child facing the maternal *grimaces* will start unconsciously imitating them and, through such a facial mimicry, will eventually come to feel, experience, the same feelings of disgust as the mother. For Bataille, then, a reflex, mimetic mechanism leads the child to reproduce the exterior, visual expression of the other, and this reproduction of a facial expression is, in turn, responsible for the emergence of an interior feeling within the ego.[73]

Interestingly, both at the level of interpersonal psychology (the mother's "communication" to the child) and at the level of collective psychology (the sovereign's "communication" to the soldiers) the same term refers to a nonverbal, automatic, unconscious transmission of affect responsible for collapsing the distinction between self and other, interior and exterior. We can now better understand why Bataille, in the context of his account of the psychology of fascism, speaks of "the affective character of this unification," an affective unification responsible for the fact that "each soldier considers the glory of the latter [i.e., of the leader] as his own" (1, 357). As the child automatically reacts to the disgusted facial expressions of the mother and comes to partake in her feelings, eventually experiencing them as its own, so the soldiers automatically march in step or give the salute to the leader (substitute father) and come to experience his "glory" as their own. Moreover, if the maternal, mimetic communication is responsible for the formation of the child's attitudes at a personal, emotional level, the leader's mimetic communication is responsible for the soldier's attitudes at the collective, ethical, and political level. In both cases, the experience of a reflex, *bodily* communication breaks down the boundaries of individuation and is responsible for the subject's automatic capitulation to the *psychic* directions of the other. Finally, as Bataille makes clear in another article of the same period, this unconscious, mimetic reaction that informs communication is predicated on a principle he assumes his readers are familiar with: "the well-known principle of contagion, or if you still want to call it that, fellow feeling, *sympathie*" (*Coll.* 109).

Through the Freudian Loop

Indeed, Bataille has taken us full circle through the Freudian loop, swinging us from identification back to sympathy. Yet by following the direction Freud indicated but did not (could not?) follow, Bataille fundamentally perverts the Freudian project: he replaces the conception of the Oedipal, repressed unconscious with the modernist conception of the mimetic unconscious Freud was trying to move away from.[74] This also means that Bataille's early account of communication brings us back to the psychophysiological conception of reflex communication with which we started, and which has been central for our understanding of mimesis in the modernist period.

Let us briefly recall that Nietzsche, in the context of his theory of empathy, made very clear that communication is, from the very beginning, predicated on an unconscious, mimetic mechanism that leads the subject to automatically reproduce the facial gestures of the other and, by doing so, to experience the affect of the other. For Nietzsche, in fact, there is a *"compulsion to imitate"* (*WP* 811) at the heart of communication. Consequently, he specifies, "One never communicates thoughts: one communicates movements, mimic signs, which we then trace back to thoughts" (809). These late affirmations reiterate a point that Nietzsche had already made at the beginning of his career. In *Human, All Too Human*, for instance, we have seen him stress the fact that the origins of this mimetic principle are rooted in childhood: "the child still understands its mother" through an imitation that is "older than speech" (216). And Nietzsche refers to the paradigmatic example of the child's reflex to reproduce the mother yawning, an immediate-automatic-mimetic-communication that breaks down the boundaries of individuation and gives the ego access to the psychic life of the other. As he puts it, the unconscious reflex of imitation is "so strong that we cannot look upon facial movements without innervation of our own face" (*HH* 216). Despite their masculinist poses and sexist prejudices, when it comes to mimesis, thinkers like Nietzsche, Conrad, Lawrence, and Bataille reveal themselves to be delicate, feminine, perhaps even maternal writers who are extremely sensitive to the tacit ways in which feelings are communicated from childhood onwards. I find it revealing that for them, the figure of the mother, more than the father, turns out to be the paradigmatic figure that allows them to follow the labyrinthine path of mimetic forms of communication that give birth to the subject.

Now, if towards the beginning of his career, Bataille refers to this facial "innervation" to account for the maternal communication to the child, here is how, towards the end of his career, he continues to account for the basic principle of mimetic contagion *en jeu* in communication:

> There is a contagiousness that rules out the possibility of dispassionate observation. It has nothing to do with that of germ-carried diseases. The contagion in question is like that of yawning or laughter. A yawn makes one yawn, repeated gusts of laughter make one want to laugh. . . . Seeing

and hearing a man laugh, I participate in his emotion from inside myself. This sensation felt inside me communicates itself to me, and that is what makes me laugh: we have an immediate knowledge of the other person's laughter when we laugh ourselves, or of excitement when we share it. (*E* 152–153)

Bataille could not have put it more clearly. As the modernist period begins to turn into postmodernism, he continues to rely on the mimetic unconscious in order to account for the contagious mechanism at work in sovereign communication. For Bataille, as for Nietzsche before him, this affective, communicative mimesis cannot be relegated to the sphere of pathology; nor can it be accounted for from a (dispassionate) theoretical distance. On the contrary, such a communication is a most ordinary phenomenon; so ordinary that it tends to go unnoticed (and, thus, unthought and, thus, untheorized), but becomes immediately apparent if we rely on a type of experiential, (passionate?) knowledge that is attentive to the contagious dimension of bodily pathos. Bataille's shift to the narrative, mimetic "I" as well as his reliance on Lévy-Bruhl's notion of "participation" is thus *à propos* in order to account for a mimetic form of communication based on a reflex, unconscious mechanism that continues to inform our ability to experience the pathos of the other. As Nietzsche had already put it, what is at stake here is a compulsion to imitate whereby "the imitated gesture led the person who was imitating back to the sensation that expressed itself in the face or body of the person being imitated" (*HH* 216).

So, it seems, we are back to where we started. The same mimetic examples are conjured to account for the mysterious force of communication; the same unconscious reflexes are invoked to account for the impersonal force of contagion. That Bataille is indebted to Nietzsche's Dionysian, squandering thought is a point that is frequently made in Bataille studies. Equally well known is the fact that Bataille's identificatory relation to Nietzsche is so profound that he confuses himself with Nietzsche: as he famously proclaims, "I am the only one who considers himself not as a commentator of Nietzsche, but as being the same as him" (VIII, 401). Virtually unknown, however, is the fact that Bataille's understanding of the precise psychic mechanism responsible for a communication between self and other that transgresses the boundaries of individuation is predicated on what Nietzsche called "genuine physio-psychology" and the "compulsion to imitate" it involves.[75] Bataille's conception of the communicative subject turns out to be Nietzschean in a more fundamental sense than has been previously recognized: Bataillean communication is Nietzschean communication insofar as it is mimetic communication.

And yet we would be misguided in rooting our genealogy of Bataille's mimetic thought in a single, Nietzschean origin, not only because Nietzsche is already indebted to a much wider psychophysiological tradition that looms large in fin de siècle psychology, but also because Bataille's communicative thought directly aligns itself with specific branches of this tradition. Hence, if our intention is to offer the tools to rethink the theoretical and affective foundations of Bataille's communicative thought and, by doing so, reevaluate how Bataille anticipates contemporary developments in mimetic theory, we must not let go of our genealogical account of communication.

The model of the mimetic unconscious Bataille relies on cannot be dissociated from what Freud, following the German philosopher and psychologist Theodor Lipps, called *Einfühlung*.[76] Here is Lipps's understanding of what he calls "the instinctive impetus (or motor power) of mimicry/imitation":

> Perhaps I see a gesture. Then the same facial expression wakens by virtue of a not further describable adjustment of my natural impulse to such movements, which are appropriate to call these gestures into existence. These movements in return are the natural expression of an affected inner condition, i.e., sadness. This condition and the questionable impulses of movement create a psychic unity.[77]

For Lipps, then, the "psychic unity" caused by what Nietzsche had already called, a few years earlier, "imitation of a gesture" is based on an adjustment that is "not further describable." Although Lipps was critical of physiology and privileged a purely psychological approach, this passage makes clear that when it comes to his central concept of *Einfühlung* and the imitation it entails, his account continues to be predicated on a model of the unconscious that reacts on immediate, mimetic reflexes—reflexes that are based on what Freud will go on to describe disapprovingly as an "irreducible primitive phenomenon" (*GP* 21). In a more positive mood, Hippolyte Bernheim had addressed the very same phenomenon in the context of his theory of hypnotic suggestion. Confronting head-on the problem that concerns Bataille in the context of Nazi Germany described in *Le bleu du ciel*, Bernheim writes: "We see a troop of young school-boys; a regiment passes with drum and band, and the boys are thrown into step as thought moved by a spring. They march to the music fatally impelled by an instinctive suggestion."[78] Bernheim is here recognizing what Dionysian philosophers from Plato to Bataille have repeatedly confirmed: namely, that "rhythm is a compulsion; it engenders an unconquerable urge to yield and join in; not only our feet follow the beat but the soul does too" (*GS* 84). Finally, Théodule Ribot sums up the paradigmatic unconscious reactions repeatedly encountered under the rubric of that mimetic pathos par excellence which is sympathy: "In man, infectious laughter or yawning, walking in step, imitating the movements of a rope-walker while watching him . . . are cases of physiological sympathy."[79]

As these paradigmatic examples make strikingly clear, Bataille, like Nietzsche, Conrad, Lawrence, and numerous theorists of mimesis before him, is a faithful inheritor of a pre-Freudian model of the mimetic unconscious. Critics of Freudian affiliation still anachronistically deride it as *l'inconscient à la française*, but the international, transnational, modernist figures we are examining place this model in a wider, forward-looking topography. What these critics do not know, in fact, is that it is precisely this reflex, psycho-physiological mechanism that troubles the mind of modernism, that is at the forefront of current empirical investigations both in the field of child psychology and in the neurosciences (as we shall see shortly). Nor do they know that they are laughing at the fundamental principle that accounts for Bataille's persistent fascination with "contagious subjectivity" (VIII, 288) and the Nietzschean theory of communication that ensues. Not only at the time of "Structure," but also in his later work, Bataille, in a period enthusiastically enthralled by the Freudian, repressed unconscious, continues until the very end to stubbornly rely on this untimely model of the mimetic unconscious. And he does so in order to account for the nonverbal power of affective communication that traverses like a current the boundaries of individuation. Thus, in *Erotism* (1957), as he returns to the topic of the formation of attitudes in childhood, Bataille writes that we "have to teach them [disgust] by pantomime" (58). In *Guilty* (1944), not limiting this mimetic communication between mother and child to the feeling of disgust, he accounts for the communication of laughter thus: "the mother provokes laughter in her child via a mimicry that engenders an emotional disequilibrium. She suddenly approaches its face, comes up with playful, surprising expressions, or utters strange little cries" (v, 390). And after accounting for the major instances of communication (such as disgust, eroticism, and laughter) by relying on the reflex model of the unconscious, Bataille concludes that "there is a contagiousness that rules out the possibility of dispassionate observation. . . . This is a disturbed state of mind, one which must normally bar methodical scientific observation" (E 152).

We seem, then, to have reached a limit in Bataille's understanding of communicative force, which is also a theoretical limit in the modernist understanding of the mimetic unconscious. And yet reaching this limit puts us in a position to better understand the principle that generates contagious forms of communication. Communication, for Bataille, as for Nietzsche, Conrad, Lawrence, late nineteenth-century psychophysiology, and modernist mimetic theory at large, is contagious and spreads from subject to subject insofar as it is predicated on an unconscious reflex mechanism that leads the subject to reproduce the gestures of the other.[80] A nonmediated, psychophysiological mimesis is thus responsible for the emergence of the feeling of the other within the ego that breaks down the distinction between ego and other. In this sense, the tradition of the mimetic unconscious we have been tracing culminates in Bataille's understanding of a communicative contagion based on immediate *pathos* (rather than discursive, linguistic *logos*).[81] We are thus beginning to realize that Bataille, one of the major precursors of the postmodern death of the subject (i.e., the subject of the signifier) and the mediation it entails, turns out to be fundamentally aligned with a model of communication that privileges the immediacy of bodily reflexes over the mediation of linguistic representation (i.e., the subject of mimesis).

Now, before pursuing this line of inquiry further and transgressing the limits of nineteenth-century psychophysiology, let us briefly recontextualize the general movement of Bataille's thought. As the 1930s are speeding towards an end, Bataille will progressively lose his spellbound fascination with the mimetic methods of monocephalic leader figures who bring about social forms of revolutionary effervescence. Yet his official project at the Collège de Sociologie (as well as its secret counterpart society, Acéphale) indicates that even after the leader's head has been symbolically severed, Bataille's preoccupations with the feelings of attraction and repulsion that swing the subject towards / away from heterogeneous matters, remain fundamentally the same. In one of his lectures (January 1938), for instance, Bataille suggests that the contradictory affective reactions triggered by heterogeneous leaders constitute but a recapitulation of a much more fundamental feeling of attraction and repulsion triggered by the heterogeneous dimension of sacrifice. Positing such a pathos of distance at the very heart of the social bond, he now speculates: "Everything leads us to believe that early human beings were brought together by disgust and by common terror, by an insurmountable horror focused precisely on what originally was the central attraction of their union" (*Coll.* 106). We can thus see how Lawrence's dramatization of the affective forces is at stake in the sacrificial bullfight, which attracts the spell-bound boy as much as it repels the skeptical lady, is still at the very center of Bataille's preoccupations. This is what he calls the *noyau central* that accounts for the human, all too human necessity to assemble.[82]

But Bataille is not only concerned with the contradictory pathos of distance that assembled humans in *illo tempore*; nor solely with the violent, sacrificial dimension of the origins of culture. He is also interested in a gay science of affective contagion responsible for assembling subjects in a what he calls a "common movement" (*Coll.* 109). In order to do so, he continues to interrogate the limits of Apollonian individuation by dissecting yet another Dionysian affect that spreads contagiously from self to others, others to self: namely laughter. Bataille does not hesitate to call this ticklish, mimetic affect the "specific form of human interaction" (*Coll.* 108), as well as "one of psychology's most complex and maddening problems" (108). And in order to account for this problem, he transgresses the limits of nineteenth-century psychophysiology and turns to consider a philosophical physician who opens up a new psychology for the future: the French philosopher and psychologist Pierre Janet.

The Psychology of the Future

Given Bataille's emphasis on the immediacy of mimetic contagion, we should expect that in order to account for the psychological mechanism that informs laughter—this most involuntary, bodily reflex—he would rely on the same psychophysiological principle of unconscious communication we have seen him consistently endorse throughout his career. This is certainly the case.[83] Thus he speaks of an "automatic, unconscious process produced .. . in the flow of communication" (II, 316). Bataille clearly situates his account of contagious forms of communication such as laughter within the tradition of the mimetic unconscious. And yet in the 1930s and 1940s Bataille is not only looking back, towards pre-Freudian conceptions of the unconscious concerned with the immediacy of bodily affects. He is equally looking forward, towards Pierre Janet's psychological research, a research that seems to advocate the necessity of distance, or mediation, with respect to this automatic, bodily pathos.

Our past, Freudian century has not been kind to Pierre Janet. It has done much to erase the memory of this long-neglected figure, and the success of this operation can be gauged by the number of critics who are familiar with his name or thought. This neglect is not an historical accident. As Ian Hacking explains in *Rewriting the Soul*, "one thing is certain, Freud personally saw Janet as a threat and a rival. . . . Janet was a victim of Freud's self-aware management of the psychoanalytic movement. Janet was a scholar; Freud, by comparison, was an entrepreneur who annihilated Janet's reputation."[84] Mimetic rivalries have winners and losers, and, thanks to Freud's entrepreneurial success, the wind has blown in favor of psychoanalysis for a while. But the wind is changing, and thanks to Henri Ellenberger's pioneering *The Discovery of the Unconscious*, and other historians and theorists of the soul, Pierre Janet is currently returning on the analytical scene, occupying center stage on cutting-edge critical debates on multiple personality disorders, trauma studies, and psychological approaches to modernism.[85] Trained both as a philosopher and as a clinical doctor, director at the Salpêtrière, professor at the Collège de France, specialist in hypnosis, hysteria, trauma, somnambulism, automatism, and dual personalities, inventor of psychological concepts like the "subconscious" and "dissociation," Janet was a strong ally, Bataille immediately sensed, to continue opening up the mind of modernism to future-oriented psychological developments. And quite rightly so; as Ellenberger argues, Janet was "the first to found a new system of dynamic psychiatry aimed at replacing those of the nineteenth century."[86]

Bataille's debt to Janet is theoretically elusive, not directly apparent, and has thus far escaped critical attention.[87] Yet Bataille was not only well read in Janet's psychology; he also collaborated with him, serving as the vice president of the short-lived Société de Psychologie Collective, founded in 1937 and presided over by Janet.[88] More important, during the same period, Bataille finds in Janet's psychology a source of theoretical inspiration that allows him to supplement his reliance on nineteenth-century psychophysiology in order to account for the riddle of communication. As he continues to dissect the contagious dimension of collective movements, Bataille writes:

> Pierre Janet in a recent article in *Annales médico-psychologiques* demonstrated the absurdity of former conceptions, or perhaps more exactly, former ignorance about the problem. Janet's explanation of the nineteenth-century psychologists' way of seeing is that, according to them, "man knows immediately." (*Coll.* 109)

If we have seen Bataille unconditionally rely on theories of automatic reflexes in order to account for what he calls "the immediate knowledge of the other person's laughter," he now abruptly changes his mind. Contrary to this way of seeing, he now posits the necessity of "recognition" and mediation for unconscious forms of communication to flow. This is, indeed, a strange turn in Bataille's otherwise Nietzschean take on the immediacy of bodily communication, but one that our diagnostic operation has taught us to expect. We must ask, then, what exactly motivates Bataille's oscillation from pathos to distance, from the immediacy of the mimetic experience to the mediation of visual recognition?

A Nod to the Master

Although Bataille does not state it explicitly, the need to posit "mediation" and "recognition" in the relationship with the other is indebted not so much to Janet—a psychologist who, after all, was very interested in automatic psychic phenomena such as somnambulism, automatic writing, and hypnosis[89]—but to Alexandre Kojève's anthropomorphic reading of Hegel. It is, in fact, well known that Kojève, in his widely influential lectures on Hegel's *Phenomenology of the Spirit* (1807), which impressed Bataille and many others so deeply, posits the necessity of the mediation of representation in that life-and-death struggle for recognition that is the master-slave dialectic.

Without entering into the details of Kojève's reading, let us recall that "mediation" and "recognition" are precisely what distinguishes animal consciousness (sentiment of self) from human consciousness (self-consciousness) or, alternatively, the slave from the master. If the master engaged in a dialectical battle for "pure prestige" is ready to confront death in order to have his desire recognized, the slave fails to do so and remains (at least in the initial stage of the dialectic) at the level of animal immediacy. "While the Slave still remains an 'immediate,' natural, 'bestial' being," comments Kojève, "the Master—as a result of his fight—is already human, 'mediated.'"[90] Bataille's emphasis on "mediation" and "recognition" is unquestionably Kojèvian/Hegelian, and in the context of his theory of sacrifice, Bataille will later posit the need for the "subterfuge" of representational distance in order to confront the phantom of death, *bien en face*.[91]

And yet we should refrain from hastily aligning Bataille with this Kojèvian/Hegelian emphasis on mediation over immediacy, the *distance* of what Bataille calls "phantasmatic representations" over the *pathos* of what we call the phantom of the ego.[92] Instead, let us take a closer look at Bataille's account of recognition and ask ourselves a more specifically mimetic question: how does recognition take place in laughter, and what, exactly, is the communicative subject supposed to recognize in the experience of communication? Bataille's answer is the following:

> Like organisms, in many instances, may well experience group movements. They are somehow permeable to such movements. What is more, I have thus only stated in other terms the well-known principle of contagion, or if you still want to call it that, fellow feeling, *sympathie*, but I believe I have done this with sufficient precision. If one acknowledges permeability in group movements [*mouvements d'ensemble*], in continuous movements, the phenomenon of recognition will appear to be constructed on the basis of the feeling of permeability experienced when confronted with an other/socius [*le phénomène de la reconnaissance apparaîtra construit à partir du sentiment éprouvé en face d'un autre/socius*]. (*Coll.* 109)

Despite his nod in the direction of master Kojève—who, by the way, was probably among the audience of this lecture at the Collège—acquiescing to the importance of mediation, Bataille, during this Hegelian period, already makes clear that recognition is *not* the condition for an affective communication to take place. On the contrary, recognition is but the effect of (*construit à partir de*) a previous, originary affectability (*sentiment éprouvé*) that overtakes the subject immediately as soon as it is exposed to the presence of an "other/socius."[93] For Bataille, then, immediate pathos is not only prior to representational distance, but is the necessary condition for mediated recognition to take place. The subject does not see the other and then feel her or his affect; it feels the pathos of the other first, and it is on the basis of this affect that recognition is based—at least in the case of communication with a socius.

Who exactly, then, is this socius responsible for that disconcerting feeling of permeability which cracks the ego up in laughter? Bataille does not point to a single identity. However, he returns to the question of the socius five days later, in another lecture delivered for the Société de Psychologie Collective. Speaking of Janet's account of *la psychologie du socius*, he now explains: "Janet insisted on the fact that the individual subject is not easily distinguished from the fellow creature with whom he is in rapport, from the socius" (II, 287). Bataille, as we shall shortly confirm, is faithful to Janet's definition of the socius as the "other" who is, paradoxically, indistinguishable from the subject. Yet he also adds a personal twist to Janet's definition, giving a specific example of a socius that is characteristically Bataillean. Thus, he writes: "the dead is a socius, which means that he is very difficult to distinguish from oneself" (II, 287). Now, if death is a socius and the socius is somebody who is difficult to distinguish from the subject, we might wonder why Bataille establishes a connection between the socius and laughter.

Laughing with the Socius

As counterintuitive as this might seem, for Bataille, the pathos triggered by the most tragic event in life, which is death, and the most comic of all affects, which is laughter, are intimately related. Thus, he gives the admittedly extreme example of "a young girl full of charm and full of humanity who cannot help laughing each time she is told of the death of someone she knows" (*Coll.* 107). More commonly, however, the sight of somebody slipping on a banana peel causes us to be overtaken, involuntarily, with laughter; and "laughter about falling is already in some manner laughter about death" (110). For

Bataille, then, it is precisely because of this other/socius with whom I am in "rapport" and is indistinguishable from myself, that I am equally shaken, like the other, by a force that pulls the rug from under my feet and dispossesses me of control over myself. And short of physically miming the other's fall, I am overtaken by an irresistible, automatic urge that surges forth from within my body, in laughter. This is, in a nutshell, also the fundamental thesis of one of the few theorists who, so far, has pointed towards the mimetic foundations of Bataille's communicative thought.

In an admirable account of Bataille's take on laughter, Mikkel Borch-Jacobsen focuses on the contagious, identificatory mechanism that is tacitly but fundamentally at work in Bataille's persistent, tragicomic confrontation with death. The concluding pages are effective in reminding us of the importance of mimesis (or identification) in Bataille's communicative thought. Moreover, through Bataille, Borch-Jacobsen gives an ontological twist to the modernist tradition that concerns us. In fact, he identifies the "being" of the Bataillean communicative subject in what he calls a "suspended instant in which we are at once ourselves *and* the other."[94] Being, according to this view, can no longer be contained within the *ipse* of a solipsistic, monadic subject, enclosed in what Bataille calls the "trap of the *ego*" (*piège du* moi) (*IE* 73; trans. modified), but is con-divided instead, in the sense that the subject shares its being *with* an other who is *divided* from itself. As Borch-Jacobsen writes: "what is needed is the other . . . in order to communicate laughter to me; what is needed is this flashing and suspended passage in which I am the other—*that I am not*."[95] In this paradoxical formula that captures the oscillating movement of communication responsible for a mimetic confusion of identity, Borch-Jacobsen is teasing out of Bataille a conclusion similar to the one that emerges from his early work on hypnosis, namely that "the subject *is* the other."[96] And indeed, who better than Bataille, a thinker of mimesis who spent his life repeatedly attempting to go beyond the distinction between self and other on the basis of a pre-Freudian conception of the unconscious, could be invoked to sustain a provocative "mimetic hypothesis" that argues for an affective con-fusion of identity at the foundations of subjectivity?

Yet at the same time, in his reading of Bataille Borch-Jacobsen now feels the necessity to stress that even at the instant of the suspension of being, the other, which "I" am, is *not* "myself." The other who falls in my place may communicate its pathos directly to me, in the instant of direct communication

that bends me in two but, in the end, leaves me standing, at a distance. This
pathos of distance, which we have identified as the structuring feature of
thinkers of mimesis, indicates that identification is necessarily always a partial failure. And quite luckily so. In fact, this failure of identity makes all the
difference insofar as it keeps the subject on the solid ground of life, shaken
to the roots of its being, yet with enough time to catch its breath. The failure
of identification is, then, responsible for driving a wedge between self and
other, so that the mimetic mechanism to which we are connected does not
reproduce simple simulacra of selfhood informed by the typographic imprint
of the mimetic other. The result of mimetic communication is not to set in
motion a mechanical reproduction of identity that churns out phantoms of
the ego without proper being; but, rather, to generate a contagious process
of becoming other that brings the ego into being *with* the other *as* other.
In short, the sovereign, communicative subject continues to have its being
suspended in the other that cracks the ego up in laughter—but the laughter
that we hear is the laughter of the socius.

Janet's Psychology of the Socius

Let us then have a closer look at Janet's psychology of the socius in order to
conclude our investigation into the intersubjective foundations of Bataille's
conception of sovereign communication and unmask the precise, mimetic
mechanism that gives birth to the phantom of the ego—out of the laughter
of the other.

Succeeding Ribot and Charcot as the president of the Congrès International de Psychologie, Pierre Janet opened the eleventh meeting, held
in July 1937, with an introductory speech titled "Les conduites sociales," a
speech that sets out to indicate what he calls his "dreams for future psychological studies."[97] In this lecture, delivered towards the end of his career,
and subsequently expanded in an article titled "Les troubles de la personnalité sociale,"[98] Janet begins with the humble recognition that despite his
career-long efforts to go beyond what he calls "a subjective psychology," his
research, he says, still remained "too much confined within a personal psychology" (C 141). The limits of such a confinement within a psychology of
the subject, which he considers symptomatic of the discipline of psychology
as a whole, he continues, are particularly visible if we realize that the ego is

not a monadic, self-contained form that comes into being in isolation but is, from the very beginning, a permeable, mimetic entity open to the affect of the other. Now, it is precisely in order to move beyond an individualist, autonomous perspective and open up a new direction of psychological research that Janet encourages young generations of psychologists to explore the role of the other in the formation of what he calls "social personality" (142). Hence, he urges future psychologists to "exit from too personal a psychology and to begin the inter-psychology Gabriel Tarde spoke of" (149). The "psychology of the socius" is Janet's major step towards this psychology of the future.[99]

Janet's account of the socius is rooted in his clinical observation of patients who suffer from a feeling of confusion between self and other, a mixing up of personalities characteristic of what Janet diagnoses as "psychasthenia." At the most fundamental level, these "personality troubles" (*troubles de la personnalité*) are characterized by the subject's feelings of being possessed by another who takes control of the subject's thoughts and actions. Characteristic complaints, as Janet reports in a diegetic narrative mode, are the following: "another person knows his own thoughts and possesses them as well as he does"; "he constantly has the feeling of a theft of his own thoughts, which are possessed by others"; "he even hears the echo of his thoughts repeated by the other who has taken possession of them" (143). As a consequence of this con-fusion of identities, where it is no longer clear who speaks and thinks (the subject or the echo of the subject?), these patients no longer know who is in control of their actions (the ego or the phantom of the ego?). For instance, Maury, a patient who suffers from psychasthenia, claims that he sees "phantoms executing movements that he would have liked to do, but that in reality was not doing."[100] Similarly, James, who suffers from the same personality trouble, succinctly communicates this indistinction of identity to Janet in a direct, mimetic narrative mode: "It is like a phantom who is there beside me or in me" (*un fantôme qui est là à côté de moi ou en moi*) (D 65).[101]

Socius is the term Janet uses in order to account for such a phantom who is experienced as being indistinguishable from the ego. This mimetic phantom, then, generates a deep sense of depersonalization, mechanization, and loss of the boundaries of individuation, which deprives the ego of its "proper" identity.[102] The socius, then, is nothing more and nothing less than the phantom

of the ego we have been tracking all along, a psychic phantom that takes possession of the subject's actions, thoughts, feelings, and soul, and is eventually
responsible for the development of severe psychic delusions, which belong
to the sphere of mental pathology. Yet, despite the clinical foundations of
Janet's psychology of the socius, he is very careful not to dismiss this "personality trouble" in terms of "rare pathological accidents" (c 149). For Janet,
in fact, the term socius does not simply designate a phantasmal psychic delu-
sion in the mind of patients who suffer from psychasthenia, or delirium of
persecution. On the contrary, following James Baldwin, he defines the socii
as those figures who are important in the formation of the subject (parents,
siblings, teachers, friends), external models who are constitutive of the child's
psychic development. Far from relegating the psychology of the socius to the
sphere of mental pathology, Janet extends its patho-*logical* implications to all
subjects who grew up in a relation of rapport with significant others.

Given that the theorists of mimesis we have encountered thus far have
repeatedly insisted on the imitative status of children, we should not be
surprised if a practicing psychologist and attentive empirical observer like
Pierre Janet links the psychology of the socius to the psychology of mimesis. Following Tarde, Janet notices that "the beginning of social life is in the
act of imitation" (T 167), and in order to supplement this mimetic line of
inquiry, he relies on child psychologists such as M. Paul Guillaume, James
Baldwin, and Henry Wallon, who argue that the development of the ego is
a social, mimetic process from the very beginning. "The act of the socius,"
Janet writes, "determines the more or less complete and exact imitations that
we see very early on among small children" (167). And he adds: "[James M.]
Baldwin has already signaled that the important consequence of imitation is
to introduce into an individual consciousness the thoughts of another" (167).
Janet is, thus, clear on the fact that it is through mimesis that the incorporation of the other/socius in the self actually takes place and, as a consequence,
the child comes into being as a social, affective subject. Further, if we have
repeatedly stressed that mimesis is a complex, intersubjective phenomenon
that eludes easy, linear explanations, Janet also reminds us that mimesis "is
far from being as simple as we think it is" and adds an extra layer of complexity to our understanding of the mimetic communication responsible for the
emergence of the phantom of the ego. Hence, he specifies the intersubjective
process of communication thus:

In the course of the same action, I must constantly modify my behavior [*conduite*] vis-à-vis a socius, depending on the reaction it provokes, a reaction I am incessantly obliged to take into account . . . the subject who imitates modifies its action in relation to the action of the other and . . . the imitated subject equally modifies its own. Thus, one is not imitated uniquely in a passive way; and there is a special attitude of the one who is imitated. (D 34)

Mimesis, for Janet, is a fundamentally relational process that transgresses neat distinctions between imitator and imitated, copy and original, in favor of a back-looping effect that short-circuits a linear causal logic. The subject's imitation of the other generates a retroactive effect whereby the other starts imitating the self imitating the other, and so on. Consequently, in behavioral mimesis there is no stable referent for the subject to imitate but, rather, a dynamic, spiraling process of mutual interaction that challenges the binary distinction between origin and copy, the subject and the echo of the subject, the ego and the phantom of the ego.[103]

Now, this spiraling process of mimetic communication, which, from childhood on, characterizes the relationship of the subject to the socii that surround it, forces a reconsideration of subjectivity in relational and reciprocal terms rather than monadic and narcissistic terms. Elaborating on the psychological implications of this reciprocal mimetic relationship, Janet adds that the socius occupies such a fundamental place in the interior, psychic development of the ego that it "troubles" the distinction between self and other so central to traditional notions of "personality":

The two personalities, the one of the subject and the one of the socius, emerge together in a confused matter [*s'édifient ensemble d'une manière confuse*]. . . . Here we come to what may seem to be a paradoxical idea. Namely, that the distinction between persons, between myself and the socius, is not as fundamental and primitive as we thought it was, and that there was a period, of which there are still traces, where my person and my acts were confused with the person and the acts of others. (C 145)

It is clear that, for Janet, clinical cases who claim "I am no longer myself," or that a "phantom" takes possession of their ego, only bring to the surface a primal confusion of identity that is, as he says, "natural and frequent" (141) and is responsible for bringing into being a *relational, affective* ego or subject. Hence, the confusion of identity that defines such a mimetic relation in childhood is not the result of two separate egos identical to themselves that later join in a common act of communication, but, rather, communication is the necessary condition for the emergence of the phantom of the ego out of the affective pathos of the other. The ego, thus understood, is not conceived as a solipsistic, self-contained monad that subsequently relates to other egos. On the contrary, for Janet, it is precisely the process of affective communication with the others/socius—what he also calls "the confusion of the subject and the socius" (T 166)—that gives birth to the subject as a relational, mimetic being. Put differently, Janet suggests that the experience of mimetic communication with the socius not only precedes the subject/object distinction, but is also the necessary condition for the formation of the psychic life of the subject instead.

Recent theoretical developments have given new impetus to Janet's dream for a psychology of the future attentive to the relational, mimetic dimension of subject formation. In the field of child psychology, for instance, Meltzoff and Moore have adopted a relational perspective in order to address the question of infants' imitation, while at the same time returning to newborns' automatic responsiveness to facial imitation, which struck modernist advocates of the mimetic unconscious as being central to communication between the newborn and its mother. Grounding their research on an empirical basis, these contemporary psychologists have established that newborns only a few hours old are already responsive to facial imitation, such as protruding the tongue or opening the mouth; records of mimetic reflexes so far being discovered in thirty-minute-olds![104] On another key area of research in mimetic theory, neurophysiological studies in the 1990s have located the presence of "mirror neurons" in the brain that are automatically triggered by the visual movements of others with whom the subject relates, the neural mechanism matching the observed behavior with the one executed. As one of the central figures of this discovery, Vittorio Gallese, puts it, "'understanding' is achieved by modeling a *behaviour* as an *action* with the help of a motor equivalence between what the others do and what the observer does."[105] Through an unconscious, embodied imitation of the actions and expressions of the other, then, we understand the intentions and feelings of the other and react accordingly. And since newborns are receptive to such mimetic communications from the very beginning, then, the focus of attention must shift from an egocentric account of ego formation to a "we-centric" communicative experience that bring a "shared mind" into being.[106] This is, indeed, a revolutionary discovery that forces us to rethink the foundations of the process of ego formation as well as of nonverbal forms of adult communication. But it is also a *re*-discovery of a mimetic principle that was once well known among modernist physicians of the soul. Nietzsche, for one, had already spoken of an "ancient association between movement and sensation," and his modernist successors were quick to echo this untimely psycho-physiological realization. In a sense, then, these recent developments in the neurosciences prove, on an experimental basis what modernist mimetic theorists have known all along: that the ego is not born in isolation but in a relation of unconscious and mimetic communication with others. Clearly, the emphasis given to unconscious forms of imitation we have repeatedly encountered in the Nietzschean current of modernism can no longer be simply dismissed as the product of an antiquated conception of the unconscious. Their unfashionable reputation in the past Freudian century simply stemmed from the fact that modernist theorists of mimesis were ahead of their time. Hence they insisted that mimetic reflexes are much more important for the formation of the ego than psychologists from Freud onwards had actually realized.

Consequently, and this is a crucial point, subjectivity, from the very beginning, must be rethought in relational, imitative terms. In fact, if the subject responds unconsciously to mimetic reflexes from the very first hours of life, then an account of ego formation must give much more attention to the relational process that takes place, at the interstices of intersubjectivity, between the ego and the socius. And if we want to account for the ego's emergence, then an inversion of perspective is in order: The ego should not be seen as the cause of mimesis but as its effect; mimesis does not follow the ego but brings it into being. This rethinking of the mimetic foundations of subjectivity, which empirical researchers are now beginning to investigate, is precisely what the authors I am concerned with have been doing all along. From Nietzsche to Conrad, Lawrence to Bataille, these modernist authors provide us with an alternative theory of the subject whose mimetic foundations are not only in line with cutting-edge scientific discoveries. They also help us to think through the social, political, and ethical implications of such discoveries. In this sense, Nietzschean modernists make our understanding of the ego quite literally *new*, bringing it up to date for our contemporary, hypermimetic times.

After this detour via the psychology of the socius we can now better understand why these others/socii are experienced as being constitutive of the psychic life of the ego. A mimetic relation with the socius in adulthood reopens those affective passages that nourished the ego in the first place, passages that convey what Janet also calls "an immediate and, in a way, reflex, certitude of the feelings of others" (T 161).[107] Characteristic examples of these unconscious, mimetic affects that trouble the stability of identity concern the mother's relations to the child and, more generally, children's imitative behavior.[108] And in order to illustrate the reenactment of such a confusion of identity at the larger, social level Janet gives the example of the leader's order (*commandement du chef*) to the soldiers and the subject's motor execution (*execution motrice imitative*) that ensues. Janet, in other words, extends his considerations on the psychology of the socius to those paradigmatic examples Bataille also relies on in order to account for the process of mimetic communication. The child automatically imitating the mother's facial expressions and the soldier mindlessly marching in step or standing at attention are not monadic subjects who communicate to other subjects—individuals (from Latin, indivisible) who are self-sufficient, self-contained, and fundamentally distinct from others. Rather, they are engaged in a process of affective, unconscious relationship that is predicated on the ego's primary mimetic openness to the affect of the socius.

The Ticklish Ego

Which conception of the subject underscores the Bataillean model of communication? What are the affective foundations of the so-called contagious subjectivity that informs his concept of sovereign communication? A direct answer, it should be clear by now, can be found in Bataille's reliance on the tradition of the mimetic unconscious in general, and Janet's psychology of the socius in particular. More precisely, for Bataille, as for Janet before him, it is because the ego is, from the very beginning, open, by reflex, to the affect of the socius that it remains subsequently vulnerable to the power of mimetic contagion.

Bataille puts it quite clearly as he pursues his discussion of the psychology of laughter and the affective permeability it generates. Anticipating contemporary developments in child psychology, Bataille stresses once again the immediate mirroring reflexes of infants: "A child, who is a few weeks old, responding to an adult's laughter, represents unambiguously the classic example of immediate laughter" (*Coll.* 107). And he specifies:

> Now I will go back to the child's laughter as a basic example [*exemple fondamental*] of permeability to a common movement. It happens when confronted with adult laughter [*Il a lieu en face du rire de l'adulte*]. It establishes between adult and child a communication that is already so profound that it later will be able to be enriched and amplified by multiplying its possibilities without its intimate nature being changed. (109)

For Bataille, then, in the beginning was laughter. Initially triggered by the *mimique* of that socius par excellence who is the mother, through an immediate, affective communication based on a reflex, involuntary mechanism, laughter, for Bataille, is the source of an originary permeability of the ego to the affect of the other/socius. Thus he writes that "we are born in the flood of hilarity" (*Ess.* 149). Or, as he will also put it, quoting Virgil, "*incipe, parve puer, risu cognoscere materm*" (v, 389).[109]

The newborn's permeability to the laughter of the socius is a foundational moment in the Bataillean conception of the communicative subject. It is also central for mimetic theory, and for at least two reasons. First, Bataille makes clear that forms of communication that have the socius as its medium do not communicate any linguistic message ("there is no pure and simple communication") insofar as for Bataille the mimetic medium *is* the mimetic message ("what is communicated is joy") (*Coll.* 110). As he specifies: "It is characteristic of this paradoxical process that it is automatic, unconscious and expressly produced not in solitude but within ordinary communication" (111). No wonder that in unconscious forms of communication the ego does not stop to reflect on the message itself, but is carried away by the electrifying current of the medium. And second, the medium of laughter serves as an affective channel through which the ego is born as a permeable, relational, intersubjective being. In fact, he specifies that the joy conveyed by the laughter of the socius establishes a communication "so profound" that it will pave the way for future forms of affective communication. As Bataille will later say, "the happiest laughter is the one that gives birth to a child [*fait naître un enfant*]" (*IE* 90; trans. modified). Bataille, then, posits a contagious yet joyful, life-affirmative affect at the origin of his genesis of the ego, fulfilling the Nietzschean dream for a gay science of mimesis.

We are thus back to the question of the birth of the ego, and, once again, what we find at the foundation of the ego is nothing original—but mimesis instead. Yet for Bataille (as opposed to, let's say, Lacan) the child's ecstatic jubilation is not the result of an identification with a static image (or *imago*) that reassuringly provides the ego with neat boundaries of individuation (or form) at the pleasing moment of narcissistic self-recognition.[110] As it was already the case for Nietzsche, Conrad, and Lawrence before him, for Bataille, the child's immediate pathos is not mediated by a prior representation. Bataille makes clear that "the laughter of satisfaction . . . comes before the laughter of recognition" (*Coll.* 109). Nor does it have its origins in a complacent feeling of narcissistic self-satisfaction at the thought that "this form is my ego!" On the contrary, laughter, for Bataille, stems from the ego's affective openness to the contagious communication of the laughter of the other (or socius) that, like an electric current (*un courant éléctrique*), transgresses the boundaries of individuation and generates the experiential realization that, "This affect is my ego"! To put it in our language, this child does not come into being by pondering its mirror-like image represented to itself from a distance ("I see myself; therefore I am") but, rather, experiences, with joy, the living pathos of the laughter of the socius whose "expressive exclamations" tickle the ego into being ("I feel—I am"). For Bataille, then, this ego is not born out of a visual imago, but out of the laughter of the socius; which also means that at the origins of the ego there is not a rigid, ideal form, but an uncontrolled burst of laughter instead.

This insight into the psychological and psychophysiological foundations of Bataille's conception of the mimetic subject puts us in a position to answer those fundamental questions addressed to Bataille's thought from a purely ontological perspective. Leslie Hill, for instance, echoing earlier theorists such as Jean-Luc Nancy and Jacques Derrida, wonders whether "despite its attempt to overcome the subject-object relation, his work does not remain hostage to it and to a metaphysics of the subject."[111] Along similar lines, François Warin, despite his awareness of the presence of mimetic elements in Bataille's thought, claims that Bataille's language "remains often prisoner of the metaphysics of the subject, a metaphysics which borrows its models and concepts from the constituted natural sciences (fusion, effusion, contagion,

dissolution, . . . concepts which always presuppose the existence of a substance, of a *upokeimenon* isolated and closed upon itself."[112] An account of
Bataille's heterogeneous theoretical sources based on a more general awareness of the longer history of mimetic theory in which Bataille's communicative thought is inscribed has taught us otherwise. Concepts like "fusion,"
"contagion," "effusion," as we have repeatedly seen, stem from a transdisciplinary tradition that challenges precisely the ontology of the subject these
critics invoke. More specifically, the Bataillean conception of the subject is
far from reposing on a self-enclosed, monadic substance (or *upokeimenon*),
but is traversed by a communicative flux of affect that renders it, from the
very beginning, vulnerable to what Bataille calls the "permeability experienced when confronted with an other" (or socius). Briefly put, the Bataillean
conception of communication does not repose on a *metaphysics of the subject*
but on a *psychology of the socius* instead.[113]

Am "I" exaggerating Bataille's reliance on a permeable conception of the
subject that slips (*glisse*) through the metaphysics of subjectivity? Are "we"
making too much of a theory of mimetic communication on the basis of
a punctual moment in Bataille's early period, unduly generalizing his take
on laughter to other forms of sovereign communication? Perhaps. And yet
Bataille is insistent in positing the centrality of laughter as *the* fundamental fact of interaction. Thus, he calls laughter the "specific form of human
interattraction" (*Coll.* 108) or, alternatively, "the fundamental phenomenon
of interattraction" (109). Moreover, Bataille considers the child's immediate
response to the laughter of the socius as the necessary form for subsequent
affective communications to take place. "This immediate joy," as he writes,
"will persist through the social alteration of laughter" (110). And he specifies:
"Laughter would be only one of the possible currents since unifying movements, transmissible from one person to another, are able to take different
forms as soon as permeability frees a passage" (109). For Bataille, then, the
child's initial openness to the reflex of mimesis is responsible for its subsequent permeability to others, opening up the neurological passages that make
it possible for future forms of communication to flow. As he pursues this line
of inquiry, Bataille makes clear that the communicative fluxes of pathos even
include what he calls mediated laughter (*rire médiatisé*)—a misleading term
insofar as, affectively speaking, this laughter is no less immediate than the
child's reflex response to the laughter of the socius.[114]

If Bataille introduces a distinction between types of laughter, it is because in this case the pathos that flows quite directly from myself to the other is "mediated" by that third, heterogeneous element, which, as we have already seen, attracts and repels Bataille so profoundly, namely death. It has been said that this kind of laughter is a manifestation of Bataille's hollow laugh (*rire jaune*) (Sartre) or, alternatively, that it is an expression of Bataille's sovereign laughter (Borch-Jacobsen). In a sense, both philosophical readings are true to Bataille.[115] What we should add is that Bataille's "tragic laughter," affectively speaking, is not different from sobbing: that is, a reflex, involuntary mechanism that shakes the foundations of the ego. At the moment of the death of the "other," a loved, intimate other who is already part of the self, there is nothing left to see, let alone to say, or think. What we have, instead, is a pathos—Bataille also says, an "open wound" (*blessure ouverte*) (v, 370)—which threatens to dissolve the boundaries of the ego in a feeling of permeability experienced, one last time, in the company of the other/socius.

In the context of this lecture at the Collège de Sociologie, Bataille will continue to delineate other passages that allow fluxes of affect that disrupt the distinction between self and other to flow, through the routes (*parcours*) initially opened by the laughter of the socius. As he puts it: "Contagious weeping and erotic contagion are the only things that, subsequently, will be able to deepen human communication" (*Coll.* 109). Sobbing and eroticism, then, will continue to deepen the mimetic passages that tie the ego to the other. This also means that affects, for Bataille, are not divided in different streams that give a theoretical, ideal form to the immanent experience of communication but, rather, are part of a single, emotional continuity of being that ties egos together. Moreover, as Bataille will pursue his exploration of what he calls "moments of intense communication" that generate an "intensity . . . devoid of personal significance" (110), he will also add other, immediate forms of affective communication that disrupt the boundaries of individuation, such as drunkenness, ecstasy, trance, poetry, and dramatization.[116] The crucial point for us is that fluxes of contagious affects continue to flow through the communicative channels initially opened by the laughter of the socius—a laughter that creates an echo in the subject and reminds us of the presence of what Bataille will later call "this *other* in me as *mine* but, at the same time, as *other*" (v, 391).

Phantoms of the Summit

A general awareness of Bataille's reliance on Janet's psychology of the socius in his earlier, less-known period helps us illuminate enigmatic, paradoxical affirmations concerning sovereign communication in his later, much-celebrated period, affirmations that have often baffled critics who have approached Bataille solely from an ontological perspective.[117] For instance, readers of *Inner Experience* have often wondered why Bataille calls the experience of communication interior (*expérience intérieure*) despite its explicit ecstatic character. From our perspective, it is clear that it is only because this other/socius is already psychologically and physiologically interior to the ego, constitutive of an identity that is not one, that a flow between interior and exterior, self and another other, can actually take place. Similarly, we can better understand why Bataille writes: "I cannot make a distinction between myself and those with whom I desire to communicate" (*IE* 42). Or, "communication is a phenomenon which is in no way added on to human reality, but constitutes it" (24; transl. modified). It is because communication with the other/socius brings the ego into being as a relational subject that dualistic categories like "self" and "other," "interior" and "exterior" are no longer tenable when the subject is, once again, confronted with the experience of sovereign communication. Communication does not entail a relation to another who is exterior to the self. Nor does it involve the assimilation of the other into the self, and thus an annihilation of the other *as* other (as commentators have repeatedly suggested). Rather communication involves an affective experience with the other that reopens those affective *passages* that brought the ego into being as a relational, mimetic subject.

Throughout his career, Bataille will continue to meditate on methods for reaching states of ecstatic, communicative intimacy that are reminiscent of those initially experienced through the laughter of the socius. To that end, he will draw on the language of dramatic impersonation, at times coming very close to the origins of mimetic theory in classical antiquity with which we started. For instance, Bataille writes: "dramatic art, using non-discursive sensation, making every effort to strike, for that reason imitating the sound of the wind and attempting to chill—as by contagion: it makes a character tremble on the stage" (*IE* 13). Bataille, like other modernists, is obviously anti-Platonic in his enthusiastic acceptance of such forms of mimetic communication.

Thus, he says that in dramatization "what counts is no longer the statement of the wind, but the wind itself" (13). Yet, faithful to the Nietzschean current in modernism, he remains Platonic in his realization that the language of dramatic impersonation (mimesis) has the power to convey contagious affects (mimesis) that transgress human, animal, and natural boundaries. As Plato had already sensed in his critical account of dramatic impersonation, mimesis does not stop at human emotions, but can stretch to give voice and body to "neighing horses, and lowing bulls, and the noise of rivers and the roar of the sea, and the thunder and everything of that kind" (*Rep.* 641; 396b).

Alternatively, Bataille equally relies on specific hypnotic techniques in order to reach a state of psychic depersonalization whereby the subject is no longer present to itself. For instance, he explains his method of reaching a state of mimetic dispossession thus: "I fix a point before me and I represent this point to myself as the geometric place of all possible existence and of all unity" (*IE* 121). If the content of this experience concerns a modern reenactment of the passion of Christ and is in line with Bataille's mystical (transcendental) bent,[118] the formal practice of visual fixation on one point, and the loss of self as well as the "dilation of [the] pupil" (17) it entails, is one of the most common (immanent) means to induce a state of hypnotic depersonalization. Under such hypnotic conditions, Bataille realizes that his ego is "of a disarming plasticity" (126) that leads him to lose all sense of boundaries and to slip (*glisser*) under the skin of other subjects. As Bataille also puts it, referring to the old, Mesmeric/hypnotic notion of rapport, in the experience of communication the subject "exists . . . only in rapport: it is a knot of real communications" (VI, 408). Or, as he had already put it earlier, in such an experience of communication the subject is "not easily distinguishable from the fellow creature with whom he is in rapport, from the socius" (II, 287). Inner experience turns out to be shared experience; sovereign communication turns out to be mimetic communication.

At the summit of experience, sovereign communication leaves the communicative subjects in midair, in an instant when the boundaries of individuation are suspended, both dissolved and sustained by the magnetic-mimetic-hypnotic-identificatory-unconscious pathos that flows through their bodies and the community at large. Quite naturally, in such a state of loss of selfhood, the subject is no longer concerned with the profane sphere of work, the realm of what is useful and can be realized through a dutiful project that unfolds in time. The experience of mimetic communication, in other words, is the general hinge that swings the subject from one pole to the other of Bataille's conceptual economy: from the profane to the sacred, from work to play, from project to chance, from time to the instant, from "slavery" to "sovereignty." At the instant of communication, the subject is "*sans emploi*," to be sure. Yet Bataille thinks that this "experience of the summit" (*expérience du sommet*) opens the gates for "sensitive emotional contacts" (VIII, 288) to flow; and this affective flux where the subject is open to the pathos of the other/socius is for him life, true Life. Thus he writes: "truth is not where men consider themselves in isolation: it begins with conversations, shared laughter, friendship, eroticism, and only takes place by passing from one to the other" (*en passant de l'un à l'autre*) (V, 282). Sovereign communication, then, continues to be possible in adulthood because it is through the other that the subject comes into being in childhood; it is an inner experience that reenacts the affective rapport that, for better or worse, brings the ego into being as a permeable, fluid entity. This also means that in the beginning is not the ego but the experience of mimetic communication, a mimetic, affective, and unconscious experience through which the ego is born *with* the other, *as* other.

From laughter to inner experience, via tears, trance, erotism, sacrifice, and dramatization, mimesis seems, indeed, to be at the center of Bataille's persistent preoccupation with sovereign forms of communication. In this last chapter, I have argued that it is only because of the subject's prior affectability by the pathos of the other/socius who is both exterior and interior to the ego, that the subject remains permeable to subsequent forms of communicative experiences. Put differently, it is because the ego is, from the very beginning, chained to another ego that such magnetic-electric-hypnotic currents characteristic of sovereign communication can actually flow. Communication, then, is not only concerned with the dissolution of the boundaries of the ego; nor solely a mystical fusion with the "continuity of Being" (though it is both these things); but also, and perhaps more importantly, with a reenactment of that very immanent, psycho-physiological process which brings the ego into being as a social, relational subject. Thus understood, the laughter of the socius opens the passages of affective communication that pave the way for the ego's future permeability to other forms of ticklish, mimetic experiences.

For Bataille and other modernists of Nietzschean inspiration, the ego is from the very beginning already a phantasmal creature. Not in the superficial sense that it is merely a copy or reproduction of other egos, but in a deeper, affective sense that it is through a unconscious form of communication with the other (or socius) that the ego is born. The experience of mimesis, in this sense, does not entail a dispossession of the ego of its "real," "original" identity, since there is no such identity to possess in the first place. It is rather the very condition that allows for an affective, relational emergence to take place. And it is because of this primary, mimetic principle that bursts open the passages of communication and brings the ego into being as a relational subject in childhood, that the ego, for better or worse, continues to respond to the haunting power of mimetic (dis)possession in adulthood. More generally, if Bataille's communicative thought can anticipate future theoretical developments concerning the intersubjective foundation of ego formation, it is also because he relies on, and extends, the interdisciplinary tradition of the mimetic unconscious that has underscored our entire investigation. In this sense, the postmodern death of the subject Bataille anticipated continues to rely on a modernist birth of the ego. After the dissolution of the ego, it is the story of this birth that Bataille allowed us to tell.

Intresting

Bataille's account of the mimetic, communicative subject does not promise any final revelation that would unmask, once and for all, the phantom of the ego we have been tracking all along, reassuringly pointing towards something original behind the mask. Nor does he offer a single, homogeneous, and definitive answer to the open question "who comes after the subject?" Yet, his account of the birth of the subject out of the laughter of the socius affirms the emergence of a mimetic being that is always open to the possibility of *becoming*—other. He also reminds us that the feelings that overtake us in the experience of communication ring an echo in the subject, if only because we are, from the very beginning, permeable to that other/socius who is ourselves while being someone other. In this sense, the ego, for Bataille, emerges, quite literally, out of the "phantom who is there next to me or in me."[119] This phantom is interlocked with the ego in such a fundamental way that it cannot be dissociated from what the ego is; it does not communicate *with* me, but *through* me, because it is already chained *into* me—part of the experience of "being multiple singular" (*être à plusieurs un seul*) (*Sur Nietzsche* VI, 279).

Mimetic Theory Revisited

Turning and turning in the widening gyre
The falcon cannot hear the falconer;
Things fall apart; the centre cannot hold . . .
                                    —W. B. Yeats, "The Second Coming"

The spiraling movement of our mimetic inquiry has been turning around contagious patho(-)logies that traverse the modernist period and are responsible for generating what Nietzsche calls "the phantom of the ego." What this ghost hunt through central figures in literary and philosophical modernism has taught us is that, in fin de siècle Europe, protean forms of psychic dispossession take place in a widening number, with increasing speed and power of infection. It also has revealed that the problematic of mimesis, though rarely discussed in the context of modernist studies, is one of the most intense preoccupations of modernity. Mimesis affects the body, thought, and soul of the modern subject; it also informs disciplines as diverse as literature, philosophy, anthropology, sociology, and different schools of dynamic psychology. Consequently, new unmasking operations and diagnostic techniques proved necessary in order to track a protean concept that changes form at will, adapting to fast-moving times. Modernist authors like Nietzsche, Conrad, Lawrence, and Bataille, read in the company of founding theorists of mimesis like Plato—but also Tarde, Burrow, and Janet—and, more recently, mimetic theorists like Girard—but also Lacoue-Labarthe, Baudrillard, and Borch-Jacobsen—have taught us that in the modernist period, it is no longer possible to point to a single, unitary, essential ego behind the turning kaleidoscope of mimetic masks that envelop it. Nor is it realistic to propose a single, unifying, and ultimately homogeneous explicative model to predict the heterogeneous manifestations of ghostly apparitions in a period when the line between appearance and reality, copy and original, the ego and the phantom of the ego, no longer holds. Mimesis can thus no longer be framed within the confines of a single mirror stage, but is fragmented in a house of mirrors instead.

And yet this does not mean that our guiding question—who is this phantom, and wherein lies its power?—remained unanswered. On the contrary, modernist figures answered the same question by consistently and insistently pointing towards the same, yet protean force of affective contagion that generates this phantom in the first place and that, for convenience's sake, I have grouped under the ancient concept of "mimesis." At the same time, the spiraling movement of mimetic patho(-)logy allowed more specific, diagnostic questions to emerge. For instance: is the phantom of mimesis a haunting force that penetrates the ego in order to deprive it of its originality from the outside, as Nietzsche seemed to initially suggest? Or is it the product of an "inner experience" that is communicated to the ego in order to bring it into being from the inside, as Bataille finally indicates? Is this phantom a deadly, life-negating presence to be condemned and rejected? Or is it a generative, life-affirming force to be celebrated and accepted? And if this phantom transgresses the barriers between origin and copy, interior and exterior, private and public, active and passive, self and other, in which direction should we read the genitive in the title phrase, "the phantom *of* the ego"? Is the *phantom* of the ego, or the *ego* of the phantom that haunts the mind of modernism? These reflections are not the product of abstract theoretical speculations. They point, rather, to the complex, unconscious process of communication that troubles the foundations of the ego in such a way that it is no longer clear if the ego comes before the phantom, or the phantom before the ego. What is clear, however, is that contagious experiences generate an identity that is, quite literally, not one, insofar as it transgresses the boundary between being singular and becoming plural.

If we started this study by chasing a mimetic phantom with the power to take possession of the ego from the outside—from the ancient theater to the modern polis, from archaic rituals to modern crowds, from mass opinion to public opinion, from Wagnerian theaters to the movie theaters—we have been progressively led to question this adventurous, perhaps still too romantic desire for a final revelation of mimesis that would expose the ego from without. Instead, in a self-reflective move characteristic of the modernist turn, the Nietzschean authors we have encountered progressively directed our diagnostic lenses inward, in order to question the unconscious foundations of the ego from within. And what we found is that at the origins of the ego there is nothing original, but the experience of mimesis itself. This originary mimetic experience that gives birth to the ego, out of the pathos of the other, points to the unconscious reflex of communication that must be understood in intersubjective, psychosomatic or, as contemporary science suggests, neurological terms. I have called the psychophysiological source of involuntary, communicative reflexes that are not under the volitional control of consciousness, but shape the malleable ego nonetheless, "the mimetic unconscious." And I did so not only to differentiate it from the Freudian variant, but also to emphasize the primacy of an embodied, affective, and relational imitation in the process of ego formation.

The conclusion of this study, then, brings us back to the "phantom" with which we started, allowing us to see it from the other end of the spectrum. And what we now see, in an inversion of perspectives reminiscent of a looking glass, is that what appeared to be a "phantom of the ego" turns out to be an "ego of the phantom." This means that the ego is an effect of mimesis, rather than its cause; there is no ego prior to imitation, but it is imitation that generates the ego in a communicative process in which mimesis comes first insofar as it is an originary, yet unoriginal, experience out of which the ego is born. This is no minor perspectival inversion. It involves a Copernican turn away from egocentric approaches to subjectivity that dominated our past, Freudian century. It also allows us to catch up with recent, post-Freudian developments that recognize the importance of behavioral forms of imitation in the formation of the ego. As Bataille has shown, anticipating recent discoveries in the neurosciences that posit automatic reflexes at the foundation of subjectivity, mimesis is not an experience that comes after the ego has been formed. Rather, mimesis is constitutive of an interior, communicative experience out of which the ego is born. The phantom of mimesis gives life to the ego by animating or, better, innervating its psycho-physiological system through a dynamic process of unconscious communication that places the reflex of the other (or socius) at the heart of subjectivity. In this sense, mimesis is at the origin of the ego; the ego is but a shadow cast by a mimetic phantom.

There are a number of important consequences that ensue from this Nietzschean inversion of perspectives. In guise of conclusion, I would like to cast a retrospective glance on the spiraling movement of our trajectory, and flesh out some of its implications for modernist studies and mimetic theory—not so much as *the* final concluding gesture but, rather, as a coda whose aim is to open up possible starting points for future inquiries.

Modernism and Mimetic Theory

What emerges from this study is not a single, homogeneous theory of mimesis, nor a unitary, structural model to contain the proliferating effects of the contagious affects that transect the social body in the modern, post-Romantic period. In a sense, what the modernist brand of mimetic theory proposes is nothing new. It reenacts a diagnostic, clinical approach whose origins are as old as the origins of mimetic theory itself and can be traced back to Plato's *Republic*. This perspectival method was, in turn, recuperated in the early-modernist period by that anti-Platonic figure par excellence who is Friedrich Nietzsche. It is based on the realization that the observer is not external to his or her observations but participates in it with its whole soul, and thus with its whole body. This "philosophical physician" is, *volens nolens*, implicated in the pathologies he diagnoses and, for this reason, is paradoxically "most skilled" in the art of psycho-physiological dissection. Given its modernist recuperation by a Nietzschean axis of modernism, it is not surprising that this old Platonic realization is also at the source of new anti-Platonic investigations. The ambition of what we have called *mimetic patho(-)logy* was thus not to propose final transcendental solutions to the riddle of mimesis; nor was it to advocate a metaphysical system of thought that would contain the physical fluxes of contagious affects in neat, ideal forms. Rather, our ambition was to diagnose, on an immanent, embodied, patho-*logical* basis, increasingly contagious forms of mimetic pathologies that infect, in a variety of historically determined contexts, the modern subject, from its early-modernist beginnings in Nietzsche, to high modernist figures like Conrad and Lawrence, eventually spilling over into postmodernism, via Bataille.

In the process, we have seen that key advocates of the modernist tradition join efforts to analyze the devastating effects of affective contagion in a period characterized by acceleration of time, conflation of space, condensation of populations, confrontation with otherness, globalized wars, technical innovations, and massive forms of psychic depersonalization. They have also offered a clinical diagnosis of the underlying psychic and somatic reasons that render the modernist ego so permeable to the pathos of the other. Last but not least, they propose an alternative model of the unconscious based on a mimetic, rather than a repressive, hypothesis. Instead of making grand, totalizing claims about being the only possible *via regia* to the riddle of the unconscious, this hypothesis functions as a starting point to rethink the foundations of the mind of modernism from relational, intersubjective presuppositions that are in line with a variety of disciplinary positions. One of the goals of this study was thus to dislocate Freudocentric approaches to the psyche in order to open up the ego to the kaleidoscopic experience of mimetic forms of communication. What we must add now is that the modernist decentering of the ego in favor of mimesis also meant positioning our approach in relation to that rival of Freud and key figure of mimetic theory who is René Girard. If Girard's theoretical presence has been in the background of this study, it is now the time to bring his theory into the foreground. This will allow us to articulate the continuities and discontinuities between our respective approaches to the old riddle of mimesis and to propose new lines of inquiry for mimetic theorists of the future.

In his first book, *Deceit, Desire and the Novel* (1961) Girard single-handedly revitalized a field that is as old as literary theory—if not Western thought itself—from an original perspective. His theoretical move was deft and forceful. Without necessarily making grand claims about his operation, he brilliantly inverted the Freudian approach to the Oedipal triangle by positing mimetic identification as the *cause* rather than the *effect* of desire, solving thus the riddle of "ambivalent" relations with father figures and of the rivalries that ensue. In many respects, then, Girard's thought remains much influenced by Freud. The rivalrous triangle is, after all, an agile inversion of a Freudian structure. Girard's emphasis on desire as a privileged door through which to access subjectivity was, however, not simply of Freudian inspiration. It was also in line with the Hegelian spirit of the 1960s.[1] In the wake of Alexandre Kojève's anthropomorphic reading of *The Phenomenology of the Spirit*, Girard integrated the Hegelian lesson about the master-slave dialectic of desire by positing the "desire of the desire of the other" at the origin of his structural model. He did so in order to account for a Romantic problematic that had so far gone unnoticed, and therefore unstudied, which he aptly called "mimetic desire." In the process, Girard developed an ambitious theoretical alternative to solipsistic and egocentric accounts of the psyche that challenged Romantic notions of the "autonomous" and "spontaneous" self, while at the same time setting out to explain, in a dynamic, structural way, the novelistic genesis of individual desires, rivalries, and interpersonal quarrels in the Romantic period and beyond. Later, in what remains, in my opinion, his most ambitious work, *Violence and the Sacred* (1972), Girard supplemented the Platonic critique of mimesis in light of the rivalrous and violent consequences of mimetic desire by opening up mimetic theory to the field of comparative anthropology. Extending his early literary investigations to the ancient sphere of myth, he shed new light on hidden phenomena that lay at the foundation of culture, such as the contagious dynamic of violence, the cathartic social function of sacrificial rituals, and the scapegoat mechanisms that have the power to resolve mimetic crises. In an unfashionable move, Girard postulated that sacrifice should not be considered an old-fashioned anthropological riddle, but an innovative solution to the abyssal problem of the origins of culture, going so far as to propose a hypothesis concerning the birth of religion, humankind, and civilization *tout court*.

In *The Phantom of the Ego*, I have benefited from Girard's insights into the logic of mimesis, the contagious dimension of violence, and the rivalries that ensue from the appropriative nature of desire—a tendency still present in early-modernist authors driven by the ambition to produce an original thought and, thus, haunted by the pathos of their mimetic models qua rivals. I have also adopted some of Girard's vital methodological principles, including his call for an interdisciplinary approach to mimesis that breaks down artificial blinders in an increasingly specialized academic world, the idea that powerful theories emerge from the texts themselves, if one takes the trouble to read them closely, and, last but not least, the realization that thoughts feed on emotions, emotions on thoughts, in a nonhierarchical, generative movement that admirable writers know how to follow. In this sense, then, the modernist brand of mimetic theory that emerges from our paradigmatic choice of transdisciplinary authors and texts is in line with the spirit of Girard's "mimetic hypothesis."

And yet being in line with this spirit also meant that the task we set ourselves was not simply to "apply" Girard's "mimetic theory" to modernist texts from the outside in, but, rather, to let the texts speak for themselves from the inside out. This hermeneutical choice led us to confront problems that are specifically modernist, to integrate the modernist solutions to these problems, and, if necessary, to reshape our hypotheses in light of new textual, theoretical, and historical evidence. As I set out to track "the phantom of the ego," my goal was thus not to offer an a priori Girardian reading of modernist texts. Nor did I particularly seek to invalidate Girard's mimetic hypothesis. Rather, my goal was to pay close attention to the polymorphous logic of mimesis in the modernist period from an open, flexible, and dynamic interdisciplinary perspective, informed by, but not limited to, Girard's work, in order to continue to further the open field of mimetic theory. As key theoretical figures—from Plato to Nietzsche, Le Bon to Tarde, Bernheim to Burrow, Durkheim to Harrison, Mauss to Janet, Bataille to Baudrillard, Lacoue-Labarthe to Borch-Jacobsen—have shown, this field is always on the move, turned towards a future increasingly haunted by real, all too real, and perhaps even hyperreal, phantoms. Hence, rather than proposing a stabilizing universal structure with unitary ambitions, modernist mimetic theory is attentive to the *movement of becoming other* in a period characterized by intense cultural, scientific, and historical transformations.

As we followed the widening spiral of mimetic patho(-)logy, we have progressively noticed that unconscious, imitative phenomena are so constitutive of the mind of modernism that they not only dissolve the centrality given to the ego and the importance given to the Romantic myth of originality, adding new strength to a project initiated by their novelistic predecessors. They also bracket the role of desire as the privileged door to subjectivity. It is as if the intensification of mimesis on massive scales characteristic of the modernist period—with its hypnotized crowds, thronged theaters, packed streets, ramified mass media, globalized wars, and totalitarian leaders—brings about a weakening of the ego's ability to passionately desire in the first place, even if this desire is but an imitation of the desire of the other. This does not mean that the modernist subject—if such a unitary fiction exists at all—is less mimetic than its Romantic counterpart. On the contrary, the types of subjects we have repeatedly encountered in fictional and theoretical texts seem *less* fixated on the single desire of the model/mediator because they are *more* (not less) imitative than their Romantic predecessors. As Lacoue-Labarthe also realized, the logic of such an apparent paradox is constitutive of the logic of mimesis.[2] In the case of the imitation of the modernists, it can be formulated as follows: the more mimetic the subject, the less will it stick to one single model, the more will it copy a multiplicity of subjects; the less formative the presence of the model, the more will the subject merge with a multiplicity of figures, the less individuated its desires will be.

In the novelistic, Romantic tradition, mimetic desires initially appear to be a debased copy of passionate, spontaneous, and autonomous desires. But as Girard recognized, mimetic desire, as well as the vanity, coquetry, and snobbism it generates, is still an individualistic, intense, and quite passionate affair; not in the *Romantic* sense that this desire is truly authentic or original, but in the *romanesque* sense that the intense pathos it generates is misrecognized as being one's own, while being directed by the Other.[3] Characters like Don Quixote, Mme de Rênal, Don Juan, and Marcel are *mimetic* individuals, to be sure, but mimetic *individuals* nonetheless whose personal and passionate intrigues occupy the center stage of the romantic novel. In the modernist period, on the other hand, it is the fiction of the individual itself that the experience of mimesis calls into question. It is as if the contagious power of mimesis has swallowed up the ego's capacity to *intensely* desire— even mimetically—in a river of impersonal confusion of affects, leaving but a phantom among phantoms in its place. Whether the focus is on the Wagnerian crowd in *The Case of Wagner*, figures like the Harlequin or Kurtz in *Heart of Darkness*, Kate Leslie in *The Plumed Serpent*, or what Bataille calls "the man among thousand" in *College de Sociologie*, the modernist subject is intensely subjected to a variety of *impersonal*, contagious phenomena that disperse the ego in the anonymous experience of the mimetic crowd. Rather than directing desire within a linear, triangular, and still familial structure, then, mimesis, for the modernists, has the power to open up the ego to a multiplicity of directions, dissolving the illusion of individuation in a river of impersonal affects that cannot be contained within the confines of fixed, universal, and still idealist, structural relations.

The modernist subject, as it is represented in the works of key Nietzschean figures in literary and philosophical modernism, is not even given a chance to think about the Romantic *mensonge* of individuality. And quite naturally so; once the ego is part of a crowd or public, there is not much space for the development of mimetic but still egocentric affects, such as vanity, snobbism, and coquetry. The modernist dissolution of the old stable ego draws the conclusion of this mimetic realization and shows that behind the mask of individuation there is no ego left to desire, but a phantom of a phantom of a phantom ... "the one forever in the head of someone else, and the head of this someone else again in the head of others: a strange world of phantasms" (*D* 105), as Nietzsche puts it. Similarly, Lawrence discusses the effects of the Great War on what he calls "*simulacrum* of a man" in a way that echoes Nietzsche: "Practically every man [is] caught away from himself, as in some horrible flood, and swept away with the ghastly masses of other men, disinclined to speak, or feel for himself, or stand on his own feet" (*K* 213). The modern crowd, then, does not allow for the still egocentric experience of a mimetic rivalry between subject and model, "copy" and "original," but dissolves the ego in a river of simulacra where the copy not only precedes the original, but explodes the very ontology of mimesis, leaving but a strange world of phantasms behind.

To be sure, seemingly individuated, original models are not lacking in the modernist period, especially charismatic, authoritarian models whose origins can be traced back to the Romantic myth of genius and, even further back, to the Platonic myth of divine inspiration. Their hypnotic will to power is not only impressed on the members of the crowd via a process Lacoue-Labarthe, following Plato, calls "typography," but is also mechanically reproduced by new mass media that powerfully echo such voices in order to inform and conform what Tarde calls the "public." Once again, given the massive doses of mimetic subjection, these models are not primarily concerned with directing the desires of individual egos considered as subjects. Rather, they shape, via an impersonal process of psychic and technical *impression*—the effects of which are now proved to mold the neurological structure of the brain—entire crowds considered as malleable raw material.[4] These models are, indeed, too exterior for the subjects of the crowd to function as their mimetic rivals and, as Girard would say, operate at the level of "external mediation." But even more importantly, the crowd is too numerous for a dialectics of desire to emerge, submerging the ego in an impersonal stream responsible for what we have called *mimetic dissolution*. In the crowd, in the jungle, at collective rituals, at large political meetings, or in the streets, the modernist generation repeatedly tells us that the ego is but a phantom among phantoms, a fluttering shadow cast on a dark screen. Even the locations in which mimetic investigations are carried out in modernist texts are no longer the same as in their novelistic counterparts. The modernist space is no longer the salon but the street; it is no longer transected by individual chivalric heroes, but by mechanical means of mass transportation; it is no longer based on personal confrontations, but on mass communication. Consequently, rather than being a heroic figure in search of an identity, the modernist subject turns out to be a "man without qualities"—to borrow the title of Robert Musil's masterpiece, itself borrowed by Lacoue-Labarthe—all the more vulnerable to the power of leaders who sell ready-made qualities in massive quantities. The modernist dissolution of the "old stable ego," then, brings about a weakening of the personal rivalries, vanities, and familial structures that once still managed to contain the polymorphous logic of mimesis.

This said, the mimetic *différend* between the Romantics and the moderns is not clear cut. What is at stake for modernist authors is not an abrupt theoretical rupture with their predecessors, but the realization that a historical, theoretical, and experiential *shift of emphasis* has gradually taken place. Although mimetic desires continue to operate in the background of modernist texts—in the form of greedy colonial exploitations for material possessions, spellbound fascination for public opinion, mindless submission to charismatic leaders—the protagonists, characters, and conceptual personae that emerge in the foreground of these texts seem less concerned with the truth and lies of the still Hegelian or, as Bataille would say, Kojèvian, master-slave dialectic of "desire" as a starting point for a theory of mimesis. Their brand of mimetic theory seems rather more directly concerned with the experience of mimesis itself, considered as a protean concept that has to be peeled off from the problematic of desire in order to be dissected on its own terms. In fact, for the modernists, it is not only desire that is contagious, but mimesis itself that is mimetic, and quite directly so. It is thus no accident that in what Nietzsche calls "the century of the masses," the modern crowd and public, as well as postmodern mass media, tend to replace the lonely figure of the Romantic hero as a privileged subject of mimetic inquiry and textual investigation. Nor is it accidental that in the modernist period, theoretical interest turns to dissect the unconscious power of collective affects that include desire, but are far from limited to it: enthusiasm, frenzy, compassion, sympathy, participation, suggestion, hypnosis, and laughter, to name a few, are all part of that sym-*pathos* (feeling with) that, for better or worse, generates phantoms on a massive scale. Rather than restricting mimesis to the specific case of mimetic desire, I thus propose the generalized concept of *mimetic pathos* as a productive starting point to account for mimesis on its own terms, at times in which this protean concept is more than ever on the move, changing form at will in order to adapt to hypermimetic backgrounds. In the modernist period, mimesis is, perhaps, the insurmountable horizon of subjectivity: it not only turns into a subject of intense literary investigations, but occupies center stage in scientific, psychological, sociological, anthropological, and philosophical discussions that are constitutive of the mind of modernism. It is thus on such textual, historical, and interdisciplinary principles that this study attempts to do clinical justice to this histrionic protagonist on the modernist stage. It does so by advocating a generalized theory of mimesis that focuses on different forms of mimetic pathos in order to diagnose its major affective, infective, at times hysterical, but always contagious, symptoms.

It seems, then, that despite their Romantic heritage and the tenaciousness of the myth of autonomy and individualistic self-sufficiency, our modernist authors are beginning to learn the *romanesque* lesson about the *mensonge* of originality. Thus, Nietzsche's still Romantic struggle with his models is progressively replaced by the realization that "actors, all kinds of actors, will be the real masters"; the "glories of exploration" Conrad romantically dreamed of in his youth give way to the impersonal reality of colonial horrors; Lawrence's triangular desires that still informed his first Romantic-oriented novels are replaced by the impersonal crowds that haunt his late, political novels; Bataille's personal concern with his father's "heterology" is replaced by his analysis of the contagious "force" of communicative patho(-)logies. Even the figure of the "universal genius" and charismatic leader, Mr. Kurtz, as Conrad's urged us to consider in *Heart of Darkness*, turns out to be a "hollow" man without opinions to call his own; a "shadow" or "phantom" whose last penetrating and presumably deep insight beyond the abyss of representation, "The horror! The horror!" turns out to be but an echo of a simple, superficial "fragment of a phrase of newspaper article" (148). What is embryonic in such a modernist realization is the dissolution of a Romantic myth that is hard to extinguish, even in postmodern, hypermimetic times when individuality, more than ever, turns out to be a fiction.

This unmasking of the figure of the Romantic genius is an important theoretical step for which modernists are grateful to their novelistic predecessors. The methodology that informs their mimetic patho-logies reflects this anti-Romantic realization. Although they are at times still complicit with the myth of originality, modernists less feel the need to disguise their disciplinary sources in order to appear truly original. Instead, they multiply references to different mimetic traditions that belong to the modernist Weltanschauung in order to account for the riddle of mimesis. They are not so anxious to differentiate themselves from other theoretical figures, but allow the different fluxes of mimetic theories to freely transect their writings. Aware of the pervasiveness of fin de siècle patho-logical discourses in different disciplinary traditions—from philosophy to crowd psychology, psychophysiology to sociology and religious anthropology—they actively rely on these *logoi* to diagnose mimetic pathos, opening up modernist studies to a transdisciplinary tradition well before the recent turn towards interdisciplinarity. If it is true that insightful novelists continue to unmask the phantom of the ego, it is equally true that we can no longer posit the noble, but somewhat restricted hypothesis that only the "great novelists" (read in the company of the evangelical texts) truly reveal what is at stake in imitation. Rather, in the modernist period, a widening number of investigations emerge to delineate, with great novelists (read in the company of atheological writers), the channels through which mimetic pathos flows. Literature must thus be reconsidered part of a generalized, transdisciplinary, immanent, and hopefully communal effort to continue to map the ever-changing laws of imitation.

I suggest that what is true for the modernist theorist of mimesis should equally apply to the contemporary mimetic theorist. Within the scope of my abilities, I have attempted to further this characteristically modernist, interdisciplinary spirit, rendering its sources fully visible when they were still masked. This involved opening up mimetic theory to central figures in the modernist tradition that have so far been neglected, or relegated to the background of the theoretical stage: From Bernheim to Janet, Le Bon to Tarde, Burrow to Harrison, Frazer to Durkheim, Lévy-Bruhl to Mauss, and, more recently, Morin to Baudrillard, Lacoue-Labarthe to Borch-Jacobsen, and many others still to be discovered, we have consistently seen that these figures, read in the company of Girard, are vital to opening up mimetic theory to a wider interdisciplinary perspective so as to account for the disconcerting power of mimetic contagion in the twenty-first century.

Furthering mimetic theory on such an open, interdisciplinary base is, indeed, more urgent than ever, if only because mimetic contagion is, perhaps, the central problem of modernity. Charismatic leaders, as we have repeatedly seen, have the will to power to subject the masses to hollow models, via a hypnotic, unconscious mechanism that communicates itself directly, through contagious affects that flow in a spiraling, cumulative movement, from the leader to the crowd, the crowd to the leader. As these ideologies are put into practice, sacrificial victims are indeed destroyed, in massive, impersonal forms, from a premeditated distance—colonial distance, but also the distance that divides invisible "enemies" at the front and, later, in camps at the margins of the totalitarian body politic, up until our hyperreal wars and contemporary versions of camps that render the ego, or better, life, as it is now called in the wake of the death of man, both "naked" and "precarious."[5] This distance not only strips life of its juridical status that renders it human; it is also intended to prevent the emergence of human sympathy in the Lawrentian sense of "feeling with," a sym-pathos still necessary, even in a posthuman world, for these rights to be recognized and granted in the first place.

In the modernist period, the violence of mimesis already fails to generate the pathos that was the necessary condition for cathartic social efficacy; violence is no longer considered sacred but profane. Modernist mimetic theory, then, challenges nothing less and nothing more than the central thesis of *Violence and the Sacred* and proposes an account of violence that is more in line with the horror, or as Adriana Cavarero calls it, "horrorism" of modernity,[6] without giving in to the temptation of apocalyptic despair. Modernists also add that if new mass media do not hesitate to reveal spectacular forms of sacrificial violence in order to "inform" public opinion, the ethical and political effects of such visual representations could not be feebler. In fact, showing the pathos of anthropogenic catastrophes from a distance has the effect of absorbing the horrors of useless forms of sacrificial carnage (World War

I being the first paradigmatic example) in the transcendental realm of the hyperreal. Modernists do not have ready-made solutions that would contain, once and for all, massive outbreaks of "hyperreal contagion" (Baudrillard's term). What they tell us is that the battles of modernity are played out on mimetic fronts whose mass media must be studied if we want to keep up with the phantom of the ego that continues to haunt our contemporary times.

In sum, the modernist brand of mimetic theory is situated in a relation of both continuity and discontinuity with its Romantic counterpart, as modernism entails both a continuation and a discontinuation of romanticism. On the one hand, mimesis remains an affective source of tremendous struggles in the modernist period, threatening more than ever the social structures of society with massive forms of sacrificial horrors. Mimesis, as Girard—read in the company of a long tradition in psychology, anthropology, and philosophy—taught us, is contagious, irrational, and potentially violent and has the power to unconsciously electrify entire crowds. In modernist times of "hyperreal contagion" it spreads even more massively through all kinds of mass media, endowed with a ramified power of suggestion that cuts across borders at an uncontrollable speed. Indeed, this is a world in which the medium of mimetic messages has the power to accentuate the pathological "escalation" of violence, as Girard explains in *Battling to the End*. On the other hand, modernist mimetic theory decenters the question of desire central to the Romantic period in order to give center stage to mimesis as the main, polymorphous conceptual protagonist of mimetic theory. For the modernists, the starting point is no longer desire, nor mimetic desire, but mimesis itself. This does not mean that the modernist tradition, in a heroic mood, attempts to *achever* its predecessors (just as I am not attempting to *achever* Girard), if only because such a move would still be in line with the Hegelian, historical spirit it seeks to overcome. Rather, it builds on them, in a constructive mood, in order to further diagnostic investigations from the angle of a generalized theory of mimesis that has the heterogeneous concept of mimetic pathos as its ultimate focus. As a consequence of this shift of perspective from mimetic *desire* to mimetic *pathos*, from an ideal triangular structure to an immanent psycho-physiological movement, a new, but not necessarily original, brand of mimetic theory emerges in order to account for the turbulent, spiraling, and infectious movement of contagious patho(-)logies in which, *volens nolens*, the moderns continue to be caught.

What we must add now is that since this spiraling movement has both disruptive and affirmative consequences, the modernist brand of mimetic theory strives to go beyond the evil implications of affective contagion in order to also account for its vitalizing, Dionysian counterpart.

The Laughter of Community

Modernist writers are, indeed, severely critical of the modern, impersonal, hypermimetic times they live in, and of the horrors these times generate. Hence, they account for the formation of phantoms in terms of a sickness that needs to be, if not completely cured, at least accurately diagnosed. And yet it is important to stress that Nietzschean modernists intent on making mimetic theory new do not forget the old Platonic lesson that mimesis is at least two faced, like the god Janus, and that mimetic patho(-)logies can quickly turn from disease into remedy, remedy into disease.[7] From Nietzsche to Bernheim, Conrad to Tarde, Lawrence to Harrison, Bataille to Janet, we have repeatedly seen that in addition to the violence of disruptive forms of contagion (what Girard calls "violent mimesis") mimetic interactions such as sympathy, imitation, participation, dance, music, and, last but not least, laughter (what Bataille calls contagious "effusions") can be turned to positive affective and social ends. In line with this balancing operation, the modernist brand of mimetic theory proposes that a critique of violent, life-negating, and dissociative forms of mimetic pathologies must be supplemented by an analysis of the healthy, life-affirming, and ultimately associative forms of mimetic communication.[8]

Laughter is a relational, communal affect that occupies a privileged position in the Nietzschean axis of modernism we have been following. I have picked that affect as a main medium by which to rethink the affective foundations of the ego for reasons that are directly in line with the theoretical message of this study. I shall just flesh out three. First, laughter is an affirmative, joyful, Dionysian effusion that has the potential to balance the critical side of mimetic theory in the spirit of a "gay science" of mimesis Nietzsche encouraged us to pursue. Second, laughter is a contagious, reciprocal affect that, well before the discovery of mirror neurons and newborns' immediate responsiveness to mimicry, offers a theoretical starting point from which to confirm the presence, efficacy, and theoretical timeliness of what we have called, for lack of a better term, "the mimetic unconscious." And third, laughter is an immanent, psychosomatic, and quite common affective experience that, from childhood on, does not take place in isolation but in the company of privileged others—what Pierre Janet calls *socii*. We have seen that the contagious experience of laughter can serve as a productive starting point for rethinking the *relational* foundations of the ego along lines that have mimesis as its generative principle. What we must add now is that this ticklish affect can equally account for the intersubjective, social, and ethical bonds that are constitutive of the experience of communal feelings as a whole. Indeed, the experience of laughter, and other gay effusions, opens up the ego to the pathos of the other, tying the other into the very tissue of the self. This realization offers an alternative, intersubjective, theoretical ground on which to reimagine the foundations of community along lines that supplement the *critical* dimension of mimetic theory from an *ethical* perspective that is attentive to the primacy of the other.[9] In short, the experience of mimesis might not only be at the origins of *historical* pathologies responsible for the crisis of modernity, but also of *theoretical* patho-logies that can help us reimagine a communal ethos the modernist generation still believed in.

Although Girard consistently emphasizes the violent, apocalyptic dimension of mimesis, he is the first to admit that the positive dimension of mimesis is "even more important,"[10] encouraging future theorists to develop this perspective as well. The modernist brand of mimetic theory proposes to further this neglected side. Indeed, the contagious reflex of an affect like laughter offers a productive starting point from which to analyze the vitalizing effects of contagion from an intersubjective, reciprocal perspective that can both benefit from and supplement Girard's theory. Many of the mechanisms Girard minutely describes are still at work in this mimetic affect par excellence; yet their effects and diagnostic conclusions are radically inverted. For instance, not unlike desire, laughter is intersubjective, contagious, and thus essentially mimetic; it does not belong originally to the self, but one catches it from another, usually an intimate, friendly other. And yet unlike mimetic desire, laughter is not confined within triangular structures, but easily affects a multiplicity of subjects. If mimetic desire generates life-negating emotions (like envy, jealousy, and ressentiment), leading to violent rivalries that culminate in dialectical struggles for pure prestige, the unconscious reflex of laughter, on the other hand, generates life-affirming emotions (like sympathy, enthusiasm, and friendship) that are as constitutive of the ego as of the other and can be shared on a non-rivalrous, joyful basis. Furthermore, not unlike violence, laughter is relational, reciprocal, and leads to uncontrollable, irrational escalations that shake the foundations of subjects to the point of tears. And yet, unlike violence, the escalation of laughter does not threaten the stability of social bonds, but opens up the boundaries of the ego to the other in order to create, vitalize, and solidify these bonds. And if laughter, like violence, has cathartic social effects that generate increasing forms of social cohesion, it does not need the mediation of tragic spectacles, but of comic spectacles instead! In this sense, the escalation of laughter goes beyond bad mimesis and proposes an alternative account of mimetic reciprocity that is rooted in the formation of subjectivity itself. As Bataille puts it, as a coda to his discussion of "the contagious movement of laughter": the members who partake in it "find again their communion by laughing with a single laughter [*en riant d'un seul rire*]" (ii, 338). One of the key modernist operations was to account for a process of affective *circulation* of communicative affects, where the mimetic flux is more important than the sum of the individual molecules that compose it.

Without invalidating the *disruptive* power of mimetic desire in competitive, rivalrous situations, or challenging the *cathartic* function of violent sacrifices in religious and nonreligious contexts,[11] an account of the *unifying* dimension of contagion furthers mimetic theory by addressing the positive, affective, and theoretical reasons responsible for the formation of social bonds. This realization has important theoretical consequences: it offers an alternative solution to the riddle of group formation that sidesteps the "economy of violence"[12] in favor of an economy of laughter.[13] Let us recall that, for Girard, social cohesion is never immediate and spontaneous, but is mediated and derived; it is not a first cause, but a secondary effect; it does not stem from the experience of communication, but is at least three times removed from the immediacy of communal experiences. In fact, for Girard, social unity emerges as a last step in a long chain that leads from mimetic desire to rivalry, from rivalry to violence, from violence to a crisis of differences, and it is only once a scapegoat has been designated and collectively sacrificed—that is, only once men follow what Girard calls, in a Freudian mood, "the royal road [*voie royale*] of violence"—that the "harmony of the community" is restored and "the social fabric" reinforced.[14] In short, for Girard, social cohesion is born out of the cathartic effects of ritual violence.

Given the importance attributed to mimetic desire as the primary structuring feature for a theory of sociality, a long and laborious sequence of theoretical steps is necessary before humans can finally assemble in a spontaneous, communal spirit. This road is definitively a well-trodden one, especially in contemporary capitalistic societies characterized by radical individualism, fierce competitiveness, and a generalized consumerism on a globalized scale.[15] But this is not the only road. In view of the Girardian realization that in these societies the logic of sacrifice has lost its cathartic and thus unifying efficacy, there is an urgent need, if not to look for prepackaged alternatives, at least to contribute to reimagining them on an alternative theoretical basis.[16] Modernist theorists of mimesis help us to do so by opening up a theoretical short-cut to the royal road of violence. For them, in fact, it is not only desire that is mimetic, or violence that is contagious, but also mimesis itself that is both mimetic and contagious. Bataille, for instance, in his "Two Fragments on Laughter" that conclude *Guilty*, does not hesitate to risk a tautology in order to stress this crucial point: "*contagion* (the intimate interpenetration of two beings) *is contagious* (susceptible of infinite repercussions)" (V, 391). Hence, Bataille, in a Nietzschean spirit, posits that the experience of "communication" in laughter has the power to trigger an intimate, immediate, and cohesive "interpenetration" that spreads contagiously across the entire social body, generating what he calls "affective unification." In this he is close to Émile Durkheim, who, in *The Elementary Forms of Religious Life*, had given an account of the feeling of "communion" and "moral unity" that ensues from what he calls "collective effervescence" generated by ritual forms of totemic communion.[17] Along similar lines, speaking of "the subjectivity of laughter" in *La Souveraineté*, Bataille writes that it is not "expressible discursively, but the laughers feel, from one to the other, an unexpected and destabilizing transparency, as if the same laughter would generate a unique interior surge" (VIII, 288). This surge creates what he calls "participants in a community" predicated on the "the communication from *subject* to *subject*" (288). Indeed, as Charles Baudelaire also put it at the dawn of modernism, for the outburst of laughter to surge forth, "the presence of two beings is needed."[18] Laughter, then, occupies a privileged place among Dionysian thinkers because it allows them to rethink the relational foundations of subjectivity from a life-affirming, immanent, and bodily perspective. It opens up the channels of communication in childhood through which other Dionysian affects (such as eroticism, dance, ecstasy, drunkenness, and friendship) will continue to flow in adulthood among consensual, egalitarian subjects who are part of what Bataille calls "elective community" (*communauté élective*) (11, 354). For Bataille, and Nietzschean modernists before him, laughter is a ticklish affect that opens up the boundaries of the ego to the pathos of the other(s) and galvanizes, on an immanent, horizontal base, the larger social body.

The modernist take on the "phantom of the ego," then, is not only important for psychological reasons; it also has larger ethical and political implications that can help us give an account of the intersubjective foundations that hold a multiplicity of subjects together.[19] Such a community is never a simple assemblage of individual egos; nor can it be considered as already given in an increasingly individualized, disembodied, and mediatized world. Rather, it emerges from the very process of alternative forms of communication that are more fundamental to the formation of the ego than previous egocentric accounts actually realized. Rethinking the foundations of subjectivity in mimetic terms in order to reimagine the foundations of community is, among other things, what the modernist tradition of the mimetic unconscious can help us do, and for at least three reasons. First, this tradition breaks free of monadic accounts of the ego that see narcissistic figures imprisoned in solipsistic repressive hypotheses and static specular reflections as the ultimate ontological horizon of subjectivity. Instead, it proposes an account of the immediate, mimetic *bonds* that, even in our mediated world, continue to be constitutive of human relations. Second, this untimely tradition of the mimetic unconscious anticipates, by more than a century, the recent discovery of involuntary reflexes and mirror neurons. In this, they are scientifically ahead of their times, but they also go beyond contemporary scientific investigations in the hard sciences. In fact, a modernist theoretical model of the foundations of subjectivity offers an account of subject formation that reveals the psychic, social, and ethico-political forms of mimetic communication responsible for generating embodied, human subjects who are themselves while being someone other. And third, a patho-logical account of immanent forms of communication invites us to think through the specific, intersubjective dynamic that gives birth to a "phantom of the ego." This phantom is not only a devalued copy of the ego but is also constitutive of it; as Nietzsche puts it, it is "communicated" (*mitgeteilt*)—con-divided, both united and divided—with the other. This ego emerges with the other as an *ipse* that is not identical to itself, but functions as a place of communication between subjects who are ready to reimagine the possibility of future communities yet to come.

The fact that the recent theoretical turn to rethinking the foundations of "community" is directly in line with Bataille's thought testifies to the timeliness of his theory of mimetic communication. We are in fact told that "Bataille has gone furthest into the crucial experience of the modern destiny of community."[20] And figures as diverse as Maurice Blanchot, Jean-Luc Nancy, and Giorgio Agamben have attempted to further Bataille's experience by emphasizing the primacy of the relation with the other and the sharing (*partage*) it entails—though these others tend to be dead rather than living others.[21] They have also opened up a "singular-plural" account of subjectivity to a relational, intersubjective perspective to account for an increasingly depersonalized, yet still singular "whatever" (*qualunque*) subjectivity that is not without echoes in the modernist account of the phantom of the ego—though these relations tend to focus on a philosophy of Being rather than on a patho(-)logy of human beings.[22] What we can add is that a Bataillean approach informed by a Nietzschean genealogy of the subject can help us account for the thus far neglected *mimetic dynamic* that renders a subject "plural-singular" in the first place. Although mimesis is rarely discussed in contemporary accounts of community, it is perhaps the singular, impersonal, yet relational pathos that is most crucial in accounting for the forces that render the ego open to a plurality of subjects, and that open up what has already been called "an *ethical* 'beyond' of the subject."[23]

Plurality, for the modernists, comes before the ego because it is through a mimetic communication with plural *socii* that a singular multiple ego can emerge; and it is through the unconscious reflex of imitation that access to the psychic life of the other can take place. This, at least, is what Nietzsche suggests as he says that it is through "the mimicking of gestures, which takes place involuntarily" that "the child still learns to understand its mother" and "people learned to understand one another" (*HH* 216). Diagnostic arrows like this one make clear that Nietzsche is not only a fierce critic of the life-negating side of the phantom of the ego; he is also one of the foremost advocates of the life-affirming side of the ego of the phantom. While destabilizing the ontology of the subject understood as a unitary, self-identical, monadic substance, this imitative process does not entail an undifferentiated "fusion" between self and other. Nor does it dissolve the otherness of the other in favor of an epistemology of "the same." Rather, this mimetic communication (*Mit-teilung*) opens up those first communicative routes (*parcours*) whereby the phantom of the ego is *con*-divided (both united and divided) with a multiplicity of others that are both interior and exterior to *ipse*.

Contemporary theorists who have turned to Nietzsche's Dionysian thought in order to rethink "the force of morality in the production of the subject" from a relational perspective tend to be critical of its violent foundations.[24] And quite rightly so since, in *On the Genealogy of Morals*, Nietzsche thinks of the affective foundations of the moral subject in terms of violent forms of mimetic will to power typographically impressed on a multiplicity of subjects along lines we have considered as socially pathological. And yet the movement of mimetic patho(-)logy has also taught us that Nietzsche's account of morality, and the type of subjectivity that emerges from it, cannot be reduced to a unitary genealogical perspective. Instead, we must be ready to trace its mimetic countermovements as they appear in his protean work. In *Beyond Good and Evil*, for instance, Nietzsche offers an account of the "inner experience" that casts new light on the "history of the human soul" (*BGE* 45) along lines Bataille will later develop. Thus, Nietzsche focuses on the relational structure of the soul understood as "multiplicity" that opens up a theoretical alternative to rethink the foundations of morality on a relational, egalitarian, and nonaggressive basis. Opening what he calls "the road to new forms and refinements of the soul-hypothesis" (*BGE* 12), he proposes the hypothesis of what he calls "'soul as multiplicity of the subject' and 'soul as social structure of the drives and emotions'" (12). This soul hypothesis rests on a deeper, mimetic hypothesis we have been concerned with all along. For Nietzsche, the soul is, in fact, multiple because the mimetic unconscious posits the presence of privileged others as formative of the very structure of subjectivity. It is, in fact, through the experience of mimesis that the ego is initially traversed by the formative pathos of a multiplicity of others/socii, predisposing it for the communal experience of what Bataille will later call, echoing Nietzsche, "being multiple singular." The door Nietzsche opens up, then, is perfectly in line with the modernist realization that the ego comes into being in a relation of communication with the other qua socius, as a relational, plural and fundamentally open *ipse* that is dependent on the affects of the socius in order to emerge. Moreover, if the child automatically mimics the mother's gestures, this unconscious mimesis gives access not only to the psychic life of the other but also to the psychic life of the ego. Consequently mimetic forms of communication, as Nietzsche understands them, are constitutive of relational bonds that posit a dependency on, and openness to, the mimetic pathos of the other as primary. This anchorage of the pathos of the other in the self is not necessarily "traumatic," nor is it based on a "linguistic" form communication[25] but, rather, takes place through the laughter of the other/socius that tickles the ego into being as an immanent, embodied, and above all communal being.

Given the primacy it gives to others in the formation of the ego, and given the consideration of the ego as a crossroads where a multiplicity of communicative experiences can take place, Nietzsche's soul/mimetic hypothesis opens up an imaginative, immanent perspective on the ethical ties that structure a community of multiple, yet singular souls. There is considerable ethical potential in this theoretical realization. Insofar as this dependency on the other/socius in order to emerge as subject is anchored in the very tissue of intersubjectivity, opening those passages through which communication will continue to flow, it becomes a livable condition not only to imagine but also to develop future relations based on mimetic interdependency.[26] Put differently, if a multiplicity already structures the soul, as Nietzsche suggests, then, a microanalysis of the affective forms of communication that brings this soul into being as singular multiple can help us account for the ties that are constitutive of a community made of multiple singular souls. What is clear, in any case, is that the psychology of the socius and the mimetic unconscious that informs it does not stop at the limits of the ego, but transgresses these limits to open up the ego to the ethos of the other along lines that will require further development. I can only suggest here that in order to further this line of inquiry along the lines opened up by Nietzschean figures, attention should be given less to the restricted principle of insufficiency, narcissistic identifications, or linguistic ontological principles, and more to the general economy characteristic of a sovereign, Dionysian excess that generates those living bonds constitutive of elective communities yet to come.

Finally, although this process of mimetic communication blurs solid distinctions between interior and exterior, self and other, private and public, this does not mean that the subject is homogeneous with the other, but that the other provides a starting point for the ego to emerge as a heterogeneous, relational subject. What is at stake in this communication is not experienced in terms of fusion, or confusion, and not even infusion, but in terms of a bodily experience that Bataille qualifies in terms of "effusion" instead. To be sure, this effusive communication is of anti-Platonic inspiration; it is in line with the Nietzschean, antimetaphysical imperative to remain faithful to the earth. And yet the idealism this immanent model attempts to counter is perhaps not directly Platonic or Christian. After all, in the wake of the death of god, the force of the "old phantom" (VI, 72), as Bataille ironically calls it, is already waning in the modernist period. Rather, it confronts the contemporary avatars of these transcendental traditions as they appear in the increasing postmodern (but still Platonic) tendency to upload embodied human subjects in the hyperreal (but still ideal) sphere of virtual "reality," a sphere where disembodied simulacra are progressively replacing what Lawrence called "solid" reality with what Nietzsche already called a "strange world of phantoms." It is because new avatars of Platonism are more alive than ever, typographically informing and conforming future generations on a massive scale, that balanced immanent perspectives are urgently needed. Tracing the process of emergence of the ego through the experience of laughter calls for a gay science of mimetic, embodied, communicative relations that take place on a horizontal plane of immanence. This, at least, is what the figures we have encountered along the path of this Nietzschean journey suggest, as they continue to open up solipsistic accounts of the psyche to the immanent social and communal forces that compose a subject that is not one.

The fact that this subject is not one does not mean that she is no one. On the contrary, the openness of communicating *passages* that structure the soul as multiplicity offers a microscopic example of the types of mimetic "drives" and "emotions" that can be reenacted, reimagined, and perhaps even performed, at the social, macroscopic level. At least in the context of a community of subjects composed by a multiplicity of chosen others ready to experience what Bataille, thinking of laughter, calls the "specific form of human interaction" (*Coll.* 108). These communities might not be *quantitatively* dominant. They never were and are certainly not so in market-oriented, capitalist, digitalized societies still driven by the fiction of the "old stable ego." But as Bataille suggests, and every subject lucky enough to be in touch with its socii—parents, lovers, teachers, friends, and, last but not least, children—knows, this mimetic communication is *qualitatively* constitutive of those fluxes of affects that have the power to give form to a life—among others.

The Center Does Not Hold

What are the psychic, ethical, political consequences of the mimetic realization that the socius generates an ego that is not one? Does this mean that stronger "ethical connection with others" should emerge from the realization that the other is already internal to the ego, as Judith Butler suggests?[27] Or does it indicate that the mimetic interpenetration of the other into the ego engenders apocalyptic cycles of "escalating" violence that lead to a "battle to the end," as René Girard prophesizes?[28] As far as I can see, there are no single, homogeneous answers to such heterogeneous theoretical alternatives. Each case of infective contagion deserves, in my view, a specific diagnostic inquiry that is attentive not only to the disruptive and productive effects of pathos, but also to the fact that pathology can quickly turn into patho-logy, and vice versa. Accounting for this movement, in both its microscopic and macroscopic loops, is what the spiral of mimetic patho(-)logy has attempted to do.

The mimetic spiral does not stop turning at the end of modernism, but it has in modernism its starting point. The writers we have been following are part of a generation of thinkers who are beginning to sense, with increasing intensity, that the power of their own medium is perhaps no longer the strongest in town to convey mimetic messages to the public. And yet this medium remains extremely sensitive to register this shift of emphasis: Nietzsche's late fascination with the actor's "will to power," Conrad's account of a "universal genius" qua journalist, the increasing fragmentation of Lawrence's "political novels," and Bataille's heterogeneous account of nonlinguistic forms of communication are symptomatic of a characteristically modernist realization that traditional artistic forms and genres, as well as the ethical, political, religious, and metaphysical certitudes they entail, are, if not entirely falling apart, at least progressively giving way to the turbulent spirit that is characteristic of the crisis of modernity.

W. B. Yeats's "The Second Coming"[29] catches, with extreme vision-
ary precision, the spiraling, centrifugal movement away from a stabilizing
human, all too human center that is characteristic of modernist times. As we
have seen, in such a period of transformation, there is no longer a stationary
axis that can hold the modernist worldview together, providing stabilizing
solutions to the unsettling riddles of mimesis. And yet this does not mean
that mimetic patho(-)logies cannot be developed in order to keep up with
the "widening gyre" characteristic of the modernist flight into the future.
Nor does the "anarchy [that] is loosed upon the world" suggest that a single
"revelation is at hand," no matter how strong the desire for a "second coming"
is, or may be, at times of decline of the West.[30] What modernist physicians
of the soul propose is perhaps less a transcendental, mythic revelation than
an immanent and untimely indication: namely, that "the best" should regain
their "conviction" in order to propose, with and against the current of our
hypermimetic times, alternative models, types, and, above all patho-*logical*
forms of inquiry that continue to critically reflect on the affective and infective power of mimetic (dis)possession. Regaining the conviction that mimesis is at the center of the crisis of modernity is the key step for continuing
to follow the widening spiral that, for better or worse, is currently turning
phantoms into egos—egos into phantoms.

Having begun with Nietzsche, we shall conclude this book with
Nietzsche. In *Twilight of the Idols* this self-proclaimed philosophical physician sums up his mimetic diagnostic about the ego along lines that modernist
physicians of the soul will be quick to echo. He restates his clinical conclusion thus: "This 'inner world' is full of phantoms.... And as for the *ego*! That
has become a fable, a fiction, a play on words" (*TI* 3; 495). *The Phantom of
the Ego* has told the story of how the ego become a fable. If our ambition
was to unmask metaphysical fictions—revealing them as fascinating plays on
words—it is not for us to predict how this fable will end.

Notes

Introduction

1. Friedrich Nietzsche, *Nachgelassene Fragmente, 1875–1879*, vol. 8 in *Sämtliche Werke: Kritische Studienausgabe*, 15 vols., ed. Giorgio Colli and Mazzino Montinari , tr. Gary Handwerk (Berlin: Walter de Gruyter, 1967–1977), 32; 8.

2. Friedrich Nietzsche, *Daybreak*, tr. R. J. Hollingdale (Cambridge: Cambridge University Press, 1982), 105.

3. The most influential account of mimetic realism is still Erich Auerbach, *Mimesis: The Representation of Reality in Western Literature*, tr. Willard R. Trask (Princeton: Princeton University Press, 2003).

4. Mark Micale, "Introduction: The Modernist Mind—A Map," in *The Mind of Modernism: Medicine, Psychology, and the Cultural Arts in Europe and America, 1880–1940*, ed. Mark Micale (Stanford: Stanford University Press, 2004), 1–20. Widely discussed mimetic phenomena included hysteria, hypnosis, suggestion, and emotional contagion.

5. Robert Pippin, *Modernism as a Philosophical Problem*, 2nd ed. (Oxford: Blackwell, 1999), 99.

6. E. R. Dodds, *The Greeks and the Irrational* (Berkeley: University of California Press, 1964), 185.

7. René Girard, "Nietzsche and Contradiction," in *Nietzsche in Italy*, ed. Thomas Harrison (Saratoga: Anna Libri, 1988), 53–66.

8. Stephen Ross defines "new modernist studies" as an "energizing turn [that] has reopened modernism to a more comprehensive gaze, taking in the full range of culture from roughly 1890 to 1950." "Introduction," in *Modernism and Theory: A Critical Debate*, ed. Stephen Ross (New York: Routledge, 2009), 1.

9. In addition to the work of René Girard, my approach to mimesis is indebted to the work of

Philippe Lacoue-Labarthe, as well as to the teaching of Mikkel Borch-Jacobsen and of Henry
Staten, all thinkers I consider to be in line with Nietzsche. See Philippe Lacoue-Labarthe,
Typography: Mimesis, Philosophy, Politics, ed. Christopher Fynsk (Cambridge: Harvard
University Press, 1989); *L'imitation des modernes (Typographies 2)* (Paris: Galilée, 1986); Mikkel
Borch-Jacobsen, *The Freudian Subject*, tr. Catherine Porter (Stanford: Stanford University Press,
1988) and *The Emotional Tie: Psychoanalysis, Mimesis, Affect*, tr. Douglass Brick et al. (Stanford:
Stanford University Press, 1992); Henry Staten, *Nietzsche's Voice* (Ithaca, N.Y.: Cornell University
Press, 1990). If Borch-Jacobsen's "mimetic hypothesis" is indebted to Girard, Lacoue-Labarthe's
take on mimesis has not been uncritical of Girard (see *Typography*, 102–121). My assumption
in what follows is that in order to further the field of mimetic theory we need to move beyond
past quarrels (both ancient and modern), learn from competing perspectives (be they Girardian,
deconstructive, or postmodern), and supplement their limitations. For useful historical and
theoretical accounts of the concept of mimesis, see Gunter Gebauer and Christopher Wulf,
Mimesis: Culture–Art–Society, tr. Don Reneau (Berkeley: University of California Press, 1995);
Arne Melberg, *Theories of Mimesis* (Cambridge: Cambridge University Press, 1995); Matthew
Potolsky, *Mimesis* (London: Routledge, 2006).

10. René Girard, *Mensonge romantique et vérité romanesque* (Paris: Éditions Bernard Grasset, 1961);
Deceit, Desire and the Novel, tr. Yvonne Freccero (Baltimore: Johns Hopkins University Press,
1965); *La violence et le sacré* (Paris: Éditions Albin Michel, 1990); *Violence and the Sacred*, tr.
Patrick Gregory (Baltimore: Johns Hopkins University Press, 1977). Dates in the body of the text
refer to the year of publication of the original French version.

11. For a Girardian reading of violence and sacrifice in the modernist period, see also William A.
Johnsen, *Violence and Modernism: Ibsen, Joyce, and Woolf* (Gainesville: University Press of Florida,
2003).

12. As Girard also recently recognized, "at the present moment, sacrificial resolutions are no longer
possible." René Girard, *Achever Clausewitz: Entretiens avec Benoît Chantre* (Paris: Carnets nord,
2007), 62 (my transl.); see *Battling to the End*, tr. Mary Baker (East Lansing: Michigan State
University Press, 2010), 23.

13. René Girard, *Evolution and Conversion: Dialogues on the Origins of Culture* (with Pierpaolo
Antonello and João Cezar de Castro Rocha) (London: Continuum, 2007), 174.

14. Friedrich Nietzsche, *Ecce Homo*, tr. R. J. Hollingdale (Harmondsworth: Penguin, 1979), 39–40.

15. Plato, *Republic*, tr. Paul Shorey, in *The Collected Dialogues of Plato*, ed. Edith Hamilton and
Huntington Cairns, tr. Lane Cooper et al. (Princeton: Princeton University Press, 1963), 575–
844, 653. For a seminal study of the pharmaceutical dimension of mimesis in Plato's thought, see
Jacques Derrida, "Plato's Pharmacy," in *Dissemination*, tr. Barbara Johnson (Chicago: University
of Chicago Press, 1981), 61–171. Robert Pippin recognizes that "perhaps modernity is a kind of
repetition of . . . Platonic themes." Pippin, *Modernism*, 25. This repetition is especially visible with
respect to *mimetic*, pharmacological themes.

16. Friedrich Nietzsche, *On the Genealogy of Morals*, tr. Douglass Smith (Oxford: Oxford University
Press, 1996), 92.

17. Plato, *Republic*, 832.

18. Nietzsche, *Genealogy of Morals*, 129.

19. If Socrates's expulsion of the mimetic poet is well known, here is a less-known passage from *Laws*
where the Athenian addresses the tragic poets in a rather different manner: "Respected visitors, we
are ourselves authors of a tragedy, and that the finest and best we know how to make. In fact, our

whole polity has been constructed as a dramatization of a noble and perfect life; that is what we hold to be in truth the most real of tragedies. *Thus you are poets, and we also are poets in the same style, rival artists and rival actors.*" Plato, *Laws*, in *Collected Dialogues of Plato*, 1387 (my emphasis). For a brilliant, and, for this study, decisive analysis of Plato's "mimetology," see Lacoue-Labarthe, "Typography," in *Typography*, 43–138.

20. D. H. Lawrence, *Phoenix* (New York: Viking Press, 1968), 520; *Phoenix II* (Harmondsworth: Penguin, 1981), 625.

21. For a lucid articulation of Girard's consideration of "literature *as* theory," see Robert Doran, "Introduction," in *René Girard, Mimesis and Theory: Essays on Literature and Criticism, 1953–2005*, ed. Robert Doran (Stanford: Stanford University Press, 2008), xiv. For a penetrating introduction to Lacoue-Labarthe's thought, which considers that, for him, "the experience of thought is also a poetic experience," see Jacques Derrida, "Introduction: Desistance," in *Typography*, 3–42, 6.

22. In Book X of *Republic*, after mimesis has already been amply discussed, Socrates returns to the subject and asks Glaucon: "Could you tell me in general what imitation is? For neither do I myself quite apprehend what it would be at." And Glaucon replies: "It is likely, then . . . that *I* should apprehend!" Plato, *Republic*, 820. On the multiple meanings of mimesis in the classical period, see Eric A. Havelock, *Preface to Plato* (Oxford: Basil Blackwell, 1963).

23. For an account of copying in contemporary culture that casts a positive light on this much despised practice, see Marcus Boon, *In Praise of Copying* (Cambridge: Harvard University Press, 2009). Http://www.hup.harvard.edu/features/boon/.

24. Micale, "Introduction: The Modernist Mind," 4.

25. The distinction between the concept of ego and the one of subject reflects the distinction between psychological and philosophical approaches to subjectivity. Since none of the authors I examine considers the notion of subject in traditional philosophical terms (as an autonomous, monadic, self-sufficient, and rational entity), and since they often use this concept interchangeably with the concept of ego, I refrain from setting up rigid boundaries between the two notions, using the former in more philosophically oriented discussions and the latter in more psychologically oriented contexts.

26. In what follows I adopt Michael Whitworth's working definition of modernism as a "set of responses to problems posed by the condition of modernity." *Modernism,* ed. Michael Whitworth (Oxford: Blackwell, 2007), 3. We shall see that when it comes to the specific *mimetic* problems posed by modernity (from the 1880s to the 1950s), the authors I consider are strikingly consistent in their patho(-)logical responses.

27. Girard, *Evolution and Conversion*, 59.

28. For an illustration of this widespread tendency, see *Modernism and the European Unconscious*, ed. Peter Collier and Judy Davies (Cambridge: Polity Press, 1990).

29. Henry Ellenberger, *The Discovery of the Unconscious: The History and Evolution of Dynamic Psychiatry* (London: Fontana Press, 1994), 111.

30. Ellenberger considers Pierre Janet the father of modern psychology. More recently, Micale reminds us that "Pierre Janet was regarded as the most sensitive and original thinker in early French depth psychology." Micale, "Introduction: The Modernist Mind," 5.

31. For Borch-Jacobsen, hypnosis and mimesis are inextricably linked insofar as both "emotional ties" are predicated on a confusion between self and other. According to this "mimetic hypothesis," "the

subject *is* the other, is *the same as* the other." Borch-Jacobsen, *The Emotional Tie*, 16. Along similar lines, Jean-Michel Oughourlian, in conversation with Girard, says that hypnosis functions as an "exceptional concentrate of all the possibilities of mimesis." René Girard, *Des choses cachées depuis la fondation du monde* (Paris: Éditions Grasset, 1978), 455 (my transl.). For a pioneering account of the relation between imitation and hypnosis, see Gabriel Tarde, *Les lois de l'imitation* (Paris: Seuil, 2001), 134–148. I am very grateful to Mikkel Borch-Jacobsen for sharing his encyclopedic historical knowledge of the hypnotic-mimetic tradition during numerous, friendly chats in Parisian cafes.

32. Judith Ryan persuasively argues that most canonical modernists did not rely on Freud as a source of inspiration, but on a variety of early psychologies of empirical orientation that circulated widely at the turn of the century. See Judith Ryan, *The Vanishing Subject: Early Psychology and Literary Modernism* (Chicago: University of Chicago Press, 1991), 1–20.

33. Micale, "Introduction: The Modernist Mind," 8. For an informative list of influential psychological figures that contributed to shaping the mind of modernism, see Micale, 5–9. For a recent study concerned with the development of the concept of the unconscious in German culture, see *Thinking the Unconscious: Nineteenth-Century German Thought*, ed. Angus Nicholls and Martin Liebscher (Cambridge: Cambridge University Press, 2010). For a cognitive account of the "new unconscious" that is currently emerging from a reconsideration of automatic, relational phenomena (including unconscious mimicry and hypnosis) that were already dominant in the modernist period, see *The New Unconscious*, ed. Ran R. Hassin, James S. Uleman, John A. Bargh (Oxford: Oxford University Press, 2005).

34. The French social psychologist Gabriel Tarde makes this point succinctly in *The Laws of Imitation*, defining imitation as an "action at a distance of a mind over another"; relying on the model of hypnotic suggesion, he specifies that "many forms of imitations are unconscious and involuntary from the beginning." Tarde, *Les lois de l'imitation*, 46, 251(my transl.).

35. Andrew N. Meltzoff, "Out of the Mouths of Babes: Imitation, Gaze, and Intentions in Infant Research—the 'Like Me' Framework," in *Mimesis and Science: Empirical Research on Imitation and the Mimetic Theory of Culture and Religion*, ed. Scott R. Garrels (East Lansing: Michigan State University Press, 2011), 55–74, 59. See also Andrew Meltzoff and Keith Moore, "Persons and Representation: Why Infant Imitation Is Important for Theories of Human Development," in *Imitation in Infancy*, ed. Jacqueline Nadal and George Butterworth (Cambridge: Cambridge University Press, 1999), 9–35. I thank Pierpaolo Antonello for discussing these developments with me during a research stay at the University of Cambridge.

36. Aristotle, *The Poetics of Aristotle*, tr. . Stephen Halliwell (Chapel Hill: University of North Carolina Press, 1987), 34.

37. For the neurophysiological discovery of "mirror neurons" that are automatically triggered by the visual movements of others, see Vittorio Gallese, "The 'Shared Manifold' Hypothesis: From Mirror Neurons to Empathy," *Journal of Consciousness Studies* 8 (2001): 33–50. On the plasticity of the human brain, see Norman Doidge, *The Brain that Changes Itself: Stories of Personal Triumph from the Frontiers of Brain Science* (New York: Penguin, 2007).

38. For a recent book-length study that initiates a stimulating dialogue between empirical researchers on imitation and mimetic theory, see Garrels, *Mimesis and Science*.

39. Henry Maudsley qtd. in Tarde, *Les lois de l'imitation*, 148 (my transl.).

40. Nietzsche, *Ecce Homo*, 39.

41. Eduardo Cadava, Peter Connor, Jean-Luc Nancy, eds., *Who Comes After the Subject?* (New York: Routledge, 1991).

Chapter 1. Nietzsche's Mimetic Patho(-)logy: From Antiquity to Modernity

1. I use the following English translations, editions, and abbreviations of Nietzsche's works: *The Antichrist* (*A*), tr. Walter Kaufmann, in *The Portable Nietzsche*, ed. Walter Kaufmann (New York: Viking Press, 1954), 568–656; *Beyond Good and Evil* (*BGE*), tr. R. J. Hollingdale (London: Penguin, 2003); *The Birth of Tragedy* (*BT*), tr. Walter Kaufmann (New York: Vintage, 1967); *The Case of Wagner* (*CW*), tr. Walter Kaufmann (New York: Vintage, 1967); *Daybreak* (*D*), tr. R. J. Hollingdale (Cambridge: Cambridge University Press, 1982); *Ecce Homo* (*EH*), tr. R. J. Hollingdale (Harmondsworth: Penguin, 1979); *The Gay Science* (*GS*), tr. Walter Kaufmann (New York: Vintage, 1974); *On the Genealogy of Morals* (*GM*), tr. Douglass Smith (Oxford: Oxford University Press, 1996); *Human, All Too Human* (*HH*), tr. Gary Handwerk (Stanford: Stanford University Press, 1997); *Nietzsche Contra Wagner* (*NW*), tr. Walter Kaufmann, in *The Portable Nietzsche*, 661–683; *Twilight of the Idols* (*TI*), tr. Walter Kaufmann, in The Portable Nietzsche, 463–563; *Untimely Meditations* (*UM*), ed. Daniel Breazeale (Cambridge: Cambridge University Press, 1997); *The Will to Power* (*WP*), tr. Walter Kaufmann (New York: Vintage, 1968). The German edition of Nietzsche's works I refer to is *Sämtliche Werke: Kritische Studienausgabe*, 15 vols., ed. Giorgio Colli and Mazzino Montinari (Berlin: Walter de Gruyter, 1967–1977). References to the primary texts will henceforth be given in the body of the text. Title abbreviations as well as part, section, and, when necessary (i.e., long sections), page numbers are given in parentheses (e.g., *GM* III, 17; 110).

2. Robert Buch writes: "Of the three means of persuasion discussed in classical rhetoric πάθος (pathos) is the one in which the orator appeals to the emotions of his audience . . . [It] was present above all in the dramatic speech: in a discourse fueled and compelled by the passion and thought to be of a quasi-contagious appeal." And he adds: "*páthos* also implies the distance and control somebody is able to maintain over his or her pain." Robert Buch, *The Pathos of the Real: On the Aesthetics of Violence in the Twentieth Century* (Baltimore: Johns Hopkins University Press, 2010), 19–20. Nietzsche often refers to the Greek notion of pathos along similar rhetorical lines, but each time this notion shifts slightly in meaning and must be understood in its proper context. What remains constant, however, is that for Nietzsche, pathos is essentially mimetic pathos, distance, mimetic distance.

3. Girard, "Nietzsche and Contradiction," 60.

4. In *Nietzsche's Voice*, Henry Staten is particularly attentive to the psychophysiological aspect of Nietzsche's thought and carefully traces the dynamic interplay of two major tendencies, or "economies," he sees at work in Nietzsche's writings: a "grand economy" characterized by affirmation and squandering of psychic energy on the one hand, and its antithesis, a "defensive/appropriative economy" characterized by a reactive self-preservation of the boundaries of individuation, on the other. In *L'imitation des modernes*, Philippe Lacoue-Labarthe articulates Nietzsche's "mimetology" by considering the "general" and "restricted" forms of mimesis that traverse his work, and in "Typography," in *Typography*, 43–138, he traces Nietzsche's take on mimesis back to Plato. My take on Nietzsche's mimetic contradictions is indebted to both Staten's and Lacoue-Labarthe's penetrating studies. It furthers them by addressing Girard's incisive question via the angle of what I shall call mimetic patho(-)logy.

5. David Krell, *Infectious Nietzsche* (Bloomington: Indiana University Press, 1996), 25.

6. Staten, *Nietzsche's Voice*, 6.

7. Compassion is a phenomenon that is rarely discussed in Nietzsche studies. For an important exception, see Staten, *Nietzsche's Voice*, 145–169.

8. Nietzsche's critique of pity is indebted to the French moralist La Rochefoucauld, as well as to Plato and Aristotle (see *HH* 50, *A* 7).

9. In *Twilight of the Idols*, Nietzsche writes that "Schopenhauer's morality of pity—a very unfortunate attempt!—is the real movement of decadence in morality; as such it is profoundly related to Christian morality" (37; 540). And, once again, he invokes the notion of "pathos of distance" in order to preserve "the cleavage between man and man" (37; 540).

10. Arthur Schopenhauer, *On the Basis of Morality*, tr. E. F. J. Payne (Indianapolis: Bobbs-Merrill, 1965), 18.

11. Schopenhauer, *Morality*, 18.

12. Schopenhauer, *Morality*, 16.

13. The notion of *Mitempfindung*, usually translated as "empathy," is broader in scope than *Mitleid* insofar as it is not confined to a sharing of suffering (*Leid*) alone, but extends to any affects (*Empfindungen*). Yet the fact that Nietzsche situates his "theory of empathy" in the context of his discussion of *Mitleid*, and that the problematic of suffering remains internal to his discussion, indicates that what Nietzsche says of *Mitempfindung* equally applies to *Mitleid*.

14. The difference between *nachmachen*, *nachbilden*, and *nachahmen* (all translated as "imitation") is slight; in his account of compassion, Nietzsche uses these terms interchangeably.

15. One of the discoverers of mirror neurons, Vittorio Gallese, explains what he calls "unconscious mimesis" on a neurophysiological basis reminiscent of Nietzsche's psycho-physiology: "When perceiving others expressing emotions by means of their facial mimicry, the observers' facial muscles activate in a congruent manner. . . . Both the production and the perception of emotion-related facial expressions or body postures impinge upon common neural structures related to viscero-motor, somato-motor, and affective aspects of the emotion experience." And in a mirroring reproduction of Nietzsche's argument, he adds: "When we witness a given facial expression and comprehend that expression as characterized by a particular emotional state, we do not accomplish this type of comprehension through explicit inference from analogy. The other's emotion is first constituted and directly understood by means of embodied simulation producing an 'as if' experience engendered by a shared body state. It is the body state shared by the observer and the observed that enables direct understanding." Gallese, "Two Sides of Mimesis," 95. Along similar lines, William Hurlbut echoes: "It appears that there is an innate (and phylogenetically ancient) capacity for translating observed actions of another into the parallel postures and muscular motions of the self." And in another mirroring confirmation of Nietzsche's argument, he adds: "It appears that even simulating the actions of another may establish an intersubjectivity that allows deeper communication than mere observation and analysis. Studies of infant imitation and the discovery of mirror neurons may provide the psychological and neurobiological explanations of this extraordinary capability." "Desire, Mimesis," 180–181.

16. As Nietzsche famously puts it, "every great philosophy has hitherto been . . . a personal confession on the part of its author and a kind of involuntary and unconscious memoir." And he adds: "above all his morality bears decided and decisive witness to *who he is*" (*BGE* 6). The "Nietzsche" I refer to progressively emerges from an intrinsic reading of his memoir, an unconscious memoir that bear witness to "who he is," or would like to be.

17. René Girard, "Superman in the Underground: Strategies of Madness—Nietzsche, Wagner, and Dostoevsky," *MLN* 91 (1976): 1257–1266; "Dionysus versus the Crucified," *MLN* 99 (1994): 816–835; "Nietzsche and Contradiction."

18. Girard, "Nietzsche and Contradiction," 58.

19. Girard, *Violence and the Sacred*, 180.

20. Girard, "Superman in the Underground," 1164.

21. Girard, *Deceit*, 99.

22. Girard, "Superman in the Underground," 1175.

23. Girard, "Superman in the Underground," 1161, 1163–1165.

24. Girard, "Nietzsche and Contradiction," 64

25. Herman Siemens, "Agonal Configurations in the *Unzeitgemässe Betrachtungen:* Identity, Mimesis and the *Übertragung* of Cultures in Nietzsche's Early Thought," in *Nietzsche-Studien* 30 (2001): 80–106, 81.

26. Borch-Jacobsen, *The Freudian Subject*, 90.

27. If I continue to refer to the Girardian notion of "mimetic rivalry," it is in this specific, Nietzschean sense that I understand it.

28. Girard, "Superman in the Underground," 1163–1169.

29. For an original precursor of the idea that the scapegoat is a *pharmakos* originally linked to rituals of purification, see Derrida, "Plato's Pharmacy," 130–133. Derrida also anticipates a key insight in mimetic theory as he writes, following Plato's account of Thoth in *Phaedrus*, tr. R. Hackforth, in *Collected Dialogues of Plato:* "In distinguishing himself from his opposite, Thoth also imitates it, becomes its sign and representative, obeys it and *conforms* to it, replaces it by violence if need be" (93). Passages like this one indicate that a full genealogy of mimetic theory still needs to be traced.

30. This no longer corresponds to Girard's current position. As he now explains: "For a long time I have tried to think of Christianity from above [*comme une position de surplomb*], and I had to renounce that. I am now convinced that mimetism needs to be thought from within." Girard, *Achever Clausewitz*, 153 (my transl.); *Battling to the End*, 82.

31. Girard claims that he has found, in the *Posthumous Fragments*, the ultimate proof of Nietzsche's enthusiasm for Wagner's most Christian work. Nietzsche, in fact, writes of "an indescribable expression of greatness *in* the compassion towards it, *whatever that means.*" And speaking of *Parsifal*, Nietzsche says: "I do not know anything that apprehends Christianity at such a depth, and that generates compassion so powerfully. I am completely transported and moved." Quoted in Girard, "Nietzsche and Contradiction," 60.

32. Girard, "Nietzsche and Contradiction," 65.

33. Girard, "Superman in the Underground," 1257.

34. Nietzsche uses this notion in a medical sense. Thus, he writes that "our physicians and physiologists confront their most interesting case in Wagner" (*CW* 5; 166).

35. Nietzsche's definition of Wagner as an "actor" and "mime" is not limited to his two books devoted to his mimetic rival, but equally appear in other books of his later period. See, *TI* 107, and book 5 of *GS*.

36. Plato, *Republic*, 832; 607b. Henceforth *Rep.*, qtd. in the body of the text (page number; line number).

37. For Nietzsche's faithful account of the Platonic critique of mimetic art, see "Richard Wagner in Bayreuth" (*UM* IV, 7).

38. Philippe Lacoue-Labarthe and Jean-Luc Nancy, "The Nazi Myth," tr. Brian Holmes, *Critical*

Inquiry 16.2 (1990): 291–312, 303. They add: "in founding Bayreuth his [Wagner's] aim will be deliberately political: it will be that of the unification of the German people, thorough celebration and theatrical ceremonial (comparable to the unification of the city in tragic ritual)" (303).

39. Jacob Golomb and Robert S. Wistrich, "Introduction," *Nietzsche, Godfather of Fascism? On the Uses and Abuses of a Philosophy*, ed. Jacob Golomb and Robert S. Wistrich (Princeton: Princeton University Press, 2002), 8.

40. For an important account that traces the continuities between Nietzsche's "mimetology" and Plato's critique of mimesis, see Philippe Lacoue-Labarthe, "Typography." What follows is indebted to this profound study. See also Lacoue-Labarthe, *La fiction du politique* (Paris: Christian Bourgois, 1987), chap. 8, "Mimétologie" and *L'imitation des modernes*. For another study particularly attentive to the affective dimension of mimesis in Plato, see Eric Havelock, *Preface to Plato*. For a comprehensive bibliography on the question of mimesis in Plato, Mihai Spariosu, "Plato's *Ion*: Mimesis, Poetry and Power," in *Mimesis in Contemporary Theory: An Interdisciplinary Approach*, ed. Ronald Bogue, vol. 2 (Philadelphia: Benjamins, 1991), 13–25.

41. Plato, *Ion*, tr. Lane Cooper, in *Collected Dialogues of Plato*, 215–228. As Spariosu puts it in his reading of *Ion*, "although Socrates does not use the word, *mimesis* in its archaic sense of play is constantly in the background in his discussion of poetry." Spariosu, "Plato's *Ion*," 19.

42. In Book III of the *Republic*, speaking of the "how" or the "manner" of poetic speech (*lexis*), Plato distinguishes between three modes of poetic enunciation: pure narrative, mimesis, and mixed style. In pure narrative, we are told, the poet "himself is the speaker and does not even attempt to suggest to us that anyone but himself is speaking." In mimetic speech, on the other hand, the poet "delivers a speech as if he were someone else [and] assimilates thereby his own diction as far as possible to that of the person whom he announces as about to speak." Finally, in the epic, the poet uses a combination of both styles (*Rep.* 637–639; 392c–394e).

43. Plato's critique of mimesis is not unilateral. In fact, Plato is far from being that systematic/ dogmatic philosopher he is often thought to be but, rather, is a thinker who follows the path of dialectical discovery. For Plato's clear celebration of the mad, enthusiastic state of the poet, as well as philosophy's entanglement in such madness, see *Phaedrus*, 491–493.

44. In *Preface to Plato*, Eric Havelock has shown that Plato's critique of mimesis can only be fully understood if it is considered against the background of an oral culture in which poetry was not read individually, but performed, heard, and memorized collectively. For Havelock, this is why Plato's critique of mimesis "focuses initially not on the artist's creative act but on his power to make his audience identify almost pathologically and certainly sympathetically with the content of what he is saying." When Plato condemns poetry, he is thus attacking "a total state of mind" in which oral performance, rhythmic patterns, collective emotions, and identificatory mechanisms lead the audience to a state of "enjoyment and relaxation" where they "were themselves partly hypnotized." Havelock, *Preface to Plato*, 45, 134, 152.

45. See Lacoue-Labarthe, "Typography," esp. 126–128.

46. Nicholas Carr writes: "Our intellectual and social lives may, like our industrial routines, come to reflect the form that the computer imposes on them." He then proceeds to give ample evidence that the Internet is indeed changing our brain. Nicholas Carr, *The Shallows: How the Internet Is Changing the Way We Read, Think and Remember* (London: Atlantic Books, 2010), 207.

47. In *Ion*, Plato famously compares the transmission of psychic energy to the effect of a magnetic stone (i.e., the "stone of Heraclea") on iron rings: "This stone does not simply attract the iron rings, just by themselves; it also imparts to the rings a force enabling them to do the same thing as the stone itself, that is, to attract another ring" (*Ion*, 220; 533d–e). For Plato, then, the mimetic

power that runs through the rhapsode is not unlike the property of magnetism. Like magnetism, mimesis is endowed with the property of attraction and of contagion. The result of this contagion, for Plato, is that "a chain of iron rings is formed" that connects different rings from God to the poet to the rhapsode and finally to the public. As Havelock points out, such considerations have a "ring of mob psychology." Havelock, *Preface to Plato*, 27. For another account of Plato's embryonic critique of crowd psychology, see J. S. McClelland, *The Crowd and the Mob: From Plato to Canetti* (London: Unwin Hyman, 1989), 35–45.

48. Nietzsche's critique of Wagner should not be limited to Nietzsche's late period. As Nietzsche puts it, "the problem of the actor has troubled [him] for the longest time" (*GS* 361), a trouble highlighted by Nietzsche's contradictory evaluation of dramatic pathos, present form the very beginning of his career. See for instance, "Richard Wagner in Bayreuth" (*UM* IV, 7; 223–225).

49. Letter to Ritschl, May 10, 1869 (*KSB* 3; 7). *Sämtliche Briefe: Kritische Studienausgabe*, 8 vols., ed. Giorgio Colli and Mazzino Montinari (New York: Walter de Gruyter, 1986).

50. Nietzsche's strategy of intellectual confrontation with his intellectual father figures is "agonal" in the sense Herman Siemens gives to this term. See Siemens, "Agonal Configurations," 82. In his analysis of the early Nietzsche, Siemens specifies how Nietzsche's antagonistic confrontation with his intellectual models is predicated on what he calls a "strategy of empowerment through and against an overwhelming opponent, an emancipatory dynamic of overcoming and acknowledgement" (82). Siemens's account of Nietzsche's agon is very close to what I call mimetic patho(-)logy. Siemens's "agonal configuration" stresses Nietzsche's "active" and "organized" (89) struggle with his educators; "mimetic patho(-)logy," on the other hand, attempts to strike a balance between the active and the passive logic of mimetic rivalry, the logical and an affective dimension of Nietzsche's mimetic thought, patho-logy and pathology.

51. Nietzsche's emphasis on the psychophysiology of the mimetic actor is also at work in the unpublished notes collected in *Will to Power* (*WP* 809–813).

52. Critics who have noticed the proximity between the Dionysian and the Wagnerian pathos have tended to follow Nietzsche's conceptual distinctions (high and low, master and slave, active and reactive, Dionysian and decadent etc.) in order to keep these two mimetic phenomena apart and create some order in the midst of these contradictions. See Peter Sloterdijk, *Thinker on Stage: Nietzsche's Materialism*, tr. Jamie Owen Daniel (Minneapolis: University of Minnesota Press, 1989), 54; Sigridur Thorgeirsdottir, *Vis Creativa: Kunst und Wahrheit in der Philosophie Nietzsches* (Würzburg: Königshausen & Neumann, 1996), 235. These accounts are faithful to Nietzsche's conceptual attempt to wrest the Dionysian apart from Wagner, good mimesis from bad mimesis, but they do not pay enough attention to the affective movement of Nietzsche's patho(-)logy, a movement that flows freely across conceptual barriers. Interestingly, when questions of intoxication, enthusiasm and contagion appear in the context of his critique of Wagner, Nietzsche is careful never to invoke the concept of the Dionysian at all, treating Wagner's enthusiastic mimomania as completely external to the same state he celebrates in the Dionysian. This gesture seems indicative of Nietzsche's inability to fully direct his critique of the Wagnerian sickness against his conception of the Dionysian.

53. The essays in *Nietzsche and Depth Psychology*, ed. Jacob J. Golomb, Weaver Santaniello, and Ronald Lehrer (Albany: State University of New York Press, 1999) are representative of the amount of critical attention that is given to Nietzsche as a precursor of psychoanalysis on the one hand, and of the lack of concern for the psychological research that fascinated Nietzsche, on the other.

54. For an informed study that testifies to the influence of the mimetic unconscious (or inconscient cérébral) on Nietzsche, see Marcel Gauchet, *L'inconscient cérébral* (Paris: Seuil, 1992), 129–136.

55. For a solid articulation of Nietzsche's take on the philosophical tradition of the unconscious, a tradition he partially inherited from Schopenhauer and von Hartmann, see Martin Liebscher, "Friedrich Nietzsche's Perspectives on the Unconscious," in Nicholls and Liebscher, *Thinking the Unconscious*, 241–269.

56. Théodule Ribot, *Les maladies de la volonté* (Paris: Alcan, 1883), 177 (my transl.).

57. As Martin Stingelin has made clear, it is in Théodule Ribot's *Revue philosophique de la France et de l'étranger* that Nietzsche finds access to the most recent French psychological theories of pre-Freudian inspiration. As he explains: "Here Nietzsche could have read articles or reviews of the works of Bergson, Bernheim, Binet, Burot, Delboeuf, Espinas . . . Lombroso, Richet, Tarde, and Wundt on topics such as comparative psychology, psychology of perception, consciousness, associations and dreams, hypnosis, multiple personality disorders, and psychophysiology." And he adds: "Given Nietzsche's intense interests in the research results of the Salpêtrière, it is not unlikely that he was familiar with Sigmund Freud's translation of Jean-Marin Charcot's *Neuen Vorlesungen über die Krankheiten des Nervensystems, insbesondere über Hysterie* (Leipzig, 1886). The nosological terminology of research on hysteria informs especially the vocabulary of *The Case of Wagner*." Martin Stingelin, "Psychologie," in *Nietzsche-Handbuch*, ed. Henning Ottmann (Stuttgart: J. B. Metzler Verlag, 2000), 424–426, 424 (my transl.).

58. Léon Chertok calls this period "the golden age of hypnosis." Léon Chertok, *Hypnose et suggéstion* (Paris: Presses Universitaires de France, 1993), 23. For a detailed account of the vicissitudes of hypnosis in the history of dynamic psychology, see Ellenberger, *Discovery of the Unconscious*, chaps. 1–3.

59. Nietzsche is closer to Bernheim of the school of Nancy than to Charcot. If Charcot stressed the pathological aspect of suggestibility to hypnotic suggestion, Bernheim argued that suggestion is a universal phenomenon that cannot be confined to the problem of hysteria.

60. Philippe Lacoue-Labarthe, *Musica Ficta* (Figures de Wagner) (Paris: Christian Bourgois, 1991), 19.

61. Hippolyte Bernheim, *Suggestive Therapeutics: A Treatise on the Nature and Uses of Hypnosis*, tr. Christian A. Herter (Westport, Conn: Associated Booksellers, 1957), 137.

62. Henry Staten, "A Critique of the Will to Power," in *A Companion to Nietzsche*, ed. Keith A. Pearson (Oxford: Blackwell, 2006), 565–582, 575.

63. Martin Liebscher points out that in Nietzsche's late period "the unconscious was to be understood against the background of the theory of the will to power," and he goes as far as claiming that Nietzsche's take on the "plurality of will to power . . . extinguishes the concept of the unconscious." Liebscher, "Nietzsche's Perspectives," 243, 257. Our approach, on the other hand, leads us to believe that the same conception of the mimetic unconscious traverses the entirety of Nietzsche's work, from *Human, All Too Human to the Nachlass*.

64. Nietzsche's definition of will to power as a pathos is in line with Gilles Deleuze's understanding of will to power as the "power of being affected." Gilles Deleuze, *Nietzsche et la philosophie* (Paris: Presses Universitaires de France, 1962), 70 (my transl.). We can now add that Nietzsche's vulnerability to all kinds of patha we have encountered so far (the pathos of compassion, Wagner's tyrannical "pathos," and now the pathos discharged via mimicry) allows us to redefine that "primitive form of affect" which is will to power in terms of power to be affected mimetically.

65. Girard, "Superman in the Underground," 1171.

66. Summing up what he calls "one of the most extraordinary discoveries of the twentieth century" (the fact that the brain is continuously subjected to change at the neurological level), Norman

Doidge writes: "Our brains are modified by the cultural activities we do—be they reading, studying music . . . learning new languages" or, we may add, being subjected to leader figures. Doidge, *Brain that Changes Itself*, 288.

67. Lacoue-Labarthe, "Typography," 227.

68. Lacoue-Labarthe, *Fiction du politique*, 127. Lacoue-Labarthe and Nancy repeat this point: "Hitlerism," they write, "could perhaps be defined as the exploitation—lucid but not necessarily cynical, for convinced of its own truth—of the modern masses' openness to [that "mimetic instrument par excellence" which for them is] myth." Lacoue-Labarthe and Nancy, "Nazi Myth," 312.

69. Nietzsche is careful not to confine his critique of the *âme moderne* to German cities. Thus he writes that "people in Paris, too, deceive themselves about Wagner, though there they are hardly anything anymore except psychologists" (*CW* 5; 165). In this sense, he diverges from Lacoue-Labarthe's and Nancy's tendency to consider vulnerability to mimetic/mythic identification as "a specifically German phenomenon." Lacoue-Labarthe and Nancy, "Nazi Myth," 297.

70. Gustave Le Bon, *The Crowd*, tr. Robert A. Nye (New Brunswick, N.J.: Transaction Publishers, 1995), 34. Serge Moscovici, in his informative genealogy of crowd psychology, points out that Le Bon considered "the dramatic stage as a model of social relationships in dramatic form and a place where those relationships were observed." Serge Moscovici, *The Age of the Crowd: A Historical Treatise on Mass Psychology*, tr. J. C. Whitehouse (Cambridge: Cambridge University Press, 1985), 89.

71. Le Bon, *The Crowd*, 51 (my emphasis).

72. For an account of Wagner's "influence" in connection to mesmerism, see Alison Winter, *Mesmerized: Powers of Mind in Victorian Britain* (Chicago: University of Chicago Press, 1998), 309–319.

73. As historians of psychology have shown, Mesmer's theory of magnetic *rapport*—i.e., of a physical fluid that could be transmitted physically through touch (magnetic passes)—was discredited in the first half of the nineteenth century. It resurfaced at the end of the century initially in France as theorists of hypnosis attempted to account for such interpersonal rapport in psychological rather than physical terms. Léon R. Chertok and Raymond de Saussure, *The Therapeutic Revolution: From Mesmer to Freud*, tr. R. H. Ahrenfeldt (New York: Brunner/Mazel Publishers, 1979), 3–60.

74. For an informed study that considers Nietzsche's thought from the angle of psychology, see Robert Pippin, *Nietzsche, Psychology, and First Philosophy* (Chicago: University of Chicago Press, 2010).

75. Lacoue-Labarthe, *L'imitation des modernes*, 282.

76. Tarde, *Les lois de l'imitation*, vii.

Chapter 2. Conrad and the Horror of Modernity

1. Francis Ford Coppola, *Apocalypse Now* (Redux) (Paramount Pictures, 2002).

2. Thomas Elsaesser and Michael Wedel write that this scene constantly reminds us of the "materiality of sound" insofar as it involves the highly conscious construction of a sound space that calls attention to itself. Thomas Elsaesser and Michael Wedel, "The Hollow Heart of Hollywood: *Apocalypse Now* and the New Sound Space," in *Conrad on Film*, ed. Gene M. Moore (Cambridge: Cambridge University Press, 1997), 151–175, 169. Their reading is predicated on

a phenomenological bracketing that leads them to conclude that "the crucial implication for the audiences would seem to be not a heightening of their listening experience but a change in the nature of cinematic perception and cognition: they 'see' differently" (167). Cinema scholars who scrutinize the scene shot by shot are indeed in a position to retain a critical distance characteristic of the subject of representation (i.e., a subject that re-presents what he sees to himself). And yet this is clearly *not* the position of the average viewer who experiences such a scene in the darkness of the movie theater. As Edgar Morin puts it, "the spectator in the 'dark room' is, on the contrary, a passive subject in a pure state. He can do nothing, has nothing to give, even his applause. Patient, he endures. Enthralled, he submits." Edgar Morin, *The Cinema, or the Imaginary Man*, tr. Lorraine Mortimer (Minneapolis: University of Minnesota Press, 2005), 97.

3. Interestingly, Coppola underestimated the affective power of the Valkyries' sequences and was "horrified" by the audience's enthusiastic response in the movie theaters. See Margot Norris, "Modernism and Vietnam: Francis Ford Coppola's *Apocalypse Now*," *Modern Fiction Studies* 44.3 (1998): 730–766, 759 n. 11. Coppola's belated *horror* at the power of his cinematic pathos indicates that as he gave the cameraman (Vittorio Storaro) directions to shoot the helicopter scene he did not fully know what he was doing. He was, indeed, enthusiastic, in the Platonic sense that he was not in control of his cinematic *techne* or, at least, of its impact on the nerves of the spectators. Lacking the necessary (Apollonian) distance, they were overwhelmed by (Dionysian) pathos.

4. For an ethical and political critique of the Vietnam War that focuses on this scene, see Norris "Modernism and Vietnam," 738–739.

5. Theodor Adorno recognized the hypnotic potential of silent films: "Suggestion and hypnosis, rejected by psychoanalysis as apocryphal, the charlatan magician masquerading before a fairground booth, reappear within its grandiose system as the silent film does in the Hollywood epic." Theodor Adorno, *Minima Moralia: Reflections on a Damaged Life*, tr. E. F. N. Jephcott (London: Verso, 2005), 64. Edgar Morin specifies that we should speak of "imitation-hypnotic state, since in the end the spectator is not asleep." Morin, *Cinema*, 96.

6. It should be clear from the above that I am not primarily interested in the question of Nietzsche's influence on Conrad. Conrad's knowledge of Nietzsche was, probably, secondhand. See David Thatcher, *Nietzsche in England, 1880–1914: The Growth of a Reputation* (Toronto: University of Toronto Press, 1972), 81–83, 170–171, 227–31. My focus is on the way modernists such as Conrad, D. H. Lawrence, and Bataille extend, from a literary, psychological, anthropological, and philosophical perspective, the diagnosis of mimesis we have encountered in Nietzsche.

7. Joseph Conrad, "An Outpost of Progress," in *Tales of Unrest* (New York: Doubleday, 1926), 86–117, 105. Henceforth "OP."

8. Jeremy Hawthorn, *Joseph Conrad: Narrative Technique and Ideological Commitment* (London: Edward Arnold, 1990), 106.

9. Hawthorn, *Joseph Conrad*, 106.

10. In a pioneering essay, Edward Said affirmed that these two authors "are best read in terms of a *common tradition* of which Nietzsche is in many ways the apogee." "Conrad and Nietzsche," in *Joseph Conrad: A Commemoration*, ed. Norman Sherry (London: Macmillan, 1976), 65–76, 66. Said considers this tradition to be rooted in a "radical attitude towards language." While I do not disregard Nietzsche's and Conrad's complex take on language, I am more attentive to the less discussed, but equally radical *affective* tradition that informs their understanding of the modern subject.

11. Le Bon, *The Crowd*, 40.

12. Tarde, *Les lois de l'imitation*, 82, n. 3, 2 (my transl.).

13. Claude Maisonnat, "Alterity and Suicide in 'An Outpost of Progress,'" *Conradiana* 28.2 (1996): 101–114, 103.

14. These two narratives have often been compared on the basis that they both stem from Conrad's Congo experience. While not indifferent to this historical connection, my reading stems from a critical engagement with Conrad's thus far unexplored *theory* of the mimetic subject—a *mimetic theory* I find internal to both texts.

15. Lombroso considered that criminal tendencies were innate in individuals, and that criminals could be recognized by the physiognomy of their heads. He formulated his notorious craniological theories in *L'uomo delinquente* (1876), a book that had an enormous impact all over Europe. As Serge Moscovici shows, criminologists' preoccupations could not be dissociated from the problematic of the crowd. Moscovici, *The Age of the Crowd*, 71–73. For an informed account of Conrad's awareness of Lombroso's theory, fin de siècle concerns with degeneration, and pre-Freudian psychology, see Martin Bock, *Joseph Conrad and Psychological Medicine* (Lubbock: Texas Tech University Press, 2002), 10–21.

16. Joseph Conrad, *Collected Letters, 1903–1907*, ed. Frederick R. Karl and Laurence Davies, vol. 3 (Cambridge: Cambridge University Press, 1988), 89.

17. For accounts of the ways gender differences inflect the Marlow/Kurtz identificatory bond see Henry Staten, "Conrad's Dionysian Elegy," in *Conrad's "Heart of Darkness" and Contemporary Thought: Revisiting the Horror with Lacoue-Labarthe*, ed. Nidesh Lawtoo (London: Bloomsbury, 2012), 201–220; Andrew Michael Roberts, *Conrad and Masculinity* (New York: St. Martin's Press, 2000), 130–136. At the general level of Victorian studies, Alison Winter usefully reminds us that Victorians "monitored their own sensibilities, took the measure of the influence they felt from each other, and speculated about the sympathies that bound them." Winter, *Mesmerized*, 12. The identificatory ties at work in *Heart of Darkness* must thus be understood in the context of a culture that is extremely sensitive to the mimetic bonds of sympathy.

18. The anonymous framing narrator adds to Marlow's claim of visibility: "It had become so pitch dark that we listeners could hardly see one another. For a long time already he, sitting apart, had been no more than a voice" (83). This passage does not preclude the possibility of communication *tout court* but, rather, introduces a shift of tropes concerning the tale's intelligibility: we move from the visible to the audible, from eyes to voice. It is in the contradictions, interruptions, and sudden changes of tonality at work in Marlow's voice that a tenuous communication begins to pierce the darkness that divides him from his listeners.

19. As Henry Staten has recognized, affirmations like this one strenghten "the solidarity of the masculine community he [Marlow] and they [the listeners] represent." Staten, "Conrad's Dionysian Elegy," 203. On Marlow's "manful effort to shore up an ideology of imperialism with an ideology of separate [gendered] spheres," see Johanna M. Smith, "'Too Beautiful Altogether': Ideologies of Gender and Empire in *Heart of Darkness*," in *Heart of Darkness: Complete Authoritative Text with Biography and Historical Contexts*, ed. by Ross C. Murfin (New York: Bedford/St. Martin's, 1996), 169–184, 196.

20. For a popular representation of Charcot's theatrical spectacles, see André Brouillet's *Une leçon de clinique à la Salpêtrière*, representing a "hysteric" woman fainting in male doctors' arms. For an informed study of these representations, see Georges Didi-Huberman, *Invention de l'hystérie: Charcot et l'iconographie de la Salpêtrière* (Paris: Éditions Macula, 1982).

21. Hippolyte Bernheim considers somnambulism a form of hypnotic suggestion. Bernheim, *Suggestive Therapeutics*, 122. This leads the French social psychologist Gabriel Tarde to

observe: "in 1884 the notion of *hypnotism* had not yet been completely substituted by that of somnambulism"; and he adds: "at the present moment [i.e., in 1890], nothing is more vulgarized than this view." Tarde, *Les lois de l'imitation*, 82, 2 n. 3 (my transl.).

22. Letters from Conrad to T. Keating, December 14, 1922, in *Joseph Conrad: Life and Letters*, ed. G. Jean-Aubry, vol. 2 (New York: Doubleday, 1927), 289.

23. Gabriel Tarde, *L'opinion et la foule* (Paris: Presses Universitaires de France, 1989), 31 (my transl.).

24. Tarde, *Opinion*, 30.

25. Tarde, *Opinion*, 38.

26. Imitation is, for Tarde, the essence of the social bond. Thus he writes: "the distinctive characteristic of every social relation is to be mimetic." Or, even more succinctly, "society is imitation, and imitation is a kind of somnambulism." Tarde, *Les lois de l'imitation*, x, 93.

27. Tarde, *Opinion*, 38.

28. Tarde specifies: "Generally, the reader is not conscious that he is subjected to the persuasive and nearly irresistible influence coming from the newspaper that he regularly reads ... he is by no means aware of the influence that the crowd of other readers has on him. This influence is nevertheless incontestable." Tarde, *Opinion*, 32–33.

29. M. H. Abrams reminds us that in seventeenth-century England "any recourse to 'enthusiasm' ... was dangerous, because it suggested the claim of disorderly religious zealots to have private access to God." M. H. Abrams, *The Mirror and the Lamp: Romantic Theory and the Critical Tradition* (Oxford: Oxford University Press, 1971), 190.

30. Garret Stewart, "Lying as Dying in *Heart of Darkness*," in *Heart of Darkness*, 3rd ed., ed. Robert Kimbrough (New York: W. W. Norton, 1988), 358–376, 371.

31. Plato links the mimetic irrationality characteristic of theatrical conduct to women. See Plato, *Rep.* 831; 605e.

32. Le Bon, *The Crowd*, 23, 39.

33. Tarde, *Opinion*, 195.

34. As Diana Fuss puts it, "essentialism is classically defined as a belief in true essence—that which is most irreducible, unchanging, and therefore constitutive of a given person or thing." Diana Fuss, *Essentially Speaking: Feminism, Nature and Difference* (New York: Routledge, 1989), 2.

35. Bernheim, *Suggestive Therapeutics*, 20.

36. Judith Butler writes in a Platonic mood: "As a young person, I suffered for a long time, and I suspect many people have, from being told, explicitly or implicitly, that what I 'am' is a copy, an imitation, a derivative example, a shadow of the real." She then proceeds to trouble the relation between original and copy. Butler, "Imitation and Gender Insubordination" in *Inside/Out: Lesbian Theories, Gay Theories,* ed. Diana Fuss (New York: Routledge, 1991), 13–31, 20.

37. Ian Hacking, *Rewriting the Soul: Multiple Personality and the Sciences of Memory* (Princeton: Princeton University Press, 1995), 70.

38. Hacking, *Rewriting the Soul*, 21.

39. Hacking, *Rewriting the Soul*, 71.

40. Extending Hacking's line of inquiry, Mikkel Borch-Jacobsen calls the delusional, artificial reality

that ensues from such a mimetic dynamic *folies à plusieurs*. Mikkel Borch-Jacobsen, *Folies à plusieurs: De l'hystérie à la dépression* (Paris: Le Seuil, 2002).

41. I would like to thank William Johnsen for bringing this connection to my attention.

42. Martin Bock usefully points out that given Conrad's medical history (he suffered from "neurasthenia"), he "was surely sensible of the extraordinary activity in the field of mental science . . . during the pre-Freudian era of the 1890s" and that "Conrad probably had more than a passing familiarity" with "pre-Freudian medical psychology." The fact that Conrad's Swiss physician at "Champel-les-Bains was, like Freud, a student of Dr. Jean-Martin Charcot, the French pioneer of hysteria studies" makes it highly improbable that Conrad was not aware of Charcot's theory of hypnotic suggestion. Bock, *Conrad and Psychological Medicine*, 6, xxi–xxii. For more details on Conrad's awareness of pre-Freudian psychopathology, see chap. 1 of Bock's study.

43. Joseph Conrad, *A Personal Record: Some Reminiscences* (London: Faber and Faber, 2008), x.

44. With respect to plot structure, it is worth signaling that the reference to Marlow's childhood precedes the references to mimetic women. If we consider Marlow's identificatory relationship with his listeners, the initial introduction of the category of mimetic childhood is of strategic importance. In fact, the listeners are very likely to recognize themselves (via identification) in the suggestible figure of the child. The introduction of the subsequent notions of enthusiasm, suggestibility, and mimetic contagion, whether directly or indirectly, involves subjects with whom identification (for the listeners on the *Nellie* but also for many readers) may be more problematic: in chronological order, the listeners are confronted with forms of enthusiasm pertaining to women, Africans, the Harlequin, and, finally, Kurtz. Importantly, the possibility of the listeners' and readers' self-recognition in the mimetic status these figures represent seems dependent upon the initial identification with the imitative status of children, a state every subject has experienced and thus can potentially sympathize with.

45. Jonathan Dollimore, "Civilization and Its Darkness," in *Conrad's "Heart of Darkness" and Contemporary Thought*, 67–86, 74.

46. Marianna Torgovnick points out that "to speak of women in *Heart of Darkness* and to speak of the primitive are, illogically, one and the same thing: fantastic, collective ('women are all alike'), seductive, dangerous, deadly." Marianna Torgovnick, *Gone Primitive: Savage Intellects, Modern Lives* (Chicago: University of Chicago Press, 1990), 156. As we will soon see, the underlying logic that links these two categories is, in good part, predicated on a mimetic logic.

47. In *Ion*, Plato compares the state of the enthusiastic rhapsode (a member of what he also calls "the poetic tribe") to "the worshiping Corybantes," followers of the cult of Dionysius who "are not in their sense when they dance . . . [since] they are seized by the Bacchic transport and are possessed." Plato, *Ion*, 220; 534a. Nietzsche, in *The Birth of Tragedy*, under the tacit influence of Plato, posited this Dionysian state at the origin of Greek culture. Since then, modern anthropology has cast more light on this mimetic phenomenon and attested to its insistent recurrence among different cultures. See Gilbert Rouget, *Music and Trance: A Theory of the Relations between Music and Possession*, tr. Brunhilde Biebuyck (Chicago: University of Chicago Press, 1985); Luc de Heusch, *La transe et ses entours* (Brussels: Éditions Complexe, 2006), 67–77, 91–93. For René Girard's discussion of "possession" in terms of "*mimesis hystérique*," see *Violence and the Sacred*, 164–166. For an article devoted to Conrad's take on trance see Nidesh Lawtoo, "A Picture of Europe: Possession Trance in *Heart of Darkness*," *Novel: A Forum on Fiction* 45.3 (2012): 409–432.

48. Sigmund Freud, "The Unconscious," in *Collected Papers*, vol. 4, ed. Ernest Jones, tr. Joan Riviere (New York: Basic Books, 1959), 98–136, 127.

49. Jean Paul Richter, *School for Aesthetics* (1804), in Nicholas T. Rand, "The Hidden Soul: The

Growth of the Unconscious in Philosophy, Psychology, Medicine and Literature 1750–1900," *American Imago* 61.3 (2004): 257–289, 258.

50. John Griffith usefully reminds us that "progressionist anthropologists like Tylor (whose *Primitive Culture* appeared in 1871) believed that human culture development followed a general law. Primitive peoples, representing the lowest rung on the cultural ladder, merely enjoyed a slower, and sometimes imperceptible, development in relation to the European civilization that occupied the highest rung. This teleological paradigm comprised three stages, savagery, barbarism, and civilization that formed a 'natural as well as necessary sequence of progress.'" John Griffith, *Joseph Conrad and the Anthropological Dilemma* (Oxford: Oxford University Press, 1995), 79.

51. Chinua Achebe, "An Image of Africa: Racism in Conrad's *Heart of Darkness*," in *Heart of Darkness*, 4th ed., ed. Paul B. Armstrong (New York: W. W. Norton, 2006), 336–349, 338.

52. Achebe, "An Image of Africa," 338.

53. For an account of the mimetic reasons that inform Achebe's critique of Conrad, see Nidesh Lawtoo, "A Picture of Africa: Frenzy, Counternarrative, Mimesis," *Modern Fiction Studies* 59.1 (2013): 26–52.

54. C. P. Sarvan, "Racism and the *Heart of Darkness*," in *Heart of Darkness*, 3rd ed., ed. Kimbrough, 280–284, 283.

55. Sarvan, "Racism," 283. In an examination of the theoretical stakes implicit in the racist/antiracist debate, Padmini Mongia indicates that such a position is shared by most critics of Achebe. "The main perspective that critics use to respond to Achebe," she writes, "is the idea that he reduces the complexity of Conrad's novel by his mean-minded appraisal of his construction of race." Padmini Mongia, "The Rescue: Conrad, Achebe, and the Critics," *Conradiana* 33.2 (2001): 153–163, 155.

56. E. B. Tylor, *Primitive Culture*, vol. 1 (London, 1871), 108.

57. Griffith, *Dilemma*, 6. Griffith adds that "the ideas of 'going native,' of colonists becoming 'decivilized,' were predicated on stereotypes of African cultures themselves as inherently debased" (72). The concept of degeneration was popularized by Max Nordau's influential study *Entartung* (1892), but as Griffith points out, its origins are older. See Griffith, *Dilemma*, 153–154, 158.

58. Le Bon, *The Crowd*, 17.

59. See also Staten, "Conrad's Dionysian Elegy," 204–209.

60. Armstrong, ed., *Heart of Darkness*, 36.

61. The anthropologist Luc de Heusch writes in this respect: "A true musical revolution, techno music triggered among youth of the opposite sex a . . . complex enthusiasm . . . The two sexes are clearly on the verge of trance, a state provoked by a chemical drug called ecstasy." Luc de Heusch, *Transe*, 121–122 (my transl.).

62. Armstrong, ed., *Heart of Darkness*, 91.

63. On Plato's take on the political dimension of music, see *Rep.* 666; 424c–d.

64. Lacoue-Labarthe, "L'horreur occidentale," *Lignes* (2007): 224–234, 230, "The Horror of the West," tr. Nidesh Lawtoo and Hannes Opelz, in *Conrad's "Heart of Darkness" and Contemporary Thought*, 111–122, 116. This collection of essays introduces Lacoue-Labarthe's newly translated philosophical reading of *Heart of Darkness* to the English-speaking world and provides a critical and theoretical context for its reception. The collection appeared prior to the present book, but *The Phantom of the Ego* had already been completed. For a shorter and revised version of the present chapter that engages with Lacoue-Labarthe's groundbreaking essay, see Nidesh Lawtoo,

"The Horror of Mimesis: Echoing Lacoue-Labarthe," in *Conrad's "Heart of Darkness" and Contemporary Thought*, 239–259.

65. Armstrong, ed., *Heart of Darkness*, 36.

66. Stephen Ross writes that "more than the simple disciplinary power of the policeman . . . , the whispers of public opinion are the markers of a fundamentally reconfigured subjectivity, one that has internalized the hailing voice of ideological authority and in turn echoes it, diffusing it throughout the cultural atmosphere." Stephen Ross, *Conrad and Empire* (Columbia: University of Missouri Press, 2004), 56. Indeed, Conrad makes us aware that such echo and diffusion is predicated on the mimetic power and *action à distance* (Tarde's term) characteristic of public opinion.

67. As an appendix to her account of the "horrorism" of contemporary violence, from Auschwitz to Abu Ghraib, Cavarero argues that both Conrad's *Heart of Darkness* and Coppola's *Apocalypse Now* serve as a "reminder of an ontological crime in which the West cannot avoid seeing itself mirrored." Adriana Cavarero, *Horrorism: Naming Contemporary Violence*, tr. William McCuaig (Columbia: Columbia University Press, 2009), 116; see also 116–124.

68. Critics have already underscored the timeliness of Conrad's critique of modern politics. Eloise Hay speaks of the "contemporary" dimension of Conrad's "political vision." Eloise K. Hay, *The Political Novels of Joseph Conrad* (Chicago: University of Chicago Press, 1963), 3; and Stephen Ross argues that Conrad anticipated "the aggressively totalitarian tactics of fascism." Ross, *Conrad and Empire*, 1. In what follows, I fundamentally agree, but for different, mimetic reasons.

69. Marlow's psychological critique of the colonial subject does not stop with the Harlequin, but stretches to encompass all colonial figures. From the Belgian secretaries to the African colonists, Marlow does not encounter any egos, but merely "phantoms" instead. Thus he defines the manager as a "papier-mâché Mephistopheles" with "nothing inside but a little loose dirt" (81), and Kurtz as "hollow at the core" (131). If the former is part of what Marlow calls "mean and greedy phantoms" (147), the latter is described as an "atrocious phantom" (133). The phantom of the ego that deprives the subject of its presence to selfhood haunts the entire colonial enterprise.

70. The realization that mimesis leads to sacrificial violence is one of Girard's fundamental intuitions; see Girard, *Violence and the Sacred*. Lawrence and, even more intensely, Bataille will continue to pursue what the latter calls "the identity of horror and the religious." Georges Bataille, *Larmes d'eros*, in *Oeuvres complètes*, 12 vols. (Paris: Gallimard, 1970–1988), X, 627.

71. As Conrad puts it in the "Author's Note" that precedes the novella, "'Heart of Darkness' is experience, too; but it is experience pushed a little (and only very little) beyond the actual facts of the case for the perfectly legitimate, I believe, purpose of bringing it home to the minds and bosoms of the readers." Joseph Conrad, *Heart of Darkness*, in *Youth: A Narrative and Two Other Stories* (London: J. M. Dent & Sons Ltd., 1923), xi.

72. Tarde, *Opinion*, 195.

73. Marlow is probably alluding to the Intended, but the structural similarity between Marlow and the Harlequin also seems to suggest a self-critique. This similarity is reinforced by their joint fascination with Kurtz: Marlow's initial description as a "lower sort of apostle" is echoed in his definition of the Harlequin as "Kurtz's last disciple" (132). Ironically, Marlow will partially inherit this position from the Harlequin. Speaking of Kurtz, he says: "it was ordered I should never betray him" (141).

74. In Part III, Marlow multiplies references to the sociopsychological notion of "crowd." He speaks of a "motionless crowd of men of dark and glittering bronze" (134), a "wild mob" (146), a "crowd

of savages" (134), and of "the murmurs of the crowds . . . speaking from beyond the threshold of an eternal darkness" (146).

75. Abbé Démanet, in Christopher L. Miller, *Blank Darkness: Africanist Discourse in French* (Chicago: University of Chicago Press, 1985), 3.

76. Lacoue-Labarthe, "The Horror of the West," 116.

77. On the power of Kurtz's voice and its implicit anticipation of Nazism, see also Lacoue-Labarthe, "Horror of the West," 116–117.

78. Conrad's antidemocratic stance should not be excused but can be better understood if we consider his awareness of the mimetic status of the subject. At stake in *Heart of Darkness* is not only a critique of Kurtz's tyrannical pathos, but also a warning that the propaganda this pathos conveys can be tacitly at work in authoritarian regimes that mask themselves under the flag of "democracy." As Edward Bernays put it at the opening of his influential *Propaganda* (1928), "The conscious and intelligent manipulation of the organized habits and opinions of the masses is an important element in democratic society." And he adds, in a mood directly informed by crowd psychology: "We are governed, our minds molded, our tastes formed, our ideas suggested, largely by men we have never heard of." Edward Bernays, *Propaganda* (New York: Ig Publishing, 2005). The fact that Bernays's study is now mostly forgotten and the word "propaganda" has been cast into disrepute does not prevent the *practice* of propaganda (redefined euphemistically as "public relations") from continuing to mold the tastes and opinions of our mass-mediatized, democratic societies.

79. As Le Bon also recognized, "most often the leader has initially been a follower hypnotized by the idea of which he will later be the apostle." Le Bon, *The Crowd*, 69. And Bernays draws a practical lesson from this theoretical insight: "If you can influence the leaders, either with or without their conscious cooperation, you automatically influence the group which they sway." Bernays, *Propaganda*, 73.

80. Tarde, *Opinion*, 38.

Chapter 3. D. H. Lawrence and the Dissolution of the Ego

1. I use editions and abbreviations of the Cambridge editions of Lawrence's following works: *Aaron's Rod* (*AR*), ed. Mara Kalnins (Cambridge: Cambridge University Press, 1988); *The Fox, The Captain's Doll, The Ladybird* (*Fox*), ed. Dieter Mehl (Cambridge: Cambridge University Press, 1992); *Kangaroo* (*K*), ed. Bruce Steele (Cambridge: Cambridge University Press, 1994); *Mornings in Mexico and Other Essays* (*MM*), ed. Virginia Crosswhite Hyde (Cambridge: Cambridge University Press, 2009); *The Plumed Serpent* (*PS*), ed. L. D. Clark (Cambridge: Cambridge University Press, 1987); *St. Mawr and Other Stories* (*STM*), ed. Brian Finney (Cambridge: Cambridge University Press, 1983); *Study of Thomas Hardy and Other Essays* (*STH*), ed. Bruce Steele (Cambridge: Cambridge University Press, 1985). *The Letters of D. H. Lawrence*, ed. G. J. Zytaruk and J. T. Boulton, vol. 2 (Cambridge: Cambridge University Press, 1989); *Psychoanalysis and the Unconscious and Fantasia of the Unconscious* (*PU; FU*), ed. Bruce Steele (Cambridge: Cambridge University Press, 2004); *Studies in Classic American Literature* (*SCAL*), ed. Ezra Greenspan, Lindeth Vasey, and John Worthen (Cambridge: Cambridge University Press, 2003); *Phoenix* (*P*) (New York: Viking Press, 1968); *Phoenix II* (*P* II), (Harmondsworth: Penguin, 1981); *Twilight in Italy and Other Essays* (*TI*), ed. Paul Eggert (Cambridge: Cambridge University Press, 2002); *The Woman Who Rode Away and Other Stories*, ed. Dieter Mehl, Christa Jansohn (Cambridge: Cambridge University Press, 2002).

2. As Lawrence puts it, "a critic must be able to feel the impact of a work of art in all its complexity

and its force." Hence, for him 'the touchstone is emotion, not reason" (*P* 539); or, in our language, pathos, not distance.

3. In the opening chapters of *The Plumed Serpent*, Ramòn makes his position on human sacrifice clear: "The Aztec horrors! The Aztec horrors! Well, perhaps they were not so horrible after all" (62).

4. See John Humma, "D. H. Lawrence as Friedrich Nietzsche," *Philological Quarterly* 53.1 (1974): 110–120; Daniel Schneider, "D. H. Lawrence and *Thus Spoke Zarathustra*," *South Carolina Review* 15.2 (1983): 96–108; Kennet Asher, "Nietzsche, D. H. Lawrence and Irrationalism," *Neophilologus* 69 (1985): 1–16. For a book-length study on the question of Nietzsche's influence on Lawrence, see Colin Milton, *Lawrence and Nietzsche: A Study in Influence* (Aberdeen: Aberdeen University Press, 1987).

5. From Bertrand Russell's claim that Lawrence's fascination with blood consciousness "led straight to Auschwitz," to Terry Eagleton's more nuanced affirmation that "Lawrence was a major precursor of fascism, which is not to say that he himself unqualifiedly accepted fascist ideology," via Michael Bell's claim that the general accusation that a "fascist tendency" is latent in his oeuvre, "has never been made by anyone who knows Lawrence's work well," the controversy concerning Lawrence's "fascism" has been amply discussed. Terry Eagleton, *Criticism and Ideology: A Study in Marxist Literary Theory* (London: NLB, 1976), 158; Michael Bell, *D. H. Lawrence: Language and Being* (Cambridge: Cambridge University Press, 1991), 183. For a succinct articulation of the reception of Lawrence's implication in fascism, see Barbara Mensch, *D. H. Lawrence and the Authoritarian Personality* (New York: St. Martin's Press, 1991), chap. 1. For a study that places Lawrence's authoritarian politics in the context of his relationship to Germany, see Carl Krockel, *D. H. Lawrence and Germany: The Politics of Influence* (New York: Rodopi, 2007).

6. Critics tend to agree that after his novelistic debut with *Sons and Lovers* (1913), *The Rainbow* (1915) and *Women in Love* (1920) represent the culmination of Lawrence's novelistic career. Yet Lawrence kept writing for a full decade thereafter, and much still needs to be said about his mature period. The Lawrence that emerges from his mature period turns out to be more theoretically sophisticated than he is often thought to be.

7. Lawrence, *Letters*, vol. 2, 183 (June 5, 1914).

8. Lawrence's last novel, *Lady Chatterley's Lover*, is clearly about sexual desire. Yet for the late Lawrence, desire, or as he also calls it, the "greater" sex (*P* 194), cannot be limited to sex as we commonly understand it, but involves a "living touch between us and other people, other lives, other phenomena" (*P* 190). As we shall see, this touch is consistently shot through with mimetic affects.

9. Anne Fernihough, *D. H. Lawrence: Aesthetics and Ideology* (Oxford: Clarendon Press, 1993), 3.

10. On Lawrence and anthropology, see Neil Roberts, *D. H. Lawrence, Travel and Cultural Difference* (New York: Palgrave Macmillan, 2004); on Lawrence and psychology, see Daniel Schneider, *D. H. Lawrence: The Artist as Psychologist* (Lawrence: University Press of Kansas, 1984); on Lawrence and psychoanalysis, see Fiona Becket, "Lawrence and Psychoanalysis," in *The Cambridge Companion to D. H. Lawrence*, ed. Anne Fernihough (Cambridge: Cambridge University Press, 2001), 217–233; on Lawrence and aesthetics, see Fernihough, *D. H. Lawrence: Aesthetics and Ideology* (hereafter *Aesthetics and Ideology*); on Lawrence and ideology, see Terry Eagleton, *Criticism and Ideology*; on Lawrence and ontology, see Michael Bell, *D. H. Lawrence*.

11. Girard, *Evolution and Conversion*, 76.

12. In this sense, he embodies a type of man who, as Plato puts it, "is able in thought to enter with understanding into the very soul and temper of a man" (*Rep*. 803; 577a).

13. For an account of modernism's take on primitivism that is critical of Lawrence's approach, see Torgovnick, *Gone Primitive*, 171–174. For a critique of Lawrence's account of Native American cultures on ethnographic grounds, see Wayne Templeton, "'Indians and an Englishman': Lawrence in the American Southwest," *D. H. Lawrence Review* 25 (1966): 18–21.

14. Roberts, *Travel*, 10. For another sympathetic account of Lawrence's "primitive sensibility" that is attentive to magic understood as a "*way* of feeling," see Michael Bell, *Primitivism* (London: Methuen, 1972), 7–20, 7.

15. Michael Taussig, *Mimesis and Alterity: A Particular History of the Senses* (London: Routledge, 1993), 47.

16. This field experience with Native Americans will be the first of a series and will serve as a source of inspiration for the ritual dimension dramatized in *The Plumed Serpent*, and for the development of his concept of "blood consciousness" and the dissolution of the ego it entails. For a detailed, biographical account of Lawrence's encounter with Native Americans, see Roberts, *Travel*, 74–99.

17. Critics who attack Lawrence on this point provide useful ethnographic corrections. See, Templeton, "Indians and an Englishman," 18–21. Yet they are knocking on an open door. Attempting to close that door by saying that "like Frazer, Lawrence claimed to be an authority" (30) is but a convenient rhetorical gesture.

18. Torgovnick, *Gone Primitive*, 162.

19. Torgovnick, *Gone Primitive*, 171.

20. As is typical in this period, Lawrence conflates ontogenesis with phylogenesis, introducing elements of his personal development in his views on the origins of the species. Thus he concludes the essay by conflating the image of old Indian men with the image of his biological father: "these old men telling the tribal tale were my fathers. I have a dark-faced, bronze-voiced father far back in the resinous ages" (*MM* 120).

21. Georges Bataille, *Erotism, Death and Sensuality*, tr. Mary Dalwood (San Francisco: City Lights Books, 1986), 152.

22. As Lawrence puts it, "instinct is largely habit" (*STH* 163); or, as he also says, "the ideas of one generation become the instincts of the next" (*P* 160).

23. Roberts, *Travel*, 89.

24. Sympathy as a heuristic principle does not translate well from the sphere of fiction to that of anthropological observation. In Templeton's words, "'intuitions, feelings,' . . . may be essential to the poet or the novelist, but are in my view potentially dangerous to the essayist." Templeton, "Indians and an Englishman," 22. In a specific ethnographic sense, this critique of the cognitive potential of affect is justified; yet again, such concerns may seem excessive. Even contemporary anthropologists have now acknowledged the importance of "empathy" in approximating the "native's point of view." See John Wengle, *Ethnographers in the Field: The Psychology of Research* (Tuscaloosa: University of Alabama Press, 1988), 160.

25. This passage resonates with Carl Jung's account of the origins of speech in *Psychology of the Unconscious*, tr. Beatrice M. Hinkle (London: Routledge, 1991), 14.

26. See Roberts, *Travel*, 77–84.

27. As he reiterates elsewhere: "Try to go back to the savages and you feel as if your very soul was decomposing inside you" (*SCAL* 127).

28. If Girard usually stresses the violent, disruptive dimension of the mimetic crisis, he also recognizes the pharmaceutical role of mimetic rituals. Thus, echoing Derrida's conception of the Platonic *pharmakon*, he says that the "phenomenon of possession . . . can appear as sickness, cure, or both at once." Girard, *Violence and the Sacred*, 166. See also Derrida, "Plato's Pharmacy," 130–132.

29. Speaking of Lawrence, Michael Bell reminds us that "the modernist generation was strongly affected by contemporary anthropology, especially by James Frazer, who was still expanding his life work, while versions of Lucien Lévy-Bruhl's notion of a 'primitive mind' were common currency." Michael Bell, "Lawrence and Modernism," in *The Cambridge Companion to D. H. Lawrence*, ed. Anne Fernihough (Cambridge: Cambridge University Press, 2001), 181.

30. John Vickery, "Myth and Ritual in the Shorter Fiction of D. H. Lawrence," in *The Critical Response to D. H. Lawrence*, ed. Jan Pilditch (Westport, Conn.: Greenwood Press, 2001), 230.

31. James Frazer, *The Golden Bough: A Study in Magic and Religion*, abridged edition, vol. 1 (New York: Macmillan, 1952), 12.

32. Frazer, *Golden Bough*, 14, 12.

33. Frazer, *Golden Bough*, 12.

34. For a similar critique of Frazer's take on sympathetic magic, see Ludwig Wittgenstein, *Remarks on Frazer's "Golden Bough"*, ed. Rush Rhees, tr. Rush Rhees and A. C. Miles (Chippenham, Eastbourne: Brynmill Press, 2010), 1–7. Girard extends this critique to Lévi-Strauss's structuralist anthropology. See Girard, *Violence and the Sacred*, esp. 241–242.

35. Michael Bell, "The Metaphysics of Modernism," in *The Cambridge Companion to Modernism*, ed. Michael Levenson (Cambridge: Cambridge University Press, 1999), 21.

36. Lawrence's repetitive use of the notion of "participation" in the context of his anthropological observations supports Bell's suggestion that he was familiar with Lévy-Bruhl's thought. He probably familiarized himself with his thought via Jane Harrison, whose work Lawrence had read.

37. Lévy-Bruhl, *La mentalité primitive* (Paris: Retz-C.E.P.L., 1976) (my transl.).

38. Lévy-Bruhl, *La mentalité primitive*, 42.

39. Lévy-Bruhl, *La mentalité primitive*, 435.

40. The unfortunate choice of the term "prelogical thinking" Lévy-Bruhl uses to qualify the modality of thought of "primitive mentality" quickly cast his work into disrepute. Yet if one takes the time to read him, one is struck by his sense of admiration for this modality of thinking, which makes the hierarchy between "logical" and "prelogical" mentality much less clear-cut than it initially sounds. Contrary to Frazer, who compares the "crude intelligence" of the "savages" to that of "dull-witted people" or, later, Freud, who likens primitive men to children and obsessive neurotics, Lévy-Bruhl specifies that this modality of thought is not due to mental "incapacity or impotence." And he adds: "the mental activity of primitives should no longer be interpreted as a rudimentary version of ours, as being infantile and nearly pathological. . . . On the contrary, it appears as normal in the conditions in which it manifests itself. It is complex and developed in its own way." Lévy-Bruhl, *La mentalité primitive*, 12, 15–16.

41. Lucien Lévy-Bruhl, *Le surnaturel et la nature dans la mentalité primitive* (Paris: Presses Universitaires de France, 1963) (my transl.).

42. Lévy-Bruhl, *Surnaturel*, 135.

43. Lévy-Bruhl, *Surnaturel*, 133.

44. Lévy-Bruhl, *Surnaturel*, 138. This analogy is not a matter of direct influence. Lévy-Bruhl first published *Surnaturel* in 1931, after Lawrence's death, but descriptions of ritual possession were common currency, and Lawrence was familiar with them through other sources. Jane Harrison, for instance, redefines Frazer's account of sympathetic magic from a psychological perspective: "sympathetic magic is, modern psychology teaches us, . . . not the outcome of intellectual illusion, not even the exercise of a 'mimetic instinct' [i.e., instinct of representation] but simply in its ultimate analysis, an utterance, a discharge of emotion and longing." Jane Harrison, *Ancient Art and Ritual* (London: Williams & Norgate, 1913), 34.

45. Frazer considered magic "a mistaken association of ideas" and concluded that "all magic is necessarily false and barren." Frazer, *Golden Bough*, 38. Freud, extending Frazer's rationalist line of inquiry, castigates magic for its belief in the "almightiness of thought" and characterizes primitive people as obsessive neurotics driven by an excess of rationality, a mistaken rationality, that is. See Sigmund Freud, *Totem and Taboo*, tr. A. A. Brill (Harmondsworth: Penguin, 1940).

46. Edgar Morin, *L'homme et la mort* (Paris: Seuil, 1974), 99 (my transl.). Like Lawrence before him, Morin supplements Frazer's and Lévy-Bruhl's accounts of magic by accentuating the role of affective mimesis. Magic, in fact, for Morin is "subjective participation and objective appropriation at the same time, . . . the objectivity of ritual and magical formulas on the one hand, and the subjectivity of the state of magical communication on the other . . . that is, the will of the microcosm to identify with the macrocosm, or to appropriate it via mimicry [*en le mimant*]." And he concludes: "in nearly all cases, magic is surrounded by rituals, that is, mimes. Rituals are magical, solemn, and hieratic mimicries of the wanted thing" (110–111).

47. For a sustained account of *Morning in Mexico*, see Roberts, *Travel*, 87–99. My emphasis differs from Roberts's insofar as I rely on an approach that combines Lawrence's interests in *both* anthropology *and* philosophy in order to unpack what I consider his most theoretically sophisticated essay, namely "Indians and Entertainment."

48. Lawrence's emphasis on the fluidity of "blood consciousness" is clearly in line with the Dionysian tradition. As E. R. Dodds reminds us, Dionysus's domain is "not only the liquid fire in the grape, but the sap thrusting in a young tree, the blood pounding in the veins of a young animal." Dodds, *Greeks and the Irrational*, xii.

49. John Foster, for instance, writes that among modernists, "it is undoubtedly Lawrence who is most willing to purse the grand cultural contrast in *Birth of Tragedy* between myth and theory." John B. Foster Jr., *Heirs to Dionysus: A Nietzschean Current in Literary Modernism* (Princeton: Princeton University Press, 1981), 92. Along similar lines, Kenneth Asher claims that with the exception of Conrad, "it is really only Lawrence, among early 20th C. British writers, who takes Dionysus as seriously as Nietzsche might have wished." Asher, "Nietzsche, D. H. Lawrence," 2.

50. Translation modified.

51. In this passage, Lawrence uses the notions of "mind" and "consciousness," as well as "ego," interchangeably.

52. Commenting on this passage, David Ellis notices that its "causal chain is highly elliptical." *D. H. Lawrence: Dying Game, 1922–1930* (Cambridge: Cambridge University Press, 1998), 179.

53. Ellis writes that in this account of the origins of Greek drama Lawrence is "relying partly on his memories of Jane Harrison's *Ancient Art and Ritual*, which he had read as long ago as 1913." Ellis, *Lawrence*, 179.

54. The Cambridge Ritualists were a group of turn-of-the-century British classical scholars (members

included Gilbert Murray, F. M. Cornford, A. B. Cook, and Jane Harrison) primarily invested in exploring the connections between the origins of Greek tragedy and ritual via anthropological theories of magic.

55. Harrison, *Ancient Art and Ritual*, 46, 47.

56. Harrison, *Ancient Art and Ritual*, 153. Interestingly, Harrison even specifies that Dionysus was "always of the people, of the 'working classes,'" introducing a connection between class and (Dionysian) mimesis that Lawrence was likely to remember and pick up.

57. Harrison, *Ancient Art and Ritual*, 204.

58. Harrison was interested in Freud and Jung, but her account also reveals her familiarity with the psychophysiological conception of the mimetic unconscious we have already encountered in Nietzsche, Conrad, and now Lawrence.

59. Harrison, *Ancient Art and Ritual*, 49.

60. Harrison, *Ancient Art and Ritual*, 42, 53.

61. Harrison, *Ancient Art and Ritual*, 191.

62. On Lawrence's rivalry with Nietzsche, see Foster, *Heirs to Dionysus*, 34, 180.

63. On Lawrence and cinema see Sam Solecki, "D. H. Lawrence's View of Film," *Literature/Film Quarterly* 1.1 (1973): 12–16; and Louis Greiff, *D. H. Lawrence: Fifty Years on Film* (Carbondale: Southern Illinois University Press, 2001).

64. Jean-Louis Baudry, "The Apparatus: Metapsychological Approaches to the Impression of Reality in Cinema," in *Film Theory and Criticism*, 4th ed., ed. Gerald Mast, Marshal Cohen, and Leo Braudy (Oxford: Oxford University Press, 1992), 693–696.

65. Bell, *D. H. Lawrence*, 95.

66. This tendency is already at work in Plato, at least in embryonic form. See Plato, *Rep.* 736–743; 500e–508a.

67. Trigant Burrow, *The Social Basis of Consciousness* (London: Kegan Paul, Trench, Trubner, 1927).

68. Burrow, *Social Basis of Consciousness*, 40, 41, 88. Critics have acknowledged Lawrence's direct debt to Burrow before. See Edward Nehls, *D. H. Lawrence: A Composite Biography*, vol. 3 (Madison: University of Wisconsin Press, 1959), 38. For an informed dissertation that focuses exclusively on the Lawrence-Burrow relationship, see Eugene Dawson, "D. H. Lawrence and Trigant Burrow: Pollyanalytics and Phylobiology, an Interpretative Analysis," PhD diss., University of Washington, 1963.

69. Ellis, *Lawrence*, 369 n. 61, 683.

70. Jacques Lacan, "Le stade du miroir comme formateur de la fonction du Je," in *Écrits* (Paris: Seuil, 1966), 95 (my transl.).

71. Lacan, "Miroir," 94.

72. Lacan, "Miroir," 113, 95. Mikkel Borch-Jacobsen defines Lacan's mirror stage and the theory of the imaginary that ensues as a "twentieth-century Platonism." Thus, he writes: "the only Being, for Lacan, is static Being—coming to a standstill before a 'theoretical' and stabilizing gaze—and this is equally true for the Being of the ego, as soon as the ego itself *is* that world at which it gazes." He continues: "for Lacan, the specular image, although admittedly an image of the ego, is simultaneously what *gives form to* the ego." And he concludes: "in the guise of the mirror, this

'image' remains an 'idea' (or 'ideal') of the ego." Mikkel Borch-Jacobsen, *Lacan: The Absolute Master*, tr. Douglas Brick (Stanford: Stanford University Press, 1991), 64, 62, 60, 64. For the full account of Borch-Jacobsen's ontological critique of the mirror stage, see 45–71.

73. Burrow, *Social Basis of Consciousness*, 119.

74. Lacan, "Miroir," 94.

75. Anticipating contemporary debates, Burrow suspects that psychoanalysis is "just another application of the method of suggestion" and that analysts are "truly the unconscious dupes of the suggestive process [they] employ." He also claims that "the attitude of the psychoanalyst and the attitude of the authoritarian are inseparable," and argues that such an attitude is an effect of the hierarchical "role" play that informs the analytic situation. Burrow, *Social Basis of Consciousness*, 3, xviii.

76. See Herbert Marcuse, *One-Dimensional Man: Studies in the Ideology of Advanced Industrial Society* (New York: Routledge, 2002), 12.

77. Burrow, *Social Basis of Consciousness*, 59, 42.

78. Burrow, *Social Basis of Consciousness*, 40.

79. Burrow, *Social Basis of Consciousness*, 48.

80. Burrow's critique of the pictorial basis of life and cinema (40–41; 88), his "organismic theory of consciousness" (6), his celebration of intersubjective relations based on a "flow" of affect (30), and the importance he gives to "sex" (as opposed to "sexuality") (205–206), are but some of the elements that powerfully resonate with Lawrence's thought. Given that often Lawrence borrows directly from Burrow's social psychology, it is strange that recent developments in Lawrence studies have not paid more attention to this figure. Such a disregard is symptomatic of the Freudocentrism that still dominates modernist studies.

81. As Lacan puts it, "the function of the imago . . . is to establish a relation between the organism and its reality—or, as they say, of the *Innenwelt* to the *Umwelt*." Lacan, "Miroir," 96.

82. In other writings of the same period, Lacan speaks of the mimetic representation that forms the ego as "the triumph of the salutary tendency." Jacques Lacan, *Les complexes familiaux dans la formation de l'individu* (Paris: Navarin Editeur, 1984), 44 (my transl.).

83. Lacan, "Miroir," 94.

84. See Burrow, *Social Basis of Consciousness*, 83–84, 130.

85. Barbara Mensch points out that "living in Italy during the period of the revolution, [Lawrence] experienced the fascist phenomenon much more clearly than did his British counterparts." Mensch, *Authoritarian Personality*, 161.

86. Gilles Deleuze, *Essays Critical and Clinical*, tr. Daniel W. Smith and Michael A. Greco (New York: Verso, 1998), 133.

87. Dollimore, *Death, Desire and Loss*, 259.

88. Deleuze, *Essays Critical and Clinical*, 4.

89. Deleuze, *Essays Critical and Clinical*, 129–130.

90. This point was already intuited by Conrad, in his account of Marlow's hypnotic fascination with the colonial map, yet Conrad lacked a critique of mimetic representation that would have allowed him to fully articulate this realization.

91. Lawrence's use of dialogue splits his narrative voice in both positions, but the fact that Aaron "smiles palely" and the different levels of critical awareness between the two characters (Lilly functioning as an initiating figure in the process of Aaron's self-discovery) suggest that Lawrence's position here is closer to Lilly.

92. Jean Baudrillard, *The Gulf War Did Not Take Place*, tr. Paul Patton (Sydney: Power Publications, 1995).

93. Michael Bell writes that "the change from Modernism to postmodernism is not a difference in metaphysics so much as a different stage in the digestion of the same metaphysics." Bell, "Metaphysics," 9. We shall confirm this point in the chapter devoted to that crossroads thinker who is Georges Bataille.

94. Jean Baudrillard, *Selected Writings*, ed. Mark Poster (Cambridge: Polity Press, 2001), 169.

95. Baudrillard, *Selected Writings*, 170.

96. Baudrillard, *Gulf War*, 72.

97. Baudrillard, *Gulf War*, 40.

98. In his ironic overturning of Platonic metaphysics, Nietzsche concludes his account of "How the True World Became a Fable" thus: "The true world—we have abolished. What world has remained? The apparent one perhaps? But no! *With the true world we have abolished the apparent one*" (*TI* 486).

99. Fernihough, *Aesthetics and Ideology*, 152.

100. Bernheim, *Suggestive Therapeutics*, 137.

101. Jean Baudrillard, *Simulacres et simulation* (Paris: Galilée, 1981), 40.

102. Anne Fernihough, for instance, suggests that Lawrence's hostility towards Freud "is rooted in what [he] sees to be a fundamental contradiction at the heart of Freud's enterprise, namely that Freud is at once attempting to subvert the Cartesian rationalist tradition and working within its confines." Fernihough, *Aesthetics and Ideology*, 12. Fiona Becket confirms this reading, adding that Lawrence's anti-Cartesian intention was to "relocate unconscious functions, or feeling in the *body*, challenging the psychoanalytical emphasis on *mind*." Becket, "Lawrence and Psychoanalysis," 221. And Anneleen Masschelein argues, from an anti-Oedipal perspective, that the Lawrentian unconscious opposes "abstraction, idealism and automatism . . . the greatest dangers threatening modern man and society." Anneleen Masschelein, "Rip the Veil of the Old Vision Across, and Walk through the Rent: Reading D. H. Lawrence with Deleuze and Guattari," in Ross, *Modernism and Theory*, 23–39, 24.

103. In a different context Girard will also speak of "Freud's Platonism." *Choses cachées*, 492. See also 488–494. As we shall see in the conclusion, this critique is partially a self-critique.

104. Freud, "The Unconscious," 109.

105. The link between dreams and the notion of "shadow" stems from Burrow. He writes that dreams are "but the shadows our lives cast behind them when we stand in the light of our own personality." Burrow, *Social Basis of Consciousness*, 180. Lawrence adds an ontological dimension by framing this connection within the Platonic myth of the cave.

106. As Lawrence puts it: "Man can inhibit the true passional impulses and so produce a derangement in the psyche. This is a truism nowadays, and we are grateful to psychoanalysis for helping to make it so" (*PU* 13).

107. Gilles Deleuze and Felix Guattari, *Anti-Oedipus: Capitalism and Schizophrenia*, tr. Robert Hurley, Mark Seem, Helen Lane (London: Continuum, 2004), 125.

108. Deleuze and Guattari, *Anti-Oedipus*, 126. A careful reading of chap. 2 of *Anti-Oedipus* reveals that Deleuze's and Guattari's critique of psychoanalysis in general and of the unconscious "as the classical theater, the classical order of representation" in particular, stems directly from Lawrence's Nietzschean/Burrowian critique of the Western ego trapped in the ideal form of mimetic representations.

109. Deleuze and Guattari, *Anti-Oedipus*, 53.

110. For a historical contextualization of the origins of psychoanalysis and the legend it produced, see Ellenberger, *The Discovery of the Unconscious*. For a foundational reevaluation of the validity of psychoanalysis, see Frank J. Sulloway, *Freud, Biologist of the Mind: Beyond the Psychoanalytic Legend* (New York: Basic Books, 1979), as well as Mikkel Borch-Jacobsen and Sonu Shamdasani, *The Freud Files: An Inquiry into the History of Psychoanalysis* (Cambridge: Cambridge University Press, 2012). For an informed collection of essays that challenges psychoanalysis and provides an overview of viable therapeutic alternatives, see *Le livre noir de la psychanalyse: Vivre, penser et aller mieux sans Freud*, ed. Catherine Meyer, 2nd ed. (Paris: Éditions des Arènes, 2010). For a bestselling anti-Oedipal reading of Freud of Nietzschean inspiration see Michel Onfray, *Le crépuscule d'une idole: L'affabulation freudienne* (Paris: Bernard Grasset, 2010).

111. Anne Fernihough points out that "Nietzsche was one of the philosophers to familiarize Lawrence with the unconscious long before he had even heard of the Freudian model." Fernihough, *Aesthetics and Ideology*, 63.

112. See Christopher Heywood, "'Blood Consciousness' and the Pioneers of the Reflex and Ganglionic Systems," in *D. H. Lawrence New Studies*, ed. Christopher Heywood (London: Macmillan, 1987), 104–108; and Schneider, *D. H. Lawrence*, 10–20.

113. Masschelein, "Rip the Veil," 26. On the influence of William James on modernism, see Ryan, *The Vanishing Subject*.

114. Wilfred Trotter, *Instincts of the Herd in Peace and War, 1916–1919* (London: Oxford University Press, 1953), 34.

115. Lawrence probably familiarized himself with the notion of suggestion via British crowd psychology. Wilfred Trotter, for instance, was familiar with Le Bon, but also with psychologist Boris Sidis, who, as he puts it, "calls attention to the intimate relation between gregariousness and suggestibility." Trotter, *Instincts of the Herd*, 14.

116. The Society for Psychical Research was founded in 1882 in order to account for a growing interest in spiritism. Frederick Myers makes the goal of this project clear in the introduction to *Phantoms of the Living*: "under our heading of 'Phantoms of the Living,' we propose, in fact, to deal with all classes of cases where there is reason to suppose that the mind of one human being has affected the mind of another, without speech uttered, or word written, or sign made.... To such transmission of thought or feeling we have elsewhere given the name of *telepathy*; and the records of an experimental proof of the reality of telepathy will form a part of the present work." Frederick Myers, "Introduction," *Phantoms of the Living*, ed. Frederick Myers and Frank Podmore (London: Trübner, Ludgate Hill, 1886), xxxv.

117. See William McDougall, *The Group Mind* (New York: G. P. Puntam's Sons, 1973), 41–43.

118. Neurophysiologists noticed that a decapitated frog continues to respond to external stimuli by movement of the limbs, and postulated that the source of such stimuli was in the spinal cord. This view had a tremendous impact in the emerging field of psychology, and authors as diverse as

Eduard von Hartman, William James, Marshall Hall, and Hippolyte Bernheim, along with the Nietzschean current in literary modernism, rely on this model of the reflex unconscious in order to account for mimetic responses in humans. Recent neurological studies proved that the neuronal source of these mirroring unconscious reflexes is actually located in the brain. Yet if the specific location is different, the general mimetic principle remains in place.

119. Ellenberger, *Discovery of the Unconscious*, 111.

120. Eagleton, *Criticism and Ideology*, 158.

121. Girard, *Deceit*.

122. Plato considers Eros in a relation of continuity with other forms of mimetic mania, such as poetic inspiration (or enthusiasm), divinatory trance, and Dionysian rites. Plato, *Phaedrus*, 475–525, 491–492; 244b–245c.

123. Raymond de Saussure and Léon Chertok, in their prehistory of psychoanalysis, remind us that "Mesmer appears to have selected, from among others, the word 'rapport' to indicate the *effective* contact, the physiological contact between individuals"; some of the descriptions of this physiological contact are highly reminiscent of Lawrence's account. Chertok and Saussure, *The Therapeutic Revolution*, 5, 21–22.

124. Torgovnick, *Gone Primitive*, 171, 170.

125. Martin Bock makes the important point that "Modernists may . . . have written psychological novels or poetry about psychic disintegration and regeneration, but they did not become Freudians until . . . late in their career." Bock, *Conrad and Psychological Medicine*, 5. Lawrence is somewhat of an exception: he encountered Freud (via his German wife, Frieda von Richthofen) relatively early on in his career. Yet his philosophical allegiance with the philosophers of the unconscious (Nietzsche and Schopenhauer) and his extensive readings of different branches of psychology provided him with a solid theoretical stance from which to question, challenge, and oppose the Freudian model.

126. Vickery, "Myth and Ritual," 231.

127. Gilles Deleuze, *Critique et Clinique* (Paris: Éditions de Minuit, 1993), 69.

128. René Girard, *To Double Business Bound: Essays on Literature, Mimesis, and Anthropology* (Baltimore: Johns Hopkins University Press), 89.

Chapter 4. Bataille's Mimetic Communication

1. Bataille had begun his literary career by describing a similar dramatic spectacle. See his first novel, *Histoire de l'oeil* (Paris: Jean-Jacques Pauvert, 1956), 143. Later Bataille would discover that a scene representing a bovid with his "bowels emptying themselves in heavy volutes, between its legs" as well as the connection with human death and sexuality already haunted man's prehistoric imagination. See *Lascaux ou la naissance de l'art* (IX, 59–60). I quote from Georges Bataille's *Oeuvres complètes*, 12 vols. (Paris: Gallimard, 1970–1988). References to volume and page number are given in the body of the text. Translations from Bataille's *O.C.* and other French authors unavailable in English are mine. Editions and/or translations from which I quote include *L'expérience intérieure* (*EI*) (Paris: Gallimard, 1954); *Inner Experience* (*IE*), tr. Leslie Anne Boldt (Albany: State University of New York, 1988); *Erotism, Death and Sensuality* (*E*), tr. Mary Dalwood (San Francisco: City Lights Books, 1986); *La sociologie sacrée du monde contemporain* (*Soc.*) (Paris: Éditions Lignes & Manifestes, 2004); *Histoire de l'oeil* (*H*); *Le Bleu du Ciel* (*BC*) (Paris: Jean-Jacques Pauvert, 1957); *Le Collège de Sociologie 1937–1939* (*Coll.*), ed. Denis Hollier

(Paris: Gallimard, 1995); *Georges Bataille: Essential Writings* (*Ess.*), ed. Michael Richardson (London: Sage, 1998).

2. As Denis Hollier puts it, "communication is nothing but this practice of repulsion, a production of repulsion as a term of attraction." Denis Hollier, *La prise de la Concorde: Essais sur Georges Bataille* (Paris: Gallimard, 1974), 125.

3. André Breton, *Manifestoes of Surrealism*, tr. Richard Seaver and Helen R. Lane (Ann Arbor: University of Michigan Press, 1969), 184.

4. Even a close friend of Bataille such as Pierre Klossowski qualified Bataille as being "pathologically engaged." Michel Surya, in a more defensive mood, opts for the conditional: "Bataille would have been pathological . . . and because of this pathology, necessarily politically derailed, confused and suspicious." Michel Surya, *Georges Bataille: La mort à l'œuvre* (Paris: Gallimard, 1992), 354 (hereafter *Mort*).

5. The question of Bataille's implication with fascism has been the subject of much controversy. For studies that tend to downplay Bataille's implication with fascism, see Surya, *Mort*, 437–438; Benjamin Noys, *Georges Bataille: A Critical Introduction* (London: Pluto Press, 2000), 39–47; Bernard Sichère, *Pour Bataille: Être, chance, souveraineté* (Paris: Gallimard, 2006), 79. On the front of accusation, see Jürgen Habermas, "The French Path to Postmodernity: Bataille between Eroticism and General Economics," in *Bataille: A Critical Reader,* ed. Fred Botting and Scott Wilson (Oxford: Blackwell, 1998), 166–190; and Richard Wolin, *The Seduction of Unreason: The Intellectual Romance with Fascism from Nietzsche to Postmodernism* (Princeton: Princeton University Press, 2004). Denis Hollier's evaluation strikes a balance between these contradictory positions by focusing on the notion of "equivocation," while ultimately leaning towards the antifascist solution: "A little equivocation gets close to fascism," he writes, "a lot of it moves away from it." Denis Hollier, "On Equivocation (between Literature and Politics)," *October* 55 (1990): 12. For an informed historical contextualization of Bataille's take on fascism, see Michel Surya "Postface," in Georges Bataille, *La structure psychologique du fascisme* (Paris: Lignes, 2009), 65–84. As usual, I am not primarily concerned with political positions per se but, rather, with the *mimetic logic* which swings thinkers of mimesis in contradictory directions, setting in motion a process of attraction and repulsion, pathos and distance, with respect to that irresistible psychic force which Jean-Pierre Faye calls, "*la force du fantasme.*" Jean-Pierre Faye, in Surya, *Mort*, 360. For a reading of Bataille's early "phantasmatolgy," which, despite its different, Hegelian and at times still Freudian orientation, echoes my Nietzschean approach, see Rodolphe Gasché, *Georges Bataille: Phenomenology and Phantasmatology,* tr. Roland Végsō (Stanford: Stanford University Press, 2012).

6. Jean-Michel Besnier, "Bataille, the Emotive Intellectual," in *Bataille: Writing the Sacred*, ed. Carolyn Bailey Gill (London, New York: Routledge, 1995), 17, 21.

7. Habermas, "French Path to Postmodernity," 171–173.

8. Habermas, "French Path to Postmodernity," 171.

9. Habermas, "French Path to Postmodernity," 167. Richard Wolin extends Habermas's philosophical critique from a cultural historical perspective and denounces "Bataille's unabashed admiration of fascist methods." Wolin, *Seduction of Unreason*, xi. Moreover, drawing on Freudian parlance, he explains that "Bataille reveres fascism insofar as it cultivates an emotional cathexis between leader and masses" (179). But again, Bataille is not the only target; he is considered as a symptom of a much profound disease. And as the subtitle of Wolin's book makes clear, the origins of this (post)modern "intellectual romance with fascism" (174) are once again rooted in the name of "Nietzsche."

10. Wolin, *Seduction of Unreason*, 59.

11. Habermas, "French Path to Postmodernity," 174.

12. Theodor Adorno and Max Horkheimer, *The Dialectic of Enlightenment*, tr. John Cumming (New York: Herder & Herder, 1972), 185. "The Fascist formula, the ritual discipline, the uniforms, and the whole apparatus, which is at first sight irrational, is to allow mimetic behavior. The carefully thought out symbols (which are proper to every counterrevolutionary movement), the skulls and disguises, the barbaric drum beats, the monotonous repetition of words and gestures, are simply the organized imitation of magic practices, the mimesis of mimesis" (183).

13. Adorno and Horkheimer, *The Dialectic of Enlightenment*, 183.

14. Habermas, "French Path to Postmodernity," 171, 174.

15. At the time of *Acéphale* (1936), Bataille, writing under the influence of Nietzsche, was already severely critical of fascism (a point that both Habermas and Wolin fail to mention). In fact, he attempts to put Nietzsche at a distance from what he now denounces as "the fascist misery" (II, 488). See also II, 452–453, 480. And in *Contre-attaque*, Bataille observes: "What especially interests us here . . . are the emotions which give human masses the powerful stimuli that free them from the domination of those who can only lead them to misery and to slaughtering houses." And he hastens to add: "But we would not want you to believe that we blindly abandon ourselves to the spontaneous reactions of the street . . . *we do not find any reasons to renounce the often decisive interventions of discernment and the methodological analysis of facts*" (I, 409, my emphasis).

16. Wolin, *Seduction of Unreason*, 156.

17. Girard, *Double Business*, 163.

18. Marcel Mauss and Henri Hubert, "Esquisse d'une théorie générale de la magie," in Marcel Mauss, *Sociologie et anthropologie* (Paris: Presses Universitaires de France), 1995, 1–141.

19. This is a widespread opinion among Bataille scholars. Leslie Hill denounces Bataille's "anthropological abstractions," which he considers "little more than wishful thinking." Leslie Hill, *Bataille, Klossowski, Blanchot: Writing at the Limit* (Oxford: Oxford University Press, 2001), 79–80. Along similar lines, Laura Frost speaks of the "highly speculative, abstract psychological structure of leaders and followers," and denounces "its reliance on a vague concept of an unnamed 'force' to explain the psychological 'unification' of heterogeneous elements that fascism supposedly brings about." Laura Frost, *Sex Drives: Fantasies of Fascism in Literary Modernism* (Ithaca, N.Y.: Cornell University Press, 2002), 63.

20. Mauss and Hubert, "Esquisse, " 102.

21. Mauss and Hubert, "Esquisse," 101.

22. Claude Lévi-Strauss, "Introduction à l'œuvre de Marcel Mauss," in Mauss, *Sociologie et anthropologie*, 49–50.

23. René Girard, "Differentiation and Reciprocity in Lévi-Strauss and Contemporary Theory," in *Double Business*, 155–177, 158.

24. Mauss and Hubert, "Esquisse," 104.

25. Mauss and Hubert, "Esquisse," 111, 105 (my emphasis).

26. As Henri Ellenberger also recognized, "an analogy could be drawn between this theory [animal magnetism] and the Polynesian concept of 'mana.'" Ellenberger, *Discovery of the Unconscious*, 62.

27. It is tempting to dismiss the notion of mimesis as a zero signifier, like the French *truc* or

machin. Yet we should recall that terms like "possession," "contagion," the "power of words," and "sympathy" (which define both *mana* and *mimesis*) point quite directly towards different manifestations of a similar state of psychic dispossession and depersonalization, a state that Borch-Jacobsen calls an "anthropological constant." Borch-Jacobsen, *The Emotional Tie*, 101.

28. Émile Durkheim, *The Elementary Forms of Religious Life*, tr. Carol Cosman (Oxford: Oxford University Press, 2001), 160.

29. Durkheim, *Elementary Forms*, 140, 155, 158.

30. Durkheim, *Elementary Forms*, 157.

31. Durkheim, *Elementary Forms*, 142.

32. Durkheim, *Elementary Forms*, 175, 158.

33. Michèle Richman's reading of Bataille first appeared in two articles: "Fascism Reviewed: Georges Bataille in *La Critique Sociale*" *South Central Review* 14 (1997): 14–30; and "The Sacred Group: A Durkheimian Perspective on the Collège de Sociologie (1937–1939)," in Gill, *Bataille*, 58–76. These articles were subsequently extended in *Sacred Revolutions: Durkheim and the Collège de Sociologie* (Minneapolis: University of Minnesota Press, 2002).

34. Richman, "Fascism Reviewed," 14.

35. Durkheim, *Elementary Forms*, 158.

36. Durkheim, *Elementary Forms*, 158, 166.

37. Durkheim, *Elementary Forms*, 166.

38. See Hill, *Bataille, Klossowski, Blanchot*, 79–80; Frost, *Sex Drives* 63.

39. Richman, "Fascism Reviewed," 24.

40. Richman, "The Sacred Group," 61.

41. Richman, "Fascism Reviewed," 24.

42. Richman, "The Sacred Group," 59.

43. If Roudinesco stresses the radical discontinuity between Freud and advocates of the *inconscient à la française*, a wide range of theorists and historians of psychoanalysis have exposed the continuity existing between these two traditions. See for instance, Ellenberger, *Discovery of the Unconscious*; Chertok and Saussure, *The Therapeutic Revolution*; Moscovici, *The Age of the Crowd*; Borch-Jacobsen, *The Freudian Subject*; Micale, *The Mind of Modernism*.

44. Richman, *Sacred Revolutions*, 111.

45. Richman, *Sacred Revolutions*, 195.

46. Le Bon, *The Crowd*, 72.

47. Richman, "The Sacred Group," 60.

48. Moscovici, *The Age of the Crowd*, 4.

49. Even exponents of the French school of anthropology do not dispute this point. Mauss, for instance writes: "One thing that, fundamentally, we never foresaw was how many large modern societies, that have more or less emerged from the middle ages in other respects, could be hypnotized [*suggestionés*] like Australians are by their dances, and set in motion like a children's roundabout." Mauss, in Hollier, *Le Collège de Sociologie*, 248. On the psychological front, a figure

like Gabriel Tarde had already recognized in 1890 that "we flatter ourselves wrongly to be less credulous and docile, in a word, less mimetic [*imitatifs*], than our ancestors." Tarde, *Les lois de l'imitation*, 84. For a more recent confirmation of the validity of this point, see Moscovici, *The Age of the Crowd*, 33.

50. Bataille specifies that "the structural knowledge of heterogeneous reality as such is to be found in the mystical thinking of primitives and in dreams: it is identical to the structure of the *unconscious*" (I, 347).

51. On Bataille's critical take on the "hypnotized masses," see also *Coll.* 223.

52. Moscovici, *The Age of the Crowd*, 219.

53. Sigmund Freud, *Group Psychology and the Analysis of the Ego* (*GP*), ed. and tr. James Strachey (New York: W. W. Norton, 1959), 37; Sigmund Freud, *The Ego and the Id*, ed. and tr. James Strachey (New York: W. W. Norton, 1960), 30. Girard's mimetic theory offers an elegant solution to the "ambivalence" generated by this Oedipal double-bind; see René Girard, "Freud and the Oedipus Complex," in Girard, *Violence and the Sacred*, 169–192.

54. For a lucid analysis of "the primal scene of Bataille's writing," see also Hill, *Bataille, Klossowski, Blanchot*, 32–35.

55. As Michel Surya puts it, Bataille was "the first in France . . . to introduce, in a useful way, the tools of psychoanalysis into the quarters of political analysis." Surya, *Mort*, 220.

56. Bataille, like Nietzsche and Lawrence before him, refers to the Platonic notion of "phantom" in order to critique the Christian underpinnings of this concept (he speaks of God as "the old phantom") (VI, 72). And, again like Nietzsche before him, Bataille connects the metaphysical conception of phantom to a psychological concern with the ego. As he declares, anticipating future proclamations of the death of man: "I don't believe in God for lack of belief in the ego. To believe in God is to believe in the ego" (V, 282).

57. This is a point that contemporary anthropologists have equally recognized. See De Heusch, *Transe*, 211.

58. See also I, 348, 357.

59. Borch-Jacobsen, *The Freudian Subject*, 10, 147. My goal here is to schematically reconstruct Freud's argument in order to assess its influence on Bataille's account of the leader's "mysterious force." For a detailed theoretical articulation of *Group Psychology* to which I am indebted, see Borch-Jacobsen, *The Freudian Subject*, 146–239, and *The Emotional Tie*, 39–61. For two key sources on Freud's social psychology on which Borch-Jacobsen as well as the present author rely, see Lacoue-Labarthe's and Nancy's "La panique politique," in *Retreating the Political*, ed. Simon Sparks (New York: Routledge, 1977), 1–28; and Girard's chapter "Freud and the Oedipus Complex," in Girard, *Violence and the Sacred*, 169–192.

60. Freud, "The Unconscious," 101. See also Sigmund Freud, "A Note on the Unconscious in Psycho-Analysis," in *Collected Papers*, vol. 4, ed. Ernest Jones, tr. Joan Riviere (New York: Basic Books, 1959), 22–29, 23–24.

61. Schematically put, the basic structure of the positive Oedipus complex involves three steps. First, initial object cathexis with the mother predicated on a direct desire to have the mother; second, progressive realization that the father is an obstacle for the possession of the object of desire which leads to the development of a rivalrous (ambivalent) identification with the father (primary identification); and third, dissolution of the Oedipal complex. This occurs when the object is given up and replaced by a positive identification with the father (secondary identification) which

brings about an incorporation of the paternal law (super ego), as well as the repression of the
child's desire for the mother in view of a future satisfaction. Freud, *Ego*, 26–27.

62. See Lacoue-Labarthe and Nancy, "La panique politique"; Borch-Jacobsen, *The Freudian Subject*
and *The Emotional Tie*; and Jean-Michel Oughourlian, *The Genesis of Desire* (East Lansing:
Michigan State University Press, 2010).

63. In this instance, Bataille links the notion of moral identification to Robertson Smith's *Lectures
on the Religion of the Semites*, a book that also serves as a direct source of Freud's account of
identification, see *GP* 42.

64. Speaking of the objective validity of psychoanalysis, Bataille offers the following methodological
observation: given that "objective knowledge is clearly insufficient ... only psychoanalyzed
patients should be able to recognize the value of psychoanalytic data" (II, 322). For a historical
invalidation of psychoanalysis from the point of view of the patients, see Mikkel Borch-Jacobsen,
Les patients de Freud: Destins (Paris: Éditions Sciences Humaines, 2011).

65. See I, 348. Freud refers to hypnosis, but negatively, in order to relegate it to the sphere of magic.
Borch-Jacobsen's *The Freudian Subject* demonstrates how the riddle of hypnosis never ceased to
haunt Freud. More generally, it continues to haunt the mind of modernism as a whole.

66. Such a disagreement can be traced back to the earliest and most influential readers of Bataille.
Michel Foucault affirms that Bataille's transgressive thought involves a "shattering of the
philosophical subject." Michel Foucault, "A Preface to Transgression," in *Language, Counter-
Memory, Practice*, ed. Donald F. Bouchard, tr. Donald F. Bouchard and Sherry Simon (Ithaca,
N.Y.: Cornell University Press, 1980), 43. Jacques Derrida, while also emphasizing the decentering
movement at work in Bataille's text, argues that "one could even abstract from Bataille's text an
entire zone throughout which sovereignty remains inside a classical philosophy of the *subject*."
Jacques Derrida, "From Restricted to General Economy: A Hegelianism without Reserve," in
Writing and Difference, tr. and ed. Alan Bass (Chicago: University of Chicago Press, 1978), 267.
And Jean-Luc Nancy writes that "perhaps Bataille did not have a *concept* of subject" and specifies
that "at least up to a point, the communication that is in excess of the subject is related to a subject,
or it erects itself as a subject." Jean-Luc Nancy, *La communauté désœuvrée* (Paris: C. Bourgois,
1983), 63.

67. Paul Hegarty reminds us that "contagion is the basis (or *is*) the communication Bataille is writing
about." Paul Hegarty, *Georges Bataille: Core Cultural Theorist* (London: SAGE Publications,
2000), 97. Mikkel Borch-Jacobsen posits "identification" at the heart of Bataille's understanding
of communication. Mikkel Borch-Jacobsen, "The Laughter of Being," in Botting and Wilson,
Bataille, 163. And Patrick ffrench argues that Bataille's early thought is characterized by what
he calls "affectivity without a subject"—by which he means "an emotional force which passes
between individuals and across groups, and which does not take the route of rational, conceptual
thought." Patrick ffrench, *After Bataille: Sacrifice, Exposure, Community* (London: Legenda,
2007).

68. Eduardo Cadava, Peter Connor, Jean-Luc Nancy, eds., *Who Comes After the Subject?* (New York:
Routledge, 1991).

69. As Bataille also puts it in one of the articles of *Contre-attaque*: "there is more to learn from the
streets of big cities, for instance, than from political newspapers or books" (I, 410).

70. Andrew Hussey, ed., *The Beast at Heaven's Gate: Georges Bataille and the Art of Transgression*.
(Amsterdam: Rodopi, 2006), 9–10.

71. There is, thus, a sense in which Bataille's thought continues to be part of the Platonic concern with

mimesis in the process of subject formation. Plato, as a coda to this critique of mimetic poetry, states that "more than anything else rhythm and harmony find their way to the inmost soul and take strongest hold upon it" (*Rep.* 646; 401d).

72. As Ian Hacking puts it, in a comparison between Freud and Pierre Janet (a figure we shall encounter shortly), "Janet was flexible and pragmatic, while it was Freud who was the dedicated and rather rigid theoretician in the spirit of the Enlightenment." And he adds: Freud's focus was on a "higher Truth about the psyche . . . he aimed at the true Theory to which all else had to be subservient." Hacking, *Rewriting the Soul*, 195, 196.

73. For a contemporary neurological account of disgust in adults that is in line with Bataille's mimetic realization, see Bruno Wicker et al., "Both of Us Disgusted in *My* Insula: The Common Neural Basis of Seeing and Feeling Disgust," *Neuron* 40 (2003): 655–664.

74. Ffrench is right to stress that Bataille's account of the psyche is "fundamentally non-Freudian," and his emphasis on the importance of immediate affectivity does much to clarify Bataille's early thought. Yet his claim that "Bataille's emphasis on affect sidesteps the issue of the unconscious and of subjectivity" as well as the emphasis on "the absence, in Bataille's thought, of the individual psyche, of the ego" needs to be qualified. Ffrench, *After Bataille*, 14. In fact, Bataille sidesteps the *Freudian* notion of the unconscious but continues to operate within the *pre-Freudian* tradition of the mimetic unconscious we have been considering so far. Aligning Bataille with this tradition will allow us to show that already in this early period he relies on a theory of the subject or ego (albeit a relational, affective one)—a theory that will continue to inform his later conception of sovereign communication.

75. Bataille shows that he is aware of this much-neglected aspect of Nietzsche's thought as he writes that "Nietzsche suggested to measure excitation through a dynamometer" (II, 331), probably alluding to Nietzsche's references to Charles Féré's psycho-physiological experiments in the fragments collected in *The Will to Power*.

76. In *The Interpretation of Dreams*, Freud had relied on Lipps's claim that "the unconscious must be assumed to be the general basis of psychical life"; but then, for the reasons explained above, he hastens to add that "'our' unconscious . . . is not the same as the unconscious of the philosophers or even the unconscious of Lipps," closing thus the door to the tradition of the mimetic unconscious. Sigmund Freud, *The Interpretation of Dreams*, ed. and tr. James Strachey (New York: Avon Books, 1998), 651–652.

77. Theodor Lipps, quoted in *Emotional Contagion: Studies in Emotion and Social Interaction*, by Elaine Hatfield, John T. Cacioppo, and Richard R. Rapson (Cambridge: Cambridge University Press, 1984), 18.

78. Bernheim, *Suggestive Therapeutics*, 129.

79. Théodule Ribot, *The Psychology of Emotions* (London: W. Scott, 1987), 232.

80. Bataille will speak of communication as being predicated on what he calls "contagious contagion" (V, 391).

81. As Bataille also puts it, "communication is never the object of discursive knowledge, but is communicated from subject to subject through a sensitive emotional contact [*contact sensible de l'émotion*]: it is communicated in laughter, tears and in the tumult of festivities" (VIII, 287–288).

82. Not unlike Girard after him and Mauss before him, Bataille is intrigued by the quasi-universal presence of sacrificial rituals among different cultures as well as by the development of artistic genres where sacrifices continue to be represented. Bataille wonders why in ritual killings (sacrifice), prehistoric paintings (visual art), or theatrical representations (tragedy) humans

continue to feel pulled towards what arouses horror and disgust. Had Bataille lived longer, he would have found evidence for his thesis in the development of cinematic genres exclusively devoted to representing slaughtering (slasher movies), the media's continuous stream of the most horrific images (under the civil and morally correct rubric, "news"), not to speak of the explosion of all kinds of heterogeneous matters represented on virtual reality. Bataille would not have been surprised to see what attracts the modern or, better, postmodern subject. But he would probably have noticed that from sacrifice to the evening news, slashers to porn, the experience of communication tends to lose its role in the creation of an immanent, social feeling of communion, progressively moving the postmodern subject towards solipsistic experiences that dissolve physical, social bonds in the ethereal network of the virtual.

83. Let me acknowledge that these concluding sections have been dictated by the pathos of loss and the joy of birth. They are dedicated to my maternal voices: Maria Succetti (1923–2007) and Natalina Lawtoo.

84. Hacking, *Rewriting the Soul*, 44. For Janet's open address to Freud about issues of theoretical priority, see Pierre Janet, *La psychanalyse de Freud* (1913) (Paris: L'Harmattan, 2004); and Pierre Janet, *La médecine psychologique* (1923) (Paris: L'Harmattan, 2005), 22–26. For an informed, historically documented account of the uncanny ways Freud and company rewrote history in order to eclipse rival psychologies, including Janet's, see Borch-Jacobsen and Shamdasani, *The Freud Files*.

85. On Janet and multiple personality, see Hacking, *Rewriting the Soul*, 44–45, 132–133; on Janet and trauma study see Ruth Leys, *Trauma: A Genealogy* (Chicago: University of Chicago Press, 2000), 83–119; on Janet and modernism, see Micale, *The Mind of Modernism*, 5–6. For a bibliographical list of Janet's writings see, Henri Ellenberger "Bibliography of the Writings of Pierre Janet," in *Beyond the Unconscious: Essays of Henri F. Ellenberger in the History of Psychiatry*, ed. Mark Micale (Princeton: Princeton University Press, 1993), 155–175.

86. Ellenberger, *Discovery of the Unconscious*, 331. See also 331–417.

87. In order to account for his conception of *le mimétisme*, Roger Caillois explicitly relied on Pierre Janet's psychological research on "legendary psychasthenia," a psychic pathology that generates among its major symptoms a feeling of dissolution of the boundaries of the ego. See Roger Caillois, "Mimétisme et psychasthénie légendaire," in *Le mythe et l'homme* (Paris: Gallimard, 1938), 86–122. Interestingly, as André Breton condemns Bataille's writings as "pathological," he specifies his medical diagnosis by saying that they manifest the "classic sign of psychasthenia." Breton, *Manifestoes of Surrealism*, 184–185. While not sharing Breton's relegation of Bataille to the sphere of mental pathology *tout court*, we shall see that Breton stumbles on something crucial, both concerning the philosophical physician who is in a best position to illuminate Bataille's communicative thought (Janet) and the "pathology" in question (mimesis).

88. See Surya, *Mort*, 330 n. 3.

89. Pierre Janet, *L'automatisme psychologique: Essai de psychologie expérimentale sur les formes inférieures de l'activité humanine* (Paris: Félix Alcan, 1903).

90. Alexandre Kojève, *Introduction to the Reading of Hegel* (Ithaca, N.Y.: Cornell University Press, 1980), 16.

91. In "Hegel, Death and Sacrifice," Bataille makes clear that identification with a victim, either in sacrifice, or later in "phantasmatic representations" (XII, 327) such as tragedy and, later, literature, is but a subterfuge for the philosophical eye to stare death in the face. As he puts it: "In tragedy, at least, it is a matter of identifying with any character who dies, and to believe to die, while at the same time remaining alive" (XII, 337).

92. Even in this most Hegelian of Bataille's texts, Bataille privileges the *"connaissance 'sensible"* characteristic of the man of sacrifice over and against Hegel's "discursive knowledge" (see XII, 338).

93. As Bataille reiterates it in a subsequent lecture: "in the end, there would be no recognition if there was no lived experience" (*Coll.* 115; translation modified).

94. Borch-Jacobsen, "The Laughter of Being," 163. See also Nidesh Lawtoo, "Bataille and the Suspension of Being," *Lingua Romana* 4.1 (2005). Http://linguaromana.byu.edu/Lawtoo4.html.

95. Borch-Jacobsen, "The Laughter of Being," 164.

96. Borch-Jacobsen sums up his thesis thus: "This ego-being (or ego-ness, as we could call it, the essence and foundation of its ego identity) is not in me: it is elsewhere, in that other—always that *alter ego*—that fascinates me, in which I love myself, in which I kill myself. *Ergo*, I am that other: *ego sum alterum.*" Borch-Jacobsen, *The Emotional Tie*, 22.

97. Pierre Janet, "Les conduites sociales," in *Onzième Congrès International de Psychologie*, ed. H. Piéron and I. Meyerson (Paris: Alcan, 1938), 138–149. Henceforth, "Conduites" (C).

98. The opening lecture is available in a written form in the congress's proceedings. The more fully developed article was reprinted in *Bulletin de Psychologie*, along with other articles dealing with the social aspects of Janet's psychology. Pierre Janet, "Les troubles de la personnalité sociale" (1937), in *Bulletin de Psychologie* 47, no. 414 (1993–1994): 156–183. Henceforth "Troubles" (T). All translations of Janet are mine.

99. For a general account of Janet's psychology of the socius, see Ellenberger, *Discovery of the Unconscious*, 388–409. For Tarde's insights into the interpsychology of imitation, see *Les lois de l'imitation*, 134–148, 250–271.

100. Pierre Janet, "Les sentiments dans le délire de persécution" (1932), in *Bulletin de Psychologie* 47, no. 413 (1993–1994), 37. Henceforth, "Délire" (D) (my transl.).

101. Other patients who suffer from psychasthenia express this state of depersonalization in a language we should be careful not to dismiss as being only symptomatic of their mimetic sickness (pathology), if only because this language testifies to a clear insight into the workings of mimetic dispossession (patho-logy). For instance, Laetitia says: "My legs walk like those of an automaton which is well reloaded. I am a mechanical woman . . . I am not responsible for anything I do; it is another who is responsible" (T 157). Another patient adds: "I am nothing more than a poor puppet pulled by strings from all sides. They steal my thoughts, they steal my soul, they lend me the soul of another"; "I am no longer myself; I no longer know who I am . . ." (157, 158). See also, Pierre Janet, *De l'angoisse à l'extase* (Paris, 1975), 54. Notice that at times Bataille's confessional language gives expression to the feeling of depersonalization expressed by Janet's patients who suffer from that mimetic trouble of the personality which is psychasthenia. As he puts it in *Sur Nietzsche*: "I am ashamed of myself. I would be soft, easily influenced . . . All resources in me seem broken . . . a continuous anxiety just finished to destroy my nerves . . . (If, in the actual conditions of my life, I let myself go for an instant, my head turns)" (VI, 104). And yet, even at these lowest moments, Bataille remains divided against himself. Thus, he specifies: "To this is opposed a consciousness sure of itself: if there is a chance to act, I will take it [*je la jouerai*], not as a secondary game but by putting my life at stake" (VI, 104).

102. In support of our genealogy of the phantom of the ego, Janet mentions that the theoretical roots of this mimetic indistinction can be traced back to Nietzsche: "In his book on psychic inferiority, a German psychiatrist quoted by M. Edg. Michaélis who inspires himself from Nietzsche has

shown that the conflict between 'mine and yours' [*'le mien et le tien'*] forms the central problem of every psychological problem" (T 162).

103. Janet is here intuiting more recent postmodern developments in mimetic theory whereby the logic of mimesis is supplemented by the logic of the simulacrum. For a theoretical extension of this theory of simulacra or artifacts within the sphere of psychology proper, see Borch-Jacobsen's *Folies à plusieurs*.

104. See Meltzoff and Moore, "Persons and Representation, 9–12; Meltzoff, "Out of the Mouths of Babes," 55–74; Braten Stein, "Introduction," in *Intersubjective Communication and Emotion in Early Ontogeny*, ed. Stein Braten (Cambridge: Cambridge University Press, 1998), 1–11.

105. Gallese, "Shared Manifold Hypothesis," 39. See also Gallese, "The Two Sides of Mimesis: Mimetic Theory, Embodied Simulation, and Social Identification," in *Mimesis and Science*, 87–108.

106. Gallese, "The Two Sides of Mimesis," 97.

107. Bataille is right to mention that Janet is not uncritical of nineteenth-century psychology, but Janet's objections do not concern his precursors' emphasis on immediate reflexes. What Janet objects to is the fact that nineteenth-century psychologists believe that "man knows immediately, *from his own personality*" rather than from a no less immediate and reflexive "knowledge of the *personality of others*" (T 161; my emphasis). Janet, on the other hand, argues that the subject knows on the basis of the affective knowledge of the other/socius. In this sense, he is sympathetic to a modernist writer like Proust, who, like Nietzsche, Conrad and Lawrence, recognizes that it is through mimesis of others' feelings that we have access not only to the psychic life of the other but to our own affects as well. "Marcel Proust said it very well: 'We only know the passions of others. What we manage to know about our own passions, we learned from others. We understand others by becoming like them, we guess others' thoughts, by imitation" (T 167).

108. Following Henri Wallon, Janet writes that "the child participate in everything that surrounds him, people and things, and we constantly observe confusions of a multiplicity of people in a single one" (T 176).

109. Bataille specifies in a note: "In a meeting at the *Collège de sociologie*, Roger Caillois . . . expressed a reserve on the meaning of this line. It is possible to translate it: 'start, little child, to recognize your mother through your laughter [*par ton rire*]' but also, 'by her laughter [*à son rire*]'" (V 389–390).

110. Lacan confidently states: "It is this captation of the human form by the *imago*, more than an *Einfühlung* demonstrably absent during early childhood [*une* Einfühlung *dont tout démontre l'absence dans la prime enfance*] which dominates the entire dialectic of the child's behavior in the presence of the other [*semblable*] between six months and two years." Jacques Lacan, "L'agressivité en psychanalyse," in *Écrits*, 101–124, 113. Recent research in the field of developmental psychology demonstrates that the opposite is true, and that newborns, from their early days of life, are receptive to the affect of the other/socius. Since Bataille's conception of mimetic communication is in line with these discoveries, he offers a more promising starting point to rethink the process of formation of the ego and to foresee who comes after the subject.

111. Hill, *Bataille, Klossowski, Blanchot*, 53.

112. François Warin, *Nietzsche et Bataille: La parodie à l'infini* (Paris: Presses Universitaires de France, 1994), 254.

113. In the context of his account of the psychology of the socius, Janet notices that the "confusions between the consciousness of the subject and the one of the socius" questions what he calls "too abstract and general philosophical notions" about subject formation (T 161). Along similar lines, Nietzsche, in his account of the origins of communication writes: "You will guess that it

is not the opposition of subject and object that concerns me here: This distinction I leave to the epistemologists who have become entangled in the snares of grammar (the metaphysics of the people)" (*GS* 354).

114. As Bataille puts it, "laughter, while unquestionably mediated, retains an aspect of pronounced immediacy in the human relations it controls" (*Coll.* 112). Bataille will continue to stick to the immediacy of laughter to the very end. Thus, he writes in *Erotism*: "we have an immediate knowledge of the other person's laughter when we laugh ourselves or of an excitement when we share it" (153).

115. Supporting Sartre's indication that the laughter in question is not funny, Bataille, writes: "It is always a distress; it is always something dispiriting that causes advanced laughter" (*Coll.* 110). The laughter he describes involves a psycho-physiological response which, like a hiccup, surprises the subject as it is confronted to an extreme fright. Yet, as Borch-Jacobsen suggests, there is an affirmative, Dionysian dimension that leads Bataille to accept and, ultimately, affirm this meaningless, involuntary laughter. Thus, Bataille is fond of quoting the following note from Nietzsche's fragments: "To see tragic natures sink and *to be able to laugh at them*, despite the profound understanding, the emotion and the sympathy—that is divine" (*IE* xxxi).

116. For an exhaustive list of the affective "effusions" that traverse Bataille's conception of sovereign communication, see *La souveraineté* VIII, 277.

117. Even later in his career, Bataille continues to have Janet explicitly in mind. For instance, he writes in a note to the introduction to *Inner Experience*: "Then I started reading Janet, imagining it necessary to use his subtlety in order to go further" (V, 430). And he specifies: "Contrary to usual tendencies in mystical studies, Janet does not confine himself to the knowledge that comes from books. He had the chance to cure an 'ecstatic' woman in a medical institution" (V, 429).

118. Bataille aligns his account of dramatization with the mystical exercises of Saint Ignace. Notoriously, Bataille tries to achieve a state of psychic depersonalization via a hypnotic identification with images of the *supplicié Chinois* Fou-Tchou-Li, a modern and real Christ/ Dionysos, literally torn to pieces. In this sense, Bataille consciously pushes to the limit the Nietzschean experience of identification with the Dionysian *sparagamos*. Both the experiences of mimetic dramatization and hypnotic depersonalization are responsible for generating a state of total dispossession whereby the ego is no longer present to itself: "I felt this state with more intensity than one normally does and as if another and not I had experienced it [*comme si un autre et non moi l'éprouvait*]" (*IE* 112).

119. Commenting on Janet's psychology of the socius, Henri Wallon writes: "these relations themselves [with others] seem to be mediated by the phantom of the other [*fantôme d'autrui*] that everyone carries within himself. The variations in intensity affecting this phantom [*fantôme*] are what govern the level of our relations with others." Henri Wallon, "The Role of the Other in the Consciousness of the Ego," in *The World of Henri Wallon*, tr. Donald Nicholson-Smith (Jason Aaronson, 1946). Http://www.marxists.org/archive/wallon/works/1946/ch7.htm.

Coda. Mimetic Theory Revisited

I would like to thank Gary Handwerk for asking a series of Nietzschean, ethical questions that provided just the right stimulus to write this coda. This last chapter is gratefully dedicated to him.

1. See Girard, "Master Slave," in *Deceit*, 96–112. Early in his career, Girard downplayed the importance of Kojève's anthropomorphic reading of Hegel in the genesis of his theory. More recently, however, he writes: "I cannot deny that Hegel was in the background. Kojève's influence

was huge in France. . . . Like Hegel, I was saying that we desire things less than we desire for ourselves the desire that others have for things; I was talking about *a desire for the other's desire*, in a way." Girard, *Battling to the End*, 30.

2. See Lacoue-Labarthe, "Diderot: Paradox and Mimesis," in *Typography*, 248–266.

3. See Girard, *Deceit*, 20–22.

4. As Nicholas Carr summarizes it, "Extensive, perpetual plasticity has been documented in healthy, normally functioning nervous systems, leading neuroscientists to conclude that our brains are always in flux, adapting to even small shifts in our circumstances and behavior." Carr, *The Shallows*, 31. And echoing a realization that is as old as Plato, Norman Doidge specifies that plasticity "produces effects we think of as both bad and good." Doidge, *Brain that Changes Itself*, 317.

5. See Judith Butler, *Precarious Life: The Powers of Mourning and Violence* (London: Verso, 2004); Giorgio Agamben, *Homo sacer: Il potere sovrano e la nuda vita* (Turin: Einaudi, 2005).

6. On the "horrorism" that informs contemporary violence see Cavarero, *Horrorism*.

7. As Jacques Derrida has famously shown, in Plato's thought mimesis already operates as a *pharmakon*, understood in the dual sense of disease and remedy. Derrida, "Plato's Pharmacy," in *Dissemination*, 61–171.

8. See also Andreas Oberprantacher, "Beyond Rivalry? Rethinking Community in View of Apocalyptical Violence," *Contagion* 17 (2010): 175–187.

9. For an account of the role of shared mimetic experiences in childhood for the creation of a "'we-centric' space" essential for establishing a feeling of "communion," see Kruger, "Imitation, Communion, and Culture."

10. Girard, *Evolution and Conversion*, 76.

11. Bataille distinguishes between "communication binding *two* beings (the laughter of the child with the mother, tickling, etc.)" and "communication through death, with a beyond of beings (essentially in sacrifice)" (V, 388).

12. Girard, *Violence and the Sacred*, 7.

13. Bataille famously speaks of "general economy" in order to account for a Dionysian squandering of energy that tightens social cohesion. Following Marcel Mauss's *The Gift*, he reminds us that "each act of generosity contributes to the cycle of generosity in general." And he adds: "Thus, throughout a limited group based on generosity there is an organic and pre-arranged communication like the multiple movements of a dance or a piece of orchestral music." Bataille, *Erotism, Death and Sensuality*, 206.

14. Girard, *Violence and the Sacred*, 8.

15. We should not forget that Girard's mimetic theory emerged in the context of U.S. academia in a period in which the "theory wars" were at their apex, generating a breeding ground for mimetic rivalry. Unfortunately, this academic, "humanistic" context all too often mimics the competitive, rivalrous, and violent spirit of the capitalist societies it is supposed to critique.

16. Benedict Anderson is right to point out that "all communities larger than primordial villages of face-to-face contact (and perhaps even these) are imagined." Benedict Anderson, *Imagined Communities: Reflections on the Origin and Spread of Nationalism* (London: Verso, 1991), 6. What we must add is that the source of this imagination is rooted in immanent, bodily reflexes that can be traced back to real face-to-face contacts with the other qua *socius*.

17. Durkheim, *Elementary Forms*, 175, 171. Speaking of the "inner experience" of "moral forces," Durkheim writes: "nothing is more contagious and, as a result, more communicable" (271).

18. Charles Baudelaire, "De l'essence du rire," in *Oeuvres complètes* (Paris: Gallimard, 1961), 975–993, 993 (my transl.).

19. Judith Butler writes that "speculations on the formation of the subject are crucial to understanding the basis of non-violent responses to injury and, perhaps most important, to a theory of collective responsibility." Butler, *Precarious Life*, 44. Butler's realization that the subject is not autonomous but is "given over to some set of primary others" (31) is indicative of a recent turn to a mimetic principle that was well known among modernists.

20. Jean-Luc Nancy, *The Inoperative Community*, ed. and tr. Peter Connor (Minneapolis: University of Minnesota Press, 1991), 16.

21. Maurice Blanchot writes that "the existence of every being is addressed to the other [*appelle l'autre*] or a plurality of others." And he adds that such a community has its "principle in the finitude of the members that compose it." Blanchot, *La communauté inavouable* (Paris: Éditions de Minuit, 1983), 16–17 (my transl.). Jean-Luc Nancy states that community "is not the space of the egos . . . but of *I*'s, who are always *others*." And he adds: "If community is revealed in the death of others, it is because death itself is the true community of *I*'s that are not *egos*." Nancy, *Inoperative Community*, 15.

22. See Jean-Luc Nancy, *Being Singular Plural*, tr. Robert D. Richardson and Anne E. O'Bryne (Stanford: Stanford University Press, 2000); Giorgio Agamben, *The Coming Community*, tr. Michael Hardt (Minneapolis: University of Minnesota Press, 1993).

23. Borch-Jacobsen, *The Emotional Tie*, 16.

24. Judith Butler, *Giving an Account of Oneself* (New York: Fordham University Press, 2005), 10. See also 10–16.

25. See Butler, *Giving an Account*, 69–87.

26. For an illuminating account of the bonds generated by what we have called, following Janet, "the psychology of the socius," see François Roustang, *Influence* (Paris: Éditions de Minuit, 1990), 149–160.

27. Butler, *Precarious Life*, 46.

28. Girard, *Battling to the End*.

29. William Butler Yeats, "The Second Coming," *Selected Poems*, ed. Richard Gill (Oxford: Oxford University Press, 2002), 26.

30. Yeats, "Second Coming," 26.

Bibliography

Abrams, M. H. *The Mirror and the Lamp: Romantic Theory and the Critical Tradition*. Oxford: Oxford University Press, 1971.

Achebe, Chinua. "An Image of Africa: Racism in Conrad's *Heart of Darkness*." In *Heart of Darkness*, 4th ed. Edited by Paul B. Armstrong, 336–349. New York: W. W. Norton, 2006.

Adorno, Theodor. *Minima Moralia: Reflections on a Damaged Life*. Translated by E. F. N. Jephcott. London: Verso, 2005.

Adorno, Theodor, and Max Horkheimer. *The Dialectic of Enlightenment*. Translated by John Cumming. New York: Herder & Herder, 1972.

Agamben, Giorgio. *The Coming Community*. Translated by Michael Hardt. Minneapolis: University of Minnesota Press, 1993.

———. *Homo sacer: Il potere sovrano e la nuda vita*. Turin: Einaudi, 2005.

Anderson, Benedict. *Imagined Communities: Reflections on the Origin and Spread of Nationalism*. London: Verso, 1991.

Aristotle. *The* Poetics *of Aristotle*. Translated by Stephen Halliwell. Chapel Hill: University of North Carolina Press, 1987.

Asher, Kenneth. "Nietzsche, D. H. Lawrence and Irrationalism." *Neophilologus* 69 (1985): 1–16.

Auerbach, Erich. *Mimesis: The Representation of Reality in Western Literature*. Translated by Willard R. Trask. Princeton: Princeton University Press, 2003.

Bataille, Georges. *Le bleu du ciel*. Paris: Jean-Jacques Pauvert, 1956.

———. *Erotism, Death and Sensuality*. Translated by Mary Dalwood. San Francisco: City Lights Books, 1986.

———. *Essential Writings*. Edited by Michael Richardson. London: Sage, 1998.

———. *L' expérience intérieure*. Paris: Gallimard, 1954.

———. *Histoire de l'oeil*. Paris: Jean-Jacques Pauvert, 1956.

———. *Inner Experience*. Translated by Leslie Anne Boldt. Albany: State University of New York, 1988.

———. *Oeuvres complètes*. 12 vols. Paris: Gallimard, 1970–1988.

———. *La sociologie sacrée du monde contemporain*. Paris: Éditions Lignes & Manifestes, 2004.

Baudelaire, Charles. "De l'essence du rire." In *Oeuvres complètes*, 975–993. Paris: Gallimard, 1961.

Baudrillard, Jean. *The Gulf War Did Not Take Place*. Translated by Paul Patton. Sydney: Power Publications, 1995.

———. *Selected Writings*. Edited by Mark Poster. Cambridge: Polity Press, 2001.

———. *Simulacres et simulation*. Paris: Galilée, 1981.

Baudry, Jean-Louis. "The Apparatus: Metapsychological Approaches to the Impression of Reality in Cinema." In *Film Theory and Criticism*, 4th ed. Edited by Gerald Mast, Marshal Cohen, and Leo Braudy, 693–696. Oxford: Oxford University Press, 1992.

Becket, Fiona. "Lawrence and Psychoanalysis." In *The Cambridge Companion to D. H. Lawrence*. Edited by Anne Fernihough, 217–233. Cambridge: Cambridge University Press, 2001.

Bell, Michael. *D. H. Lawrence: Language and Being*. Cambridge: Cambridge University Press, 1991.

———. "Lawrence and Modernism." In *The Cambridge Companion to D. H. Lawrence*. Edited by Anne Fernihough, 179–196. Cambridge: Cambridge University Press, 2001.

———. "The Metaphysics of Modernism." In *The Cambridge Companion to Modernism*. Edited by Michael Levenson, 9–32. Cambridge: Cambridge University Press, 1999.

———. *Primitivism*. London: Metheuen, 1972.

Bernays, Edward. *Propaganda*. New York: Ig Publishing, 2005.

Bernheim, Hippolyte. *Suggestive Therapeutics: A Treatise on the Nature and Uses of Hypnosis*. Translated by Christian A. Herter. Westport, Conn.: Associated Booksellers, 1957.

Besnier, Jean-Michel. "Bataille, the Emotive Intellectual." In *Bataille: Writing the Sacred*. Edited by Carolyn Bailey Gill, 13–26. New York: Routledge, 1995.

Blanchot, Maurice. *La communauté inavouable*. Paris: Les Éditions de Minuit, 1983.

Bock, Martin. *Joseph Conrad and Psychological Medicine*. Lubbock: Texas Tech University Press, 2002.

Boon, Marcus. *In Praise of Copying*. Harvard: Harvard University Press, 2009. Http://www.hup.harvard.edu/features/boon/.

Borch-Jacobsen, Mikkel. *The Emotional Tie: Psychoanalysis, Mimesis, Affect*. Translated by Douglass Brick et al. Stanford: Stanford University Press, 1992.

———. *The Freudian Subject*. Translated by Catherine Porter. Stanford: Stanford University Press, 1988.

———. *Folies à plusieurs: De l'hystérie à la dépression*. Paris: Le Seuil, 2002.

——. *Lacan: The Absolute Master.* Translated by Douglas Brick. Stanford: Stanford University Press, 1991.

——. "The Laughter of Being." In *Bataille: A Critical* Reader. Edited by Fred Botting and Scott Wilson. 146–166. Oxford: Blackwell, 1997.

——. *Les patients de Freud: Destins.* Paris: Éditions Sciences Humaines, 2011.

Borch-Jacobsen, Mikkel, and Shamdasani, Sonu. *The Freud Files: An Inquiry into the History of Psychoanalysis.* Cambridge: Cambridge University Press, 2012.

Breton, André. *Manifestoes of Surrealism.* Translated by Richard Seaver and Helen R. Lane. Ann Arbor: University of Michigan Press, 1969.

Buch, Robert. *The Pathos of the Real: On the Aesthetics of Violence in the Twentieth Century.* Baltimore: Johns Hopkins University Press, 2010

Burrow, Trigant. *The Social Basis of Consciousness.* London: Kegan Paul, Trench, Trubner, 1927.

Butler, Judith. *Giving an Account of Oneself.* New York: Fordham University Press, 2005.

——. "Imitation and Gender Insubordination." In *Inside/Out: Lesbian Theories, Gay Theories.* Edited by Diana Fuss, 13–31. New York: Routledge, 1991.

——. *Precarious Life: The Powers of Mourning and Violence.* London: Verso, 2004.

Cadava, Eduardo, Peter Connor, and Jean-Luc Nancy, eds. *Who Comes After the Subject?* New York: Routledge, 1991.

Caillois, Roger. *Le mythe et l'homme.* Paris: Gallimard, 1938.

Carr, Nicholas. *The Shallows: How the Internet Is Changing the Way We Read, Think and Remember.* London: Atlantic Books, 2010.

Cavarero, Adriana. *Horrorism: Naming Contemporary Violence.* Translated by William McCuaig. Columbia: Columbia University Press, 2009.

Chertok, Léon R., and Raymond de Saussure. *The Therapeutic Revolution: From Mesmer to Freud.* Translated by R. H. Ahrenfeldt. New York: Brunner/Mazel, 1979.

Collier, Peter, and Judy Davies, eds. *Modernism and the European Unconscious.* Cambridge: Polity Press, 1990.

Conrad, Joseph. *Collected Letters, 1903–1907.* Edited by Frederick R. Karl and Laurence Davies. Vol. 3. Cambridge: Cambridge University Press, 1988.

——. *Heart of Darkness,* in *Youth: A Narrative and Two Other Stories* by Joseph Conrad. 45–162. London: J. M. Dent & Sons, 1923.

——. *A Personal Record: Some Reminiscences.* London: Faber and Faber, 2008.

——. *Tales of Unrest.* New York: Doubleday, 1926.

Coppola, Francis Ford. *Apocalypse Now (Redux).* Paramount Pictures, 2002.

Dawson, Eugene. "D. H. Lawrence and Trigant Burrow: Pollyanalytics and Phylobiology, an Interpretative Analysis." PhD diss., University of Washington, 1963.

De Heusch, Luc. *La transe et ses entours.* Brussels: Éditions Complexe, 2006.

Deleuze, Gilles. *Critique et clinique* (Paris: Éditions de Minuit, 1993).

——. *Essays Critical and Clinical*. Translated by Daniel W. Smith and Michael A. Greco. New York: Verso, 1998.

——. *Nietzsche et la philosophie*. Paris: Presses Universitaires de France, 1962.

Deleuze, Gilles, and Felix Guattari. *Anti-Oedipus: Capitalism and Schizophrenia*. Translated by Robert Hurley, Mark Seem, and Helen Lane. London: Continuum, 2004.

Derrida, Jacques. "From Restricted to General Economy: A Hegelianism without Reserve." In *Writing and Difference*. Edited and translated by Alan Bass, 251–277. Chicago: University of Chicago Press, 1978.

——. "Introduction: Desistance." In *Typography: Mimesis, Philosophy, Politics*. Edited by Christopher Fynsk, 3–42. Cambridge: Harvard University Press, 1989.

——. "Plato's Pharmacy." In *Dissemination*. Translated by Barbara Johnson, 61–171. Chicago: University of Chicago Press, 1981.

Didi-Huberman, Georges. *Invention de l'hystérie: Charcot et l'iconographie de la Salpêtrière*. Paris: Éditions Macula, 1982.

Dodds, E. R. *The Greeks and the Irrational*. Berkeley: University of California Press, 1964.

Doidge, Norman. *The Brain that Changes Itself: Stories of Personal Triumph From the Frontiers of Brain Science*. London: Penguin, 2007.

Dollimore, Jonathan. *Death, Desire and Loss in Western Culture*. New York: Routledge, 1998.

——. "Civilization and Its Darkness." In *Conrad's "Heart of Darkness" and Contemporary Thought: Revisiting the Horror with Lacoue-Labarthe*. Edited by Nidesh Lawtoo, 67–86. London: Bloomsbury, 2012.

Durkheim, Émile. *The Elementary Forms of Religious Life*. Translated by Carol Cosman. Oxford: Oxford University Press, 2001.

Eagleton, Terry. *Criticism and Ideology: A Study in Marxist Literary Theory*. New York: NLB, 1976.

Ellenberger, Henry. *Beyond the Unconscious: Essays of Henry F. Ellenberger in the History of Psychiatry*. Edited by Mark Micale. Princeton: Princeton University Press, 1993.

——. *The Discovery of the Unconscious: The History and Evolution of Dynamic Psychiatry*. London: Fontana Press, 1994.

Ellis, David. *D. H Lawrence: Dying Game, 1922–1930*. Cambridge: Cambridge University Press, 1998.

Elsaesser, Thomas, and Michael Wedel. "The Hollow Heart of Hollywood: *Apocalypse Now* and the New Sound Space." In *Conrad on Film*. Edited by Gene M. Moore, 151–175. Cambridge: Cambridge University Press, 1997.

Fernihough, Anne. *D. H. Lawrence: Aesthetics and Ideology*. Oxford: Clarendon Press, 1993.

Ffrench, Patrick. *After Bataille: Sacrifice, Exposure, Community*. London: Legenda, 2007.

Foster, John B., Jr. *Heirs to Dionysus: A Nietzschean Current in Literary Modernism*. Princeton: Princeton University Press, 1981.

Foucault, Michel. "A Preface to Transgression." In *Language, Counter-Memory, Practice*. Edited by Donald F. Bouchard and translated by Donald F. Bouchard and Sherry Simon, 29–52. Ithaca, NY.: Cornell University Press, 1980.

Frazer, James. *The Golden Bough: A Study in Magic and Religion*. Vol. 1. New York: Macmillan, 1952.

Freud, Sigmund. *The Ego and the Id*. Edited and translated by James Strachey. New York: W. W. Norton, 1960.

———. *Group Psychology and the Analysis of the Ego*. Edited and translated by James Strachey. New York: W. W. Norton, 1959.

———. *The Interpretation of Dreams*. Edited and translated by James Strachey. New York: Avon Books, 1998.

———. "A Note on the Unconscious in Psycho-Analysis." In *Collected Papers*, vol. 4. Edited by Ernest Jones and translated by Joan Riviere, 22–29. New York: Basic Books, 1959.

———. *Totem and Taboo*. Translated by A. A. Brill. Harmondsworth: Penguin, 1940.

———. "The Unconscious." In *Collected Papers*, vol. 4. Edited by Ernest Jones and translated by Joan Riviere, 98–136. New York: Basic Books, 1959.

Frost, Laura. *Sex Drives: Fantasies of Fascism in Literary Modernism*. Ithaca, N.Y.: Cornell University Press, 2002.

Fuss, Diana. *Essentially Speaking: Feminism, Nature and Difference*. New York: Routledge, 1989.

Gallese, Vittorio. "The 'Shared Manifold' Hypothesis: From Mirror Neurons to Empathy." *Journal of Consciousness Studies* 8 (2001): 33–50.

———. "The Two Sides of Mimesis: Mimetic Theory, Embodied Simulation, and Social Identification." In *Mimesis and Science: Empirical Research on Imitation and the Mimetic Theory of Culture and Religion*. Edited by Scott R. Garrels, 87–108. East Lansing: Michigan State University Press, 2011.

Garrels, Scott R. "Imitation, Mirror Neurons, and Mimetic Desire: Convergence between the Mimetic Theory of René Girard and Empirical Research on Imitation." *Contagion* 12–13 (2006): 47–86.

———, ed. *Mimesis and Science: Empirical Research on Imitation and the Mimetic Theory of Culture and Religion*. East Lansing: Michigan State University Press, 2011.

Gasché, Rodolphe. *Georges Bataille: Phenomenology and Phantasmatology*. Translated by Roland Végsō. Stanford: Stanford University Press, 2012.

Gauchet, Marcel. *L'inconscient cérébral*. Paris: Seuil, 1992.

Gebauer, Gunter, and Christopher Wulf. *Mimesis: Culture-Art-Society*. Translated by Don Reneau. Berkeley: University of California Press, 1995.

Girard, René. *Achever Clausewitz: Entretiens avec Benoît Chantre*. Paris: Carnets nord, 2007.

———. *Battling to the End*. Translated by Mary Baker. East Lansing: Michigan State University Press, 2010.

———. *Deceit, Desire and the Novel*. Translated by Yvonne Freccero. Baltimore: Johns Hopkins University Press, 1965.

———. *Des choses cachées depuis la fondation du monde*. Paris: Éditions Grasset, 1978.

———. "Dionysus versus the Crucified." *MLN* 99 (1994): 816–835.

———. *Evolution and Conversion: Dialogues on the Origins of Culture* (with Pierpaolo Antonello and João Cezar de Castro Rocha). London: Continuum, 2007.

———. *Mensonge romantique et vérité romanesque*. Paris: Éditions Bernard Grasset, 1961.

——— . *Mimesis and Theory: Essays on Literature and Criticism, 1953–2005*. Edited by Robert Doran. Stanford: Stanford University Press, 2008.

——— . "Nietzsche and Contradiction." In *Nietzsche in Italy*. Edited by Thomas Harrison, 53–66. Saratoga: Anna Libri, 1988.

——— . "Superman in the Underground: Strategies of Madness—Nietzsche, Wagner, and Dostoevsky." *MLN* 91 (1976): 1257–1266.

——— . *La violence et le sacré*. Paris: Éditions Albin Michel, 1990.

——— . *To Double Business Bound: Essays on Literature, Mimesis, and Anthropology*. Baltimore: Johns Hopkins University Press, 1978.

——— . *Violence and the Sacred*. Translated by Patrick Gregory. Baltimore: Johns Hopkins University Press, 1977.

Golomb, Jacob, Weaver Santaniello, and Ronald Lehrer, eds. *Nietzsche and Depth Psychology*. Albany: State University of New York Press, 1999.

Golomb, Jacob, and Robert S. Wistrich, eds. *Nietzsche, Godfather of Fascism? On the Uses and Abuses of a Philosophy*. Princeton: Princeton University Press, 2002.

Greiff, Louis. *D. H. Lawrence: Fifty Years on Film*. Carbondale: Southern Illinois University Press, 2001.

Griffith, John. *Joseph Conrad and the Anthropological Dilemma*. Oxford: Oxford University Press, 1995.

Habermas, Jürgen. "The French Path to Postmodernity: Bataille between Eroticism and General Economics." In *Bataille: A Critical Reader*. Edited by Fred Botting and Scott Wilson, 166–190. Oxford: Blackwell, 1998.

Hacking, Ian. *Rewriting the Soul: Multiple Personality and the Sciences of Memory*. Princeton: Princeton University Press, 1995.

Harrison, Jane. *Ancient Art and Ritual*. London: Williams & Norgate, 1913.

Hassin, Ran R., James S. Uleman, and John A. Bargh. *The New Unconscious*. Oxford: Oxford University Press, 2005.

Hatfield, Elaine, John T. Cacioppo, and Richard R. Rapson. *Emotional Contagion: Studies in Emotion and Social Interaction*. Cambridge: Cambridge University Press, 1984.

Havelock, Eric. *Preface to Plato*. Oxford: Basil Blackwell, 1963.

Hawthorn, Jeremy. *Joseph Conrad: Narrative Technique and Ideological Commitment*. New York: Edward Arnold, 1990.

Hay, Eloise K. *The Political Novels of Joseph Conrad*. Chicago: University of Chicago Press, 1963.

Hegarty, Paul. *Georges Bataille: Core Cultural Theorist*. London: Sage, 2000.

Heywood, Christopher. "'Blood Consciousness' and the Pioneers of the Reflex and Ganglionic Systems." In *D. H. Lawrence: New Studies*. Edited by Christopher Heywood, 104–108. London: Macmillan, 1987.

Hill, Leslie. *Bataille, Klossowski, Blanchot: Writing at the Limit*. Oxford: Oxford University Press, 2001.

Hollier, Denis. "On Equivocation (between Literature and Politics)." *October* 55 (1990): 3–22.

——— , ed. *Le collège de sociologie 1937–1939*. Paris: Gallimard, 1995.

——— . *La prise de la Concorde: Essais sur Georges Bataille*. Paris: Gallimard, 1974.

Humma, John. "D. H. Lawrence as Friedrich Nietzsche." *Philological Quarterly* 53.1 (1974): 110–120.

Hussey, Andrew. *The Beast at Heaven's Gate: Georges Bataille and the Art of Transgression.* Amsterdam: Rodopi, 2006.

Janet, Pierre. *De l'angoisse à l'extase.* Paris, 1975.

———. *L'automatisme psychologique: Essai de psychologie expérimentale sur les formes inférieures de l'activité humaine.* Paris: Félix Alcan, 1903.

———. "Les conduites sociales." In *Onzième Congrès International de Psychologie.* Edited by H. Piéron and I. Meyerson, 138–149. Paris: Alcan, 1938.

———. *La médecine psychologique.* Paris: L'Harmattan, 2005.

———. *La psychanalyse de Freud.* Paris: L'Harmattan, 2004.

———. "Les sentiments dans le délire de persécution." *Bulletin de Psychologie* 47, no. 413 (1993–1994): 3–73.

———. "Les troubles de la personnalité sociale." *Bulletin de Psychologie.* 47, no. 414 (1993–1994): 156–183.

Johnsen, William A. *Violence and Modernism: Ibsen, Joyce, and Woolf.* Gainesville: University Press of Florida, 2003.

Jung, Carl. *Psychology of the Unconscious.* Translated by Beatrice M. Hinkle. London: Routledge, 1991.

Kojève, Alexandre. *Introduction to the Reading of Hegel.* Assembled by Raymond Queneau, edited by Allan Bloom, and translated by James H. Nichols Jr. Ithaca, N.Y.: Cornell University Press, 1980.

Krell, David. *Infectious Nietzsche.* Bloomington: Indiana University Press, 1996.

Krockel, Carl. *D. H. Lawrence and Germany: The Politics of Influence.* New York: Rodopi, 2007.

Kruger, Ann Cale. "Imitation, Communion, and Culture." In *Mimesis and Science:Empirical Research on Imitation and the Mimetic Theory of Culture and Religion.* Edited by Scott R. Garrels, 111–128. East Lansing: Michigan State University Press, 2011.

Lacan, Jacques. "L'agressivité en psychanalyse." In *Écrits,* 101–124. Paris: Seuil, 1966.

———. *Les complexes familiaux dans la formation de l'individu.* Paris: Navarin Editeur, 1984.

———. "Le stade du miroir comme formateur de la fonction du Je." In *Écrits,* 93–100. Paris: Seuil, 1966.

Lacoue-Labarthe, Philippe. *La fiction du politique.* Paris: Christian Bourgois, 1987.

———. "L'horreur occidentale." *Lignes* (2007): 224–234.

———. "The Horror of the West." Translated by Nidesh Lawtoo and Hannes Opelz. In *Conrad's "Heart of Darkness" and Contemporary Thought: Revisiting the Horror with Lacoue-Labarthe.* Edited by Nidesh Lawtoo, 111–122. London: Bloomsbury, 2012.

———. *L'imitation des modernes (Typographies 2).* Paris: Galilée, 1986.

———. *Musica Ficta (figures de Wagner).* Paris: Christian Bourgois, 1991.

———. *Typography: Mimesis, Philosophy, Politics.* Edited by Christopher Fynsk. Cambridge: Harvard University Press, 1989.

Lacoue-Labarthe, Philippe, and Jean-Luc Nancy. "The Nazi Myth." Translated by Brian Holmes. *Critical Inquiry* 16.2 (1990): 291–312.

———. "La panique politique." In *Retreating the Political*. Edited by Simon Sparks, 1–28. New York: Routledge, 1977.

———. *Retreating the Political*. Edited by Simon Sparks. New York: Routledge, 1977.

Lawrence, D. H. *Aaron's Rod*. Edited by Mara Kalnins. Cambridge: Cambridge University Press, 1988.

———. *The Fox, The Captain's Doll, The Ladybird*. Edited by Dieter Mehl. Cambridge: Cambridge University Press, 1992.

———. *Kangaroo*. Edited by Bruce Steele. Cambridge: Cambridge University Press, 1994.

———. *The Letters of D. H. Lawrence*. Edited by G. J. Zytaruk and J. T. Boulton. Vol. 2. Cambridge: Cambridge University Press, 1989.

———. *Mornings in Mexico and Other Essays*. Edited by Virginia Crosswhite Hyde. Cambridge: Cambridge University Press, 2009.

———. *Phoenix*. New York: Viking Press, 1968.

———. *Phoenix II*. Harmondsworth: Penguin, 1981.

———. *The Plumed Serpent*. Edited by L.D. Clark. Cambridge: Cambridge University Press, 1987.

———. *Psychoanalysis and the Unconscious* and *Fantasia of the Unconscious*. Edited by Bruce Steele. Cambridge: Cambridge University Press, 2004.

———. *St. Mawr and Other Stories*. Edited by Brian Finney. Cambridge: Cambridge University Press, 1983.

———. *Studies in Classic American Literature*. Edited by Ezra Greenspan, Lindeth Vasey, and John Worthen. Cambridge: Cambridge University Press, 2003.

———. *Study of Thomas Hardy and Other Essays*. Edited by Bruce Steele. Cambridge: Cambridge University Press, 1985.

———. *Twilight in Italy and Other Essays*. Edited by Paul Eggert. Cambridge: Cambridge University Press, 2002.

———. *The Woman Who Rode Away and Other Stories*. Edited by Dieter Mehl and Christa Jansohn Cambridge: Cambridge University Press, 2002.

Lawtoo, Nidesh. "Bataille and the Suspension of Being." *Lingua Romana* 4.1 (2005). Http:// linguaromana.byu.edu/Lawtoo4.html.

———. ed. *Conrad's "Heart of Darkness" and Contemporary Thought: Revisiting the Horror with Lacoue-Labarthe*. London: Bloomsbury, 2012.

———. "A Picture of Africa: Frenzy, Counternarrative, Mimesis." *Modern Fiction Studies* 59.1 (2013): 26-52.

———. "A Picture of Europe: Possession Trance in *Heart of Darkness*." *Novel: A Forum on Fiction* 45.3 (2012): 409-432.

Le Bon, Gustave. *The Crowd*. Translated by Robert A. Nye. New Brunswick, N.J.: Transaction Publishers, 1995.

Léon Chertok. *Hypnose et suggestion*. Paris: Presses Universitaires de France, 1993.

Lévi-Strauss, Claude. "Introduction à l'œuvre de Marcel Mauss." In *Sociologie et anthropologie*, by Marcel Mauss, ix–lii. Paris: Presses Universitaires de France, 1995

Lévy-Bruhl, Lucien. *La mentalité primitive*. Paris: Retz-C.E.P.L., 1976.

———. *Le surnaturel et la nature dans la mentalité primitive*. Paris: Presses Universitaires de France, 1963.

Leys, Ruth. *Trauma: A Genealogy*. Chicago: University of Chicago Press, 2000.

Liebscher, Martin. "Friedrich Nietzsche's Perspectives on the Unconscious." In *Thinking the Unconscious: Nineteenth-Century German Thought*. Edited by Nicholls Angues and Martin Liebscher, 241–269. Cambridge: Cambridge University Press, 2010.

Maisonnat, Claude. "Alterity and Suicide in 'An Outpost of Progress.'" *Conradiana* 28.2 (1996): 101–114.

Marcuse, Herbert. *One-Dimensional Man: Studies in the Ideology of Advanced Industrial Society*. New York: Routledge, 2002.

Masschelein, Anneleen. "Rip the Veil of the Old Vision Across, and Walk through the Rent: Reading D. H. Lawrence with Deleuze and Guattari." In *Modernism and Theory: A Critical Debate*. Edited by Stephen Ross, 23–39. New York: Routledge, 2009.

Mauss, Marcel, and Henri Hubert. "Esquisse d'une théorie générale de la magie." In *Sociologie et anthropologie*, by Marcel Mauss, 1–141. Paris: Presses Universitaires de France, 1995.

McClelland, J. S. *The Crowd and the Mob: From Plato to Canetti*. London: Unwin Hyman, 1989.

McDougall, William. *The Group Mind*. New York: G. P. Putnam's Sons, 1973.

Melberg, Arne. *Theories of Mimesis*. Cambridge: Cambridge University Press, 1995.

Meltzoff, Andrew N. "Out of the Mouths of Babes: Imitation, Gaze, and Intentions in Infant Research—the 'Like Me' Framework." In *Mimesis and Science: Empirical Research on Imitation and the Mimetic Theory of Culture and Religion*. Edited by Scott R. Garrels, 55–74. East Lansing: Michigan State University Press, 2011.

Meltzoff, Andrew N., and Keith Moore. "Persons and Representation: Why Infant Imitation Is Important for Theories of Human Development." In *Imitation in Infancy*. Edited by Jacqueline Nadal and George Butterworth, 9–35. Cambridge: Cambridge University Press, 1999.

Mensch, Barbara *D. H. Lawrence and the Authoritarian Personality*. New York: St. Martin's Press, 1991.

Meyer, Catherine, ed. *Le livre noir de la psychanalyse: Vivre, penser et aller mieux sans Freud*. 2nd ed. Paris: Éditions des Arènes, 2010.

Micale, Mark, ed. *The Mind of Modernism: Medicine, Psychology, and the Cultural Arts in Europe and America, 1880–1940*. Stanford: Stanford University Press, 2004.

Miller, Christopher L. *Blank Darkness: Africanist Discourse in French*. Chicago: University of Chicago Press, 1985.

Milton, Colin. *Lawrence and Nietzsche: A Study in Influence*. Aberdeen: Aberdeen University Press, 1987.

Mongia, Padmini. "The Rescue: Conrad, Achebe, and the Critics." *Conradiana* 33.2 (2001): 153–163.

Morin, Edgar. *The Cinema, or the Imaginary Man*. Translated by Lorraine Mortimer. Minneapolis: University of Minnesota Press, 2005.

————. *L'homme et la mort*. Paris: Seuil, 1974.

Moscovici, Serge. *The Age of the Crowd: A Historical Treatise on Mass Psychology*. Translated by J. C. Whitehouse. Cambridge: Cambridge University Press, 1985.

Myers, Frederick, and Frank Podmore, eds. *Phantoms of the Living*. London: Trübner, Ludgate Hill, 1886.

Nancy, Jean-Luc. *Being Singular Plural*. Translated by Robert D. Richardson and Anne E. O'Bryne. Stanford: Stanford University Press, 2000.

————. *La communauté désœuvrée*. Paris: C. Bourgois, 1983.

————. *The Inoperative Community*. Edited and translated by Peter Connor. Minneapolis: University of Minnesota Press, 1991.

Nehls, Edward. *D. H. Lawrence: A Composite Biography*. Vol. 3. Madison: University of Wisconsin Press, 1959.

Nicholls, Angues, and Martin Liebscher, eds. *Thinking the Unconscious: Nineteenth-Century German Thought*. Cambridge: Cambridge University Press, 2010.

Nietzsche, Friedrich. *The Antichrist*. In *The Portable Nietzsche*. Edited and translated by Walter Kaufmann, 568–656. New York: Viking Press, 1954.

————. *Beyond Good and Evil*. Translated by R. J. Hollingdale. London: Penguin, 2003.

————. *The Birth of Tragedy*. Translated by Walter Kaufmann. New York: Vintage, 1967.

————. *The Case of Wagner*. Translated by Walter Kaufmann. New York: Vintage, 1967.

————. *Daybreak*. Translated by R. J. Hollingdale. Cambridge: Cambridge University Press, 1982.

————. *Ecce Homo*. Translated by R. J. Hollingdale. Harmondsworth: Penguin, 1979.

————. *The Gay Science*. Translated by Walter Kaufmann. New York: Vintage, 1974.

————. *Human, All Too Human*. Translated by Gary Handwerk. Stanford: Stanford University Press, 1997.

————. *Nietzsche Contra Wagner*. In *The Portable Nietzsche*. Translated and edited by Walter Kaufmann, 661–683. New York: Viking Press, 1954.

————. *On the Genealogy of Morals*. Translated by Douglass Smith. Oxford: Oxford University Press, 1996.

————. *Sämtliche Werke: Kritische Studienausgabe*. 15 vols. Ed. Giorgio Colli and Mazzino Montinari. Berlin: Walter de Gruyter, 1967–1977.

————. *Twilight of the Idols*. In *The Portable Nietzsche*, translated by Walter Kaufmann, 463–563. New York: Viking Press, 1954.

————. *Untimely Meditations*. Edited by Daniel Breazeale. Cambridge: Cambridge University Press, 1997.

————. *The Will to Power*. Translated by Walter Kaufmann. New York: Vintage, 1968.

Norris, Margot. "Modernism and Vietnam: Francis Ford Coppola's *Apocalypse Now*." *Modern Fiction Studies* 44.3 (1998): 730–766.

Noys, Benjamin. *Georges Bataille: A Critical Introduction*. London: Pluto Press, 2000.

Oberprantacher, Andreas. "Beyond Rivalry? Rethinking Community in View of Apocalyptical Violence." *Contagion* 17 (2010): 175–187.

Onfray, Michel. *Le crépuscule d'une idole: L'affabulation freudienne*. Paris: Bernard Grasset, 2010.

Oughourlian, Jean-Michel. *The Genesis of Desire*. East Lansing: Michigan State University Press, 2010.

Pippin, Robert. *Modernism as a Philosophical Problem*. 2nd ed. Oxford: Blackwell, 1999.

———. *Nietzsche, Psychology, and First Philosophy*. Chicago: University of Chicago Press, 2010.

Plato. *The Collected Dialogues of Plato*. Edited by Edith Hamilton and Huntington Cairns. New York: Bollingen Series, 1963.

Potolsky, Matthew. *Mimesis*. London: Routledge, 2006.

Ribot, Théodule. *Les maladies de la volonté*. Paris: Alcan, 1883.

———. *The Psychology of Emotions*. London: W. Scott, 1987.

Rand, Nicholas T. "The Hidden Soul: The Growth of the Unconscious in Philosophy, Psychology, Medicine and Literature 1750–1900." *American Imago* 61.3 (2004): 257–289.

Richman, Michèle. "Fascism Reviewed: Georges Bataille in *La Critique Sociale*." *South Central Review* 14 (1997): 14–30.

———. "The Sacred Group: A Durkheimian Perspective on the Collège de Sociologie (1937–1939)." In *Georges Bataille: Writing the Sacred*. Edited by Carolyn Bailey Gill, 58–76. New York: Routledge, 1995.

———. *Sacred Revolutions: Durkheim and the Collège de Sociologie*. Minneapolis: University of Minnesota Press, 2002.

Roberts, Andrew Michael. *Conrad and Masculinity*. New York: St. Martin's Press, 2000.

Roberts, Neil. *D. H. Lawrence: Travel and Cultural Difference*. New York: Palgrave Macmillan, 2004.

Ross, Stephen. *Conrad and Empire*. Columbia: University of Missouri Press, 2004.

Ross, Stephen, ed. *Modernism and Theory: A Critical Debate*. New York: Routledge, 2009.

Rouget, Gilbert. *Music and Trance: A Theory of the Relations between Music and Possession*. Translated by Brunhilde Biebuyck. Chicago: University of Chicago Press, 1985.

Roustang, François. *Influence*. Paris: Les Éditions de Minuit, 1990.

Ryan, Judith. *The Vanishing Subject: Early Psychology and Literary Modernism*. Chicago: University of Chicago Press, 1991.

Said, Edward. "Conrad and Nietzsche." In *Joseph Conrad: A Commemoration*. Edited by Norman Sherry, 65–76. London: Macmillan, 1976.

Sarvan, C. P. "Racism and the *Heart of Darkness*." In *Heart of Darkness*, 3rd ed. Edited by Robert Kimbrough, 280–284. New York: W. W. Norton, 1988.

Schneider, Daniel. *D. H. Lawrence: The Artist as Psychologist*. Lawrence: University Press of Kansas, 1984.

———. "D. H. Lawrence and *Thus Spoke Zarathustra*." *South Carolina Review* 15.2 (1983): 96–108.

Schopenhauer, Arthur. *On the Basis of Morality*. Translated by E. F. J. Payne. Indianapolis: Bobbs Merrill, 1965.

Sichère, Bernard. *Pour Bataille: Être, chance, souveraineté.* Paris: Gallimard, 2006.

Siemens, Herman. "Agonal Configurations in the *Unzeitgemässe Betrachtungen:* Identity, Mimesis and the *Übertragung* of Cultures in Nietzsche's Early Thought." *Nietzsche-Studien* 30 (2001): 80–106.

Sloterdijk, Peter. *Thinker on the Stage: Nietzsche's Materialism.* Translated by Jamie Owen Daniel. Minneapolis: University of Minnesota Press, 1989.

Smith, Johanna M. "'Too Beautiful Altogether': Ideologies of Gender and Empire in *Heart of Darkness.*" In *Heart of Darkness: Complete Authoritative Text with Biographical and Historical Contexts, Critical History, and Essays from Five Contemporary Critical Perspectives.* Edited by Ross C. Murfin, 169–184. New York: Bedford / St. Martin's, 1996.

Solecki, Sam. "D. H. Lawrence's View of Film." *Literature/Film Quarterly* 1.1 (1973): 12–16.

Spariousu, Mihai. "Plato's Ion: Mimesis, Poetry and Power." In *Mimesis in Contemporary Theory: An Interdisciplinary Approach.* Edited by Ronald Bogue, vol. 2, 13–25. Philadelphia: Benjamins, 1991.

Staten, Henry. "A Critique of the Will to Power." In *A Companion to Nietzsche.* Edited by Keith A. Pearson, 565–582. Oxford: Blackwell Malden, 2006.

———. "Conrad's Dionysian Elegy." In *Conrad's "Heart of Darkness" and Contemporary Thought: Revisiting the Horror with Lacoue-Labarthe.* Edited by Nidesh Lawtoo, 201–220. London: Bloomsbury, 2012.

———. *Nietzsche's Voice.* Ithaca, N.Y.: Cornell University Press, 1990.

Stein, Braten, ed. *Intersubjective Communication and Emotion in Early Ontogeny.* Cambridge: Cambridge University Press, 1998.

Stewart, Garret. "Lying as Dying in *Heart of Darkness.*" In *Heart of Darkness,* 3rd ed. Edited by Robert Kimbrough, 358–376. New York: W. W. Norton, 1988.

Stingelin, Martin. "Psychologie." In *Nietzsche-Handbuch.* Edited by Henning Ottmann, 425–426. Stuttgart: J. B. Metzler Verlag, 2000.

Sulloway, Frank J. *Freud, Biologist of the Mind: Beyond the Psychoanalytic Legend.* New York: Basic Books, 1979.

Surya, Michel. *Georges Bataille: La mort à l'œuvre.* Paris: Gallimard, 1992.

———. "Postface." *La structure psychologique du fascisme,* by Georges Bataille, 65–84. Paris: Lignes, 2009.

Tarde, Gabriel. *Les lois de l'imitation.* Paris: Seuil, 2001.

———. *L'opinion et la foule.* Paris: Presses Universitaires de France, 1989.

Taussig, Michael. *Mimesis and Alterity: A Particular History of the Senses.* London: Routledge, 1993.

Templeton, Wayne. "'Indians and an Englishman': Lawrence in the American Southwest." *D. H. Lawrence Review* 25 (1966): 18–21.

Thatcher, David. *Nietzsche in England, 1880–1914: The Growth of a Reputation.* Toronto: University of Toronto Press, 1972.

Thorgeirsdottir, Sigridur. *Vis Creativa: Kunst und Wahrheit in der Philosophie Nietzsches.* Würzburg: Königshausen & Neumann, 1996.

Torgovnick, Marianna. *Gone Primitive: Savage Intellects, Modern Lives.* Chicago: University of Chicago Press, 1990.

Trotter, Wilfred. *Instincts of the Herd in Peace and War, 1916–1919.* London: Oxford University Press, 1953.

Tylor, Edward Burnett. *Primitive Culture.* Vol. 1. London: Murray, 1871.

Vickery, John. "Myth and Ritual in the Shorter Fiction of D. H. Lawrence." In *The Critical Response to D. H. Lawrence.* Edited by Jan Pilditch, 230–244. Westport, Conn.: Greenwood Press, 2001.

Wicker, Bruno, Christian Keysers, Jane Plailly, Jean-Pierre Royet, Vittorio Gallese, and Giacomo Rizzolatti. "Both of Us Disgusted in *My* Insula: The Common Neural Basis of Seeing and Feeling Disgust." *Neuron* 40 (2003): 655–664.

Wallon, Henri. "The Role of the Other in the Consciousness of the Ego." In *The World of Henri Wallon.* Translated by Donald Nicholson-Smith. Jason Aaronson, 1946. Http://www.marxists.org/archive/wallon/works/1946/ch7.htm.

Warin, François. *Nietzsche et Bataille: La parodie à l'infini.* Paris: Presses Universitaires de France, 1994.

Wengle, John. *Ethnographers in the Field: The Psychology of Research.* Tuscaloosa: University of Alabama Press, 1988.

Whitworth, Michael. *Modernism.* Edited by Michael Whitworth. Oxford: Blackwell, 2007.

Winter, Alison. *Mesmerized: Powers of Mind in Victorian Britain.* Chicago: University of Chicago Press, 1998.

Wittgenstein, Ludwig. *Remarks on Frazer's "Golden Bough."* Edited by Rush Rhees, translated by Rush Rhees and A. C. Miles. Chippenham, Eastbourne: Brynmill Press, 2010.

Wolin, Richard. *The Seduction of Unreason: The Intellectual Romance with Fascism from Nietzsche to Postmodernism.* Princeton: Princeton University Press, 2004.

Yeats, William Butler. "The Second Coming." In *Selected Poems.* Edited by Richard Gill. Oxford: Oxford University Press, 2002.

Index